CONNECTING CORE COM

Connecting Core Competencies:
A Workbook for Social Work Students

Quienton Nichols, *Kennesaw State University*

Available in 2 versions:
MySocialWorkLab and Printed Workbook

MySocialWorkLab version:

Contains hundreds of questions that test student knowledge of CSWE's core competencies!

Bundle with any Pearson Social Work text at no extra charge; also sold standalone.

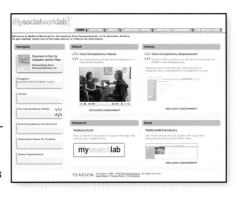

- A complete **etext** of the Nichols workbook (see below) with-
  - Audio file of the text
  - Note-taking & Highlighting features
- **Numerous Videos** illustrating CSWE's Core Competencies with assessement
- **75+ cases** with assessment
- **Career interviews**
- Assessment that feeds into your **Gradebook** so you can track student progress
- And More

Printed Workbook version:

Contains hundreds of questions that test student knowledge of CSWE's core competencies!

Bundle with any Pearson Social Work text; also sold standalone.

Each chapter covers one of CSWE's 10 core competencies and includes:

- Detailed explanation of the competency
- Assessment questions that test student knowledge and mastery of skills in the competency-
  - multiple choice questions
  - What Would You Do?: Case Vignette Scenarios and questions
  - reflective essay questions

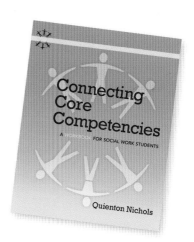

www.pearsonhighered.com/showcase/swcccs/workbook

PEARSON mysocialworklab™

MySocialWorkLab website helps students develop and master the skills articulated in CSWE's core competencies.

Features include:

- **NEW! Hundreds of assessment questions**, organized by each of the 10 competencies. Most are written in a similar format as on the licensing exam.
- Complete **eText with audio files** and **chapter tests**
- **Numerous videos** demonstrate the skills in CSWE's core competencies.
- MySocialWorkLibrary—**75 case studies**, each with accompanying assessment
- A **Gradebook** that **allows you to monitor student progress** on all assessment questions on the site
- **MySearchLab**—a collection of tools that **aid students in mastering research assignments and papers**
- **And much more!**

MySocialWorkLab can be bundled at no extra cost with any Pearson social work text. Contact your sales representative for details.

Professional Identity

2.1.1 Identify as a professional social worker and conduct oneself accordingly.

Necessary Knowledge, Values, Skills

- Social workers serve as representatives of the profession, its mission, and its core values.
- Social workers know the profession's history.
- Social workers commit themselves to the profession's enhancement and to their own professional conduct and growth.

Operational Practice Behaviors

- Social workers advocate for client access to the services of social work;
- Social workers practice personal reflection and self-correction to assure continual professional development;
- Social workers attend to professional roles and boundaries;
- Social workers demonstrate professional demeanor in behavior, appearance, and communication;
- Social workers engage in career-long learning; and
- Social workers use supervision and consultation.

Ethical Practice

2.1.2 Apply social work ethical principles to guide professional practice.

Necessary Knowledge, Values, Skills

- Social workers have an obligation to conduct themselves ethically and engage in ethical decision-making.
- Social workers are knowledgeable about the value base of the profession, its ethical standards, and relevant law.

Operational Practice Behaviors

- Social workers recognize and manage personal values in a way that allows professional values to guide practice;
- Social workers make ethical decisions by applying standards of the National Association of Social Workers Code of Ethics and, as applicable, of the International Federation of Social Workers/ International Association of Schools of Social Work Ethics in Social Work, Statement of Principles;
- Social workers tolerate ambiguity in resolving ethical conflicts; and
- Social workers apply strategies of ethical reasoning to arrive at principled decisions.

Critical Thinking

2.1.3 Apply critical thinking to inform and communicate professional judgments.

Necessary Knowledge, Values, Skills

- Social workers are knowledgeable about the principles of logic, scientific inquiry, and reasoned discernment.
- They use critical thinking augmented by creativity and curiosity.
- Critical thinking also requires the synthesis and communication of relevant information.

Operational Practice Behaviors

- Social workers distinguish, appraise, and integrate multiple sources of knowledge, including research-based knowledge, and practice wisdom;
- Social workers analyze models of assessment, prevention, intervention, and evaluation; and
- Social workers demonstrate effective oral and written communication in working with individuals, families, groups, organizations, communities, and colleagues.

Diversity in Practice

2.1.4 Engage diversity and difference in practice.

Necessary Knowledge, Values, Skills

- Social workers understand how diversity characterizes and shapes the human experience and is critical to the formation of identity.
- The dimensions of diversity are understood as the inter-sectionality of multiple factors including age, class, color, culture, disability, ethnicity, gender, gender identity and expression, immigration status, political ideology, race, religion, sex, and sexual orientation.
- Social workers appreciate that, as a consequence of difference, a person's life experiences may include oppression, poverty, marginalization, and alienation as well as privilege, power, and acclaim.

Operational Practice Behaviors

- Social workers recognize the extent to which a culture's structures and values may oppress, marginalize, alien-ate, or create or enhance privilege and power;
- Social workers gain sufficient self-awareness to elimi-nate the influence of personal biases and values in working with diverse groups;
- Social workers recognize and communicate their understanding of the importance of difference in shaping life experiences; and
- Social workers view themselves as learners and engage those with whom they work as informants.

Human Rights & Justice

2.1.5 Advance human rights and social and economic justice.

Necessary Knowledge, Values, Skills

- Each person, regardless of position in society, has basic human rights, such as freedom, safety, privacy, an ade-quate standard of living, health care, and education.
- Social workers recognize the global interconnections of oppression and are knowledgeable about theories of justice and strategies to promote human and civil rights.
- Social work incorporates social justice practices in organizations, institutions, and society to ensure that these basic human rights are distributed equitably and without prejudice.

Operational Practice Behaviors

- Social workers understand the forms and mechanisms of oppression and discrimination;
- Social workers advocate for human rights and social and economic justice; and
- Social workers engage in practices that advance social and economic justice.

Research Based Practice

2.1.6 Engage in research-informed practice and practice-informed research.

Necessary Knowledge, Values, Skills

- Social workers use practice experience to inform research, employ evidence-based interventions, evalu-ate their own practice, and use research findings to improve practice, policy, and social service delivery.
- Social workers comprehend quantitative and qualitative research and understand scientific and ethical approaches to building knowledge.

Operational Practice Behaviors

- Social workers use practice experience to inform scientific inquiry; and
- Social workers use research evidence to inform practice.

Human Behavior

2.1.7 Apply knowledge of human behavior and the social environment.

Necessary Knowledge, Values, Skills

- Social workers are knowledgeable about human behavior across the life course; the range of social systems in which people live; and the ways social systems promote or deter people in maintaining or achieving health and well-being.
- Social workers apply theories and knowledge from the liberal arts to understand biological, social, cultural, psychological, and spiritual development.

Operational Practice Behaviors

- Social workers utilize conceptual frameworks to guide the processes of assessment, intervention, and evaluation; and
- Social workers critique and apply knowledge to understand person and environment.

Policy Practice   2.1.8 Engage in policy practice to advance social and economic well-being and to deliver effective social work services.

Necessary Knowledge, Values, Skills

- Social work practitioners understand that policy affects service delivery and they actively engage in policy practice.
- Social workers know the history and current structures of social policies and services; the role of policy in service delivery; and the role of practice in policy development.

Operational Practice Behaviors

- Social workers analyze, formulate, and advocate for policies that advance social well-being; and
- Social workers collaborate with colleagues and clients for effective policy action.

Practice Contexts
2.1.9 Respond to contexts that shape practice.

Necessary Knowledge, Values, Skills

- Social workers are informed, resourceful, and proactive in responding to evolving organizational, community, and societal contexts at all levels of practice.
- Social workers recognize that the context of practice is dynamic, and use knowledge and skill to respond proactively.

Operational Practice Behaviors

- Social workers continuously discover, appraise, and attend to changing locales, populations, scientific and technological developments, and emerging societal trends to provide relevant services; and
- Social workers provide leadership in promoting sustainable changes in service delivery and practice to improve the quality of social services.

Engage, Assess, Intervene, Evaluate   2.1.10 Engage, assess, intervene, and evaluate with individuals, families, groups, organizations, and communities.

Necessary Knowledge, Values, Skills

- Professional practice involves the dynamic and interactive processes of engagement, assessment, intervention, and evaluation at multiple levels.
- Social workers have the knowledge and skills to practice with individuals, families, groups, organizations, and communities.
- Practice knowledge includes
  - identifying, analyzing, and implementing evidence-based interventions designed to achieve client goals;
  - using research and technological advances;
  - evaluating program outcomes and practice effectiveness;
  - developing, analyzing, advocating, and providing leadership for policies and services; and
  - promoting social and economic justice.

Operational Practice Behaviors

(a) Engagement
- Social workers substantively and affectively prepare for action with individuals, families, groups, organizations, and communities;
- Social workers use empathy and other interpersonal skills; and
- Social workers develop a mutually agreed-on focus of work and desired outcomes.

(b) Assessment
- Social workers collect, organize, and interpret client data;
- Social workers assess client strengths and limitations;
- Social workers develop mutually agreed-on intervention goals and objectives; and
- Social workers select appropriate intervention strategies.

(c) Intervention
- Social workers initiate actions to achieve organizational goals;
- Social workers implement prevention interventions that enhance client capacities;
- Social workers help clients resolve problems;
- Social workers negotiate, mediate, and advocate for clients; and
- Social workers facilitate transitions and endings.

(d) Evaluation
- Social workers critically analyze, monitor, and evaluate interventions.

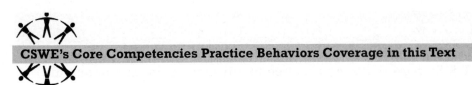

CSWE's Core Competencies Practice Behaviors Coverage in this Text

Practice Behavior	Chapter
Professional Identity (2.1.1)	
Social workers advocate for client access to the services of social work	1
Social workers practice personal reflection and self-correction to assure continual professional development	1
Social workers attend to professional roles and boundaries	
Social workers demonstrate professional demeanor in behavior, appearance, and communication	12
Social workers engage in career-long learning	12
Social workers use supervision and consultation	
Ethical Practice (2.1.2)	
Social workers recognize and manage personal values in a way that allows professional values to guide practice	2, 6, 9
Social workers make ethical decisions by applying standards of the National Association of Social Workers Code of Ethics and, as applicable, of the International Federation of Social Workers/International Association of Schools of Social Work Ethics in Social Work, Statement of principles	2, 6, 9
Social workers tolerate ambiguity in resolving ethical conflicts	2, 9
Social workers apply strategies of ethical reasoning to arrive at principled decisions	2
Critical Thinking (2.1.3)	
Social workers distinguish, appraise, and integrate multiple sources of knowledge, including research-based knowledge, and practice wisdom	2, 3, 5, 7, 8
Social workers analyze models of assessment, prevention, intervention, and evaluation	2, 3, 5, 7, 8
Social workers demonstrate effective oral and written communication in working with individuals, families, groups, organizations, communities, and colleagues	2, 5
Diversity in Practice (2.1.4)	
Social workers recognize the extent to which a culture's structures and values may oppress, marginalize, alienate, or create or enhance privilege and power	4
Social workers gain sufficient self-awareness to eliminate the influence of personal biases and values in working with diverse groups	3, 4
Social workers recognize and communicate their understanding of the importance of difference in shaping life experiences	1, 2, 3, 4, 8, 9, 12, 13
Social workers view themselves as learners and engage those with whom they work as informants	
Human Rights & Justice (2.1.5)	
Social workers understand the forms and mechanisms of oppression and discrimination	1, 2, 3, 7, 8, 9, 12
Social workers advocate for human rights and social and economic justice	1, 12
Social workers engage in practices that advance social and economic justice	1, 2

Practice Behavior	Chapter
Research Based Practice (2.1.6)	
Social workers use practice experience to inform scientific inquiry	1, 4, 5, 6, 7, 8, 9, 10, 12
Social workers use research evidence to inform practice	1, 4, 5, 6, 7, 8, 9, 10, 12
Human Behavior (2.1.7)	
Social workers utilize conceptual frameworks to guide the processes of assessment, intervention, and evaluation	4, 11
Social workers critique and apply knowledge to understand person and environment	4
Policy Practice (2.1.8)	
Social workers analyze, formulate, and advocate for policies that advance social well-being	1, 12
Social workers collaborate with colleagues and clients for effective policy action	1, 12
Practice Contexts (2.1.9)	
Social workers continuously discover, appraise, and attend to changing locales, populations, scientific and technological developments, and emerging societal trends to provide relevant services	5, 6, 8 ,10,11
Social workers provide leadership in promoting sustainable changes in service delivery and practice to improve the quality of social services	11
Engage, Assess, Intervene, Evaluate (2.1.10(a)–(d))	
A) ENGAGEMENT	
Social workers substantively and effectively prepare for action with individuals, families, groups, organizations, and communities	3, 5, 9, 10, 11
Social workers use empathy and other interpersonal skills	3
Social workers develop a mutually agreed-on focus of work and desired outcomes	9, 11
B) ASSESSMENT	
Social workers collect, organize, and interpret client data	3, 5, 9, 10, 11
Social workers assess client strengths and limitations	9
Social workers develop mutually agreed-on intervention goals and objectives	9, 11
Social workers select appropriate intervention strategies	3, 5, 9, 10, 11
C) INTERVENTION	
Social workers initiate actions to achieve organizational goals	3, 5, 9, 10, 11
Social workers implement prevention interventions that enhance client capacities	9, 11
Social workers help clients resolve problems	9, 11
Social workers negotiate, mediate, and advocate for clients	3, 10
Social workers facilitate transitions and endings	9
D) EVALUATION	
Social workers critically analyze, monitor, and evaluate interventions	9, 11

CONNECTING CORE COMPETENCIES **Chapter-by-Chapter Matrix**

Chapter	Professional Identity	Ethical Practice	Critical Thinking	Diversity in Practice	Human Rights and Justice	Research-Based Practice	Human Behavior	Policy Practice	Practice Contexts	Engage, Assess, Intervene, Evaluate
1	✔				✔	✔		✔		
2		✔	✔	✔	✔					
3			✔	✔		✔				✔
4				✔		✔	✔			
5			✔			✔			✔	✔
6		✔				✔			✔	
7			✔	✔	✔	✔				
8			✔		✔	✔			✔	
9		✔			✔	✔				✔
10				✔		✔			✔	✔
11				✔			✔	✔		✔
12	✔				✔	✔		✔		
Total Chapters	2	3	5	6	6	10	2	3	4	5

Social Worker as Researcher

Integrating Research with Advocacy

Tina Maschi
Fordham University

Robert Youdin
Fordham University

PEARSON

Boston Columbus Indianapolis New York San Francisco Upper Saddle River
Amsterdam Cape Town Dubai London Madrid Milan Munich Paris Montreal Toronto
Delhi Mexico City São Paulo Sydney Hong Kong Seoul Singapore Taipei Tokyo

Editorial Director: Craig Campanella
Editor in Chief: Dickson Musslewhite
Executive Editor: Ashley Dodge
Editorial Product Manager: Carly Czech
Director of Marketing: Brandy Dawson
Executive Marketing Manager: Jeanette Koskinas
Senior Marketing Manager: Wendy Albert
Marketing Assistant: Jessica Warren
Media Project Manager: Felicia Halpert
Production Manager: Meghan DeMaio

Creative Director: Jayne Conte
Cover Designer: Suzanne Duda
Cover Image: © Tetra Images/Tetra Images/Corbis
Interior Design: Joyce C. Weston
Editorial Production and Composition Service:
   Chitra Sundarajan/PreMediaGlobal
Printer/Binder: Edwards Brothers
Cover Printer: Lehigh-Phoenix Color
Interior Images: © Christopher M. Mooney

Library of Congress Cataloging-in-Publication Data

Maschi, Tina.
Social worker as researcher : integrating research with advocacy / Tina Maschi Robert
   Youdin. —1st ed.
      p. cm.
   Includes bibliographical references and index.
   ISBN-13: 978-0-205-59494-8 (alk. paper)
   ISBN-10: 0-205-59494-8 (alk. paper)
   ISBN-13: 978-0-205-02242-7 (Instructor ed. : alk. paper)
   ISBN-10: 0-205-02242-1 (Instructor ed. : alk. paper)
   [etc.]
   1. Social service—Research. 2. Social workers. 3. Public welfare.   I. Youdin, Robert.
II. Title.
   HV11.M3497 2012
   361.0072—dc23

                                                                              2011018293

10 9 8 7 6 5 4 3 2 1 EB 15 14 13 12 11

Student Edition
ISBN-10: 0-205-59494-8
ISBN-13: 978-0-205-59494-8

Instructor Edition
ISBN-10: 0-205-02242-1
ISBN-13: 978-0-205-02242-7

à la Carte Edition
ISBN-10: 0-205-02272-3
ISBN-13: 978-0-205-02272-4

Contents

9. Tapping the Evidence-Based Practitioner Within: Single-Subject Design   185

10. The Qualitative Approach: Tapping the Artist and Scientist Within   199

12. Writing for a Change and Other Advocacy Tips   267

Preface

Social Worker as Researcher: Integrating Research with Advocacy was inspired by the collective works of frontline social workers who put research into action on a daily basis. This book also comes at an ideal time as the profession celebrates over 100 years of humanitarian efforts. In fact, there has never been a more exciting time to be a social worker, except for perhaps the turn of the 20th century. In this new century, social work has come of age; the possibilities are endless for the next generation of social workers to build on the solid professional foundation. With a professional mission that has an ultimate collective goal of achieving human rights and social justice and well-being among individuals and communities, our work is cut out for us.

Research has always been a systematic agent of change and an organizing frame used to develop individual- and community-level interventions and to monitor the desired outcomes. As the contents of this book will reveal, social work's history, particularly with the rise of social work research, can be used to rejuvenate and reclaim research for practice and action. We have the option to coordinate the compassionate, passionate, and rational minds within ourselves and the collective by integrating research, practice, and action for change.

This book's broad scope and practical approach and infusion of experiential learning techniques help social workers prepare for evidence-based excellence in practice. It will also help social workers make a difference by providing them with the knowledge, values, and skills grounded in understanding the history and methods of "who, what, where, and why we do it" of social work research for practice to achieve permanent excellence.

Connecting Core Competencies Series

This new first edition is a part of Pearson Education's *Connecting Core Competencies* series, which consists of foundation-level texts that make it easier than ever to ensure students' success in learning the 10 core competencies as stated in 2008 by the Council on Social Work Education. This text contains:

- **Core Competency Icons throughout the chapters,** directly linking the CSWE core competencies to the content of the text. Critical thinking questions are also included to further students' mastery of the CSWE standards. For easy reference, page iv displays which competencies are used in each chapter, in a chapter-by-chapter matrix.
- **End-of-chapter Practice Tests,** with multiple-choice questions that test students' knowledge of the chapter content.
- **Your competence** at the end of each chapter to evaluate students' mastery of the skills and competencies learned.
- **Additional questions pertaining to the videos and case studies found on MySocialWorkLab** at the end of each chapter to encourage students to access the site and explore the wealth of available materials. If this text did not come with an access code for MySocialWorkLab, you can purchase access at www.mysocialworklab.com.

Acknowledgments

We would like to acknowledge our family, friends, colleagues, and students for the unwavering support of this book. We are especially grateful to Amy Gugig, Maryann Hom, and Jennifer Ristow, who kept us grounded in understanding what is most helpful to students to connect research with practice and advocacy. We also acknowledge Myron Youdin's (1918–1994) love of research and teaching that was an inspiration for this book, Naomi Sarah Browar whose clinical social work insights were most helpful, and Joanne Maschi who make this book possible. And finally, to Micah Dylan, may you grow up to learn about human rights, social justice, and research and use it to make a difference. And to Ashley and Sasha, whose canine wisdom continually reminds us that it is not just about throwing the Frisbee but also bringing it back. This book is dedicated to all of you.

1

Social Work Research and Evaluation: Foundations in Human Rights and Social Justice

Core Competencies in This Chapter (Check marks indicate which competencies are demonstrated)				
✓ Professional Identity	☐ Ethical Practice	☐ Critical Thinking	☐ Diversity in Practice	✓ Human Rights and Justice
✓ Research-Based Practice	☐ Human Behavior	✓ Policy Practice	☐ Practice Contexts	☐ Engage, Assess, Intervene, Evaluate

BACKGROUND

Social Work and Its Scientific Roots

Social work has reached a significant developmental milestone in its professional identity as it collectively celebrates over a century of professional practice that targets individual and societal transformation (Popple & Leighninger, 2007). Historically, social workers have used a combination of research and practice strategies to advocate for improved social conditions for underserved populations, such as the poor, immigrants, political refugees, child abuse victims, and criminal offenders (Day, 2008; Maschi, Bradley, & Ward, 2009). In fact, social workers' striving for "new possibilities" for humankind parallels the global social movement for human rights (United Nations [UN], 1994), particularly with the emphasis on the "intrinsic" value of *every* person, and the use of individual and group action to promote social justice as a form of "equitable social structures that provide people security and development while upholding their dignity" (International Federation of Social Work [IFSW], 1988, p. 1).

In pursuit of new possibilities and a better world, research and evaluation strategies for practice have been a common thread woven throughout social work history.

In pursuit of new possibilities and a better world, research and evaluation strategies for practice have been a common thread woven throughout social work history. Social work research and evaluation continue to evolve as a mechanism that gathers data that can be used toward enhancing well-being and socially just outcomes (Wronka, 2008). Since the beginning of the profession, research in the form of the scientific method has been used to understand individual and social problems and to guide, assess, and intervene with underserved populations, especially the poor (Zimbalist, 1977). In fact, the United Nations (1994) has made a distinct reference to social work as a human rights profession because of its long-standing commitment to well-being and justice. Research and evaluation are important aspects for helping the profession achieve its mission. According to the Council on Social Work Education (CSWE, 2008):

> The purpose of the social work profession is to promote *human and community well-being*. Guided by a person and environment construct, a global perspective, respect for human diversity, and knowledge based on *scientific inquiry*, social work's purpose is actualized through the *quest for social and economic justice*, the *prevention of conditions that limit human rights*, the *elimination of poverty*, and the *enhancement of the quality of life for all persons*. (p. 1)

Definitions

Social workers need to be clear about the meaning of common terms. As noted earlier, scientific inquiry informs the profession's purposes. *Scientific inquiry* commonly refers to the process of gathering fact-based information in a systematic way. In social work, it refers to the process by which social workers ask questions, develop and carry out investigations, make hypotheses or predictions, gather evidence, and propose explanations or corroborate evidence (Gibbs & Gambrill, 1998). An essential component of scientific inquiry is critical thinking, which is the intellectually disciplined process of "actively and skillfully conceptualizing, applying, analyzing, synthesizing, and/or evaluating information gathered from, or generated by, observation, experience, reflection, reasoning, or communication, as a guide to belief and action" (Fisher & Scriven, 1997, p. 1).

Research and evaluation comprise a central feature of social work practice that can foster and appraise the profession's progress toward its mission (Wronka, 2008). Research and evaluation are important because they give social workers permission to be curious and creative, as well as systematic and thorough in their activities that involve assessment, prevention, and intervention efforts with individuals, families, and communities.

The term *research* generally refers to a systemic and thorough search or examination that involves the collection of data (Engel & Schutt, 2010). As a verb, *research* often refers to conducting an exhaustive investigation. The term *evaluation* often refers to the careful appraisal and study about the effectiveness of an intervention (Barker, 2003). The use of the scientific methods with the distinct purpose of generating information to apply to practice has historically made social work research and evaluation unique.

Functions of Science and Research in Social Work

Although some aspects of social work practice are an art, science and research comprise an essential component of social work practice activities (Kirk & Reid, 2002). Reid (1997) articulated three major functions for social work practice. First, scientific perspectives and methods can provide a framework for practice activities and help obtain the best results possible. It is a way of thinking that offers strategies for action. According to Reid (1997):

> Such an orientation calls for the use of concepts that are clearly tied to empirical events; the systematic collection of data; the cautious use of inference and the consideration of alternative explanations; the application when possible, of research-based knowledge, and the discriminating evaluation of the outcomes of one's efforts. (p. 2040)

Second, research is an essential tool toward building knowledge that can be used for practice. Research can serve as a generative tool to develop and refine theories for practice and can be used to evaluate practice effectiveness. When knowledge is empirically grounded, it strengthens practice decisions.

Third, research serves a practical function for social workers in the field, to evaluate their own practice with individuals, agencies, or communities. It is common for social workers to conduct needs assessment, quality assurance, program and practice evaluation, productivity studies, and program evaluation. Data gathered for specific practice situations can be used to make practice decisions and actions.

The professional social work organization, the National Association of Social Workers (NASW, 2010), underscores the diversity of social issues addressed in social work research and its benefits. Social work research targets an array of psychosocial problems; prevention and intervention efforts; and community, organizational, policy, and administrative concerns. Some areas of research for practice include research on mental health, child maltreatment, community violence, HIV/AIDS, juvenile delinquency, productive aging, substance abuse, and international community development. Other areas of research address risk and resilience, such as community violence, among individuals, families, groups, neighborhoods, and society to generate information that can be used to develop or refine practice. Other areas of research examine the effectiveness of service delivery and public policies, achieving human and community well-being and social and economic justice. Moreover, these areas of research can be used to benefit stakeholders that include consumers, practitioners, policy makers, educators, and society.

Research and Social Work's Core Values

Core professional values emphasized in contemporary practice, such as scientific inquiry, also can be traced throughout the profession's history. In fact, the CSWE emphasizes these core values in its Educational Policy and Accreditation Standards (EPAs) in which Policy 1.1 refers to values. The policy states that "service, social justice, dignity and worth of the person, the importance of human relationships, integrity, competence, human rights, and *scientific inquiry* are among the core values of social work. These values frame the profession's commitment to respect for all people and the quest for economic and social justice" (CSWE, 2008, p. 2).

An important component of social work practice has been its efforts in integrating scientific methods with the art of practice, particularly to understand the causes of poverty and give relief to the poor (Zimbalist, 1977). The integration of science with social work practice was first advanced in the late 1800s as part of the scientific philanthropy movement to address poverty (Orcutt, 1990), which was scientific research used as a mechanism to uncover the causes of poverty, to assess individual families, and to evaluate the effectiveness of social work efforts to assist the poor (Kirk & Reid, 2002).

Professional Identity

Critical Thinking Question: How do the core values of scientific inquiry and human rights and social justice help shape your personal professional identity and the profession as a collective?

Perhaps the profession's biggest developmental challenge has been integrating the passionate, action-oriented reformer with the compassionate counselor/helper, and the objective scientific observer.

THE HISTORY OF SOCIAL WORK AND RESEARCH: EVIDENCE AND THE ALTRUISTIC IMAGINATION

As the social work profession moves forward into 21st-century practice, a clear understanding of its historical roots can be used to inform current practices, especially those related to the roles and functions of social work research and evaluation. A review of history reveals the birth of the profession based on humanitarianism during turbulent times in which poverty, discrimination, and political corruption were rampant, and two world wars were waged killing millions of world citizens.

In the late 19th century, a group of like-minded citizens banded together in the pursuit of humanistic ideals to help reinvent a better and more just world. Social workers actively used scientific methods, such as descriptive surveys and outcome studies, to achieve their aims of identifying adverse societal conditions or evaluating their practice. Significant progress in educational, practice, and policy reform was made using evidence that it was research that guided practice and practice that guided research. Table 1.1 provides a significant timeline of life events for social work, with an emphasis on research and evaluation milestones.

Perhaps the profession's biggest developmental challenge has been integrating the passionate, action-oriented reformer with the compassionate counselor/helper, the objective scientific observer within each individual social worker, and the collective profession. In the following review, social work history suggests that some of the most advanced achievements occurred

Table 1.1	**Social Work Research History: Developmental Milestones**
Dates	Social work research history
1800s	Rise of the Scientific Philanthropy Movement
1841	Dorothea Dix first advocates for conditions of mentally ill in prison
1884	National Conference on Charities and Corrections (NCCC)
1860s	Board of Charities and Corrections formed; Rise of Charity movement and friendly visitors and the settlement house movement (research, reform, and residence); Dorothea Dix continues to advocate mentally ill in prisons; creation of state hospitals
1865	American Social Science Association established; Organized by Franklin Sanborn, gen sec of MA Board of Charities
1878	National Conference of Charities and Corrections formed
1884	The settlement house, Toynbee Hall, in England established
1889	Jane Addams and Ellen Starr establish Hull House, the first settlement house in the United States
1890	U.S. Jacob Riis publishes *How the Other Half Lives*, photographic survey of how NY poor lived
1894	*American Charities: A Study of Philanthropy and Economics* A.G. Warner published—on mixed methods study on poverty
1895	"U.S. Hull House Maps and Papers" published, documenting problem of Chicago's new immigrants
1897	"1897—The Influential Pittsburgh Survey Study" conducted by Charity workers. *The Philadelphia Negro: A Social Study*—documented the trials of urban AA
1898	The City Wilderness Robert Wood's-Boston-New Immigrants and Poverty
1899	Juvenile court is established in Chicago
1900–1920	Separation takes place between professional SW education and academic social sciences
1900	Educator Simon Patten coins the term *social worker* to describe friendly visitors and settlement house workers; Staggering youth statistics spur growth of child-saving movement; journals *Charities* and *Commons* published
1902	London—Charles Booth's *The Life and Labour of the People of England* published
1906	School social work programs are established in New York and other U.S. cities, journals *Charities* and *Commons* are combined to become the journal *Charities and Commons*
1907–1916	Jane Addams publishes six books and numerous essays
1907	Russell Sage Foundation formed; Pittsburgh Study begins, establishes a department of surveys and exhibits, provides grants to establish social research in schools of social work
1909	Jane Addams—First woman to be elected president of the NCCC; Last American Social Science Association held
1912	U.S. Children's Bureau established—Julia Lathrop of Hull House instrumental in data gathering, local and national; Robert Chapin's report is published "The Standard of Living among Working-men's Families in NYC"

(continued)

Table 1.1	**Social Work Research History: Developmental Milestones (Continued)**
Dates	Social work research history
1915	Abraham Flexner's famous address "Is Social Work a Profession" at the 42nd annual session of the National Conference of Charities and Corrections
1917	NCCC now National Conference of Social Workers; Mary Richmond publishes social diagnosis
1919	School of Social work forms an association that later becomes CSWE
1920s	Sigmund Freud's theories gain prominence in social work; Sophie van Senden conducts research on youth in foster care through charity organization
1920	U.S.—Mary Richmond came up with first experimental code of ethics
1921	Tuft report on SW education; Mary Richmond receives honorary degree from Smith College for establishing the scientific base of SW
1922	Mary Richmond's *What Is Social Casework?* published
1923	Tufts (1923) published education and social work
1927	*Social Service Review Journal* is started by Abbott and Breckinbridge of Hull House
1928	The Milford Conference reports distinguished general and specific components of social work practice
1929	Growth of Freudian thought in social work casework to examine individual problems; Rise of diagnostic and functional schools of thought
1930	Functional school of social casework develops psychosocial approach; 1931 Conference of Social Work, Cabot's speech urges social workers to evaluate their practice
1931	Jane Addams receives the Nobel Peace Prize; Edith Abbott advocates for the use of scientific method in SW
1937	1937 SW Yearbook—distinction is made between social research and social work research
1938	Conference of Evian is held in response to Third Reich
1939	"The Lane Report"—text on community organizing builds on Lindeman's 1921 text; Cabot starts Cambridge-Somerville Youth Study focused on juvenile delinquency
1945	Emily Green Balch, SW reformer and SW educator, receives Nobel Peace Prize
1947	Landmark conference that distinguishes between social research and social work research; Social Work Research Group is established
1948	Universal Declaration of Human Rights is adopted, National Conference of Social Workers 1948
1949	Establishment of the Institute of Mental Health
1950s	Community Planning for Human Services-Community Level Research Project; research becomes centered in schools of social work; SW doctoral education programs grow
1951	SWRG begins to index social work research abstracts
1952	Council on Social Work Education forms after merging of educational organizations; French prepare an Approach to Measuring Results in Social Work, published to examine service effectiveness; SW schools include a research thesis in MSW programs

Table 1.1	**Social Work Research History: Developmental Milestones (Continued)**
Dates	Social work research history
1955	Specialty section in NASW—Council on SW Research; National Association of Social Workers is formed when SW groups merged, including SWRG
1959	Boehm's (1959) Social Work Curriculum Study Project
1960s–1970s	Shift from social work research conducted in agencies to universities, expansion of SW doctoral education; Russell Sage is no longer a major funder of SW research
1960	NASW first Code of Ethics is established (one page); First SW Research text published, edited by Norman Polansky under auspices of NASW
	1961 legislation establishing the President's Committee on Juvenile Delinquency and Youth; Crime-funded community demonstration projects
1964	War on Poverty is launched and beginning of community action projects
1965	NASW publishes *Research and Abstracts*
1970s	Concerns about the bridge between research and practice grow in SW profession
1972	Fordham University Symposium reviews 13 direct service research projects from 1960s
1973	Fischer—*Is Social Case Work Effective?*: A review is published; caused an ongoing debate about practice effectiveness
1974	1974 reorganization of NASW; subsumes disparate SW organizations under one umbrella; NASW abolished special interest groups for one unified definition
1975	Group for the Advancement of Doctoral Education-Social Work (GADE) is formed
1976	IFSW—adopts first international code of ethics
1977	Zimbalist publishes *Historic Themes and Landmarks in Social Welfare Research*; NIMH funds research conference for CSWE to document gap between research and practice in MH
1978	NIMH funds research conference for NASW to document gap between research and practice in MH
1979	NASW Code of Ethics expand to 10-page document conduct provisions (1990 and 1993) Jayartne & Levy (1979) *Empirical Clinical Practice Model* published
1980s–	NIMH funding shifts from funding clinical practitioners to research on treatment
1981	Dinerman (1981) report—documents the disconnect between research and practice
1982	"1982 CSWE Curriculum Policy Statement"—integration of research in practice
1981	Heineman's The Obsolete Scientific Imperative in SW Research—ignites ongoing debate about research for practice
1984	CSWE accreditation requirement for practice-based research
1986	IFSW Code of Ethics is supplemented by a declaration of ethical principles; NIMH director authorizes the creation of task force on SW Research

(continued)

Table 1.1	Social Work Research History: Developmental Milestones (Continued)
Dates	Social work research history
1988	"1988 CSWE Curriculum Policy Statement"—curriculum should impart knowledge for practice and evaluate services
1990s	NIMH funds eight developing research centers; Rise of evidence-based practice in medicine followed by social work
1991	1991 report—"Task Force on SW Research," supported by NIMH, published report, "Building SW Knowledge"
1993	Establishment of Institute for the Advancement of Social Work Research (IASWR)
1994	Society for Social Work Research is formed
1994	NASW establishes SW Research journal, founding of the Society for Social Work Research
1994	United Nations (1994) publishes "Human Rights and Social Work" manual
1996	1996 Code of Ethics by NASW; ANSWER is established—advocacy network for increased support for SW research
1998	A Report on Progress in the Development of Research Resources in Social Work (IASWR, 1998)
1999	Legislation is filed to establish a National Center for SW Research
2000	National Institute on Drug Abuse creates the SW Research Development Program and provides grants
2001	Ife (2001) publishes *Human Rights and Social Work*
2002	Kirk and Reid (2002) publish *Science and Social Work*, which critically appraises past efforts to make SW more scientific
2003	Reichert (2003) publishes *Social Work and Human Rights*
2004	IFSW and IASSW adopt new ethical document—*Ethics in SW: Statement of Principles*
2008	Wronka (2008) publishes *Social Justice and Human Rights*
2009	SWRnet is established; IASWR is disbanded
2010	*Journal of Society for Social Work Research* is established

when these three aspects of passion, compassion, and rationality were respected. Also, passionate debates among social workers resulted in new understanding of the roles and functions of research in social work.

Evidence and the Altruistic Imagination

In the mid-19th century, many concerned citizens and volunteers began their humanitarian efforts to address growing social problems, particularly in urban America where poverty and substandard living and working conditions were rampant. They began to use a variety of research methods to understand and assist disenfranchised populations, which included people with mental illness, the poor, racial and ethnic minorities, at-risk youth, and prisoners.

Perhaps one of the most notable 19th-century humanitarians who used research strategies for advocacy purposes was Dorothea Dix (Viney & Zorich, 1982). In the early 1840s, Dorothea Dix began her in-depth observation of the treatment of people with mental illness in jails and prisons. She used the findings of her observational notes to increase awareness of the inhumane treatment meted out behind closed correctional doors. She also used her findings to advocate for improved conditions for this population. The following excerpt is an appeal she made to the Massachusetts Legislature in 1845:

> In illustration of my subject, I offer the following extracts from my Note-Book and Journal. I found, near Boston, in the Jails and Asylums for the poor, a numerous class brought into unsuitable connection with criminals and the general mass of Paupers. I refer to Idiots and Insane persons, dwelling in circumstances not only adverse to their own physical and moral improvement, but productive of extreme disadvantages to all other persons brought into association with them.

As Dix has stated, her observational notes were a source of documented evidence of the mistreatment of the mentally ill. Her use of this data to persuade state legislatures and the media was quite fruitful. Dix is attributed with almost single handedly leading social reform efforts for the treatment of the mentally ill and the establishment of state hospitals for their institutional care, both nationally and abroad (Dix, 1975).

In the late 19th century, a growing number of concerned citizens joined the ranks of the charity and settlement house movements, volunteers (Day, 2008). In 1884, Toynbee Hall in England was established to address community problems including poverty and overcrowding. Inspired by this work, five years later in 1889, Jane Addams and Ellen Starr established Hull House in Chicago, Illinois. The success of their efforts has been attributed to three words that begin with *r*: *residence, research,* and *reform.* Residence was in the form of living in the midst of the community. Research involved quantitative and qualitative approaches that included community mapping and observational and interview data. Reform efforts included legislative advocacy at the local, state, federal, and international levels.

Other related but notable social reform efforts included public awareness efforts by the media. Jacob Riis (1890) was an innovative photojournalist of the New York City slums. In 1890, in his book *How the Other Half Lives,* Riis wrote about children in slums:

> I counted the other day the little ones, up to ten years or so, in a Bayard Street tenement that for a yard has a triangular space in the centre with sides fourteen or fifteen feet long, just room enough for a row of ill-smelling closets at the base of the triangle and a hydrant at the apex. There was about as much light in this "yard" as in the average cellar. I gave up my self-imposed task in despair when I had counted one hundred and twenty-eight in forty families. (p. 58)

This photographic survey of how the New York poor lived was an eye-opener to many American citizens who were unaware of the substandard living conditions of the urban poor.

Social Work and the Social Sciences: A Shifting Alliance

In the late 1800s, the rise of the scientific philanthropy movement and the use of the scientific method helped social scientists to understand and intervene with pressing social problems. These problems included mental health, political corruption, crime-ridden streets, juvenile delinquency, exploitative work conditions, and immigrants living in urban slums. Social scientists, from disciplines such as history, anthropology, political science, and psychology, banded together to help understand the nature of these pressing social problems. In 1865, an interdisciplinary collaboration of social scientists formed the American Social Science Association (ASSA) (forerunner of the American Sociological Association) (Broadhurst, 1971; Kirk & Reid, 2002).

The social problem-solving aims of the social scientists were consistent with members of state boards of charity organizations engaged in the field. Both parties also were eager to break away from the prevailing religious prescriptions for society's ills and instead adopt a rational-minded scientific method to understand and combat societal ills. A common ground between the charity organization members and social scientists was their shared concern over the wide-scale social problems and the need for social and legislative reforms. In 1874, Franklin Sanborn, who was the general of the Massachusetts Board of Charities, organized a historic meeting between state boards of charities members and the ASSA social scientists at their annual ASSA meeting (Austin, 2003; Zimbalist, 1977).

With these similar agendas, an organizational alliance was formed, and the social welfare group met under an ASSA special section, titled Social Economy. However, this union was short-lived (1874 to 1879). Although they shared common concerns over social problems, the charity board members and social scientists differed on the purpose and especially on the importance of the application of their research and evaluation findings.

Eventually, the charity board members found the social scientists' fixation with abstract social theory development limiting, especially when they were faced with practical management issues facing frontline practitioners (Broadhurst, 1971). A philosophical split seems to have occurred between scientific detachment and the pursuit of humanitarian ideals and passionate social change efforts. To address their specific aims, the state boards of charities started their own organization, the National Conference of Charities and Correction, in 1878. It included Charity Organization Societies (COS) and emphasized their agenda, which was the use of the scientific methods for practical applications. This system included philanthropic, nongovernmental social welfare organizations that focused on the problems of urban poverty and other social problems, such as orphaned and abandoned children, as well as a network of state-administered institutions, such as orphanages, mental institutions, and correctional institutions (Austin, 2003; Zimbalist, 1977).

The ASSA social scientists disbanded in 1909. Social scientists from their respective disciplines developed associations for their own specializations. The debate about the purpose of research eventually had a winner. As history has shown, the emphasis on objective theory building and knowledge building, often referred to as *social research*, and not its practical applications to address social problems, became the major focus of academic social science departments during the first half of the 20th century.

The gap in the field for more directly applied research and evaluation efforts was largely filled by members of the emerging social work profession.

The loosely knit group of charity workers and community volunteers became known as *social workers* when Simon Patten, a social work educator, coined the term in 1900. The profession wanted to move beyond pure armchair theorizing to compassion in action. However, it would be another 33 years before the profession's developmental milestones in which ownership of the unique features of research in social work took root. In 1933, the publication *Social Work Yearbook* included an article titled "Research in Social Work" (Hall, 1937). The author, Helen Jeter, wrote, "research in social work is inquiry into the techniques used by social workers in meeting certain human problems, whether these are individual or community-wide" (Jeter, 1933, p. 98). In addition to practice techniques, research involved the investigation of social needs and problems to which social work services actually or potentially apply (Zimbalist, 1977).

Similarly, in 1937, the *Social Work Yearbook* published another article that clearly distinguished "social work research" or "research in social work" from "social research" of other social sciences. Collective ownership of the research arm of practice was reiterated in 1947 when the landmark conference also articulated a clear distinction between social work research and social research.

The Convergence of Research and Evaluation and Social Reform

Zimbalist (1977) identified six major themes in social work research history before 1980: research on the causes of poverty, measurement of the prevalence of poverty, the social survey movement, quantification indexes in social work, evaluative research on social service effectiveness, and study of the multiproblem family. Since that time, the rise of prevention and intervention research, emancipatory and empowerment methods, and community-based participatory action research methods have become part of the diverse repertoire of social work research techniques that foster the profession's mission.

Many of the late 19th-century social work research studies examined the causes and consequences of poverty. For example, in 1894, Amos Griswold Warner (1894) attempted to make social work its own scientific discipline and published the book *American Charities: A Study of Philanthropy and Economics*. Warner's social work used mixed methods research to explore common social work problems, such as poverty and social work practice methods. At the time, it was a definitive text in social work practice; however, it was critiqued by contemporaries for its methodological research limitations.

Also noteworthy are community-based research and evaluation efforts of the settlement house and charity movements during the first half of the 20th century. Ely's edited book *Hull House Maps and Papers,* published in 1895, included a compilation of research reports and other writings that documented the problems of Chicago's poor neighborhoods and the substandard conditions endured by new immigrants (Ely, 1895). Two years later, in 1897, charity workers conducted an influential study titled "The Philadelphia Negro: A Social Study," which documented the poor living conditions experienced by many African American city residents.

Other research projects addressed the living conditions of immigrants in poverty and at-risk youth. In 1898, in Boston, Robert Wood's City Wilderness Study documented poverty conditions among new immigrants. Beginning in the 1920s, Sophie van Senden Theis conducted her landmark adoption research as a part of the New York State Charities Aid Association. This large-scale outcome study sampled 910 children placed in foster homes between 1898 and 1922. In 1924, she published her findings in the book *How Foster Children Turn Out*. This study was the prototype for many later foster care outcome studies. Almost 20 years later, in 1939, Cabot started the Cambridge-Somerville Youth Study, which focused on the causes and consequences of juvenile delinquency.

Although these early research studies have been scrutinized for their methods, they did serve an important development milestone for improving social work research studies and their application for improving service and social reform efforts.

An important aspect of the profession's development was fostering scholars or experts and leaders among its collective ranks to help improve practice. Journals also were an important mechanism to share knowledge among social workers. In 1900, the charity and settlement house movement published their own professional journals, *Charities* and *Commons*, respectively. In 1906, both journals were merged to become the *Charities and Commons* journal. In 1927, one of the most well-respected journals, the *Social Service Review*, was started by Abbott and Breckinbridge as part of the Chicago School of Philanthropy. In 1951, the Social Work Research Group (SWRG), which was a collective of social work researchers, began to index *Social Work Research* and *Abstracts*. In 1965, the NASW published *Research and Abstracts* (Austin, 2003; Graham, Al-Krenawi, & Bradshaw, 2000).

Combined leadership and scholarly contributions among social workers were also noteworthy. For example, between 1907 and 1915, Jane Addams published six books that addressed social problems of the time, including juvenile delinquency. Jane Addams is also noted as the first woman elected president of the National Council on Charities and Corrections (NCCC) in 1909. Perhaps her greatest achievement came from her international peace movement efforts, which earned her the Nobel Peace Prize in 1931 (Elsthain, 2002).

Similarly, Mary Richmond also had an impressive number of achievements. In 1899, Richmond published *Friendly Visiting the Poor* in an attempt to systematize friendly visiting, which was often referred to at the time as *doing good*. Partially in response to the Flexner speech, which is detailed later in this chapter, Mary Richmond integrated the scientific methods in social work. In 1917, she published the seminal text *Social Diagnosis* and in 1922, she published *What Is Social Casework*. In 1921, Mary Richmond received an honorary degree from Smith College for establishing the scientific base of social work. She is also credited with drafting the first experimental code of ethics for social work (Agnew, 2002).

Educational and Community Resources

Other important aspects of social work's professional development in the 19th century were the development of professional education and other resources. By 1906, school social work programs were established in New York and other major American cities (Leighninger, 2000). Around the same time, in 1907, the Russell Sage Foundation, a private philanthropic foundation, was formed and became an important funding source for social work until the 1950s (Kirk & Reid, 2002).

The Russell Sage Foundation was instrumental in social work research development through providing grants to establish a research arm in these newly formed schools of social work (Austin, 2003). These grants started the shift from conducting research and evaluation in communities and agencies to schools of social work. The Russell Sage Foundation also provided funding for social workers to conduct the groundbreaking Pittsburgh Study, which provided descriptive information of the poor urban conditions that was used for Progress Era reforms. The foundation also established a department of surveys and exhibits for social work. The social survey movement was important to social work, so much so that the journal *Charities and Commons* changed its name to *Survey*. In fact, community survey and needs assessment can be traced back to the survey movement (Kirk & Reid, 2002).

There were also some notable situations in which social workers used research-based evidence to advocate for legislative change, community development, and the improvement of service provision during the first half of the 20th century. Child-saving movement advocates, such as Jane Addams, Julia Lathrop, Sophonisba Breckinridge, and Edith Abbott, gathered statistics on at-risk youth, including delinquents (Breckinbridge & Abbott, 1912). In 1900, the outcomes of these collective efforts resulted in the establishment of the juvenile court in Chicago. This model was later adopted nationally and internationally. In 1912, the U.S. Children's Bureau was established; Julia Lathrop was its first director. She was instrumental in data-gathering on children at the local and national levels. Robert Chapin also published the report "The Standard of Living Among Workingmen's Families in New York City," which brought attention to exploitative employment conditions and local reform efforts (Killian & Maschi, 2009; Platt, 1977).

Perhaps the most critical incident in this young profession's history was in 1915 when Abraham Flexner delivered his legendary keynote address titled "Is Social Work a Profession?" during the 42nd annual session of the NCCC (Kirk & Reid, 2002). Flexner, a young education reformer from New York, was well respected for his rigorous review and was instrumental in the reform of medical education. Although he noted his lack of competence to properly assess a profession with which he was not familiar, he did conclude that social work is "hardly eligible" for status as a profession (Flexner, 1915, p. 588). To attain status as a profession, social workers would need to clarify autonomous responsibility for their client outcomes, refine the goals or aims of their profession from being too broad to more specific, further develop academic training and a specialized knowledge base, and firmly establish a scientific body of knowledge. Although Flexner publicly admitted his limited experience with social work, his speech forever changed social work, particularly his critique of the lack of a scientific knowledge base (Austin, 1983; Kirk & Reid, 2002).

Toward a Separate but Collective Identity

As the profession began to forge a professional identity, organizational alliances evolved and merged, and separated between the education, research, and practice factions of social work. In 1919, schools of social work formed an association that later became the Council on Social Work Education (CSWE) in 1952 (Leighinger, 2000). The SWRG was established in 1948 in an effort to advance the growth of social work research (Graham et al., 2000). In 1948, the NCCC was renamed to the National Conference of Social Workers to underscore a professional social work identity. In 1955, the NASW was formed to merge disparate social work groups, including SWRG, into one unified organization. Under one umbrella, NASW specialty sections were formed, including a Council on Social Work Research. Another merger occurred in 1974 with the reorganization of the

NASW. The NASW merged the different social work organizations under one common umbrella. NASW abolished special interest groups to foster one unified definition (Orcutt, 1990). The pattern of convergence and divergence of social work's community, clinical, and research specializations suggests a profession struggling with how to best realize common goals and a unified identity among professionals with divergent interests and world views.

Efforts were made to further develop and coordinate professional education and the growth of a knowledge and scientific base of social work. In 1917, Mary Richmond published *Social Casework*, which advocated for the application of the scientific method to social work. In an attempt to draw from a knowledge base, in the 1920s, Freud's theories about examining individual problems gained prominence in social work (Deal, 2007). In the 1930s, the functional school of social casework applied a psychosocial approach to understanding and intervening in problems (Reid & Edwards, 2006). People such as Edith Abbott attempted to reinforce the accountability of the profession. In 1931, Abbott advocated for greater efforts to adopt the scientific method in social work. She asserted, "the failure in the past to apply scientific methods and scientific leadership to the needs of the poor has wasted the taxpayers' money and left behind a trail of good intentions and futile efforts" (Abbott, 1942, p. 5).

Echoing Abbott's plea, Richard B. Cabot made a keynote address at the Conference of Social Work in 1931. He critiqued social work for its lack of rigor in research studies. He urged his fellow social workers to move beyond mere assumptions of helping to gathering observable evidence that they had actually done so.

Research and Practice Integration and Effectiveness

As the social work profession matured, around the 1950s, there was a shift from conducting social work research at agencies to conducting it at universities, and there was growing alarm about the lack of research and practice integration. Another significant milestone was the establishment of the National Institute of Mental Health (NIMH) in 1949. NIMH became the major funder of social work when the Russell Sage Foundation folded and social work funding ended. During the 1950s, there was a significant expansion of social work doctoral education to accommodate the need for PhD-level social workers. The Group for the Advancement of Doctoral Education-Social Work (GADE) was formed in 1975 to meet this demand.

In the 1970s, concerns about the effectiveness of social work and a growing chasm between research and practice grew louder. In 1972, a Fordham University Symposium reviewed 13 direct service research projects conducted in the 1960s and deemed or found them to be ineffective (Kirk & Reid, 2002). Similarly, in 1973, Joel Fischer (1973) published the article "Is Social Case Work Effective?" This classic piece continues to fuel the ongoing debate about practice effectiveness (Fischer, 1979, 2005).

There were efforts to address the concerns about service effectiveness and practice and research integration. In 1978, NIMH funded a research conference for NASW to document gaps between research and practice in mental health. One year later, Jayartne and Levy (1979) published *Empirical Clinical Practice Model* in an attempt to systematize the use of single-subject design research to evaluate practice.

Educational organizations, such as CSWE, echoed their support for the integration of research and practice. For example, in 1983, the CSWE

(1983) Curriculum Policy Statement emphasized the integration of research and practice. In 1988, the CSWE Curriculum Policy Statement was revised to indicate the curriculum should impart knowledge for practice and evaluation of services (Commission on Accreditation, 1988). Most recently, the 2008 CSWE (2008) accreditation standards advocate that social workers be competent in the use of research to inform practice and practice to inform research.

Foundational Shifts

In the 1980s, research conducted at agencies almost completely shifted to university schools of social work. Also, the NIMH shifted from funding the training of social workers in mental health practice to funding research on the etiology of mental illness and intervention effectiveness.

Despite this growth, the direction of social work research was the subject of intense debate among academics and practitioners. In 1981, Martha Heineman called into question the logical empiricism for social work aims and argued that qualitative methods which drew data from the ground up were more suitable for the profession. In her 1981 article "The Social Work Research Imperative," she argued:

> In a misguided attempt to be scientific, social work has adopted an outmoded, overly restrictive paradigm of research. Methodological rather than substantive requirements determine the subject matter to be studied. As a result, important questions and valuable data go unresearched. (p. 1)

Despite philosophical debates about the nature of social work research, efforts to grow research infrastructure flourished, and targeted attempts to close the research-practice divide were made. In 1986, the NIMH director authorized the creation of the Task Force on Social Work Research (Graham et al., 2000). In the 1990s, NIMH funded eight developing research centers that were housed in schools of social work. In 1991, the task force published a report, "Building Social Work Knowledge." One of the report's recommendations resulted in the establishment of the Institute for the Advancement of Social Work Research (IASWR) in 1993, and a self-standing organization called the Society for Social Work Research (SSWR) in 1994.

Two years later, in 1996, the group ANSWER was established as an advocacy network for increased support for social work research. In addition, in 2000, the National Institute on Drug Abuse created the Social Work Research Development Program and provided grants to social work researchers (Zlotnick, Biegel, & Solt, 2002; Zlotnick & Solt, 2006). NASW also reinforced the development of social work research in the 1990s, which included the establishment of the *Social Work Research* journal to disseminate social work knowledge.

A Taste of Evidence-Based Medicine for Practice

Evidence-based practice (EBP) was first developed in the 1990s in medicine and became influential in social work (Strauss, Richardson, Glasziou, & Haynes, 2005). Sackett, Rosenberg, Gray, Haynes, and Richardson (1996) defined EBP as the "conscientious, explicit, and judicious use of the current best evidence in making decisions about the care of individual patients" (p. 2). The EBP movement has been steadily growing as a staple of social work practice efforts to enhance practice effectiveness (Rubin, 2008). EBP is reviewed in more detail in Chapter 3.

Recent Developmental Milestones

More recent efforts to disseminate social work research have been achieved. IASWR was disbanded as of 2009 for achieving its aims. The establishment of SWRnet (Social Work Research Network) was launched in October 2009 to continue serving the social work research community by providing regular updates on funding opportunities, calls for papers, conference deadlines, and newly published research (http://www.bu.edu/swrnet).

In 2010, the inaugural issue of the *Journal of the Society for Social Work and Research* (JSSWR) was published. This journal represents a timely way to disseminate social work research in an open journal format (http://www.jsswr.org). *JSSWR* boasts an editorial review board that mentors authors by providing extensive detailed critiques and guidance in refining their manuscripts.

HUMAN RIGHTS AND SOCIAL JUSTICE: IMPLICATIONS FOR SOCIAL WORK RESEARCH

Social work's enduring role in fostering human rights and social justice aims has distinguished it as a human rights profession.

As evidenced in the profession's history, social workers have been on the frontline of seeking solutions for a myriad of societal problems across the globe. Social work's enduring role in fostering human rights and social justice aims has distinguished it as a human rights profession (Healey, 2008). Social work's core ethical principles are consonant with human rights philosophy, such as honoring the "intrinsic value of *every* person," and its use of individual and collective action to promote social justice in the form of "equitable social structures that provide people security and development while upholding their dignity" (International Federation of Social Workers [IFSW], 1988, p. 1).

Echoing this theme, the Council on Social Work Education's (CSWE, 2008) Educational Policy (2.1.5), dictates that social workers be competent in advancing human rights and social and economic justice to achieve social work aims, including the use of research and evaluation strategies. This policy states:

> Each person, regardless of position in society, has basic human rights, such as freedom, safety, privacy, an adequate standard of living, health care, and education. Social workers recognize the global interconnections of oppression and are knowledgeable about theories of justice and strategies to promote human and civil rights. Social work incorporates social justice practices in organizations, institutions, and society to ensure that these basic human rights are distributed equitably and without prejudice. Social workers understand the forms and mechanisms of oppression and discrimination; advocate for human rights and social and economic justice; and engage in practices that advance social and economic justice. (CSWE, 2008, p. 15)

Definitions: Human Rights and Social Justice

So what is meant by *human rights* and *social and economic justice*? And how are they related to research and evaluation? Human rights are generally described as inherent and necessary for human survival (Reichert, 2003). These rights are universal and belong to every person. Honoring the inherent dignity and worth of each person suggests that all people are deserving of respect and protection (UN, 1994). Human rights offer guiding principles or codified values, and laws, to best ensure a high quality of life for all persons (Wronka, 2008).

Human rights are based on civil and political rights; economic, social, and cultural rights; and collective or solidarity rights and are represented in the Universal Declaration of Human Rights (Reichert, 2003; UN, 1948). Wronka (2008) described human rights as a set of guiding principles that are interdependent and have implications for macro, mezzo, and micro practice. Human rights also have been described as the "cornerstone or bedrock of social justice" (Wronka, 2008; p. 5). Human rights provide a global mechanism to pursue a socially just world.

Social justice consists of two essential terms, *social* and *justice*. The Latin root of the term *social* means "companion," "ally," and "associate." Similarly, the definition of *social* refers to a situation involving allies or relating to human society, the interaction of the individual and the group, or the welfare of human beings as members of society (Reichert, 2003). The second term, *justice*, emphasizes the principles of fairness and equity, especially related to morals, ethical standards, or legal protections (Wronka, 2008). Wronka (2008) described social justice as a "struggle to unite friends, allies, and partners in fair and equitable practices" (p. 5).

Traditionally, social work has defined social justice as an ideal condition in which all individual citizens have equal rights, equality of opportunity, and equal access to social resources (UN, 1994). Similarly, *economic justice* is referred to as an ideal condition in which all individuals have access to the sociopolitical resources necessary to reach their full human potential (UN, 1994).

Social justice also refers to the obligations between individuals and society. These mutual obligations fall into three domains: legal justice, distributive justice, and commutative justice. *Legal justice* refers to what an individual owes to society. For example, every person should contribute their time or resources to a larger cause. In contrast, *distributive justice* refers to what a society owes a person. For example, governments and other social institutions should create conditions to ensure fair access to social, cultural, civil, and economic well-being in that all people receive adequate incomes above an agreed-upon threshold. *Commutative justice* refers to what people owe to one another (Humphries, 2008; Van Soest, 1995). For example, individuals must treat one another with dignity and respect.

SOCIAL WORK AT THE INTERSECTION OF HUMAN RIGHTS HISTORY

The profession has also continued to develop amidst a world struggling with war, peace, and human rights. World War I (1914–1918) was quickly followed by the rise of Adolf Hitler and the Nazi regime as well as Japanese Imperialism, over which World War II was fought (1939–1945). For three decades of the 20th century the world witnessed two of the most destructive and wide-scale wars ever fought. The inhumane and cruel treatment inflicted by humans on other humans, particularly during World War II, seemed unfathomable. This treatment included the attempted extermination of Jews and other groups, such as homosexuals and persons with disabilities. The dropping of the atom bomb on the Japanese cities of Nagasaki and Hiroshima transformed a seemingly harmless mushroom cloud into an unprecedented weapon of mass destruction that could wipe out large cities in a matter of minutes (Gilbert, 2004; Strachan, 2003).

From the ashes of war, most world citizens and their leaders were ready for a new approach to human rights in which dignity and respect for all humans were honored. World leaders sought new ways to address world problems, which included the establishment of the United Nations in 1945. With Eleanor Roosevelt at the helm, and in conjunction with the UN Commission on Human Rights, the Universal Declaration of Human Rights (UDHR) was crafted and then ratified on December 10, 1948. The initial proclamation in the UDHR preamble continues to resound: "We the peoples of the United Nations [are] determined to reaffirm faith in fundamental human rights, in the dignity and worth of the human person, in the equal rights of men and women and of nations large and small" (UN, 1948, p. 1).

The UDHR authors crafted the declaration to be a relatively short, inspirational, and energizing document usable by common people. The UDHR consists of 30 articles that are often described by three generations of rights. The first generation of rights (articles 2–21) are referred to as *negative rights*, both civil and political. Generally, these are rights to standards of good behavior by governments or protection of the rule of law, including the right to life, to freedom from torture, to own property, and to limiting where government may intrude. The second generation of rights (articles 22–27) are often referred to as *positive rights* or economic, social, and cultural rights. These rights include the right to social security, the right to work, and the right to participate freely in cultural life. Third generation rights (articles 28–30) are collective or solidarity rights, such as everyone is entitled to a social and international order (Reichert, 2003; UN, 1948; Wronka, 2008).

Social workers have put forth their efforts to improve human rights in all three domains, particularly in the area of international peace. For example, social work leaders, such as Jane Addams and Emily Green Balch, were instrumental in international peace efforts and are internationally recognized for these efforts; they received the Nobel Peace Prize in 1931 and 1960, respectively (Ehrenreich, 1985; Elsthain, 2002).

In addition to the UDHR (UN, 1948), the United Nations has additional documents further delineating these rights and has also developed organizations or implementation mechanisms to help monitor countries' adherence to them (UN, 1994). Wronka (2008) referred to the *Human Rights Triptych* as a triangle, with the UDHR at the center; other UN documents, such as declarations and conventions, which further elaborate upon the UDHR, on the right side; and implementation mechanisms, such as the Human Rights Council and other UN special commissions, on the left side.

The International Federation of Social Workers' (1996) international policy on human rights delineated basic documents concerning human rights, which included instruments, covenants, and conventions that concern social

Table 1.2	**Human Rights Documents**

Basic global instruments for human rights are:

1. Charter of the United Nations (1945)
2. Universal Declaration of Human Rights (1948)
3. The Covenants on Human Rights (1966)
   a. International Covenant on Civil and Political Rights
   b. International Covenant on Economic, Social, and Cultural Rights
4. International Convention on the Elimination of All Forms of Racial Discrimination (1965)
5. Convention on the Elimination of All Forms of Discrimination Against Women (1979)
6. Convention Against Torture and Other Cruel, Inhuman, and Degrading Treatment or Punishment (1984)
7. Convention on the Rights of the Child (1989)
8. International Convention on the Protection of the Rights of All Migrant Workers and Members of Their Families (1990)

These global instruments are reinforced by:

1. The European Convention on Human Rights (1950)
2. The American Convention on Human Rights (1969)
3. The African Charter on Human Rights and Peoples Rights (1981)

The covenants and conventions are supported by United Nations declarations:

1. The Rights of Mentally Retarded Persons (1971)
2. The Protection of Women and Children in Armed Conflicts (1974)
3. The Elimination of All forms of Religious Intolerance (1981)
4. The Right to Development (1986)

Source: United Nations. (1994). *Human rights and social work: A manual for schools of social work and the social work profession.* Geneva: United Nations Centre for Human Rights.

workers. As outlined in Table 1.2, these include the UDHR, the International Covenant on Civil and Political Rights (ICCPR), the International Covenant on Economic, Social, and Cultural Rights (ICESCR), and Conventions on the Rights of the Child (CRC). Social workers should be aware of the documents relevant to their area of practice and/or research interests.

Advanced Generalist/Public Health Model to Human Rights and Social Justice

In Wronka's (2008) Advanced Generalist/Public Health (AGPH) model, research and evaluation assume a pivotal and essential role (see Figure 1.1). Whereas the public health model articulates these levels of intervention, this model uses a

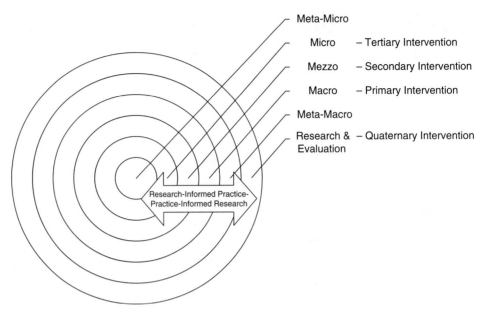

Figure 1.1
AGPH Model: Types of Interventions to Advance Human Rights and Social Justice
Source: Based on Wronka, J. (2010). *Human rights and social justice: Social action and service for the helping and health professions.* Thousand Oaks, CA: Sage Publications.

whole population approach through the lens of human rights and social justice aims, in which research and evaluation play a central role in achieving these aims. Although the demarcation across them is not always distinct, the model conceptualizes four levels of intervention designed to prevent or alleviate social problems: primary, secondary, tertiary, and quaternary, which target macro, mezzo, micro, meta-micro, meta-macro, and research levels of intervention. Although research has its own level, it also informs all intervention levels. Interestingly, none of the levels offer a perfect solution and definitive answer to social problems. Therefore, interventions at all levels can best help achieve research and social action and/or service aims (Wronka, 2008).

Macro and Meta-Macro Levels

In the AGPH model, the macro level is a target of primary intervention strategies because it targets a whole population, mostly on a national level, such as the total population of the United States. The purpose of primary intervention strategies is to prevent individuals from compromising their health and well-being (Wronka, 2008). An example of a primary intervention strategy is the development and implementation of a national campaign for substance abuse awareness. The even larger meta-macro level focuses on the international level, which acknowledges the global interconnectedness of people and places. An example of a global prevention initiative is a social media campaign that promotes the importance of universal education.

Mezzo Levels

The mezzo level is the target of secondary intervention strategies among groups at risk. These strategies may involve interventions in high-risk environments such as crime-ridden neighborhoods. For example, a social worker can develop a crime prevention program and monitor its effectiveness on outcomes such as neighborhood violence.

Micro and Meta-Micro Levels

The micro level is the target of tertiary intervention strategies and symptomatic populations. Tertiary level interventions commonly entail clinical interventions on an individual level using one-on-one or group counseling. For example, a social worker employed at a nursing home may design and implement a reminiscent therapy group for older adults and monitor its effectiveness on the overall cognitive functioning of the group participants.

The meta-micro level also is the target of tertiary intervention strategies. However, not all problems require clinical intervention but rather can be effectively dealt with in everyday life with families and communities. Although clinical interventions help with problems, everyday life social connections, such as family, friends, and others, can have therapeutic benefits. For example, a conversation between a grandchild and a grandparent may have mutual beneficial effects on their social well-being.

Research and Evaluation Level

In the AGPH model, research and evaluation are the methods used in quaternary intervention strategies. Findings from research and evaluation studies provide informed knowledge for prevention and intervention strategies across the other intervention levels. In turn, the primary, secondary, and tertiary levels influence the research questions to be asked and the methodologies used (Wronka, 2008).

The Relationship between Human Rights, Social Justice, and Research

Problem Formulation

As a quaternary intervention strategy, research and evaluation can be defined using a human rights and social justice framework. In fact, using a human rights and social justice framework, social workers may view a study as having two purposes, which include the purpose of the study for the particular problem under investigation and a higher purpose to advance human rights and social justice in that area.

Human Rights and Justice

Critical Thinking Question: What are the pros and cons of using a human rights and social justice framework for social work research, including problem formulation and implications?

Human rights scholars note that human rights documents, such as the UDHR, are a means of defining the research problem (Ife, 2001a, 2001b). Social workers can consult human rights documents to help clearly define their research problem and research questions.

Using a human rights framework, social workers also should consider the historical context in understanding the research problem. This includes closely examining the historical experiences of a minority population under investigation, such as the African American and Native American communities (Wronka, 2008).

On a micro and mezzo level, social workers can engage in research and evaluation by defining problems in their community settings. This includes conducting needs assessments to identify gaps in services, developing programs to fill those gaps, and evaluating the outcomes. Social workers can also engage in practice evaluation, including the use of EBPs, to ensure that the individuals and families served obtain the best services possible. Carefully monitoring interventions will assist social workers with modifying interventions as needed for an individual or family.

On a meta-macro or macro level, some research and evaluation projects may involve gathering information that can be used as a gauge for countries' progress on a host of human rights and social justice issues, including human and community well-being. For example, some researchers may conduct descriptive studies to determine the prevalence of human trafficking on a national and international level. Clearly identifying the problem can lead to potential solutions to stop illegal behavior and promote improved well-being among its victims.

Social workers can also use research for policy reform efforts by critically examining legal and public discourse and the extent to which they comply with human rights principles. For example, whereas the United States has political and civil rights as part of its legal system, there is a paucity of economic, social, and cultural rights in the United States in both federal and state constitutions. This area is ripe for exploration among social workers.

Methods

After determining a research question, a social worker should choose the best available methods to answer that question. Social workers have a host of quantitative, qualitative, and mixed methods designs at their disposal for use in the field. These will be detailed in the remainder of this text; therefore, only a brief overview is provided here. Quantitative research, mostly using numeric data and large population samples, is a means of documenting the magnitude and severity of a problem among target populations.

Qualitative research methods, often using narrative data and smaller sample sizes, are an effective means of exploring relatively unknown areas and elevating the voices of subjugated groups, such as mental health consumers, so they are heard. Qualitative approaches also can provide a thick description of lived experiences of individuals, such as political refugees, holocaust survivors, or incarcerated offenders.

Mixed methods studies often offer the best of both the quantitative and qualitative worlds. They also can offer wide-scale comparative analysis of international policies on work conditions, family violence, or the well-being of children, adults, and/or older adults.

Alternative methodologies, such as community mapping, participatory action research, empowerment evaluation, and community-based participatory research, involve central stakeholders in partnerships with the researchers (e.g., Guitierrez, 2003; Hillier, 2007; Patton, 2002; Secret, Jordan, & Ford, 1999).

The importance of knowledge of ethics

Using a human rights and social justice framework, social workers must carefully weigh protections for research participants with methods decisions that employ the most rigorous research designs possible. For example, social workers should be well aware of how the research ethics guidelines arose in response to international human rights abuses, especially the Nazi experiments conducted during World War II and the establishment of the Nuremberg Code, which outlined essential research ethics. As will be detailed in chapter 2, research ethics underscore participants' right to self-determination and voluntary participation, justice, and beneficence.

Findings, Dissemination, and Action

Using a human rights and social justice framework, social workers should also consider the historical context of minorities when interpreting findings. To be consistent with this framework, it is imperative that social work research and evaluation efforts be shared. Social workers commonly communicate their research findings through writing and speaking. Getting the message out includes publishing reports and journal articles, giving public presentations, and using the media (Ife, 2001a; UN, 1994; Wronka, 2008).

Social workers should use language that can be understood by laypeople as well as scholars. Therefore, both their speech and writing should be clear and succinct and easy for readers to grasp. The use of effective oral and written communication also is an effective tool to move an audience to action. Aristotle's (350 B.C./2000) rhetoric for persuasion includes three forms: *ethos, logos,* and *pathos.*

The following example applies the three forms of rhetoric to a speech or oral presentation commonly used with practice and research activities.

Ethos represents a speaker's authority or honesty as to how he or she demands authority to speak on a topic. The speaker exerts a demeanor of sincerity and fair-mindedness and uses appropriate language, including vocabulary and grammar (Wisse, 1989).

Logos represents the use of logic, in the form of evidence and reason, to persuade an audience. For example, logos mostly describe the use of evidence to support an important point, such as the national statistics on children who were maltreated. The use of logic to persuade an audience might include the use of definitions, factual data and statistics, quotations, and/or informed opinions or citations from experts and authorities. The use of logos often supplements the speaker's ethos appeal as an authority to speak on a designated topic. The speaker also appeals to reason using established theories and/or cause-and-effect arguments (Wisse, 1989).

Pathos, on the other hand, represents an appeal to emotions. This emotional appeal can be in the form of passionate delivery, including the assertion that a topic is a human rights and social justice issue. Techniques for pathos include the use of vivid descriptions, emotionally charged language, emotional tone, and figurative or metaphorical language. The use of pathos is most effective when a speaker makes the connection with an underlying value, such as fairness and equity, and when it is coordinated with the character of ethos and logic of logos (Aristotle, 350 B.C./2000; Wisse, 1989).

These findings also should be put into action that is consistent with the professional value of social justice. Social workers are expected to engage in social action (NASW, 1999) as a part of their ethical commitment to the profession. Social work advocacy efforts can be done alone or in tandem with other stakeholders. This might include using research findings to advocate policy reform (Thomas & Mohan, 2007).

Social workers as collaborators for human rights also use sound research and evaluation findings for the purposes of action. The United Nations (1994) has recommended intervention strategies to help advance human rights that social workers can adapt. These intervention strategies include to

Social workers as collaborators for human rights also use sound research and evaluation findings for the purposes of action.

- work with local, regional, and national organizations to promote, develop, and implement needed changes in policy, planning, and programming on human rights issues,
- recognize and adapt existing services to maximize effectiveness,

◗ develop and involve appropriate and qualified leaders from the community to identify, plan, and implement needed services and advocacy efforts,

◗ develop self capacities of those disadvantaged in their human rights,

◗ organize previously unorganized disadvantaged groups for self-help,

◗ form alliances with like-minded social and political movements,

◗ develop mechanisms to enhance local and global awareness, including the use of mass media,

◗ fundraise for the cause,

◗ assess the impact of actions undertaken in collaboration with persons and groups affected and associated groups and organizations,

◗ document and disseminate information on human rights abuses, and

◗ promote legislation that benefits disadvantaged groups (UN, 1994).

The following interview excerpt illustrates the use of research and statistics for advocacy purposes. The interviewee is Marian Wright Edelman, president and founder of the Children's Defense Fund (Goodman, 2007). During her interview with radio host Amy Goodman, she described her view for the expansion of children's healthcare during a time when then President George W. Bush promised to veto a bill expanding the Children's Health Insurance Program. Using child well-being data, she advocates for children's rights to quality healthcare and the necessity for the government to act. Edelman made the following impassioned plea:

> We [the Children's Defense Fund] believe that the richest nation on earth should not leave thirteen million children behind in poverty and nine million children behind without healthcare. 80% of our black and Latino children are unable to read and write in fourth grade; 60% of our white children are unable to read. And we believe that this is something that is going to be an Achilles' heel of this nation. But the President of the United States simply appropriated—in our view, illegally—our trademarked slogan and then proceeded to use it as a fig leaf to hide policies that gave massive tax cuts to the rich at the expense of the poor, to widen the gap between rich and poor, to say he was going to do education while he put far more money into people who did not need it. And they refused to cease and desist. (Goodman, 2007, p. 1)

Social Work Leaders—Researchers, Practitioners, and Advocates

This section highlights the leadership efforts of early social work leaders, such as Mary Richmond and Jane Addams, to integrate research with practice activities that ranged from the individual to community level (Addams, 1910; Richmond, 1917). At the individual level with social work casework, Mary Richmond (1917) advocated for the newly formed social work profession to integrate a scientific approach to understanding social problems and evaluating practice. In her 1917 book *Social Diagnosis*, Richmond urged social

Policy Practice

Critical Thinking Question: Use current or historical examples; how might the use of research for policy practice have a positive or negative effect on individuals, families, or communities?

workers to go beyond the assumption of "helping" to critically appraise whether in fact their interventions were helpful. On the opening page of her historic text, she asserted:

> "Doing good" was the old phrase used for "social service." It begged the question, as do the newer terms, "social work" and "social service"—unless society is really served. We should welcome, therefore, the evident desire of social workers to abandon their claims to respect based upon good intentions alone. (p. 1)

In her seminal text *Social Diagnosis*, Mary Richmond (1917) delineated the principles of casework and the use of the scientific method. Borrowing from the medical professional, Mary Richmond advocated for the use of scientific problem-solving method to make a "social diagnosis" (Richmond, 1917). To support hypotheses about individuals and families served, data were gathered in the field, which could then be tested by obtaining relevant evidence (Orcutt, 1990). Mary Richmond also was instrumental in establishing professional social work education and advocated for the inclusion of a field-based component to the academic curriculum (Colcard & Mann, 1930).

On the community level, Jane Addams was instrumental in social change efforts of which community-level research was an essential part (Linn, 2000). Her community practice activities included the establishment of the Hull House in Chicago (Addams, 1910). Hull House was a catalyst for the settlement house movement that served urban immigrant families in the United States (Day, 2008). In the classic text that was a compilation of writings by the residents of Hull House (Ely, 1895), *Hull-House Maps and Paper: A Presentation of Nationalities and Wages in a Contested District of Chicago*, research, including community mapping, generated essential data used in advocating for social reform. In this text Jane Addams contributed a piece in which she documented unfair labor practices and poverty. In her piece, the "Settlement as a Factor in the Labor Movement," Jane Addams wrote:

> No trades are so overcrowded as the sewing-trades; for the needle has ever been the refuge of the unskilled woman. The wages paid throughout the manufacture of clothing are less than those in any other trade. . . . The residents of Hull House have carefully investigated many cases, and are ready to assert that the Italian widow who finishes the cheapest goods, although she sews from six in the morning until eleven at night, can only get enough to the keep her children clothed and fed; while for her rent and fuel she must always depend upon charity or the hospitality of her countrymen. (p. 186)

Additionally, other Hull House members, such as Julia Lathrop, Florence Kelly, and Ellen Gates Starr, also were instrumental in conducting community-level research and advocacy efforts. In Julia Lathrop's (1895) book, in a chapter entitled "Cook County Charities," she wrote:

> As the study of these [community] maps reveals an overwhelming proportion of foreigners, and an average wage-rate so low as to render thrift, even if existed, an ineffective insurance against emergencies, we are led at once to inquire what happened when the power of self-help is lost. (p. 143)

Jane Addams and her colleagues at the Hull House worked collaboratively among themselves, and with other professionals, for social and political change at the national and international governmental levels. They successfully collaborated with other social workers and activists of their time on the reform of child labor laws, the establishment of a separate juvenile court system for delinquent youth, women's right to vote, and international peace (Ehrenreich, 1985; Platt, 1977). Some of these efforts were also noted internationally; for example, with Jane Addams's Nobel Peace Prize in 1931 (Linn, 2000).

Furthering Research, Practice, and Advocacy Integration

Research-Based Practice

Critical Thinking Question: What factors facilitate or create barriers for research and practice integration among social workers?

As illustrated by past social work leaders, social work intervention successes consistently comprised an integrated approach to facilitating change. This integrated approach of research-practice-advocacy was part and parcel of individual practitioners or practitioners in collaboration with other interested stakeholders to work toward individual and social/political-level change. Historically, social workers have assisted individuals and families to improve their psychosocial functioning through casework and clinical practice. Additionally, they have combated unjust and unfair societal conditions through legal and policy advocacy, such as for women's and children's rights (Bartlett, 1958, 1970; Zimbalist, 1977).

Many social workers may be less aware of the historic role of scientific inquiry and its function in developing and improving practice and advocacy efforts at an individual, community, and societal level. In fact, students and practitioners often are initially drawn to the social work profession because of a strong desire to help others and/or to combat societal injustice and the unfair treatment of individuals or groups (Grobman, 2004, 2005; Le Croy, 2006; Limb & Organista, 2003). A host of social work activities, such as research, clinical practice, community organizing, program administration, and advocacy, can be viewed as a means to this end (Bogo, Raphael, & Roberts, 1993; Butler, 1990; D'Aprix, Dunlap, Able, & Edwards, 2004). In fact, progress toward social work's mission of promoting well-being and just outcomes appears to be most effective when research and practice aims are coordinated.

Social work students often embrace practice activities, such as clinical and community practice, but are unsure of the role of research and evaluation activities in the promotion of well-being, human rights, and social justice (Bogo et al., 1993; Butler, 1990; D'Aprix et al., 2004). In their social work educational experience, research coursework is often a new experience, and many students approach it with trepidation (Epstein, 1987; Maschi et al., 2007). However, evidence suggests that with increased exposure to the research and involvement in projects, the use of research and practice evaluation strategies becomes a seamless part of the social work students' and practitioners' knowledge, values, and skill set (Unrau & Grinnell, 2005).

This text is about the integration of research into professional practice and action. It is composed of a practice trinity of practitioner-researcher-activist. The term *trinity* is used to represent three closely related activities of practice, research, and activism in which the boundaries are often blurred. We refer to integration of these activities in combination of parts that work together well. When these activities are in alignment, great strides are made in advocating at the individual and community levels for individual and social change. This integration must occur within individual practitioners, as well as the profession as a whole.

Professional social work organizations underscore the integration of research and practice to foster their missions (CSWE, 2002, 2008; NASW, 1996). Social work organizations, such as the Council on Social Work Education (CSWE, 2008) and the National Association of Social Workers (NASW, 1996), mandate that social workers should be proficient in using research and in evaluation skills. CSWE's (2008) most recent educational policy initiative deepens the commitment to research and practice integration. According to CSWE's accreditation standards, social work education programs must equip students to understand and use research and evaluation, knowledge, and skills (Education Policy 2.1.6). Thus, social work students must not only be prepared to use "practice experience to inform scientific inquiry" but also to use "research evidence to inform practice" (CSWE, 2008, p. 5). Social work students also must be educated to "critically analyze, monitor, and evaluate interventions" (Educational Policy 2.1.10d; CSWE, 2008, p. 7).

Similarly, the NASW's (1996) Code of Ethics considers the integration of research and practice as part of social workers' ethical responsibility to the profession. Section 5.0.1 outlining principles related to the *Integrity of the Profession* clearly delineates that practicing with integrity includes conducting research and monitoring and evaluating policies, programs, and practice interventions. Additionally, social workers' ethical responsibilities also include keeping current with emerging social work knowledge and applying research evidence to professional practice as outlined in Section 5.02 on *Evaluation and Research* (NASW, 1996).

Despite these efforts, a residual tension remains among some social workers on how to integrate the objective scientific observer with the empathic counselor and passionate action-oriented reformer (Briar, Weissman, & Rubin, 1981; Flexner, 1915; Fraser, Jensen, & Lewis, 1993). This unresolved tension seems to impact social work students in their integration of a professional social work identity. It also is a source of tension among different specializations of social work practice, such as research, clinical practice, and community practice, in which misunderstanding may occur about the importance and relevance of these activities toward meeting the profession's mission to enhance well-being and social justice outcomes. This text will help social work students embrace the multifaceted aspects of social work, which include scientific inquiry, service, and activism. It will also provide the skills to integrate research into practice and to collaborate with other professionals in social work and other disciplines.

The EBP model used in social work and allied professions, such as medicine, is receiving a great deal of attention because it uses scientific methods and has scientific support for effectiveness. The EBP process assists practitioners with integrating preexisting scientific evidence with their practice experience on which to base their real-world practice decisions (Rubin, 2008). The EBP model is discussed in detail in Chapter 3.

An ongoing assessment of research competence that can be used throughout the semester to monitor research-related confidence and anxiety about obtaining competence in research is provided in Table 1.3 and Figure 1.2. After reviewing single-subject design, students can use this weekly exercise to monitor their research learning experience.

Table 1.3	**Research Competence Assessment Survey and Graph: Research Anxiety and Confidence Single-Subject Design Project**

For this exercise, you will need to analyze your thoughts, feelings, and confidence about research.
Directions: PLEASE COMPLETE ONE SURVEY PER WEEK (Preferably on the same day and at the same time). This assignment is ongoing throughout the semester. All students are expected to complete one survey per week for the semester.

Part 1. Using the following subjective rating scale (between 1 and 9) that measures research confidence class, (1 = not confident at all, 5 = somewhat confident, 9 = completely confident), please complete the following questions:

Week#: _____ Date: _____ Time: _____

(please complete each week for sessions 1–15)

Part A: How confident are you in

_____A1. Formulating a research problem consistent with human rights and social justice?

_____A2. Gathering empirical literature relevant to my topic of interest?

_____A3. Adhering to ethical standards in conducting research?

_____A4. Conducting a research project?

_____A5. Using research to inform practice and practice to inform research?

_____A6. Analyzing results using quantitative and qualitative methods?

_____A7. Writing a research report?

_____A8. Analyzing the impact of a study's findings for social work practice?

_____A9. Analyzing the impact of a study's findings for social policy?

_____A10. Analyzing the impact of a study's findings for human rights and social justice?

_____ Part A Total Score (for questions 1–10) *(scores can range from 10 through 90)*

Part AB. Anxiety Scale: Circle the number that best represents how anxious you feel about research.

0	10	20	30	40	50	60	70	80	90
Not anxious at all				Moderately anxious					Extremely anxious

Part B: Please answer these additional questions:

_____B1. How many hours this week did you attend research class (or classes)?

_____B2. How many hours this week did you read research materials?

_____B3. How many hours this week did you conduct research?

_____ Part B Total Hours Per Week

11. Please write a paragraph on your thoughts and feelings about research this week.

Source: Maschi, T. (2010). *Research Competence Survey and Graph.* New York: Community Research and Evaluation Collaborative.

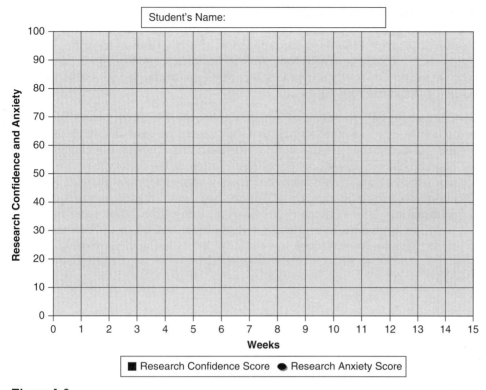

Figure 1.2

Research Competence Assessment and Graph: Graphing Research Anxiety and Confidence

Based on the graphed results (and integrating your qualitative results where possible), briefly explain your experience with research related–anxiety and confidence before, during, and at the end of the semester. How (if at all) do you see your research-related anxiety and confidence related? Please explain.

Source: Maschi, T. (2010). *Research competence survey and graph.* New York: Fordham University Community Research and Evaluation Collaborative.

SUMMARY

Research and evaluation strategies for practice have been a common thread woven throughout social work history as social workers pursue new possibilities and help create a better world. Since the beginning of the profession, research in the form of the scientific method has been used to understand individual and social problems and to guide, assess, and intervene with underserved populations, especially the poor (Zimbalist, 1977).

Social work has been touted as a human rights profession mostly based on a shared value system with human rights philosophies and the use of practices to enhance human and community well-being and fairness in society. From a human rights framework, social work research and evaluation are a quaternary intervention level and have an essential role in primary, secondary, and tertiary prevention. Social workers' knowledge of human rights philosophies and documents can be used to inform all phases of the research and evaluation process.

A review of social work history reveals a profession that has undergone a process of integrating scientific inquiry with humanistic values and passionate action. Social work research has periods of convergence and divergence and tension with social work practice. The recognition of this creative tension is a first step in the process toward a peaceful and long-standing union. Eleanor Roosevelt (1958), in her speech to the UN Commission on Human Rights at the United Nations in New York on March 27, 1958, suggests where and how we might approach our practice contexts, both large and small, toward evidence-based reforms. She said:

> Where, after all, do universal human rights begin? In small places, close to home—so close and so small that they cannot be seen on any maps of the world. Yet they are the world of the individual person; the neighborhood he lives in; the school or college he attends; the factory, farm, or office where he works. Such are the places where every man, woman, and child seeks equal justice, equal opportunity, equal dignity without discrimination. Unless these rights have meaning there, they have little meaning anywhere. Without concerted citizen action to uphold them close to home, we shall look in vain for progress in the larger world.

Succeed with PEARSON mysocialworklab

Log onto **www.mysocialworklab.com** and answer the following questions. (*If you did not receive an access code to MySocialWorkLab with this text and wish to purchase access online, please visit www.mysocialworklab.com.*)

1. **Watch the professional identity video "Advocating for the Client."** Using the chapter's human rights framework, determine the intervention level. How can research and evaluation inform the intervention?

2. **Watch the policy practice video "Participating in Policy Changes."** After listening to the commentary, indicate how research and evaluation were used to promote human rights and social justice?

PRACTICE TEST
The following questions will test your knowledge of the content found within this chapter. For additional assessment, including licensing-exam type questions on applying chapter content to practice, visit **MySocialWorkLab**.

1. A social worker engaging in primary interventions social work research would most likely:
   a. Target only select at-risk individuals
   b. Be conducted in one neighborhood
   c. Target the whole population, mostly on a national level
   d. Not be conducted

2. Scientific inquiry in social work's history is best represented by:
   a. Collective curiosity
   b. Systematically gathering information
   c. Gathering information and setting a goal for change
   d. Regularly continually asking questions

3. "Social work research" was first differentiated from "social science research" in which year?
   a. 1910
   b. 1925
   c. 1937
   d. 1948

4. Jane Addams and the settlement house movement attributed their collective social change successes to:
   a. Opening Hull House
   b. Advocating at the legislative level
   c. The rise of the charity movement
   d. The three *r* strategies: residence, research, and reform

5. On a scale of 0 to 10 (in which 0 = no confidence and 10 = complete confidence), rate your confidence about using research to inform practice and practice to inform research. Identify one strategy you can use to improve confidence.

ASSESS YOUR COMPETENCE
Use the scale below to rate your current level of achievement on the following concepts or skills associated with each competency presented in the chapter:

1	2	3
I can accurately describe the concept or skill.	I can consistently identify the concept or skill when observing and analyzing practice activities.	I can competently implement the concept or skill in my own practice.

_____ can demonstrate knowledge of social work research history.

_____ can apply research or evaluation strategies that promote human rights and social and economic justice at different intervention levels.

_____ can use scientific inquiry to inform social work practice.

_____ can engage in policy practice that advances human rights and social justice.

2

The Value of Values and Ethics in Social Work Research and Evaluation

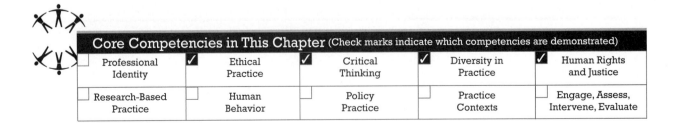

Core Competencies in This Chapter (Check marks indicate which competencies are demonstrated)									
	Professional Identity	✓	Ethical Practice	✓	Critical Thinking	✓	Diversity in Practice	✓	Human Rights and Justice
	Research-Based Practice		Human Behavior		Policy Practice		Practice Contexts		Engage, Assess, Intervene, Evaluate

INTRODUCTION

Social work often has been described as a values-based profession. That is, social workers belong to a profession in which professional values and ethical principles comprise a core philosophical base that guides social work thought and actions, including research activities (Bartlett, 1958; Congress, 1999; Wronka, 2007). In fact, professional values might be thought of as the heartbeat of social work, whereas ethics represent the conscience of social work practice.

As illustrated in this chapter, the history of social work values and ethics is intertwined with human rights and research ethics history. Many of the social work professional core values and ethical principles are consistent with human rights values. Research ethics history seeks to promote dignity and worth of the person, beneficence, justice, and scientific integrity (Wronka, 2008). Contemporary social workers engaged in research and evaluation must continually consider the role of professional values and ethics in their practice decision-making processes (NASW, 1999).

The history of social work values and ethics is intertwined with human rights and research ethics history.

This chapter first reviews the role of social work values and ethics in research practice, and then looks at the history and impact of biomedical research ethics on contemporary social work research and evaluation. This chapter concludes with an ethical decision-making model that can be used for planning and implementing research and evaluation projects.

Values and Ethics

To engage in ethical research and evaluation practices, social workers must first understand the critical distinctions between values and ethics. *Values* often refer to the customs, beliefs, and rules of conduct that a group, culture, or society desire (Reamer, 1995). In other words, values represent strong beliefs or feelings that are, in general, not empirically verifiable but that guide human actions and behaviors (Congress, 1999). Individuals' personal values may differ on issues such as social welfare services for the poor or the use of the death penalty as a punishment for violent crime. Values differ from knowledge in that *values* are the "beliefs, preferences, or assumptions about what is desirable for people," and *knowledge* is "observations about the world and people which have been verified or [are] capable of verification" (Pincus & Minahan, 1973, p. 37). As illustrated in this chapter, social workers who engage in research and evaluation activities must be aware of and negotiate their personal and professional values while they use scientific methods.

National and international social work organizations (International Federation of Social Workers [IFSW] and International Association of Schools of Social Work [IASSW], 2004; NASW, 1999) have articulated professional values that provide a foundation of ethical principles in their ethical codes. For example, the NASW Code of Ethics (1999) stipulates six core professional values: service, social justice, dignity and worth of the person, importance of human relationships, integrity, and competence. This constellation of core values influences the attitudes and approaches of social workers, in all aspects of their work, including research and evaluation activities. For example, the core values of service and social justice suggest that research in social work best represents these values when it is used to improve service provision or increase social justice outcomes for the population under investigation (NASW, 1999).

Ethics

Whereas the term *values* commonly refers to strong beliefs or feelings, the term *ethics* refers to a standard of conduct or moral duty. The word *ethics* originates from the Greek language and means "character" (Merriam-Webster, 2007). Similarly, *ethics* refers to moral principles and people's perceptions about right and wrong (Congress, 1999). Values and ethics differ in that values reflect what is good and desirable, whereas ethics reflect what is right or correct. However, values commonly form the philosophical base from which ethics are deduced, and therefore they must be consonant with each other (Congress, 1999). For example, the right to privacy is an American value and a social work professional value and relates closely to confidentiality, a central aspect of most social work practice, especially research and the protection of participants.

PROFESSIONAL CODE OF ETHICS: HISTORY AND MEANING

Ethical principles are most often based on the larger culture's beliefs and values (Reamer, 1995). Western values that guide ethical codes for many global helping professions, including social work, include respect for all persons, the provision of service, the obligation to "do no harm," integrity, and trustworthiness (American Counseling Association [ACA], 2005; American Medication Association [AMA], 2001; IFSW, 1988). Social work is unique as a helping profession in that it combines traditional helping professional values with the value of human rights and social justice in the form of honoring the dignity and worth of all persons, the fair distribution of societal resources, and eliminating all sorts of oppression related to age, race and ethnicity, sexual orientation, and socioeconomic status (IFSW & IASSW, 2004).

Code of Ethics

Most helping professions have a code of ethics to guide professional conduct. A code of ethics often is an explicit statement of a profession's values, principles, and codes of conduct (Barker, 2003). In other words, a code of ethics for a profession generally provides guidelines as to how members of the profession translate their values into action. Professional codes of ethics guide decision making, regulate professional behavior, protect the rights and welfare of clients, set standards for research and evaluation, and are a basis for improving practice and ensuring accountability. In particular, the social work profession has the IFSW (2000) and NASW (1999) codes of ethics that delineate the profession's values, ethics, and rules, which in turn inform social workers' research activities. The NASW code of ethics has standards for the use and practice of social work research and evaluation (section 5.02), which will be discussed later in this chapter.

International Ethics for Social Work

The International Federation of Social Workers (IFSW) and International Association of Schools of Social Work (IASSW) (2004) developed the first international code of ethics for social work in 1976 and last revised it in 2004.

This four-page document titled "Ethics, Statement of Principles Code" consists of general principles divided into five parts titled preamble, definition of social work, international conventions, principles (human rights and dignity and social justice), and professional conduct.

The IFSW (2000) code emphasizes the importance of ethical awareness as a fundamental part of the professional practice and research of social workers across the globe. The IFSW and IASSW promote ethical debate and reflection among their individual members and member organizations. Some ethical challenges and problems facing social workers are specific to particular countries; others are global. The authors of the document purposely devised general principles to guide social workers around the globe to engage in thoughtful reflection on the ethical dilemmas they experience and to use an ethical decision-making process to guide their actions in particular practice contexts. Some common areas in which conflicting priorities challenge social workers' loyalties include having to assume the dual and conflicting roles of helper and controller; the conflicts between their duty to protect the interests of populations they serve and societal demands for efficiency, utility, and accountability; and needing environmental resources to best serve while resources in society are limited (IFSW & IASSW, 2004). As discussed later in this chapter, these types of problems and dilemmas are faced by all social workers, including those engaging in research and evaluation. A complete copy of this code can be found at http://www.ifsw.org/f38000032.html.

NASW Code of Ethics

Developed in the United States, the NASW Code of Ethics (1999) is a set of standards for the professional conduct of social workers. All NASW members are expected to abide by the code of ethics. The NASW Code of Ethics (1999) has evolved from a 1-page to a 25-page document that delineates the values, rules, and principles of ethical conduct for all professional social workers (Reamer, 1995). The original code of ethics for social workers was implicit in the 1951 Standards for Professional Practice of the American Association of Social Workers (AASW). NASW developed a formal code in 1960 and has since made subsequent revisions; the latest update occurred in 2008 when recently immigrated (*immigration status)* was added to the list of vulnerable populations (Congress, 1999, 2008).

The NASW Code of Ethics (1999) is composed of a preamble that states the mission and core values, ethical principles, and ethical standards that address responsibilities to clients, colleagues, the profession, practice settings, and the broader society. The document underscores respect and dignity and worth of the person, self-determination, integrity, competence, and advocacy and social action. It is a social worker's responsibility to engage in ethical conduct by adhering to the profession's code of ethics, which includes providing the highest-quality services and acting honorably (Congress, 1999). As described earlier, this document also explicates the use of standards for research and evaluation. Social workers engaged in ethical research must conform to the accepted standards of conduct set forth by the NASW as well as the international research ethics codes. The preamble states: the "primary mission of the social work profession is to enhance human well-being and help meet the basic human needs of all people, with particular attention to the needs and empowerment of people who are vulnerable, oppressed, and living in poverty" (NASW, 1999, p. 1).

Table 2.1	**Values and Ethical Principles in NASW Code of Ethics (1999)**
Value	Ethical Principle
Service	Social workers' primary goal is to help people in need and to address social problems.
Social Justice	Social workers challenge social injustice.
Dignity and Worth of the Person	Social workers respect the inherent dignity and worth of the person.
Importance of Human Relationships	Social workers recognize the central importance of human relationships.
Integrity	Social workers behave in a trustworthy manner.
Competence	Social workers practice within their areas of competence and develop and enhance their professional expertise.

Source: Adapted from National Association of Social Workers. (1999). *Code of ethics of the National Association of Social Workers.* Washington, DC: NASW Press.

Social workers promote social justice and social change and enhance the capacity of individuals, families, organization, and communities to address social injustices. These activities may be in the form of direct practice, community organizing, supervision, consultation, administration, advocacy, social and political action, policy development and implementation, education, and research and evaluation.

Ethical principles

As illustrated in Table 2.1, social work's ethical principles are based on the six core values listed earlier. These principles set forth ideals to which all social workers should aspire. The NASW Code of Ethics (1999) reflects the commitment of all social workers to uphold the profession's values and to act ethically. "Principles and standards must be applied by individuals of good character who discern moral questions and, in good faith, seek to make reliable ethical judgments" (p. 2). Although the Code of Ethics provides ethics guidelines, social workers are responsible for putting them into practice.

THE RESEARCH TO EVALUATION CONTINUUM

Values, Ethics, and the Research Process

Ethics influence all stages of the research and evaluation process.

Ethics influence all stages of the research and evaluation process. Social workers must balance the requirement for ethical responsibilities and research rigor during each stage of research planning and implementation. For example, social work research has been described as a systematic and objective inquiry that applies the science or research method to examine social problems to generate generally applicable new knowledge (Grinnell, 1997). Practice evaluation, on the other hand, is the systematic, ongoing, and more or less objective determination of whether practitioners are achieving their objectives and goals of practice with their clients (Bloom, Fischer, & Orme, 2009, p. 10).

Table 2.2   Comparison of Research and Practice Evaluation on Knowledge Building and Client Outcome Objectives

Goals	Objective: Primary or Secondary			
	Practice only	Practice evaluation	Research for practice	Research only
Generalizable knowledge	None	Secondary	Primary	Primary
Client outcomes	Primary	Primary	Secondary	None

As shown in Table 2.2, practice evaluation and research differ as to whether client outcomes are secondary or primary to building knowledge. Research often is conducted to generate knowledge; and the research may have broader implications but may not help the practitioner at hand. The main objective of practice evaluation is to assist with client outcomes; its secondary objective is to aid research. Practice evaluation is, therefore, often a breath of fresh air for social workers whose primary objective is to help clients; their secondary aim is to contribute to knowledge building. The history of ethics in research shows us that in some cases when scientific aims were not balanced with respect and human dignity and the protection of participants, tragic consequences resulted, mostly for participants.

NASW ETHICAL STANDARDS FOR SOCIAL WORK RESEARCH AND EVALUATION

The NASW Code of Ethics has guidelines for ethical research practice that involve protections. The ethical standards are consistent with biomedical research ethics guidelines and will be detailed in the next section. Overall, the NASW code delineates ethical standards and can be classified into two broad categories: (a) the promotion of research and evaluation (5.02, a–c) and (b) protections of participants (5.02, e–p). The standards pertaining to the first category stipulate that social workers should actively participate in research and evaluation at the policy and practice levels, contribute to the development of knowledge, and keep current with the literature. The research or evaluation project is subject to rigorous and responsible review so that it meets acceptable ethical standards (see Table 2.3).

The ethical standards pertaining to the second category address research and evaluation project planning and implementation. For project planning, the Code specifies that social workers should weigh the consequences of their research design decisions by following ethical guidelines for participant protections and consulting an Institutional Review Board (IRB). For project implementation, ethical standards are delineated for: (a) informed consent, (b) protection from harm, (c) privacy and confidentiality, (d) conflicts of interest, and (e) dissemination and education.

Ethical practice guidelines stipulate that informed consent must be voluntary for participants with some exceptions. In general, informed consent should be written and signed by participants to record their consent. If a participant is unable to give consent (e.g., children, those who are mentally ill), written

Table 2.3   NASW Code of Ethics: Evaluation and Research Section 5.02: Responsible Research Practices

Promotion of Research and Evaluation Practice and Dissemination

(a) Social workers should monitor and evaluate policies, the implementation of programs, and practice interventions.

(b) Social workers should promote and facilitate evaluation and research to contribute to the development of knowledge.

(c) Social workers should critically examine and keep current with emerging knowledge relevant to social work and fully use evaluation and research evidence in their professional practice.

Protection of Research Participants for Research and Evaluation Projects

Planning Phase

(d) Social workers engaged in evaluation or research should carefully consider possible consequences and should follow guidelines developed for the protection of evaluation and research participants. Appropriate institutional review boards should be consulted.

Implementation Phase

Informed Consent

(e) Social workers engaged in evaluation or research should obtain voluntary and written informed consent from participants, when appropriate, without any implied or actual deprivation or penalty for refusal to participate; without undue inducement to participate; and with due regard for participants' well-being, privacy, and dignity. Informed consent should include information about the nature, extent, and duration of the participation requested and disclosure of the risks and benefits of participation in the research.

(f) When evaluation or research participants are incapable of giving informed consent, social workers should provide an appropriate explanation to the participants, obtain the participants' assent to the extent they are able, and obtain written consent from an appropriate proxy.

(g) Social workers should never design or conduct evaluation or research that does not use consent procedures, such as certain forms of naturalistic observation and archival research, unless rigorous and responsible review of the research has found it to be justified because of its prospective scientific, educational, or applied value and unless equally effective alternative procedures that do not involve waiver of consent are not feasible.

(h) Social workers should inform participants of their right to withdraw from evaluation and research at any time without penalty.

Ensuring Prevention of and Protection From Harm

(i) Social workers should take appropriate steps to ensure that participants in evaluation and research have access to appropriate supportive services.

(j) Social workers engaged in evaluation or research should protect participants from unwarranted physical or mental distress, harm, danger, or deprivation.

Privacy and Confidentiality

(k) Social workers engaged in the evaluation of services should discuss collected information only for professional purposes and only with people professionally concerned with this information.

(l) Social workers engaged in evaluation or research should ensure the anonymity or confidentiality of participants and of the data obtained from them. Social workers should inform participants of any limits of confidentiality, the measures that will be taken to ensure confidentiality, and when any records containing research data will be destroyed.

Table 2.3   NASW Code of Ethics: Evaluation and Research Section 5.02: Responsible Research Practices (Continued)

(m) Social workers who report evaluation and research results should protect participants' confidentiality by omitting identifying information unless proper consent has been obtained authorizing disclosure.

Conflicts of Interest

(n) Social workers engaged in evaluation or research should be alert to and avoid conflicts of interest and dual relationships with participants, should inform participants when a real or potential conflict of interest arises, and should take steps to resolve the issue in a manner that makes participants' interests primary.

Dissemination and Education

(o) Social workers should report evaluation and research findings accurately. They should not fabricate or falsify results and should take steps to correct any errors later found in published data using standard publication methods.

(p) Social workers should educate themselves, their students, and their colleagues about responsible research practices.

Source: Adapted from National Association of Social Workers. (1999). *Code of ethics of the National Association of Social Workers.* Washington, DC: NASW Press.

consent may be obtained from a designated guardian while also obtaining assent from a participant. The informed consent form should include information about the nature, extent, and duration of participation requested and disclose the risks involved in the research along with the benefits of participation. It should also make clear that there is no penalty for participants who decline to participate or withdraw, and it should address assurances for privacy and confidentiality or anonymity and protection from harm.

The ethical standards stipulate that social workers should respect participants' privacy, well-being, and dignity. As for privacy, research and evaluation projects should be designed and carried out such that they protect the anonymity (identity unknown) or confidentiality (identity known but not disclosed) of participants. Social workers should discuss information collected only for professional purposes and with appropriate staff. Social workers must also omit identifying information unless authorized disclosure is obtained. Participants also must be informed of limits to confidentiality and measures taken to ensure confidentiality, and they should be informed of the length of time data collected will be held until destroyed. In addition, participants should be protected from unwarranted physical or mental harm. Social workers should provide participants access to appropriate support services in case of physical or mental distress.

Also in this section of the ethical standards is the stipulation that conflicts of interest and dual relationships should be avoided. Social workers should disclose any potential conflicts to participants. Social workers must keep the interests of the participants as their primary concern when resolving any conflict of interest.

The ethical standards also underscore that research findings should be reported and disseminated accurately such that educational data are not fabricated or falsified. Steps should be taken if data need to be corrected. It is the responsibility of social workers to educate themselves, their students, and colleagues about responsible research practices.

HISTORY AND MEANING-MAKING IN 20TH CENTURY RESEARCH ETHICS

Ethical Practice

Critical Thinking Question: Why is knowledge of research ethics history important (if at all) to conducting social work research today?

The development of ethical principles and rules for biomedical and behavioral research also strongly influence past and present social work research and evaluation practice. The following section provides relevant information about the history and meaning behind 20th century research ethics. Because social workers often practice in interdisciplinary settings, they are likely to interact with diverse professionals, such as medical and law professionals, on research projects. Social workers who are knowledgeable about research ethics history and its significance for protections for research participants will be well prepared to work in multidisciplinary practice settings and situations in which common philosophical and ethical principles are adhered to across disciplines such as medicine and psychology, and they will understand jargon used in intra- and inter-professional dialogue. For example, central ethical principles shared by contemporary biomedical research ethics, human rights documents, and social work codes of ethics are respect, beneficence, and justice. That is, research should be conducted in a manner in which participants are treated with respect, the benefits for the participants must outweigh risks of participation, and the representation and risk must be distributed fairly across different groups of people.

In the midst of great scientific strides in the 20th century, such as the development of penicillin to cure once-incurable diseases such as syphilis, there were some setbacks in the treatment of human subjects of experimental research. In Europe, Nazi doctors conducted research experiments for 5 years (1940–1945) on concentration camp prisoners that often resulted in significant mental and physical harm, including death. In America, the U.S. Public Health Service (PHS) conducted the Tuskegee Study for 40 years (1932–1972) on a sample of poor black male sharecroppers with syphilis in which they were purposefully not treated despite the discovery of penicillin in the 1940s.

As a result of these tragic events, resounding reform occurred at national and international levels as ethical practice developed from mere promises to more formal laws and policies designed to protect human subjects. To that end, the scientific community has developed formal definitions to describe research practice. In the U.S. Federal Regulation and Ethical Guidelines, research is defined as:

> A systematic investigation, including research development, testing and evaluation, designed to develop or contribute to generalizable knowledge. Activities which meet this definition constitute research for purposes of policy, whether or not they are conducted or supported under a program which is considered research for other purposes. For example, some demonstration and service program may include research activities. (USDHHS, 2005, p. 6)

A human subject is a "living individual about whom an investigator conducting research obtains data through intervention or interaction with the individual, or identifiable private information" (USDHHS, 2005, p. 6). In contrast to biomedical research, which uses the term *human subject*, it is more common in social work research to use the term *participant* or *respondent*. Therefore, social workers should be familiar with these different terms, and they should contemplate how this difference in language may influence the research process.

The next section reviews, in chronological order, the major research experiments that led to human subject atrocities including the Tuskegee Study, the Nazi experiments, the Milgram experiments, and the Willowbrook Study. Major documents, policies, and laws included in the review include the Hippocratic Oath, the Nuremberg Code, the Declaration of Helsinki, the 1974 National Research Act, the Belmont Report, the Beecher Study, and the USDHHS Federal Research Guidelines.

Research Ethics Chronology

400 B.C.: Hippocratic Oath

The use of ethical principles and practice in medical practice and research can be traced to the Hippocratic Oath around 400 B.C. Its development is attributed to Hippocrates, who is noted as the father of Western medicine. Medical professionals still take the Hippocratic Oath today. The oath includes practicing with competence and integrity, inflicting no harm, keeping privacy rights, and respecting all life, including patients' (Coller, 2006).

1932–1950: The Tuskegee Study Beginnings

One of the most notorious unethical research studies conducted by the PHS is a 40-year study often referred to as the Tuskegee Study. The purpose of the Tuskegee Study was to observe the natural course of syphilis and racial differences in human health outcomes. The study used a sample of black male sharecroppers from Tuskegee, Alabama, who were poor and had limited education. The study recruited 309 black males with syphilis and a matched sample of 210 black males without syphilis. The participants were not informed about the nature of the study or that they had syphilis, and despite the discovery of penicillin as an effective treatment for syphilis in the 1940s, the PHS actively withheld this treatment from study participants.

1941–1945: Nazi Experiments

To advance the Nazi regime's war efforts in Europe during World War II, Nazi doctors conducted a series of almost unfathomable and gruesome human subject experiments on concentration camp prisoners, which included Jews, homosexuals, and individuals with disabilities. These research studies used human subjects for freezing and hypothermia experiments in which participants were placed naked in below-freezing water; painful medical experiments, such as the administration of eye injections, were conducted on twins; and bone, muscle, and nerve transplantation experiments were conducted without the use of anesthesia. Participation often resulted in serious physical and mental consequences for prisoners. Many research subjects died or were murdered for postmortem testing. Clearly, the Nazi doctors did not give the prisoners the opportunity to willingly volunteer, nor did they explain the nature of the studies and the potential risks of participation. The Nazi experiments became exposed internationally during the Nazi War Crimes Trial (Lifton, 1986; Spitz, 2005).

1947: Nuremberg Code for Human Medical Experiments

When World War II ended, the Nazi doctors were prosecuted at the Nuremberg Tribunal in Germany (Tisa & Tisa, 2010). Once these experiments were exposed, the international community expressed collective outrage at the gruesome scientific experiments conducted on human beings (Ehrenfreund, 2007). The Nuremberg Code for Human Medical Experiments (1947) was adopted in response and became the first internationally recognized code of ethics for human subject research.

At the trial, several of the doctors argued in their defense that there was no international law regarding medical experimentation (Spitz, 2005). The judgment of the Nuremberg War Crimes Tribunal established 10 standards for medical doctors when conducting human subject research. Many basic principles were outlined, including voluntary informed consent, which includes the capacity to consent; freedom from coercion; the minimization of risk and harm; a favorable risk–benefit ratio; qualified investigators using appropriate research designs; and freedom for the subject to withdraw at any time (Dewbry, 2004). The Nuremberg Code (1949/n.d.) can be reviewed at http://ohsr.od.nih.gov/guidelines/nuremberg.html.

1948: Universal Declaration of Human Rights

The content of the Universal Declaration of Human Rights (UDHR) was influenced by the Nuremberg Code's standards (UN, 1948). The UDHR was ratified unanimously by 51 nations, including the United States. Despite it wide-scale adoptions, most countries had no legal mechanism for implementing the provisions of the declaration directly following its ratification.

1953: National Institute of Health Federal Policy for Protection of Human Subjects

In 1953, the National Institute of Health (NIH) created the first U.S. federal policy to protect human subjects. This federal policy infused the principles of Nuremberg but also provided a mechanism for ethics review committees to review research protocols for potential ethical issues. This important policy led to the beginning of the research review mechanism or the establishment of the Institutional Review Board. Currently IRBs are a central mechanism for evaluating ethical research practices.

1961–1963: The Milgram Experiments

Despite notable national and international accomplishments in support of human subject protections, some controversial research studies continued. Between 1961 and 1963, Dr. Stanley Milgram conducted a series of social psychology experiments to explore the role of obedience, regardless of consequences, to authority, such as what occurred in Nazi Germany. During the simulated experiments, the research participants were persuaded or even ordered to administer what appeared to be progressively more painful electroshocks to human recipients. Milgram found that many participants obeyed orders even when they perceived the orders to be painful and immoral. In 1974, Milgram published the book *Milgram Experiment: An Experimental View*, which vividly describes the study's controversial methods (Milgram, 2009). At the time, the scientific community heavily criticized the study methods, which remain controversial and continue to be a subject of debate about what constitutes ethical research methods, including the use of deception in research studies (Blass, 2000).

1963–1966: Willowbrook Hepatitis Studies

Another notable study was conducted on children with disabilities. From 1963 to 1966, the Willowbrook Study, a medical experiment, involved a group of children diagnosed with mental retardation who were under the care of the Willowbrook State Hospital in Staten Island, New York. Due to overcrowding in other areas of the hospital, many children were denied entry to the Willowbrook State Mental Hospital unless parents enrolled them into a less-crowded hepatitis ward. While children were placed in the hepatitis ward, scientists infected them with a Hepatitis virus to study the progression of the disease and to test vaccinations under development. To transmit the hepatitis virus, initially the child "subjects" were fed extracts of stools from other infected individuals or injected with purified virus preparations. The researchers defended the controlled spread of hepatitis with the argument that most of the children would have acquired the infection while housed on that ward (Murphy, 2004).

Overall, the hospital's treatment of residents, both youth and adults, was substandard. Robert F. Kennedy toured the Willowbrook Institution in 1962 and publicly stated Willowbrook was a disgrace. Despite Kennedy's outrage, nothing was done about it. Ten years later, in 1972, Geraldo Rivera hosted one of the first television exposés on Willowbrook. In the film *Willowbrook: The Last Great Disgrace*, Rivera reported his first impressions of the facility as patients lying naked on the floor. The exposé led to the closing of Willowbrook and increased awareness of treatment of people with disabilities (Primo, 1972).

1964: The Declaration of Helsinki

In 1964, another important milestone for protections for research participants was advanced. The World Medical Association (WMA), in its *Declaration of Helsinki: Recommendations Guiding Medical Doctors in Biomedical Research Involving Human Subjects*, expanded the protections of human subjects established in the Nuremberg Code. It was first adopted by the 18th World Medical Assembly in Helsinki, Finland, in 1964 and revised in 1975 and 1989. The declaration established a philosophical foundation for conducting ethical research, including that dignity and respect for human beings supersedes scientific aims (WMA, 1964). The declaration proclaims:

> It is the duty of the physician to promote and safeguard the health of the people. The physician's knowledge and conscience are dedicated to the fulfillment of this duty. In medical research on human subjects, consideration related to the well-being of the human subject should take precedence over the interests of the science and society. (WMA, 1964, p. 1)

The declaration provided principles for subjects unable to provide informed consent and established a precedent for the independent review by an ethics committee to review research protocols or proposals (available at http://ohsr.od.nih.gov/guidelines/helsinki.html).

1966: The Beecher Study

In 1966, a greater public awareness of ethical issues in research was a result of Dr. Henry K. Beecher's (1966) article titled "Ethics and Clinical Research," published in the *New England Journal of Medicine*. Although an anesthesiologist by trade, Beecher provided a wake-up call for the medical research community about continued ethical violations in research in both the United States and abroad.

In his seven-page article, Beecher (1996) highlighted 22 research studies conducted by well-known researchers and published in major journals. His review exposed questionable research practices including unclear informed consent procedures, the withholding of known effective treatment, and at least 20 preventable deaths of research participants. Beecher concluded "an experiment is ethical or not at its inception; it does not become ethical post hoc—ends do not justify the means" (p. 1360). The Beecher article underscored the importance of science for improving practice. However, he also was realistic that an oversight mechanism was needed to monitor ethical practice.

1972: The End of the Tuskegee Study

In the early 1970s, efforts were made in the United States to codify human subject protections. Most notable was the exposure of the Tuskegee Study methods and the governmental response that followed. In 1972, the Tuskegee experiment moved into its fourth decade. By that time some study participants were still alive, and at least 28 to 100 had identifiable advanced stages of syphilis (Jones, 1993).

In the end, Peter Buxtun, a social worker by training, with the assistance of the media, was instrumental in stopping the Tuskegee Study. In 1965, Buxtun was hired by the PHS as a venereal disease interviewer. After starting his job at the Hunt Street Clinic in San Francisco, California, Buxtun overheard his coworkers discussing the Tuskegee Study. He had difficulty believing the stories. "It didn't sound like what a PHS institution should be doing" (Jones, 1993, p. 123). He had attempted to consult with the PHS and other members of the scientific and legal community. He later left the PHS and entered law school and continues to lobby for justice.

In 1972, Buxtun went to the press, after other efforts within the scientific community had failed, and exposed the study. The assigned journalist Jean Heller's investigative reporting efforts uncovered more information, mostly from officials at the Centers for Disease Control and Prevention (CDC), including estimates of how many participants died from late-stage syphilis. On July 25, 1972, the story broke in the *Washington Star* with the headline "Syphilis Victims in U.S. Study Went Untreated for 40 Years." On August 24, 1972, an ad hoc panel was created at the PHS to review the experiment. Two months later (October, 1972), the ad hoc panel recommended ending the study (Jones, 1993). The panel determined that the PHS syphilis study should be stopped immediately and that the overseeing of human research was inadequate. The panel recommended that federal regulations be designed and implemented to protect human research subjects in the future.

1973: Governmental Hearings on the Tuskegee Study

In 1973, Senator Edward Kennedy, viewed as an expert in healthcare, began hearings in the Senate Committee on Labor and Human Resources about the Tuskegee Study and addressed other alleged healthcare abuses of prisoners and children. Senator Kennedy described the Tuskegee Study as "an outrageous and intolerable situation which this government never should have been involved in" (Jones, 1993, p. 214). These congressional hearings presaged a national review of federal guidelines on human experimentation. Subsequently, there was a revamping of the U.S. Department of Health Education and Welfare (HEW) regulations on human experimentation.

In addition to policy reform, reparations to the study participants were made. On March 3, 1973, the HEW secretary, Casper Weinberger, ordered treatment for the Tuskegee Study participants. In July 1973, a $1.8 billion lawsuit was filed against the PHS by participants and their families. About 18 months later (December 1974), the U.S. government settled the lawsuit out of court and paid $37,500 to living survivors and $15,000 to the survivors' heirs. In 1975, the government extended treatment to the wives and children of study participants who contracted syphilis. However, it took another 22 years for a U.S. president, Bill Clinton, to formally apologize to participants for the government's part in this study.

One of the 40-year participants said after the study ended, "I ain't never understood the study" (Jones, 1993, p. 219). Interestingly, the initial "purpose" of the study to examine the progression of syphilis across the life course was trumped by an ethical "higher purpose." In fact, the Tuskegee experiment was among the most influential in shaping public perceptions of research involving human subjects. The Tuskegee Study was a rallying cry for reform. The Study has long-standing repercussions in the African American and minority communities against trusting, helping professions to provide fair and effective services.

1974: National Research Act (Pub. L. 93-348)

The outcome of the governmental hearings on Tuskegee was the catalyst for the development of the passage and enactment of the National Research Act of 1974. Voted into law by the 93rd U.S. Congress, this federal law required the HEW to codify its human subjects protection policy into federal regulations often referred to as the *common rule*, a group of similar requirements that cover the various forms and standards for human subjects research.

With the historic passage of the National Research Act, the National Commission for the Protections of Human Subjects of Biomedical and Behavioral Research was formed. The purpose of the National Commission was to oversee and regulate the use of human experimentation, particularly in medicine. Its charge was to identify the fundamental ethical principles that undergird research on human subjects. To accomplish this task, the National Commission examined writings and discussions on human subjects research that had taken place to date and asked, "What are the basic ethical principles that are used to judge the ethics of human subject research?" Congress also asked the National Commission to develop guidelines to ensure that human research is conducted in accordance with those principles. The National Commission developed the Belmont Report: Ethical Principles and Guidelines for the Protection of Human Subjects of Research from 1974 through 1978.

1979: Belmont Report

In 1979, the National Commission published the Belmont Report (available for review in its entirety at http://ohsr.od.nih.gov/guidelines/belmont.html). The Belmont Report represented a major advancement in public policy related to human subject research. Five fundamental ethical principles can be derived from the report that apply to conducting human subject research: (a) respect for persons, (b) beneficence, (c) justice, (d) trust, and (e) fidelity and scientific integrity.

Respect for persons and their autonomy is a core ethical principle in which significant value is placed on the self-determination of participants. For participants with diminished autonomy, such as children, prisoners, and persons with mental disabilities, special protection is essential. Overall, this principle clearly delineates guidelines for research design in which respect for participants' inherent dignity and rights takes precedence over the expected benefits of knowledge building. This principle is consistent with the social work value and ethical principle related to the respect for the dignity and worth of the person (NASW, 1999).

Beneficence is an ethical principle in which researchers are obligated to promote good and do no harm. That is, researchers must design projects to maximize the benefits to participants and minimize their potential harm in any of the following domains: physical, emotional, psychological, economic, and social. If there is a risk of harm or discomfort to the participants, precautions must be taken, including termination of the study, if needed. In general, using placebos is considered unethical if treatment is available. This principle is consistent with the social work value and ethical principle related to service (NASW, 1999).

Justice generally refers to fair practices in sampling and treatment of participants. There also should be a fair distribution of burdens and benefits of research among groups that differ by socioeconomic status, race and ethnicity, gender, and therapeutic versus nontherapeutic research. Studies should be free of coercion and solicitation, compensation of participants should be fair, there should be compensation for injury, and research outcomes should be accessible to participants. This principle is consistent with the social work value and ethical principle of human rights and social justice (IFSW & IASSW, 2004; NASW, 1999).

The ethical principle of trust suggests that researchers are expected to foster a relationship of trust with the research participants. Trust is facilitated by the researcher making the participants fully aware of the purpose of the study, what is expected from their participation, rights to privacy and confidentiality and voluntary participation, and risks and benefits of participation. This principle is consistent with the social work values and ethical principles related to the importance of human relationships and integrity (NASW, 1999).

The ethical principle of fidelity and scientific integrity underscores researchers' commitment to the discovery and promotion of "truth" and to work within their level of competence. In accord with this principle, researchers should design research that contributes to knowledge and understanding and is justifiable by its potential benefits that outweigh the risks (Sales & Folkman, 2002). This principle is consistent with the social work values and ethical principles related to integrity and competence (NASW, 1999).

Human Rights and Justice

Critical Thinking Question: To what extent are human rights and social justice values represented in research ethics?

1981: Code of Federal Regulations (45 CFR 46)

Since 1974 the HEW sought to revise the original federal regulations. It was not until two years after the release of the Belmont Report that the primary set of federal regulations regarding the protection of human subjects in research was finalized. In 1981, the renamed HEW became the Department of Health and Human Services (DHHS). During the same year, approval was obtained for the Code of Federal Regulations (45 CFR 46), which is often referred to as *the Common*. This regulation was later revised from being applicable to only the DHHS research to cover all federally supported research.

This 27-page document defines the laws for human subject protections, the definition and formulation of IRBs to provide oversight and evaluation for proposed research projects that meet human subject standards, and criteria for IRB review exemptions (Sieber, 1992; USDHHS, 2005). This document has four major parts. Subpart A is the basic HHS policy for protection of human subjects. Subpart B has information on additional protections for pregnant women, human fetuses, and neonates involved in research. Subpart C has additional protection pertaining to biomedical and behavioral research involving prisoners as subjects. Subpart D has additional protections for children involved as subjects in research (USDHHS, 2005). This federal regulation can be reviewed in its entirety at http://ohsr.od.nih.gov/guidelines/45cfr46.html.

Probably the most formal mechanism derived from the passage of this law is that studies involving human subjects need to be reviewed to obtain approval from an independent panel of professionals called an institutional review board (IRB). IRB approval for a study is based on the "determination of the IRB that the research has been reviewed [and] may be conducted at an institution within the constraints set forth by the IRB and by other institutional and federal requirements" (USDHHS, 2005, p. 7). Researchers must take a mandatory human subjects assurance training before beginning a study. The Office of Human Research Protections (OHRP)'s Human Subjects Assurance Training provides one example of online training certification (http://ohrp-ed.od.nih.gov/CBTs/Assurance/login.asp). Visit the OHRP at http://www.hhs.gov/ohrp for more information.

Based on IRB suggestions, researchers often modify their research designs to maximize human subject protections. Once approved, IRB certification is the official notification that a research project or activity involving human subjects has been reviewed and approved by an IRB in accordance with an approved assurance (USDHHS, 2005, p. 7).

1997: Clinton's Presidential Apology for the Tuskegee Study

Another milestone in reparations to participants occurred on May 16, 1997, when President Clinton offered a public apology for the government's role in the Tuskegee Study. The White House invited the eight surviving members of the Tuskegee Study to this public apology. President Clinton's words included:

> The United States government did something that was wrong—deeply, profoundly, morally wrong. It was an outrage to our commitment to integrity and equality for all our citizens. . . . The American people are sorry—for the loss, for the years of hurt. You did nothing wrong, but you were grievously wronged. I apologize and I am sorry that this apology has been so long in coming. (Clinton, 1997, p. 1)

One of the requests of Tuskegee survivors was the establishment of an educational memorial. The president announced the building of a lasting memorial at Tuskegee University in Alabama to commemorate the Tuskegee Institute and established a center to serve as a museum of the Tuskegee Study. The text of the presidential apology (http://clinton4.nara.gov/textonly/New/Remarks/Fri/19970516-898.html) and information on the Tuskegee Institute (http://www.nps.gov/tuin/index.htm) are available online.

CORE ETHICAL PRINCIPLES AND PRACTICES

The following section reviews in more detail core ethical principles and practices for voluntary participation, privacy and confidentiality, risks versus benefits, informed consent, and diversity and cultural sensitivity. The core principles should be addressed in any informed consent procedures for research. Table 2.4 is a sample informed consent form for use with an adult prison population.

Core ethical principles and practices for research are voluntary participation, privacy and confidentiality, risks versus benefits, informed consent, and diversity and cultural sensitivity.

Table 2.4	**Sample Informed Consent**

Fordham University Graduate School of Social Service
New York, NY
Title of Study: Pathways of Risk and Resilience Project
Principal Investigator: Tina Maschi, PhD
Contact Information for Dr. Maschi: 212-636-6633/collab@fordham.edu
Informed Consent

Purpose of Study

The New Jersey Department of Corrections (NJDOC) has given permission to Dr. Tina Maschi from the Fordham University Graduate School of Social Service to conduct a research study of inmates in the New Jersey Prison system. Funding for this study has been provided by Fordham University. The purpose of the study is to learn about how important life experiences and people have influenced individuals who are now in prison and how they cope with the being in prison. We are interviewing individuals, like you, who are serving time in prison, about their thoughts and feelings about important relationships and life experiences. Findings from this study will be used to create new or improve services in the criminal justice system.

What You Will Be Asked to Do in This Study

You are invited to participate in this study because you are either 18 to 24 years old or at least 55 years old, the two age groups that we are studying, and were randomly chosen by the researchers. If you decide to participate in the study, you would be interviewed for about one-and-a-half hours by one of the members of the research team. The interview would include questions about your participation in programs or treatment services in the community, important experiences and people in your life and how they affected you, and how you cope with stress. If you agree to participate in this interview, you will also be asked if we can review your case files. You can say no to this request and still take part in the interview.

If you agree to participate in this interview, you may also be invited to participate in an additional interview to discuss your life experience in much more detail. That additional interview would last for about two-and-a-half to three hours. Participating in the first interview does not mean you have to participate in the additional interview. You do not have to decide now about the additional interview. You will be asked at a later time whether you want to participate in the additional interview.

Voluntary Participation

Your participation is completely voluntary. You are free to choose not to answer any questions that you don't want to answer. You can also stop or end the interview at any time.

Risks and Benefits to Participation

Participating in this research study will not benefit you directly. It will not change anything about the parole eligibility date nor influence the length of your prison sentence. There is only a very minor possible risk to you if you participate in this study, which could happen if you feel uncomfortable answering questions about your past experiences.

If for some reason you become upset because the interview made you think about unpleasant things in your life, and you would like to talk with a professional about this, you can inform a correctional officer that you need to speak to a counselor or mental health specialist immediately. If it is not an emergency, you also may place a slip in the inmate mail system for mental health services and receive counseling within 24 to 48 hours.

Confidentiality

If you agree to participate, everything you say during the interview would be strictly confidential, with some exceptions. This means that what you say during the interview will NOT be shared with anyone but the person who is interviewing you and the other two researchers. No one from the Department of Corrections, or anyone else, will be able to know what you said during the interview.

However, there are some exceptions to this protection of confidentiality. If you say that you want to harm yourself or another person, if you talk about a crime that is unknown to authorities, or if you say that you are dealing illegal drugs in prison, the interviewer is legally required to report the information to the prison warden.

Table 2.4	**Sample Informed Consent (Continued)**

Your confidentiality is protected by not putting your name or other information that could identify you on any documents for this study. All data will be collected by trained research staff from Fordham University or the New Jersey Department of Corrections who were approved to participate only after passing a background check. Survey results will be stored at Fordham University's Graduate School of Social Service in a secure place and destroyed within 5 years of collection to further guarantee your privacy.

Who to Contact With Questions and Your Rights as a Participant in a Research Study:

If you have any questions about the study at any time, you may contact Dr. Tina Maschi (Address: Fordham University Graduate School of Social Service, 113 West 60th Street, Room 721G, New York, NY 10023; telephone number: 212-636-6633; e-mail: collab@fordham.edu). If you have any questions about your rights as a participant in a research study, you may contact the Fordham University Institutional Review Board, which is responsible for making sure that research is conducted in a way that protects study participants. (Address: Fordham University, 113 West 60th Street, Room LL203C, New York, NY 10023; telephone number: 212-636-7946; e-mail: irb@fordham.edu).

You may keep a copy of this information for your records. If you would like to participate in the first interview in this study, please print and sign your name on the attached page. We ask that you sign two copies so that you may keep one of the copies and the other copy will be for the study. The copy for the study will be placed in a locked file cabinet in Dr. Maschi's office, which will be a different locked file cabinet from the one in which the interviews for this study are stored.

Agreement

If you have read and understood the information above about this study, have had a chance to have all of your questions answered, and if you agree to participate in the first interview, please check the boxes below and sign form below.

I agree to participate in an interview _____Yes _____ No

I give permission to the research team to review my case records: _____Yes _____ No

_____	_____
Participant Signature and Date	Witness Signature and Date
_____	_____
Please Print Name	Please Print Name

Voluntary Participation

Voluntary participation is an essential ethical principle underscored in research ethics documents and laws, including the NASW Code of Ethics and the Federal Ethical Guidelines (USDHHS, 2005). Voluntary participation also is consistent with the social work value of self-determination. Adhering to voluntary participation can compromise a research design goal of recruiting a representative and generalizable sample. However, the general rule in which ethical principles supersede research design considerations elevates voluntary participation as most important.

The first standard of the Nuremberg Code (Office of Human Subjects Research [OHSR], 1949/n.d.) described voluntary participation and informed consent as "absolutely essential" (p. 1). Voluntary participation was described as the person involved should have legal capacity to give consent; should be situated as to be able to exercise free power of choice, without the intervention of any element of force, fraud, deceit, duress, overreaching, or other ulterior form of constraint or coercion; and should have sufficient knowledge and comprehension of the elements of the subject matter involved as to enable him to make an understanding and enlightened decision. (OHSR, 1949/n.d., pp. 1–2)

Privacy and Confidentiality

An essential ethical principle is that participants should be made aware of the nature of a research project so that they can make an informed decision about participation. *Confidentiality* refers to the situation in which the researcher, although knowing what data describe which subjects, agrees to keep that information confidential. In contrast, *anonymity* refers to the situation in which the researcher cannot identify the individual by the specific information that has been supplied. In other words, the researcher cannot connect the supplied data to participants. An example is a self-administered anonymous questionnaire. A general rule for maximizing human subject protection is to design a study in which anonymity is feasible.

Self or Other Harm (Duty to Warn)

During the course of a research project, a participant may disclose thoughts about harming himself or herself, or intent or plans to harm himself or herself. This situation is similar to those that arise in a practice setting in which such information supersedes confidentiality, and assistance must be provided to the client. For example, if a study participant communicates a threat toward a specific person and either has the intent or ability to implement a violent act or has a history of such acts, the social worker is required to take appropriate actions. This may include warning the victim, calling the police, asking the client to accept voluntary hospitalization, or attempting to arrange an involuntary hospitalization. Social workers should clearly state this clause in an informed consent, especially when dealing with a population known for violence (Sales & Folkman, 2000; Sieber, 1992).

Child Maltreatment Reporting

Another situation that may affect a research study is the disclosure of child maltreatment victimization during the course of the study. All 50 states have passed some form of a mandatory child abuse and neglect reporting law. This type of law is required to qualify for funding under the Child Abuse and Prevention Treatment Act (CAPTA [January 1996 revision]), 42 U.S.C. 5101, et seq. Most standards mandate filing require a report when individuals have reasonable cause to suspect that a child they encounter in their professional or official capacity is abused or maltreated. Some states mandate that any person can report if there is reasonable cause (USDHHS, 2009). If this might be an issue, especially when interviewing about trauma, the exceptions to confidentiality should be addressed in the informed consent.

Informed Consent

Voluntary participation is demonstrated through the process of informed consent. An informed consent form that is reviewed with participants should spell out all aspects of the study, including the purpose, the procedures, the topics that will be covered, possible harms, incentives, and remuneration.

Informed consent refers to informing potential research participants about all aspects of the research that might reasonably influence their decision to participate. Informed consent is linked with the principle of respect for persons in the informed consent process. According to federal research guidelines, informed consent "requires that participants, to the degree they are capable, be given the opportunity to choose what shall or shall not happen to them" (USDHHS, 2005, p. 6). Informed consent should contain and address the following three features: information, comprehension, and voluntariness.

The informed consent is a document signed by the participants or their legal guardians or representatives. Special conditions exist for children in which parent consent and youth assent is needed. Steps in the process involve the participants reading the informed consent form and the researcher explaining the content, including the study purpose, procedures, risks and benefits, and remuneration, if any. The participant is given time to ask for clarification. If the subject decides to participate, he or she must sign the informed consent form (unless a telephone or online interview) before he or she participates in research.

No one should be forced or coerced to participate. All participants must be aware that they are participating in a study, be informed of all consequences, and give consent to participate. If the research entails sensitive topics, such as sexual or physical abuse and substance abuse, a debriefing statement is often recommended. (See Table 2.5 for a sample debriefing statement.) The federal regulations outline the criteria for informed consent (see USDHHS, 2005, pp. 13–14).

Table 2.5   Sample Debriefing Statement

Fordham University Graduate School of Social Service
New York, New York
Title of Study: Pathways of Risk and Resilience Project
Principal Investigators: Tina Maschi, PhD
Contact Information for Dr. Maschi: 212-636-6633, collab@fordham.edu

Thank you for participating in this research study. The purpose of this study was to learn how about the influence of important people and life events influence individuals in the criminal justice system. If participating in the study has made you feel uncomfortable in any way, or if it caused you to think about things that upset you, please contact the confidential counseling service available to you in the prison. If you find you need someone to talk to about what we discussed, please tell a correctional officer that you need to speak to a counselor or mental health specialist immediately. If it is not an emergency, you also may place a slip in the inmate mail system for mental health services and receive counseling within 24 to 48 hours.

Please keep the information sheet that you were given about this study. It describes your rights as a participant in a research study. The information on contacting the researcher is on the information page and is also repeated here.

If you have any questions about the study at any time, you may contact Dr. Tina Maschi (Address: Fordham University Graduate School of Social Service, 113 West 60th Street, Room 721G, New York, NY 10023; telephone number: 212-636-6633; e-mail: collab@fordham.edu).

If you have any questions about your rights as a participant in a research study, you may contact the Fordham University Institutional Review Board, which is responsible for making sure that the research is conducted in a way that protects study participants: (Address: Fordham University, 113 West 60th Street, Room LL203C, New York, NY 10023; telephone number: 212-636-7946; e-mail: irb@fordham.edu).

Your answers during the interview are very important and greatly appreciated. If you would like to receive a copy of any reports written based on the information collected from all of the inmates who participated in this study, please tell the researcher now, or send a letter at the address above or an e-mail to Dr. Maschi to tell her you want a copy of the report. Please e-mail your request to Dr. Maschi at collab@fordham.edu.

You may keep this information sheet for your records.

Risks and Benefits

Protection from harm is a consideration for all phases of the research project from planning and implementing the study to disseminating the findings. Research studies should be designed and implemented with a full account of the potential risks as well as benefits to participants and society at large. A study must be designed and carried out in a manner in which the benefits outweigh the risks.

Minimal risk to research participants is generally sought. *Minimal risk* is defined as "the probability and magnitude of harm and discomfort anticipated in the research [that] are not greater in and of themselves than those ordinarily encountered in daily life or during the performance of routine physical and psychological examinations of tests" (USDHHS, 2005, p. 7). Researchers should minimize physical or mental distress or avoid exposing subjects to physical or mental distress or danger. Participants should be fully informed of any potential adverse consequences that may result as a part of their participation. IRBs determine the risk versus benefit ratios by evaluating risks to participants, such as undesirable physical, psychological, economic, legal, or other types of immediate, short- and long-term adverse effects. If there is a potential risk, the research team provides a debriefing statement for participants to remind them of potential consequences of participation and where they can obtain assistance, if needed.

Diversity in Practice

Critical Thinking Question: How might bias and insensitivity compromise a research study, and how might it be avoided?

Diversity and Cultural Sensitivity

Ethical issues for social work research also should be extended to address diversity and cultural sensitivity. Social workers refer to *diversity* in a broad sense to include age, race and ethnicity, gender, sexuality, disabilities (physical and mental health), socioeconomic status, and immigration status. The presence of bias and insensitivity in the research design can compromise the quality of a study (Potocky & Farmer, 1998). The culturally competent research and practice literature identifies common steps to building diversity awareness knowledge and skills (NASW, 2001).

Some of the recommendations are:

1. Adopt a strengths or resilience perspective to minimize pathologizing the targeted group.
2. Attend cultural events or visit historic sites to get immersed in the culture of population under study. *Cultural immersion* refers to being immersed in the culture of the population under investigation.
3. Seek ongoing consultation with the central stakeholder and community stakeholders that include scholars and community leaders of the group under investigation.
4. Employ local community members as research staff or as bilingual representatives of the target population when implementing a study.
5. Develop and assess existing measures for diversity sensitivity and cultural competence.
6. Treat respondents with respect.
7. Provide inducement for participation; conduct the study in the natural setting of participants, or provide assistance with transportation and child care.

8. Provide adequate compensation and facilitate participation; choose a natural setting with provisions made for barriers to transportation and childcare.

9. Use and train culturally competent interviewers.

10. Use anonymous enrollment procedures with stigmatized populations.

11. Use tracking methods and anchor points to foster ongoing participation. (e.g., Potocky & Farmer, 1998; Rothman, 2008; Rubin & Babbie, 2010; Saleebey, 1996)

ETHICAL RESEARCH DECISION-MAKING PROCESS

Once professional values and ethical principles and practices become familiar, they can be used to inform the ethical decision-making process. Ethical decision-making is often a complex process. Oftentimes, social workers are faced with no simple answers for resolving complex ethical issues. Social workers should be clear about their personal and professional values. First, when designing a research or evaluation project, social workers should thoroughly assess the impact of their decision making on the population under investigation. It is the responsibility of social workers to do an honest self-assessment that identifies any conflicts between personal and professional values. Social workers can seek guidance from the relevant literature about receiving consultation from an agency, IRBs, colleagues, supervisors or legal counsel to explore personal and professional values dilemmas.

When designing a research or evaluation project, social workers should thoroughly assess the impact of their decision making on the population under investigation.

Second, social workers should consider all the ethical principles and standards and the many other sources of research ethics information when conducting research. Knowledge about research ethics must be counterbalanced by knowledge of social work theory and research methods, relevant laws, regulations, and policies. Social workers also must consider the NASW (1999) statement that when consulting other professions' ethical codes for decision making, "social workers should consider the NASW Code of Ethics as their primary source" (p. 5).

Based on all the competing decisions required to design research and evaluation activities, it is quite likely that an ethical dilemma may arise. *Ethical dilemma* often refers to a situation in which an individual must make the best possible choice among two or more conflicting values (Congress, 1999). Ethical dilemmas occur in situations in which the social worker must choose between two or more relevant, but contradictory, ethical principles or when every alternative results in an undesirable outcome for one or more persons.

Research Ethical Decision-Making Model

For the purposes of this exercise, let us say you have identified an original idea for a research or evaluation project. You spoke with some colleagues who suggested that your project has the potential to contribute to improving your agency service provision and/or contribute to the larger social work field. Your plan is to systematically evaluate it and receive IRB approval at your university to conduct the study. Because research and design choices and ethical practice are intricately intertwined, you must consider both at all times during the research and evaluation processes. When striving for a sound research design, you may want to ensure that the protections of participants are of paramount concern.

You begin to conceptualize the study and ponder the methods choices to carry out the project. First, you ask yourself the following questions: In what ways is the study ethical? Have efforts to ensure voluntary participation been adequately considered? How will informed consent and minimization of risks to participants be ensured? What is the best alternative among those identified? You review the related empirical literature and check with experienced colleagues for potential pitfalls in implementing such a design.

You also remind yourself that the same questions you ask yourself also will be asked by IRB member(s) or the research ethics board reviewing your application for IRB approval. Having an almost superego-like function, the IRB members will scrutinize your study methods to best ensure human subject protections.

Therefore, it is important to engage in thoughtful ethical decision-making to ensure sound research and evaluation design. Because ethical issues influence the initial planning and implementation stages of a study, we offer an ethical decision-making model to assist with the process. The use of a model can help identify the potential areas where the rights of participants may be violated.

Ethical Decision-Making Stages

(1) **Identify the research question(s):** First, the social worker should identify the research or evaluation question(s) that will guide his or her investigation.

(2) **Weigh options:** Based on the research questions identified, the social worker should survey the menu of different methods to answer the study question(s). The types of methods choices that the social worker must undertake include type of research design (quantitative or qualitative, longitudinal or cross-sectional, secondary or primary data, experimental or nonexperimental designs), sampling strategies (probability or nonprobability), measures used, data analysis, and dissemination strategies. Each method should be carefully appraised as to how well it addresses considerations such as participant protections, sound research methodology, project timelines, and costs. These options also must be weighed carefully before finalizing the methods choices. Consultation with colleagues and methods and ethics literature is helpful at this stage to weigh the pros and cons of methods choices.

(3) **Choose a study plan:** Once the alternative methods choices are carefully reviewed, the next essential step is to choose a study plan. This decision should weigh heavily toward the least risky method with the greatest likelihood of advancing knowledge. Based on your assessment, the final design balances participants' rights with your efforts to derive new and important knowledge for your agency and/or the field. The IRB proposal serves as a blueprint of the study that will be implemented in the field. The overall research or evaluation plan also needs to meet IRB scrutiny, which ensures human subject protections.

(4) **Implement**. Once the research or evaluation plan is selected and approved, the project can be implemented. This step often places social workers in contact with research participants, including the administration of informed consent.

Critical Thinking

Critical Thinking Question: What are some ways critical thinking skills can facilitate or hinder ethical decision-making processes in social work research activities?

(5) Monitor: Throughout the process, the social worker is responsible for ensuring that ethical mandates are followed and that no unintended consequences have arisen in the study. The social worker should continually evaluate his or her choices and assume responsibility for any unintended consequences that may arise. If anything changes such that participants' rights are jeopardized, the social worker may need to modify the study plan. The designated IRB or ethics review board can be consulted during any stages of the project to discern ethical dilemmas and potential resolutions.

(6) Document and share: Once a project is completed, study findings should be shared, and their implications and applications for social work practice should be delineated. This information can then be used by policy makers, practitioners, and other stakeholders to improve conditions for the population under investigation. Researchers should make the effort to share best practices in adhering to research ethics and choosing a sound research design.

SUMMARY

The history of social work ethics, particularly with research, is intricately entwined with biomedical and behavioral research ethics and the 20th-century human rights movement. Central principles common to medical, social science, and social work disciplines involve a stream of historical events, including some human rights atrocities. These events led to legal mandates and regulations that guide the design and implementation of research and evaluation. Core principles that transcend disciplines include the common principles or rules. First and foremost, research participants' welfare and rights supersede scientific aims. Participants' rights and well-being must not be violated during the course of a research study. Potential participants have the right to be fully informed about the study's purpose or methods, the potential risks and benefits of participation, and the availability of alternative treatments. Informed consent procedures should document these protections in a written statement to participants. Social workers can use an ethical decision-making process for research and evaluation, which includes identifying the research question(s), weighing design options, choosing a study plan, implementing the plan, and monitoring the process and outcomes.

Succeed with **PEARSON** **mysocialworklab**

Log onto **www.mysocialworklab.com** and answer the following questions. (*If you did not receive an access code to* **MySocialWorkLab** *with this text and wish to purchase access online, please visit* www.mysocialworklab.com.)

1. **Watch the ethical practice video "Recognizing Personal Values."** After listening to the commentary, explain how personal values awareness can help inform conducting research with participants with different personal views than one's own.

2. **Watch the human rights and justice video "Social and Economic Justice: Understanding Forms of Oppression and Discrimination."** After listening to the commentary, describe what similar types of oppression and discrimination led to the establishment of research ethics.

PRACTICE TEST
The following questions will test your knowledge of the content found within this chapter. For additional assessment, including licensing-exam type questions on applying chapter content to practice, visit **MySocialWorkLab**.

1. A social worker conducting research should allow ethics to influence what part of the research process?
   a. Problem formulation
   b. Data collection
   c. Data analysis
   d. All stages of the research process

2. The Universal Declaration of Human Rights was influenced by what historical research ethics document?
   a. The Nuremberg Code
   b. The Belmont Report
   c. The Declaration of Helsinki
   d. The NASW Code of Ethics

3. An exception to confidentiality during a research study may be when a 45-year-old participant discloses:
   a. Using illegal substances
   b. Having a history of suicide attempts
   c. Having the intent with a plan to harm another person
   d. Having a criminal record

4. A social worker engaging in culturally competent research is more than likely to do which of the following?
   a. Engage central stakeholders, especially from the group under study, in the research process.
   b. Not offer incentives to participants because it might bias results.
   c. Use an open enrollment procedure to recruit participants.
   d. Use existing measures with no adaption to the measures.

5. What kinds of ethical issues might arise in designing a study of substance abuse treatment for an agency that serves mainly ethnic minorities?

ASSESS YOUR COMPETENCE
Use the scale below to rate your current level of achievement on the following concepts or skills associated with each competency presented in the chapter:

1	2	3
I can accurately describe the concept or skill.	I can consistently identify the concept or skill when observing and analyzing practice activities.	I can competently implement the concept or skill in my own practice.

_____ can apply ethical issues to professional practice.

_____ can apply critical thinking to inform and communicate professional research and evaluation judgement.

_____ can demonstrate cultural competent strategies in social work research and practice evaluation.

_____ can use research and evaluation to promote human rights and social and economic justice.

3

Problem Solving, Critical Thinking, and Evidence-Based Practice

CHAPTER OUTLINE

Core Competencies in This Chapter (Check marks indicate which competencies are demonstrated)				
☐ Professional Identity	☐ Ethical Practice	☑ Critical Thinking	☑ Diversity in Practice	☐ Human Rights and Justice
☑ Research-Based Practice	☐ Human Behavior	☐ Policy Practice	☐ Practice Contexts	☑ Engage, Assess, Intervene, Evaluate

INTRODUCTION

Social work is a helping profession designed to assist individuals, families, and communities build upon their strengths. Social workers may write psychosocial assessments, assess suicidal risk or physical or sexual abuse, make court recommendations to terminate parental rights, write probation or parole dispositions, or assess the competency of subjects to participate in a research or evaluation project, or social workers may supervise or evaluate others in these activities. Community-level research practices also may involve conducting a needs assessment or community mapping, or evaluating the impact of a policy.

All of the aforementioned activities incorporate some aspect of defining or solving an identified problem or challenge. Defining the problem is an essential part of sound assessment. When Einstein was asked what he would do if he had 1 hour to save the world, he replied he would spend 55 minutes defining the problem and only 5 minutes finding the solution (Calaprice, 2005). The use of research knowledge and skills can be an essential tool in moving from problem definition to resolution for both research and practice. In particular, disciplined inquiry for practice and research issues can be used to facilitate empirically based understanding and explanation which, in turn, informs action (Davies, 2000).

This chapter reviews problem formulation in research and evaluation by anchoring the discussion in generalist practice problem-solving stages. Because research and practice involves a systematic decision-making process, this chapter also reviews critical thinking, cultural competence, and evidence-based practice (EBP). The importance of bridging cultural competence and EBPs is reviewed, and practical assessment techniques are discussed.

Generalist Practice and Problem-Solving Processes

Across all social work research and practice evaluation activities, the generalist practice phases undergird the research process.

Across all social work research and practice evaluation activities, the generalist practice phases undergird the research process. These phases are (a) engage, assess, and define the problem; (b) brainstorm potential solutions; (c) choose goal-oriented action or intervention plan; (d) implement the chosen action or the plan; and (e) evaluate and conclude the results (Dubois & Miley, 2010; Marlow, 2010). This process is represented in Figure 3.1.

Phase One: In phase one, social workers build partnerships and alliances with central stakeholders from diverse backgrounds and views to formulate the problem. They gather evidence to identify challenges and resources. This information can be used to define a problem or establish a problem statement. For example, a social worker in clinical practice may work collaboratively with an individual, a family, or a group in defining the problem. For policy practice, the social worker should develop a clear and concise statement on the issue. The social worker collaborates with the client and/or other stakeholders to define the problem or challenge as well as capacities and resources (Dubois & Miley, 2010).

Social workers conducting a research study use problem formulation to identify the problem. Problem formation may involve engagement processes that include recruiting participants for preliminary focus groups. Researchers also may engage in research practices that include building partnerships using such methods as community-based participatory action research. The information gathered from these collaborations is used to identify the problem and/or

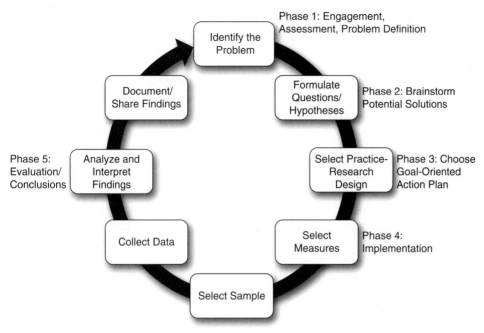

Figure 3.1

Problem Solving, Research and Evaluation, and Generalist Practice

concerns. At this stage, social workers develop a mutual understanding of situations in which there are gaps in the lives of individuals and families. Social workers also must address community resources, services, or policies that affect individuals and families (Marlow, 2010).

Social workers engaged in research and evaluation activities decide on a problem and research question, most often based on either a literature gap or need in the field (Monette, Sullivan, & De Jong, 2008). For example, a social worker using participatory action research methods may identify a group of urban minority youth who define their problem as daily exposure to community violence in the form of trash-ridden communities such as those found in Alice McIntyre's (2000) study, *Inner City Kids: Adolescents Confront Life and Violence in an Urban Community.*

Phase Two: In phase two, the social worker collaboratively brainstorms with stakeholders for potential solutions. As reviewed in Chapter 2, social workers should use culturally competent practices such as engaging leaders of key constituents in the community. A research or practice evaluation design at this stage includes a systematic scrutiny of the methods used to gather data as well as scrutiny of any relevant ethical concerns. During this phase, the researcher writes a report with analyzed results and recommendations for practice and research, and policy implications for improving well-being and advancing human rights and social justice (Monette et al., 2008).

Phase Three: Phase three involves choosing a goal-oriented action or intervention plan. Based on the designated target or essential problem, goals are established to address the targeted problem/s. In a practice evaluation situation, it is important to formulate goals as an essential action step. This includes ascertaining the implications and applications of research and evaluation findings to develop or improve practice and policy efforts. The details are often documented as part of a treatment or intervention (Dubois & Miley, 2010).

Phase three also can involve determining what is known in the empirical literature to help develop and prioritize program and policy options. It is important to identify the implications and applications for practice in working with communities to implement these strategies (Marlow, 2010). For example, a social worker can work with a community to implement an evidence-based home health-aid program for older adults in the community and measure the outcomes of program participants' health and well-being.

The social worker's research report documents the implications and applications for practice. It is essential that researchers make an effort to translate their research findings so that social workers can use them in the field. The research team can develop interventions based on the findings or can work collaboratively with community stakeholders to implement programs or interventions. A sufficiently detailed implications section of a report can be used as a blueprint for others. Using clear and precise language that lay persons can understand is another important factor in enabling translation of research into practice (Marlow, 2010).

Phase Four: In phase four, the social worker in practice implements a planned action or intervention that other stakeholders have agreed to. Both parties are accountable for completing specific tasks agreed to within the contract. Implementation may involve developing alliances and working on goals. At this stage it is important that research be used to monitor the effectiveness of the intervention (Marlow, 2010; Patton, 2002).

Phase Five: In phase five, the social worker assesses the extent to which the agreed-upon goals have been attained and evaluates how well the research or evaluation advanced knowledge and improved real-world practice conditions. Conclusions are drawn about the next step in individual and social change efforts. For research and evaluation projects, social workers can reflect on the limitations of studies, assess their overall qualities, and determine future directions. New insight occurs when research and practice evaluation efforts are modified. This line of inquiry begins the process all over again (Marlow, 2010; Patton, 2002).

Engage, Assess, Intervene, Evaluate

Critical Thinking Question: How does the social work research process involve the different phases of practice (i.e., engage, assess, intervene, and evaluate)?

How Do Social Workers Know What They Know?

Social workers often use various methods to sort and sift through multiple sources of evidence to discern the problem for investigation or intervention. This new information can be used to revise working hypotheses or policies, or for theory refinement (Gettier, 1963; Russell, 1940). Therefore, social workers should have a foundation in the different "ways of knowing" that may influence how they interpret problems and make decisions.

In epistemology, which is the science of knowing, knowledge has been described as the intersection in which "truth" or facts converge with beliefs (Armstrong, 1973). For example, an individual must believe a "fact" before it can become a part of his or her knowledge base. In discerning what a "problem" is, we need to know how we came to define the problem. The social worker should ask: How do I know what I know? Historically grounded in philosophy, contemporary social workers ask this question every day as they gather and process information. For example, a social worker involved in child protective services must determine how he or she came to a case disposition of child neglect or sexual abuse.

Ways of knowing, that is, how we know what we know, influence our understanding.

Ways of knowing, that is, how we know what we know, influence our understanding. Six common ways of knowing are (a) authority, (b) personal experience,

(c) intuition or inspiration or revelation, (d) empiricism/observation, (e) rationalism and the scientific method, and (f) culture. As noted by scholars, each way of knowing has both strengths and limitations, which preclude depending on it as a sole method (Dobson & Avery, 2009; Huitt, 1998; Woolman, 2000). These ways of knowing can contribute to our individual and collective understanding of human behavior in the social environment.

Authority

Individuals can access information from an authority or expert in an area they would like to learn about. In some instances, this involves tapping into the knowledge of those much more informed about an issue or situation. Yet, there are also insurmountable limitations to obtaining knowledge exclusively from an authority. There is no guarantee that the authority figure has unearthed all aspects of an issue, is completely accurate, or is not affected by personal biases. Depending on an external authority for knowledge can impede one's use of personal critical judgment and inner knowledge (Engel & Schutt, 2010).

Personal Experience

Personal experience is a way of knowing based on knowledge via one's senses. A strength of personal experience is that it clearly identifies an individual's subjective perceptions that can be confirmed or disconfirmed based on prior experiences. Similar to information received from authority figures, personal experiences may be subject to biases or faulty interpretations. Personal experience often will not capture the full breadth of another individual's experience of the same phenomenon (Engel & Schutt, 2010).

Intuition, Inspiration, and Revelation

Intuition, inspiration, and revelation have also been referred to as *emotional* or *spiritual wisdom* and are often associated with intuition or instinctive knowledge. A strength of this way of knowing is that it enables individuals to access information that has profound personal impact and that is not accessible via other ways of knowing. However, emotional or spiritual wisdom is limited because internal experiences are not easily shared with others and therefore are not easily verifiable (Woolman, 2000).

Empiricism/Observation

Empiricism, which is sensory perception and observation, is a way of knowing based on the scientific method that utilizes observable facts and objectivity. A strength of the empirical way of knowing is that it is based on observation and therefore can be shared and even critiqued by others. As noted in Chapter 1, the scientific method involves the use of careful thought and systematic use of methods, which make it more easily verifiable and replicable by others. Empiricism also has limitations. Perhaps one of the largest drawbacks is that not all experiences, such as internal attitudes, thoughts, and feelings, are easily visible and observable as behaviors. Additionally, sensory perceptions can be imprecise; conscious efforts need to be taken to identify and evaluate faulty thinking and beliefs (Dobson & Avery, 2010).

Rationalism and the Scientific Method

Rationalism combines reasoning and logic. *Reasoning* is the act or process of drawing conclusions from facts and evidence. It is often described as a careful and judicious process used to determine which beliefs and actions are most well-founded. *Logic*, which is the basis of the scientific method, involves thinking in a linear, step-by-step manner about how a problem can be solved. However, limitations to this approach include that logical arguments may hide logical fallacies (Barnes, 1984; Cohen & Nagel, 1934). What may seem like a logical conclusion may be actually socially or culturally influenced.

The scientific method is a widely accepted way of knowing in the physical and social sciences because it uses systematic methods to draw conclusions and make inferences. However, it is important to note that culture is another form of knowing that must be addressed during the research and practice process.

Culture

Ways of knowing also can be influenced by cultural and ethnic worldviews. *Culture* is defined as a "system of shared values, beliefs, ideas and learned patterns of behavior, grounded in a common history and experiences shared by a group" (Rothman, 2008, p. 5). Cultural worldviews are often distinct. Similarly, *ethnicity* refers to membership in a group that is based on ancestry, nationality, or race, which shares a common experience and a common set of beliefs and identities that are passed through the generations (Lum, 1999). Therefore, tradition is an important element in cultural worldviews.

It also is important to note that different cultures hold different ways of knowing in higher esteem. For example, Barnhardt and Kawagley (2005) noted that indigenous populations, such as Alaskan Natives, have alternative worldviews about ways of knowing. According to Barnhardt and Kawagley (2005), indigenous people are much more in tune with observing natural processes; this orientation is different from an outcome-oriented Western world. The different ways of knowing can contribute to our understanding of the different interpretations of human behavior in the social environment. Agreement in interpretation across these ways of knowing can corroborate or confirm knowledge. Disagreement in interpretation can be advantageous when it necessitates reevaluation of the conflict, which might result in a higher level of understanding (Grinnell & Unrau, 2005; Tashakkori & Teddlie, 1998). Social workers also must carefully assess the influence of cultural worldviews when working in partnership with different cultural groups in research or evaluation activities.

Critical Thinking and Reflection

As noted earlier, each of the different ways of knowing has differing strengths and limitations. For example, rational and logical thought processes have many benefits for practice and research decision-making. Any potential pitfalls and biases in our everyday thought processes are carefully examined and refined to increase the likelihood that professional decisions and actions will do more good than harm for the population served.

It is quite fitting then that the Council on Social Work Education (2008) mandates critical thinking as a core competency for social workers. Gambrill (2005) described critical thinking as a "unique kind of purposeful thinking in which we use standards, such as clarity and fairness" (p. 11). Moreover it involves the "careful examination and evaluation of beliefs and actions in order to arrive at well-reasoned decisions" (p. 11). Critical thinkers are empowered and independent thinkers yet good listeners of internal dialogue, curious yet focused, and flexible yet in control of their own thoughts (Gibbs & Gambrill, 2002).

Consistent with human rights and social justice aims, critical thinking underscores accuracy and fairness as a key aspect of decision-making processes and actions. Critical thinking includes high-quality thought processes represented by clarity, precision, specificity, accuracy, relevance, consistency, logic, depth, completeness, significance, adequacy, and fairness. The opposite end of the spectrum involves low-quality thoughts represented by lack of clarity, imprecision, vagueness, inaccuracy, inconsistency, illogicality, incompleteness, triviality, inadequacy, and bias. The quality of our thoughts, in turn, impacts the quality of our decision making which, in turn, impacts the quality of our actions. Quality decisions that continually need to be made include classifying clients into categories, making causal assumptions, and making predictions about the effectiveness of interventions, policies, or laws (Gambrill, 2005).

Critical thinking gives permission to move beyond "thinking as usual" to incorporate more precise thinking for use in professional practice decision-making and actions. For example, the social worker who actively uses critical thinking skills during the problem formulation process might ask the following questions about information gathered from the field or literature:

> *Critical thinking gives permission to move beyond "thinking as usual" to incorporate more precise thinking for use in professional practice decision-making and actions.*

- How reliable is the information source?
- Does this information seem accurate?
- Are the claims corroborated by other sources?
- Has any important information been left out?
- Is there confirming or disconfirming evidence across multiple sources?
- Are there subjugated viewpoints that have not yet been voiced in regard to this issue or problem?
- How would alternative worldviews or other ways of knowing describe or explain the problem?

Common Thinking Errors

Social workers can avoid common errors in thinking by increasing their awareness of those errors. Gibbs (2002) referred to common errors in thinking and reasoning that represent over thinking, stagnant or stalled thinking, relying on nontraditional or traditional thinking, split thinking, and disempowered thinking. These errors in thinking may occur at both the individual and societal level. A social worker may intervene to help improve negative attitudes about mental illness among mental health consumers and their families or even combat stigma against individuals with mental illness at the larger societal level. Oftentimes, the goal is to use reasoning that represents precise, dynamic, clear, pragmatic, and empowered thinking (Gibbs & Gambrill, 1999).

Over Thinking

Over thinking occurs when an individual uses overgeneralization or overreliance on testimonials. A social worker may overgeneralize when drawing conclusions about a specific case and mistakenly infer relevance to the larger population (Gibbs, 2002). For example, a social worker had an older adult female client who received a ticket for reckless driving. The social worker's initial thought was "women do not know how to drive." However, upon closer examination of her thoughts, she realized that she was overgeneralizing.

Overreliance on testimonials occurs when a social worker claims that a practice method is effective based on one's own experience only (Gibbs, 2002).

For example, a social worker who was experiencing job-related stress began writing poetry, which helped to relax her. Her initial thought was that this technique would work for all social workers experiencing job-related stress. Upon closer examination, she realized she used the thinking error of overreliance on her own personal testimony. She reframed her thinking to reflect all that she had evidence for: Poetry was effective in reducing her job-related stress.

Stagnant or Stalled Thinking

Other errors in cognition include the use of stagnant or stalled thinking, which consists of resistance to change or overreliance on untraditional or traditional thinking. A social worker who is resistant to change is reluctant to change his or her ideas in light of new practice information (Gibbs, 2002). For example, a social worker in clinical practice disregards statements from a client, who is a married man with children, that he thinks he is homosexual. The social worker at first disregards this statement because it seems to conflict with the client's heterosexual orientation. The social worker then realizes she was resistant to change; she reframes her thinking and realizes that her client is questioning his sexual orientation and asks him to tell her more about it.

Relying on Nontraditional or Traditional Thinking

Relying on traditional or new thinking occurs when a social worker makes assumptions about the effectiveness of interventions because they have historically been used or are new (Gibbs, 2002). For example, a social worker may conclude that an intervention is effective after having successfully used it once as a community organizing strategy. However, upon close examination, the social worker determines that he does not have enough information about intervention effectiveness and consults the literature and with colleagues to obtain more detailed information about the effectiveness of intervention.

Unclear Thinking

Unclear thinking is represented by the use of vague thoughts (Gibbs, 2002). For example, a social worker in the community may advocate for assistance for the homeless population. When she speaks to community stakeholders about homelessness, she uses vague descriptions by saying there are just too many people on the streets. She realizes she was expressing vague thoughts about the significance of the problem and follows up her statement saying, "A statewide report about homelessness found that there are 75,000 state residents who are homeless, of which one half are children 12 years old and younger."

Split Thinking

Split thinking is represented by dichotomous or dualistic thinking. When a social worker uses dichotomous thinking, he or she sees the world in either black or white without grey areas. For example, a social worker may perceive a split between rational thought and emotions and interpret that to mean that he or she cannot be warm, empathic, and caring while also being analytical, scientific, and rationale in practice (Gibbs, 2002). After realizing that she was engaging in dichotomous thinking, the social worker reassured herself that she could be both compassionate and rational in her practice.

Disempowered Thinking

Disempowered thinking consists of uncritical agreement with authority (Gibbs, 2002). For example, a social worker engaging in disempowered thinking assumed that an intervention is effective based on one expert's lecture on the topic of the link between borderline personality disorder and childhood sexual abuse because she assumed the information to be fact, although she felt a mild sense of disagreement with the conclusions. After realizing she was engaging in uncritical agreement with authority, she decided to find out more about the topic and began to read more on it.

Cultural Overcompetence

Cultural overcompetence occurs when a social worker perceives that he or she has the ability to work and respond in a culturally competent manner without preparation to do so. An example is the social worker who insists that he acknowledges and respects other groups' culturally based beliefs, attitudes, behaviors, and customs without having explored his knowledge, values, and skills related to inner self-awareness of culture or learning about diverse populations he serves. After realizing he was engaging in cultural overcompetence, the social worker decides to assess his own cultural beliefs and potential biases, read the literature, and talk with relevant community stakeholders to learn more about the populations he serves.

Practicing Critical Reflection

In conclusion, problems related to practice may remain inadequately addressed because social workers do not carefully review the accuracy of their thought processes. A social worker should continually ask himself or herself: How did I come to this conclusion about this problem or practice situation? Did I revert to any of the common cognitive thinking errors to draw conclusions? Are there alternative ways of looking at the problem or other possible conclusions or solutions?

Social workers motivated to help others can do so by making every effort to reduce bias in their thinking and optimize accurate assessments and interventions. Actively engaging in personal reflection before making decisions is an essential strategy for enhancing human rights and social justice outcomes and the well-being of the populations social workers serve. There is much merit to the argument that the populations social workers serve deserve the right to effective treatment and interventions (Thyer & Myers, 1999).

Critical Thinking

Critical Thinking Question: How can critical thinking skills improve practice decision-making processes in social work research and evaluation?

EVIDENCE-BASED PRACTICE

The rise of the Evidence-Based Practice (EBP) movement in social work has gained momentum over the past two decades (Gibbs, 2003). EBP assists social workers in managing the complex thinking and tasks of professional practice. The crux of EBP is managing combining the best available empirical evidence with professional experience and client and constituents values and preferences (Cournoyer & Powers, 2002; Gambrill, 1999).

The term *evidence-based practice* was initially developed in the 1990s for the medical profession and was referred to as *evidence-based medicine* (Haynes, Devereaux, & Guyatt, 2002). The EBP movement has steadily been adopted among the allied professions, which include social work, child welfare, education, mental health, and criminal justice. The EBP movement offers a common mechanism and language for use in interdisciplinary practice (Satterfield et al., 2009).

This history of the EBP movement has relevance to social work, a profession built on enhancing well-being and increasing social justice outcomes. Before the rise of EBP, practice knowledge was based mostly on authority and tradition. In essence, experts were in charge of how issues and practices were perceived and implemented. In the 1970s, a number of published empirical studies debated the ineffectiveness of social work practice, especially clinical practice (Fischer, 1973; Fraser & Taylor, 1991).

In the late 1980s and after the development of EBP medicine, practitioners' expertise began to be conceptualized as an essential component of practice decision-making and actions. This process included using the best available evidence to make clinical decisions for individualized care. Although models of EBP have been evolving, EBP commonly integrates the use of the best research evidence with professional expertise, and client preferences and values. Incorporation of critical thinking skills to manage the process is therefore essential (Rubin, 2008; Sackett, Rosenberg, Gray, Haynes, & Richardson, 1996).

Evidence-Based Practice as an Outcome and a Process

In social work, *EBP* refers to both an outcome and a process. As an outcome, *EBPs* commonly refer to treatment or other interventions that have accumulated a body of sound research evidence to support their effectiveness. Drake and colleagues (2001) defined *EBP* as "any practice that has been established as effective through scientific research according to a set of explicit criteria" (p. 79).

Evidence-based practices stake their claims on a body of strong empirical evidence that corroborates effectiveness. EBPs may reliably produce the intended outcomes such as increased child safety or reduced accidental injury or poverty among older adults. Social workers must feel confident in using their research knowledge and skills to increase their proficiency in developing, improving, or evaluating EBPs for the populations (e.g., children, adults, older adults) they serve in different practice settings (e.g., schools, community agencies, hospitals, prisons). For a social worker searching for EBP practices, there are a number of resources, such as websites, treatment manuals, and guides available to help facilitate the use of EBP interventions.

Evidence-based practices are available for a wide range of populations from infants to older adults and for practice settings from hospitals to education and corrections facilities. They differ on the extent to which they have been used with diverse populations. Social workers working in agencies as administrators or service providers often are expected to identify and/or implement and evaluate EBP practices. An example of evidence-based, family-focused interventions for at-risk youth that have been evaluated internationally is outlined next.

Example: Family Functional Therapy (FFT)

An example of an EBP is Family Functional Therapy (FFT [Waldron & Turner, 2008]), an internationally recognized EBP intervention for at-risk youth (ages between 11 and 18 years old). Consisting of 12 sessions over 3–6 months, FFT has been effective in reducing recidivism among juvenile offenders and increasing family protective factors and is flexible across practice contexts and populations (e.g., Alexander & Sexton, 2002; Gordon, Graves, & Arbuthnot, 1995). More information about FFT is available at http://www.fftinc.com/.

EBP as a Decision-Making Process

Evidence-based practice also refers to a decision-making process. It involves critical thinking combined with knowledge of research and practice, and a long-term commitment to learning (Rubin, 2008). EBP is different from authority-based practice, which relies on testimonials from respected experts (Gambrill, 1999). If social workers understand that EBP offers a balanced approach to practice decision-making, they can evaluate the nature and quality of the evidence using the empirical literature, practice wisdom or experience, and the personal and cultural values and preferences of their constituents and the system.

Definitions

According to the Institute of Medicine (2001), EBP has been defined as the "the integration of best researched evidence and clinical expertise with patients' values" (p. 147). Health professionals Sackett, Rosenberg, Gray, Haynes, and Richardson (1996) published a model commonly used in social work practice (see Figure 3.2). Sackett et al. (1996) described the EBP process as entailing the "conscientious, explicit and judicious use of the current best evidence in making decisions about the care of individual patients" (p. 1). Similarly, Rubin (2008) described EBP as a "process for making practice decisions in which practitioners integrate the best research evidence available with their practice expertise and with client attributes, values, preferences, and circumstances" (p. 17).

Mechanism for Decision Making

Proponents of EBP note a number of strengths toward achieving benefits for individuals and communities served. The EBP process provides social workers with an organizing mechanism on which to base their decision making and actions; the mechanism includes the current best research evidence, professional judgment and practice wisdom, clients' (or constituents') values and preferences, and the environmental context. It is important to note that a common

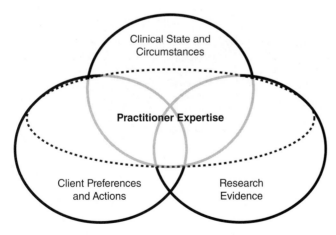

Figure 3.2
Evidence-Based Practice Model
Source: Haynes, R. B., Devereaux, P. J., & Guyatt, G. H. (2002). Editorial: Clinical expertise in the era of evidence-based medicine and patient choice. *ACP Journal Club*, March/April.

misconception is that the practitioner's judgment has no place in the process. In fact, quite the opposite is true. The practitioner's judgment is the hub of the decision making (Haynes et al., 2002; Sackett et al., 1996). For example, a social worker can modify an intervention to address the specific cultural needs of an individual, a family, or a community, such as including extended family members within the parameters of a family intervention.

Using critical thinking skills, EBP provides a mechanism for social workers to engage in a systematic thought process to answer here-and-now practice-based questions based on the best research evidence and stakeholder input; social workers also consider the environmental context before making a final judgment or assessment and intervention. Because many of social workers' practice interventions entail policy practice or macro-level interventions at the community or governmental level, we propose an evidence-based practice model that includes all levels of intervention and language that is inclusive of all levels of practice. Figure 3.3 features traditional factors that comprise the EBP model. It also includes agency-level practice and social-environmental factors that may influence the EBP process or which the social work intervention may target.

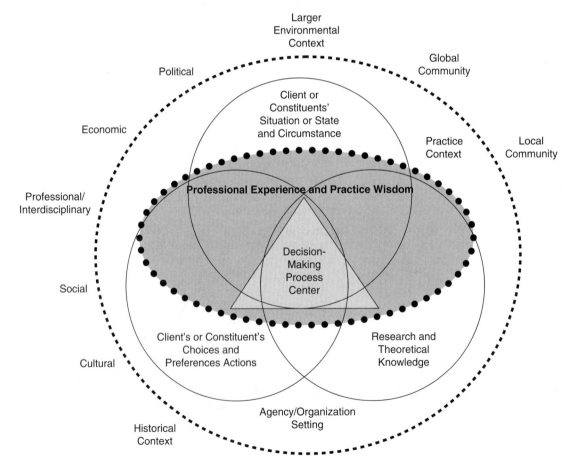

Figure 3.3
The Evidence-Based Practice Process in the Larger Context

Table 3.1	**EBP Steps**
	Evidence-Based Practice Steps
Step 1	Formulate a practice-based question
Step 2	Search for evidence
Step 3	Evaluate the quality of the evidence
Step 4	Identify intervention options
Step 5	Choose intervention
Step 6	Monitor intervention progress
Step 7	Evaluate outcomes and document results

EBP Steps

Although the steps may vary, common steps in the EBP process include starting with answerable practice-based questions when working with individuals, families, organizations, and communities. The next step is to find and review the relevant empirical literature related to addressing the target problem. Next, the literature must be evaluated for the rigor of the research design on which conclusions were drawn and its relevance to the population served (Rubin, 2008).

As shown in Table 3.1, the EBP steps outlined are as follows: (a) formulate a practice-based question, (b) search for evidence, (c) evaluate the quality of the evidence, (d) identify intervention options, (f) choose an intervention, (f) monitor intervention options, and (g) evaluate outcomes and document results. A brief description of the steps is reviewed next. Steps 1 to 3 are reviewed in Chapter 5 on conducting a literature review. Steps 5 to 7 are reviewed in Chapters 6 through 11 related to research design and program evaluation.

Step 1 involves formulating a practice-based question. This question commonly refers to which interventions, programs, or policies have the best evidence supporting their effectiveness. Social workers must formulate an EBP question to guide an intervention decision for their practice or program (Howard, Bricout, Edmond, Elze, & Jenson, 2003). Examples of practice-based questions include: (a) What interventions have the best research support for interventions with a 65-year-old woman with depression who was a victim of elder abuse? (b) What interventions have the best empirical support for treating adolescent boys with mental health problems who engage in juvenile delinquency?

In step 3, *the search for evidence* refers to finding the literature that can best help the social worker answer that question. In step 3, social workers evaluate the quality of the evidence collected for use with their client population. The empirical evidence found must be used to carefully evaluate to what extent the literature reviewed represents a similar practice context, diverse population served, cultural competence, and targeted outcomes. Step 4 is to identify intervention options. Steps 5 through 7 represent the outcome of the decision-making process in which an intervention is chosen, implemented, monitored for progress, and then evaluated for outcomes. The social worker using a human rights and social justice framework works collaboratively with clients to choose an intervention that considers clients' or constituents' personal and cultural values and preferences, research evidence, the environmental context, and professional experience.

Research-Based Practice

Critical Thinking Question: Using Figure 3.2 or 3.3, explain how you would use the model for practice decision-making. What are its strengths and limitations for your practice setting?

Professional experience comprises an essential component of the EBP model. As noted in Figure 3.2, the intersection of professional experience, client and constituents' personal and cultural values and preferences, and the theoretical and research evidence is what the practitioner uses as part of his or her decision-making processes.

Professional experience is associated with practice wisdom, which is described as social workers' accrual of practice-based information, assumptions, and judgments for use in practice. Practice wisdom is often equated with common sense and may or may not be validated when subjected to empirical or systematic analysis and may or may not be consistent with prevailing theory (Powell, 2008).

Practice wisdom is linked to tacit or implicit knowledge that influences the decision-making process (Powell, 2008). This represents the exchange of deductive empirical knowledge (i.e., use theory and research to inform practice) as a source of evidence combined with the use of practice wisdom generated from prolonged engagement in field (i.e., use practice experience to inform research). Dybicz (2004) referred to this latter process as *practice-linked knowledge* that is the result of a "process of 'incipient induction,' as involving processes or actions, including knowing-in-action and reflection-in-action" (p. 25). Weighing the different sources of evidence with an emphasis on diversity can help social workers to optimize their ability to engage in culturally competent social work research and evaluation, which is consistent with the human rights and social justice framework.

Hierarchy of Evidence: Appraising

Research is often presented within a hierarchy of evidence to help social workers design or evaluate studies from the most to least rigorous designs for establishing intervention effectiveness. An example of such a hierarchy of evidence, in which systematic reviews or meta-analyses are considered to be the most rigorous and personal experience, is considered the least rigorous, is:

1. A systematic review or meta-analyses
2. Randomized control group designs
3. Quasi-experimental designs
4. Case control design or cohort studies
5. Single group pretest-posttest design
6. Single-subject design
7. Survey-descriptive and correlational designs
8. Qualitative research designs
9. Evidence from expert committee reports
10. Expert opinions
11. Anecdotal case reports
12. Personal opinion or experience

Although there is no consistent agreement on the hierarchy of the best available research, the highest level is often attributed to systematic reviews and meta-analyses. See Table 3.2 for an EBP Hierarchy of Evidence Checklist.

Table 3.2   Evidence-Based Practice Hierarchy of Evidence Checklist

Directions: After conducting your literature review on your chosen topic area, describe how you would organize your literature in the hierarchy of evidence below. Based on your classification, how would you rate the body of evidence related to this area of research or evaluation?

Hierarchy of Evidence	Articles Found (Use the First Author's Name and Year of Publication)
A systematic review or meta-analyses	
Randomized control group designs	
Quasi-experimental designs	
Case control design or cohort studies	
Single group pretest-posttest design	
Single-subject design	
Survey-descriptive and correlational designs	
Qualitative research designs	
Evidence from expert committee reports	
Expert opinions	
Anecdotal case reports	
Personal opinion or experience	
Other—not noted above	

Rate the evidence found on a scale of 1 to 5: 1 = poor, 2 = fair, 3 = good, 4 = very good, 5 = excellent. Briefly explain your rationale for your rating.

The Campbell Collaboration conducts systematic reviews in which the review process and decision-making criteria are prepared in advance and are carefully documented (Littell, Corcoran, & Pillai, 2008). Next in the hierarchy are singular studies that use randomized controlled trials (RCTs). RCTs use randomly selected experimental and control groups and are commonly viewed as the gold standard to which all other methods are compared. The use of RCTs is commonly viewed by researchers to have a stronger design for establishing that the intervention worked (causality) (Rubin, 2008).

Example of Rating EBP

A growing number of organizations and communities are developing rating systems to appraise the strength of the evidence for interventions. One example is the California Evidence-Based Clearinghouse for Child Welfare (CEBCCW, 2010) (available at http://www.cebc4cw.org/). It has adopted two rating scales for research rigor and practice relevance related to a scientific rating scale and the child welfare rating scale.

Scientific Rating

The scientific rating scale is used to evaluate the empirical evidence generated from an intervention. It uses a scale of 1 to 5 with 1 representing the strongest research evidence and 5 representing a concerning practice that may pose substantial risk to children and families. Programs without enough accumulated research evidence are not included.

Relevance Rating

The second rating, the Child Welfare Relevance Rating Scale, examines the degree to which the program or model was designed for families served within the child welfare system, which include racial and ethnic minorities. This scale is needed as some well-researched practices may never have been intended for child welfare applications and the research, upon which the scientific rating is made, may have little relevance to child welfare environments. On a scale of 1 to 3, 1 is rated as high relevance because this program is designed or commonly used among child welfare populations. A rating of 2 represents medium relevance with populations similar to child welfare populations. A score of 3 is low and assigned to programs that were limited or had no relevance to child welfare.

Child Welfare Outcomes

Child welfare outcomes are evaluated by examining peer-reviewed empirical literature. Three major federal goals and outcomes that public child welfare services are accountable to address are (a) safety, (b) permanency, and (c) child and family well-being. Some programs or practices target one or more of these goals (CEBCCW, 2010).

Critiques of Evidence-Based Practice

Many debates and critiques of EBP have been put forth. One of the critiques is that it has limited application, especially for diverse cultural groups. Additionally, a number of interventions have not as of yet accumulated a body of research evidence. This may complicate the decision-making process for social workers in the field because there is limited evidence available.

Sometimes there are difficulties in implementing an intervention. For example, the social worker may not be trained in the best available method and the agency has no plans to provide the training. Limited time and resources may make it difficult for individuals and agencies to adapt. There also has been difficulty in translating EBP into interdisciplinary practice or making it easily translatable from micro-level to macro-level interventions. The extent to which EBPs can bridge the cultural divide has not yet been adequately determined (Gibbs & Gambrill, 2002; Satterfield et al., 2009; Straus & McAlister, 2000).

Evidence-Based Practice and Diversity and Cultural Competence

As noted earlier, important factors in the selection of an EBP intervention are the level of empirical support, the relevance to the population served, and success with reaching targeted outcomes. A central concern is how well individual social worker and organization is prepared to address diversity and cultural competence among their constituents. Interventions that have been conducted with homogenous or similar groups, such as mostly adult Caucasian men, may have limited relevance to the practice settings in which there are a large number of older adult women of diverse racial or ethnic backgrounds.

A central concern is how well each individual social worker and organization is prepared to address diversity and cultural competence among their constituents.

Cultural Diversity and Cultural Competence

Conceptions of cultural diversity in social work have evolved from concerning only race and ethnicity to also include gender, age, social class, religion, sexual orientation, immigration status, and physical and mental abilities (National Association of Social Workers [NASW], 2006; Rothman, 2008). Therefore, social workers who use EBPs can incorporate cultural competence. So what exactly is meant by *cultural competence*? NASW (2001) defines cultural competence as a "set of congruent behaviors, attitudes, and policies that come together in a system or agency or among professionals and enable the system, agency, or professionals to work effectively in cross-cultural situations" (p. 61).

Cultural competence is the process by which individuals, service systems, and communities respond both respectfully and effectively to people of all cultures, languages, classes, races, ethnic backgrounds, religions, and other diversity factors. Therefore, social workers can infuse in the research and evaluation processes a culturally competent response that recognizes, affirms, and values the worth of individuals, families, and communities, and protects and preserves their dignity (NASW, 2006).

NASW Standards of Cultural Competence (2006) has 10 standards for reaching cultural competence among individuals, organizations, and communities. These standards are as follows: (1) ethics and values, (2) self-awareness, (3) cross-cultural knowledge, (4) cross-cultural skills, (5) service delivery, (6) empowerment and advocacy, (7) diverse workforce, (8) professional education, (9) language diversity, and (10) cross-cultural leadership.

Bridging Cultural Competence and Evidence-Based Practices

To bridge the cultural competence and EBP divide, culturally competent practices need to be embedded within all stages of program development and implementation practices. Cave (2004) recommended strategies for planning culturally competent, evidence-based services that include skill development and policy guidance to ensure clinical and administrative practices are culturally competent. It is important to: (a) assess the effectiveness of EBPs across diverse cultural groups, (b) continue to build the evidence base so it is effective for all populations served, and (c) disseminate and share "what works" so that other agencies in the community or other communities may learn and adapt these practices.

These recommendations for building culturally competent EBP are classified under agency-level practices, research and evaluation, and community outreach (Cave, 2004). They are as follows:

Agency-level practices

⬧ Develop a written strategic plan to address disparities.
⬧ Know and understand the various cultural groups present in the community served.

▶ Recruit and retain a diverse staff that is representative of the community.
▶ Include readily accessible bilingual and bicultural staff or interpreters.
▶ Provide language assistance at all points of contact as needed.
▶ Provide translated vital service documents, program documents, and rights and grievance information.
▶ Provide ongoing training about the cultural groups served and assure strategies employed are effective across cultures.
▶ Adapt service environments, practices, and delivery to match the individuals and families served.

Research and evaluation

▶ Include assessment of cross-cultural interactions as part of the employee evaluation and supervisory processes.
▶ Examine agency and individual outcomes to determine whether specific groups within the service population are over- or under-represented, to track consumer satisfaction, and to promote consumer-driven services.
▶ Collect demographic data about the community at large and service recipients to determine future directions for program development.

Community outreach

▶ Consider various methods and media for mental health information exchange and education and promotion.
▶ Develop partnerships with community leaders, cultural brokers, and natural networks to facilitate increased service access and to provide feedback that will guide service design.

Diversity in Practice

Critical Thinking Question: Using the cultural competence survey, identify and evaluate areas of strength and in need of improvement. What are three strategies for improvement?

Conducting Self- and Organizational Assessment for Cultural Competence

In the current age of accountability, many grants require evidence of cultural competence and sensitivity, including social worker self-assessments and training. Therefore, it is strongly recommended that agencies monitor their progress in achieving evidence of cultural competence. The Georgetown University National Center for Cultural Competence (NCCC) provides invaluable resources including the Assessment of Self and Organizational Cultural Competence Survey (Association of University Centers on Disabilities [AUCD], 2004).

The survey documents progress in cultural competence at both the individual and organizational level (AUCD, 2004). Cultural competence assesses the services, supports, or other assistance that is conducted or provided in a manner that is responsive to the beliefs, interpersonal styles, attitudes, language, and behaviors of individuals who receive them, and in a manner that has the greatest likelihood of ensuring their maximum participation in the program involved (AUCD, 2004, p. 1). It consists of the following three sections: (a) assessment of organizational cultural competence, (b) respondent information, and (c) assessment of individual cultural competence (AUCD, 2004). The assessment of individual cultural competence is provided in Table 3.3.

Table 3.3   Individual Assessment of Cultural Competence

Individual Assessment of Cultural Competence

As a member of the organization, the knowledge you have of yourself and others is important and reflected in the ways you communicate and interact. This individual assessment instrument was developed to assist you in reflecting upon and examining your journey toward cultural competence. **The following statements are about you and your cultural beliefs and values as they relate to the organization. Please check the ONE answer that BEST DESCRIBES your response to each of the statements (from never to always).**

Statements	Rate from Never to Always				
I reflect on and examine my own cultural background, biases and prejudices related to race, culture and sexual orientation that may influence my behaviors.	Never 0	Almost never 1	Sometimes 2	Often 3	Always 4
I continue to learn about the cultures of the consumers and families served in the program, in particular attitudes toward disability; cultural beliefs and values; and health, spiritual, and religious practices.	Never 0	Almost never 1	Sometimes 2	Often 3	Always 4
I recognize and accept that the consumer and family members make the ultimate decisions even though they may be different compared to my personal and professional values and beliefs.	Never 0	Almost never 1	Sometimes 2	Often 3	Always 4
I intervene, in an appropriate manner, when I observe other staff engaging in behaviors that appear culturally insensitive or reflect prejudice.	Never 0	Almost never 1	Sometimes 2	Often 3	Always 4
I attempt to learn and use key words and colloquialisms of the languages used by the consumers and families served.	Never 0	Almost never 1	Sometimes 2	Often 3	Always 4
I utilize interpreters for the assessment of consumers and their families whose spoken language is one for which I am not fluent.	Never 0	Almost never 1	Sometimes 2	Often 3	Always 4
I have developed skills to utilize an interpreter effectively.	Never 0	Almost never 1	Sometimes 2	Often 3	Always 4
I utilize methods of communication, including written, verbal, pictures, and diagrams, which will be most helpful to the consumers, families, and other program participants.	Never 0	Almost never 1	Sometimes 2	Often 3	Always 4
I write reports or any form of written communication in a style and at a level which consumers, families, and other program participants will understand.	Never 0	Almost never 1	Sometimes 2	Often 3	Always 4
I am flexible, adaptive, and will initiate changes, which will better serve consumers, families, and other program participants from diverse cultures.	Never 0	Almost never 1	Sometimes 2	Often 3	Always 4
I am mindful of cultural factors that may be influencing the behaviors of consumers, families, and other program participants.	Never 0	Almost never 1	Sometimes 2	Often 3	Always 4
Total Score (0–44)					

Source: Association of University Centers on Disabilities. (2004). *Assessment of organizational cultural competence.*

SUMMARY

This chapter reviewed research and evaluation through the lens of the culturally competent generalist phases of practice and EBP methods, and the promotion of human rights and social justice aims. The generalist phases of practice include (a) engage, assess, and define the problem, (b) brainstorm potential solutions, (c) choose a goal-oriented action or intervention plan, (d) implement the chosen intervention, and (e) evaluate the intervention and conclude the results.

The "ways of knowing" influences how social workers know what they know. The different ways include (a) authority, (b) personal experience, (c) intuition, inspiration, and revelation, (d) empiricism or observation, (e) rationalism, and (f) culture. Each of the ways of knowing has both strengths and limitations. Critical thinking is a core social work practice skill that can increase the accuracy of practice decision-making processes, including problem definition.

The term *evidence-based practice* is used to describe empirically supported interventions as well as the decision-making process that social workers use based on empirical evidence and evidence from the field. EBP is a mechanism in which evaluation of evidence can be weighed with professional experience, client preferences and values, and environment context, including at the social, cultural, and structural levels. Cultural competence is an essential aspect of individual, organizational, and community practice and is essential to achieving EBPs that incorporate sensitivity to diversity. Some available resources to learn more about EBP are listed below:

- California Evidence-Based Clearinghouse for Child Welfare provides current information on evidence-based child welfare practices.

  http://www.cebc4cw.org/

- Campbell Collaboration is a global nonprofit organization that provides systematic reviews and meta-analyses on the effectiveness of psychological, social, and behavioral interventions relevant to social work, criminal justice, and education fields.

  http://www.campbellcollaboration.org

- Cochrane Collaboration is an international, nonprofit organization that produces and disseminates systematic reviews of health care interventions.

  http://www.cochrane.org

- Family-focused EBP interventions.

  http://www2.dsgonline.com/mpg/

- National Alliance of Multi-Ethnic Behavioral Health Associations (NAMBHA) addresses disparities in behavioral health services and provides information on culturally appropriate, best practice models.

  http://www.nambha.org/

- National Association of State Mental Health Program Directors Research Institute (NRI) has useful information about defining EBPs.

  http://www.nasmhpd.org/

- National Initiative for the Care of the Elderly (NICE).

  http://www.nicenet.ca/

- ▶ OJJDP Prevention Model Programs Guide.
  http://www2.dsgonline.com/mpg/
- ▶ Substance Abuse and Mental Health Services Administration (SAMHSA) National Registry of Evidence-based Programs and Practices (NREPP).
  http://www.nrepp.samhsa.gov/
- ▶ SAMHSA Guide to Evidence-Based Practices (EBP).
  http://www.samhsa.gov/ebpwebguide/index.asp
- ▶ National Center for Cultural Competence provides information on evaluating cultural competence.
  http://www11.georgetown.edu/research/gucchd/nccc/
- ▶ NASW Standards for Cultural Competence.
  http://www.naswdc.org/practice/standards/NASWCulturalStandards.pdf

Succeed with **PEARSON mysocialworklab**

Log onto **www.mysocialworklab.com** and answer the following questions. (*If you did not receive an access code to* **MySocialWorkLab** *with this text and wish to purchase access online, please visit* www.mysocialworklab.com.)

1. **Watch the critical thinking video "Applying Critical Thinking."** After listening to commentary and gaining a better understanding about critical thinking for

practice decision-making, describe how your decision-making process would be different or similar in this situation.

2. **Watch the research-based practice video, "Engaging in Research-Informed Practice."** After listening to the commentary, explain how effective the social worker was in assessing for an appropriate evidence-based therapy.

PRACTICE TEST
The following questions will test your knowledge of the content found within this chapter. For additional assessment, including licensing-exam type questions on applying chapter content to practice, visit **MySocialWorkLab**.

1. Consistent with generalist practice, the initial problem-solving process of research involves:
   a. Project implementation
   b. Engagement, assessment, and problem formulation.
   c. Evaluation and conclusion
   d. Choosing a goal-oriented action plan

2. Evidence-based practice as a process generally refers to:
   a. Interventions based on a body of sound research evidence
   b. Evidence derived exclusively from practice wisdom
   c. The development of innovative interventions
   d. Conscientious and judicious use of the current best evidence in practice decision-making

3. Which of the following is most often considered a more rigorous source of research evidence?
   a. Single-subject designs
   b. Survey-descriptive designs
   c. Randomized control group design
   d. Expert committee reports

4. A research and evaluation strategy for culturally competence in an agency is not which of the following?
   a. Collecting local demographic data to inform program development
   b. Assessing cross-cultural interactions on an employee evaluation
   c. Examining agency services for over- or underrepresentation of certain groups
   d. Providing language assistance for certain programs

5. Describe at least one strength and limitation of the evidence-based practice model (see Figure 3.2).

ASSESS YOUR COMPETENCE
Use the scale below to rate your current level of achievement on the following concepts or skills associated with each competency presented in the chapter:

1	2	3
I can accurately describe the concept or skill.	I can consistently identify the concept or skill when observing and analyzing practice activities.	I can competently implement the concept or skill in my own practice.

_____ can apply generalist problem-solving process to the research process.

_____ can use critical thinking to identify and modify errors in thinking.

_____ can apply the evidence-based practice model to practice situations.

_____ can engage diversity and difference in evidence-based practice decision-making.

4

Problem Formulation
From Conceptualization
to Operationalization

Core Competencies in This Chapter (Check marks indicate which competencies are demonstrated)									
	Professional Identity		Ethical Practice		Critical Thinking	✓	Diversity in Practice		Human Rights and Justice
✓	Research-Based Practice	✓	Human Behavior		Policy Practice		Practice Contexts		Engage, Assess, Intervene, Evaluate

INTRODUCTION

Social workers committed to advancing human rights and social and economic justice can use research and evaluation to plan and evaluate progress toward these goals. This entails social workers continually refining their skills at navigating the research process. They commonly use both abstract and concrete thinking to understand how research paradigms are linked to theories, hypotheses, concepts, and variables, as well as the choice of certain research and evaluation methods or the appraisal of studies conducted by others (Rubin, 2008).

Social workers often combine inductive and deductive processes.

Social workers often combine inductive and deductive processes. When using deductive thinking, the social worker begins with theory and derives one or more hypotheses to test in research. When using deductive thinking, the social worker also begins with a prediction or hypothesis, then gathers data and analyzes the findings. When using inductive thinking, the social worker begins with observed data and develops hypotheses to explain observations. These are distinct processes but often can be used as part of a cyclical thought process (Jordan & Franklin, 2003) (see Figure 4.1).

Individuals may naturally tend to lean toward inductive processes, deductive processes, or a mixed approach. Therefore, social workers should be aware of their natural orientation and how this might affect their practice

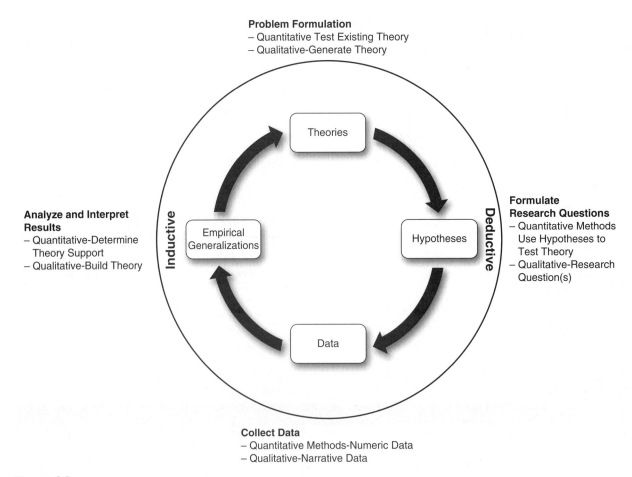

Figure 4.1
The Cycle of Inductive and Deductive Processes for Research and Practice Evaluation

decision-making process. Exhibit 4.1 of "Conducting a Literature Review" section provides a survey to evaluate inductive and deduction orientation.

This chapter begins with describing the philosophy behind research, which includes the paradigms or worldviews—such as positivism, social constructivism, pragmatism, and critical social science—that guide it. This chapter next reviews the role of theory as it relates to the research and practice integration, including an overview of the inductive and deductive processes that inform qualitative, quantitative, and mixed methods approaches and study types. The phases in the research and practice evaluation cycle include: (a) identify the problem, (b) formulate research questions and hypotheses, (c) select practice–research design, (d) select measures, (e) select sample and identify client, (f) collect data, (g) analyze and interpret the findings, and (h) document, share the findings, and take action. These phases will be elaborated on in chapters 5 through 12. (See Figure 4.2).

Social workers who understand how research and practice inform each other will be at a greater advantage for tapping all potential sources of evidence for practice decision making and action. The clients and constituents served can be more confident that the services being provided are designed to help and empower them.

Philosophy: The Science of Knowing

Philosophy shapes the way we define and seek to resolve problems. The different research approaches of quantitative, qualitative, and mixed methods are influenced by different philosophical worldviews. Philosophy, or the science

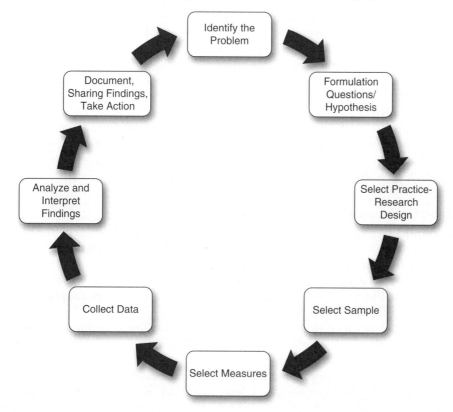

Figure 4.2
The Research and Practice Evaluation Cycle

of knowing, in both Eastern and Western traditions examines and seeks to understand the nature of reality and existence, often referred to as *ontology* (Osborne & Van Loon, 2003; Popper, 1959).

Historically, philosophy has examined collective beliefs about fundamental human concerns often related to the nature of existence, truth, reality, knowledge, values, meaning, language, and reason. Classic questions associated with philosophical thought include What is existence? What is truth? What is reality? How do we know what we know? What is the meaning of life? (Morgan, 2001; Popkin, 1999). The answers may vary depending upon the paradigm, or philosophical worldviews used.

Paradigms

A paradigm is a collective worldview that includes a set of assumptions, concepts, values, and practices that constitute a way of viewing reality.

A paradigm is a collective worldview that includes a set of assumptions, concepts, values, and practices that constitute a way of viewing reality for the community of individuals that shares them (Kuhn, 1962). Paradigms are general frameworks for understanding aspects of life. A paradigm may be visualized as a large umbrella that encompasses a common way of seeing the world and interpreting social reality. Paradigms act as an organizing framework or umbrella, which helps give us a general sense of our observations and our worldview. In reference to science, *paradigms* refer to a broad philosophical framework that guides science and social science theories and generalizations and the types of research methods used (Kuhn, 1970).

For example, most helping professions are closely allied with particular worldviews. The medical profession, often referred to as a "hard" science, commonly assumes an objective or neutral stance to diagnose and treat health issues. In contrast, the social or "soft" sciences, such as anthropology, often assume a socially constructed worldview, which contains many interpretations of the problem and possible solutions.

Other social science disciplines, such as social work, move between objective and subjective worldviews in understanding and intervening with individual- and social-level problems (Fox, Martin, & Green, 2007). When working in interdisciplinary contexts, such as hospitals or correctional settings, social workers should be aware of potential differences in worldviews among different professionals. It also is important to one's own core philosophical perspectives on reality, including linear versus holistic thinking.

Scientific Revolutions

The import of paradigms in the social sciences can be attributed to Kuhn's (1962) book, *The Structure of Scientific Revolutions*. This groundbreaking text examines the history and nature of philosophical thought in science. Kuhn found that shifts occurred in the dominant paradigm when an anomaly or inconsistency in evidence contradicted it and challenged assumptions and "the existing tradition of scientific practice" (p. 6).

The transformation in collective thought that occurs in response to anomalies may result in a "scientific revolution." This shift in collective scientific thought is dynamic and evolves over time based on new discoveries. According to Kuhn (1970), competing paradigms may exist simultaneously, especially within young disciplines, such as social work. Coexisting paradigms may be perceived as a source of intellectual conflict and heated irresolvable debate or a means for the creative integration of opposing viewpoints.

Research Paradigms That Inform Social Work

Research paradigms, which include positivism, postpositivism, construc- tivism, pragmatism, and critical social science paradigms, commonly influ- ence the social work research process throughout, from problem formulation to the choice of methods used (see Table 4.1). Distinctions among them have been the subject of heated debates and traditionally have been discussed as the "paradigm wars." Although the paradigms as a source of knowledge genera- tion are commonly debated, at other times, social workers integrate them in thought and practice (Patton, 2002).

The positivist and postpositivist approaches are most often associated with quantitative deductive research approaches (Klemke, Hollinger, & Kline, 1988). In contrast, the constructivist and critical social science approaches are most often associated with qualitative inductive research approaches (Guba & Lincoln, 1994). The pragmatist approach is most often associated with mixed (quantitative and qualitative) methods (Patton, 2002).

Diversity in Practice

Critical Thinking Question: How might diversity in thought among the different paradigms (i.e., postpositivism, constructivism, and critical social science) influence, if at all, problem formulation in research?

Positivism

Rising out of 19th-century scientific thought, the defining features of posi- tivism (or realism) are objectivity and neutrality. Positivism embraces the

Table 4.1	**Research Paradigms for Social Work**				
Paradigm	Positivism	Postpostivism	Constructivism	Pragmatism	Critical social science
Methods	Quantitative	Quantitative	Qualitative	Mixed methods	Qualitative
Logic	Deductive	Deductive	Inductive	Deductive and inductive	Inductive- deductive awareness
Epistemology viewpoint	Objective	Mostly objective	Subjective	Subjective and objective	Subjective- objective awareness
Knower–known relationship	Dualism—knower separate from known	Dualism—light	Merger of knower and known	Dualism and indivisible	Indivisible but awareness of dualism
Role of values	Value-free	Controllable values	Value- influenced	Values play a role in interpreting results	Collective values embedded in history
Ontology (nature of reality)	One reality	Some collective agreed up reality	Multiple, socially constructed realities	Mixed	Liberation reality with awareness of oppression
Causality	Causal effects— use hypotheses	Some causal effects	Reciprocal interactions	Possibility of causal relationship	Action— individual and social change
Generalizations	Yes	Yes	No	Maybe	No

belief that there is a separate reality that exists quite apart from our own perception of it. It assumes the position that a real objective world exists separately from a socially constructed subjective world that we can generally agree upon. You see a bird, others see the bird, and therefore it is the same bird that everyone saw. In philosophical terms, the *knower* (the person) and the *known* (the knowledge) are separate or independent from each other (Popper, 1959).

When social workers use a positivist approach to scientific inquiry, individuals are viewed as objective and value-free (not influenced by values) and are not subject to external constraints, such as time or context. The positivist approach assumes a mechanistic and linear view of the world in which cause-and-effect relationships exist and can be collectively observed and from which generalizations can be made. This approach uses deductive logic, moving from general (e.g., abstract theory or concepts) to specific (e.g., real-world data) (Compte, 2009; Patton, 2002).

However, the positivist paradigm was discredited in the late 1940s. The rigid stance on the objective and value-free nature of postpositivists were contradicted by the influence of subjectivity and values in the research process. Similar to Kuhn's description of a shift in scientific paradigms, it was debunked partially by the rise of constructivism. A modified version called postpositivism emerged (Tashakkori & Teddlie, 1998).

Postpositivism

The rise of pospositivist positions during the 1960s is often attributed to Carl Popper's (1959) influence. The postpositivist position modified the rigid beliefs of positivism in a number of ways. As opposed to a value-free position, a postpositivist approach to research recognizes that the values of the researcher or evaluator may influence the research process. For example, research is influenced by the researcher's personal values and/or by the theory or hypotheses or framework that an investigator uses (Klemke et al., 1988; Patton, 2002).

A postpositivist approach acknowledges some level of subjectivity in interpreting reality, aspects on which most people agree. For example, many people agree that relationships influence their lives, but they can disagree on how to interpret these relationships. To account for this discrepancy, the postpositivist position acknowledges "inter-subjective agreement" in which different observers may be influenced by biases; there are still areas of collective agreement about the nature of the social world (Rubin & Babbie, 2010).

Constructivist Paradigm

Rising during the 1960s, constructivist (or interpretivist or naturalist) approaches offered a contrast to the dominant postpositivist views (Lincoln & Guba, 1985). Constructivist views are based on a core belief that reality is socially constructed. This paradigm differs from the postpositivist's argument for the existence of an objective reality. The constructivist position counterargues that multiple realities and interpretations of the social world exist. For example, one individual who looks at a dove may associate it with a bird, whereas another individual looks at the same dove and associates it with a peace symbol.

Because reality is socially constructed, the purpose of research is to unravel the diverse meanings of people's realities (Creswell, 2006). Additionally, in contrast to postpositivist deductive approaches, constructivism uses an inductive approach. Using this approach, social workers gather firsthand narrative data from the field, which are then used to make empirical generalizations and/or build theories as opposed to testing existing theories.

In contrast to the postpositvist position, the constructivist approach assumes a subjective stance and acknowledges how values influence the research process, and merges the knower with the known. Contextual factors, such as time, place, and culture, decrease an individual's confidence in the ability to make predictions about cause-and-effect relationships or generalizations about findings (Creswell, 2006). Now let us apply this information to real-world examples. Attitudes toward individuals with mental illness have varied throughout history. Attitudes toward gays and lesbians differ in different parts of the world or even different regions in the United States. The contextual influence of culture can be seen in the fact that views on older adults vary across different cultures.

Pragmatism

In the 1980s, the pragmatist paradigm arose out of irreconcilable differences between postpositivist and positivist camps. The war between the two paradigms resulted in a creative dissonance, which created the conditions for an integrated approach called *pragmatism* (Patton, 2002). Pragmatism offered a cease-fire between proponents of postpositivist and constructivist positions in order to use both of their strengths (Creswell, 2006).

As the term *pragmatic* suggests, this approach is practical when choosing a research approach; pragmatists base their decisions on the best approach to answer a research or practice evaluation question. The pragmatist view is that postpositivist and constructivist approaches are compatible and both contribute to improving practice. Pragmatism uses integrated inductive-deductive and mixed method approaches to research design (Patton, 2008).

Using the pragmatist lens, the human mind can try on different philosophical lenses to observe and interpret psychological or social phenomena. A pragmatic approach allows for the use of any approach to define the problem and potential solutions.

Critical Social Science Paradigm

The critical social science paradigm emphasizes social critique and empowerment. Gaining momentum in the 1990s, this paradigm and the methods that flow from it, such as participatory action research and antioppressive social work research, are purported to be consistent with human rights–based social work aims (Healey, 2001; McIntyre, 2008; Stier, 2006).

As the word *critical* suggests, this approach critically explores the social world to critique it and achieve individual and social transformation (Foucalt, 1980). This paradigm moves from a stage of critical reflection to action steps. It examines subjective and shared realities among groups, which are reinforced through language (Foucalt, 1982).

The critical social science approach asserts that there is an intergenerational transmission of a historically based collective reality. Although individual and group empowerment is a goal, it is tempered by the reality that structural barriers, such as institutional oppression and social and economic disadvantage, create barriers to achieving this goal. Building upon constructivist approaches, the critical paradigm assumes that reality is both socially and structurally constructed. A constructivist approach includes an examination of social, political, cultural, and economic forces as well as other aspects, such as ethnicity and gender (Buchanan, 2010; Foucalt, 1982).

Critical social science has some similar yet distinct characteristics from other research paradigms. Similar to the pragmatist paradigm, the critical approach acknowledges the reciprocal interaction of the subjectivity and objectivity paradigms. Similar to constructivism, the critical paradigm separates us from what we know except during the direct interaction among a social worker, study site, or group (Held, 1980).

The distinctive feature of the critical social science paradigm is its examination of group oppression with an action orientation. This approach rejects the false dichotomies of either/or black-and-white thinking (positivist versus constructivist) and instead delves into shades of intellectual grey. Another unique feature is the use of reflective dialogue that moves toward action-oriented solutions, with the purpose of challenging existing viewpoints. A central aspect is community involvement in the process at all stages from problem formulations, to methods, to implications and applications. The research endeavor aims to create individual and social transformation (Healey, 2006; Held, 1980; McIntyre, 2008).

Quantitative and Qualitative Research Methods

The two major research approaches, quantitative (deductive) and qualitative (inductive) research, flow from research paradigms.

The two major research approaches, quantitative (deductive) and qualitative (inductive) research, flow from research paradigms (see Table 4.2).

Quantitative Research Methods

Quantitative research has been seen as systematic investigations that include descriptive or inferential statistical analysis. Consistent with a postpositivist approach, quantitative research generally tests a hypothesis (or hypotheses) based on an existing theory or empirical support. The research is based on a nomothetic causal model that seeks to understand a part of a problem using only a few factors (Rubin & Babbie, 2010). For example, a nomothetic and quantitative research question might be: What parental factors predict sexual risk behavior among Latina youth?

Steps   The steps to quantitative deductive research are (a) use a research question to formulate hypotheses from existing theoretical or empirical literature, (b) develop research procedures, and (c) collect data to test the hypotheses.

Table 4.2	**Steps in the Measurement Process: A Quantitative–Qualitative Comparison**	
Paradigms/ philosophical roots	Postpostivism	Constructivism
Approaches	Quantitative	Qualitative
Theory	Test theory	Build theory
Research question and hypotheses	Uses research question and hypotheses	Uses research question
Concepts	Translate to variable and operational definition	Use sensitizing concepts as a guide
Variables	Operationally define, include values or attributes	Generally N/A

Most quantitative investigations use closed-ended questions and numeric data to make comparisons and draw conclusions (Grinnell & Unrau, 2005). Common quantitative research methods use descriptive surveys and experimental designs. Grounded in a postpositivist tradition, quantitative (deductive) research attempts to draw a large and representative sample of people so that findings are "generalizable," and can be extended to the larger population (Engel & Schutt, 2010).

Qualitative Methods

In contrast, qualitative methods most often use an inductive approach and holistic and circular thought processes (Patton, 2002). Strauss and Corbin (1998) defined *qualitative research* broadly as "any kind of research that produces findings not arrived at by means of statistical procedures or other means of quantification" (p. 5). Qualitative methods generally use an ideographic model of causation and strive to obtain the complete picture of an individual or a case, and they commonly include all factors that might be influential on a case (which might be an individual, a family, a group, an agency, or a community). A broader qualitative research question might be, What factors facilitate empowerment among urban minority adolescents? (Engel & Schutt, 2010).

Using a holistic approach, qualitative research explores the richness, depth, and complexity of phenomena. Using an inductive process, qualitative methods generate narrative data from information-rich cases (Guba & Lincoln, 1994). Qualitative methods (inductive) emphasize deeper meanings of experience. Common qualitative methods include ethnography, grounded theory, phenomenology, case study, and biographical and narrative methods (Creswell, 2006; Padgett, 2008).

Steps A qualitative investigation generally starts with a research question and then gathers data about sensitizing concepts (Patton, 2002). Sensitizing concepts for a study might be "internal and external resources" and "well-being" among retired older adults in the community. After data are gathered and analyzed, empirical generalizations can be drawn and/or developed into a theory (Padgett, 2008). Qualitative research methods will be reviewed in chapter 11.

Similarities Between Quantitative and Qualitative Research Methods

The similarities between quantitative and qualitative methods underscore their compatibility, especially if integrated in mixed methods projects. First, both quantitative and qualitative methods can be used to study any social problem or to answer the same research question. Additionally, both approaches are guided by systematic procedures and pay careful and diligent attention to detail during all stages of the research process (Monette, Sullivan, & DeJong, 2008).

LINKING APPROACHES TO STUDY TYPES

There are different types of studies informed by the different research approaches, quantitative and qualitative. These different types of studies can be classified into six study types: descriptive, exploratory, explanatory, predictive, evaluative, and action research (see Table 4.3).

Research-Based Practice

Critical Thinking Question:
How can social workers effectively use quantitative and qualitative methods for integrating research and practice?

Table 4.3   Study Types and Sample Research Questions

Preexisting knowledge base	Most commonly used methods	Design types	Example research questions
Extensive knowledge on topic		Predictive	What predicts late onset substance use among older adults?
	Quantitative	Explanatory	What are the risk and protective factors that link early victimization experience to adverse health outcomes?
Some knowledge on topic	Quantitative/ qualitative	Evaluative	What is the impact of an economic literacy on women survivors of domestic violence?
		Action research	What do collaborators report about the problem and steps to solution?
		Descriptive	What are the characteristics of adolescents who take psychotropic medication?
Lack of knowledge on topic	Qualitative	Exploratory	What is the lived experience of homeless individuals with serious mental illness?

Common Study Types

Descriptive research attempts to define and/or describe a population or phenomenon. Exploratory research attempts to explore or uncover what might be happening with individuals or situations in which little is known. In contrast, explanatory research attempts to identify causes and effects. Predictive research attempts to predict outcomes, such as risk or resilience, among different populations that may vary by personal, geographic, or other characteristics. Evaluation research attempts to discern how effective a program, an agency, or a policy is at attaining its expected outcomes (Monette et al., 2008).

Examples   Examples of research questions for these different study types using youth gang involvement follow. A descriptive study might ask, "What are the social and environmental characteristics of American communities with high concentrations of juvenile gang members?" An exploratory study might ask, "What is the lived experience of parents who are aware their child is an active gang member?" An evaluation study might ask, "What is the effect of this gang prevention program in reducing gang membership among juveniles?" An explanatory study might ask, "What psychosocial and environmental factors can explain why juveniles join gangs?" A predictive study might ask, "What factors predict gang involvement among juveniles?"

Action Research

Action research is a sixth type of study gaining increased importance in social work. Action research is practitioner-generated research conducted in collaboration with relevant stakeholders and has a goal of social change (Stringer, 2007). Applying this model to practice, practitioners can examine their existing practices; formulate practice-based questions; design and implement evaluations; and use the results to improve their personal, agency, or community based practice (Stringer & Dwyer, 2005).

Example   Action research questions related to a community-based juvenile gang program for youth might be, How do juveniles involved in gangs describe their problems? What solutions do they suggest? How can the feasible solution(s) be implemented? Was the implementation of the chosen solution(s) effective?

Decision Making

The initial challenge in decision making is to figure out what type of study design to choose for research or evaluation practice purposes. An explanatory or predictive motive often suggests an emphasis on an explanatory or predictive design using deductive hypothesis testing and quantitative methods. An evaluative motive suggests an evaluation design that examines the effectiveness of an existing program or policy. The social worker can choose from quantitative, qualitative, or mixed methods approaches to answer the study question(s).

If little is known about a specific topic area, it often is appropriate to conduct an exploratory or descriptive study to gain more information about it. This suggests a qualitative inductive or mixed methods approach. Based on situations in the field in which community partners seek solutions, an action research approach that incorporates qualitative methods or possible mixed methods approaches is warranted.

INTEGRATING RESEARCH AND PRACTICE USING THEORY

Theories in social work research and practice evaluation can serve as a guiding force in the research and practice evaluation processes. Theories are composed of concepts that provide the doorway that connects practice and research. Therefore, it is important that social workers identify precise and essential concepts of theories. These identification skills will help in developing ways to measure concepts and working hypotheses for assessment and intervention purposes. This next section describes theories that range from broad-based meta-theories to more specific middle-range explanatory and practice theories. Practical examples that illustrate central concepts and their relationships to one another are provided. Directly following is a discussion of how theories are constructed that further clarifies this point.

Theories in social work research and practice evaluation can serve as a guiding force in the research and practice evaluation processes.

Theories defined   Theories for the social sciences often refer to a systematic set of interrelated statements about human nature, the social work, or the facilitation of individual and/or social change. Social work theory is defined as a body of thought that provides an "organized description and explanation of the purposes and content of social work as both a social phenomenon and as an activity" (Payne, 2000, p. 332).

Usefulness of theory   Theories are useful for understanding aspects of clients' internal and external worlds and for explanations that can facilitate individual or social transformation. Theories help us make sense of the world and offer explanations as to the common patterns in psychological and social behavior and the nature of social work practices. Useful theories are grounded in real-world biopsychosocial concepts and help frame research and practice evaluation activities (Turner, 1996).

Understanding Different Levels of Theories

Social workers often combine theories and perspectives to guide research and practice evaluation. Therefore, to best understand how to move from the world of abstract theory to the specific observable outcomes, clarity about the different levels of theories, which include meta-theories or middle-range explanatory or practice theories, is helpful.

Meta-theories   Meta-theories are perspectives that are abstract and offer the highest level of generality to describe human behavior (Bisman & Hardcastle, 1999). However, these perspectives offer a frame in which research and practice is constructed. For example, the commonly used ecological systems theory can be classified as a meta-theory because of its broad general application. Based on the work of the developmental psychologist, Urie Bronfenbrenner (1979), the ecological theory asserts that individual-level and social and environmental factors impact human psychosocial development. The ecological system consists of many levels, which include the micro level (individual biological level), the mesosystem (family, peers, and school), the exosystem (external social settings), and the macrosystem (culture).

According to ecological systems theory, the reciprocal interaction, which exists among the different subsystems, suggests that a change in one system will affect changes in other parts of the system (Bronfenbrenner, 1979). This perspective is particularly relevant to social work because it addresses areas of micro- and macro-level social work research and practice evaluation aims toward increasing human well-being and social justice outcomes.

Middle-range theories   Middle-range theories, in contrast, are more narrow in focus, and may be classified as explanatory theories or theories for research and practice evaluation (Bisman & Hardcastle, 1999). Basically, both explanatory and practice theories explain a phenomenon as it relates to conditions of adaptive and maladaptive functioning. Practice theories add an intervention component. Examples of an explanatory theory (cumulative disadvantage theory) and a practice theory (rational emotive behavioral therapy) follow.

Explanatory theory example   Cumulative advantage and disadvantage theory, a middle-range sociological theory, examines the cumulative impact of stress across the life course (e.g., Ross & Mirowsky, 2001). Cumulative disadvantage theory uses micro-level and macro-level contextual factors. These factors include belonging to a member of a racial or ethnic minority or socioeconomically disadvantaged group, being female or unemployed, belonging to a single-parent household, and living in an impoverished neighborhood. The accumulation of stressors or deficits may impact overall well-being across the life course (Mirowsky & Ross, 2005; Ross & Mirowshy, 2001; Sampson & Laub, 1997).

Cumulative disadvantage theory is an example of an explanatory theory, which does not include a practice component. However, it is very relevant to informing social work research and practice. The theory helps social workers to conceptualize the pathways to health disparities among disadvantaged groups in society. Based on this conceptual framework, multilevel interventions can be designed to help eradicate poverty and increase overall well-being among all individuals in society, which are essential goals of the social work profession and its commitment to human rights and social justice.

Practice theory example   As noted earlier, practice theories take one step further and provide an understanding of how problems may arise and also guidelines for facilitating change. For example, whereas both social learning theory (an explanatory theory) and cognitive behavioral theory (a practice theory) focus on the learning of maladaptive attitudes and behaviors, cognitive behavioral theory offers intervention strategies, such as cognitive restructuring devised to change maladaptive thoughts and behaviors (Coady & Lehman, 2008).

Rational emotive behavioral therapy (REBT) is a specific type of cognitive behavioral practice theory that will be used as an example. Developed by the psychologist, Albert Ellis (1994), the theory purports that the relationship between an antecedent event and adverse emotional or behavioral consequences is mediated (or influenced) by beliefs. Because beliefs are an essential link between an antecedent event and outcomes, an essential practice intervention is to dispute these beliefs (Ellis, 2003). This theory is discussed in more detail in the next section.

Social justice practice theory innovations   More recent innovative practice theories relevant to social work view the rise of social and psychological distress as a response to individual and systemic oppression. For example, antioppressive practice theories with empirical support, such as relational-cultural theory, are designed to help individuals or groups to gain an insight into how oppression affects them and to promote individual and social transformation, mutual support, and empowerment (Jordan, 2010; Payne, 2000). Targeting oppressed groups such as women and racial or ethnic minorities, relational-cultural theory practice strategies target the improvement of psychological, relational, and social justice outcomes (Jordan, 2010; Comstock et al., 2008).

Overall, theories that inform social work research and evaluation help to foster (a) individual and social transformation and (b) practice or the provision of services (Payne, 2000). Whether these theories are explanatory or practice theories, they often are tested for their "explanatory power" in a research study in which large samples are used. As suggested in the evidence-based practice model, social workers who use these in practice can evaluate the explanatory power of these theories in assessments or interventions for use with their particular clients or constituents.

Additionally, prior empirical studies that have tested these theories can provide information on how the different concepts or constructs relevant to these theories were measured. As noted earlier, gaining an in-depth understanding of these central concepts is helpful toward moving from vague concepts to measurable practice outcomes. The next section focuses on how concepts can move from the process of conceptualization to operationalization.

FROM CONCEPTUALIZATION TO OPERATIONALIZATION

Theory Construction and Deconstruction

To understand how to move from concepts to operational definitions and hypothesis testing, social workers must understand how theories are constructed. Social workers commonly apply theories to help guide assessment and intervention with individuals, families, organizations, and communities. Therefore,

Human Behavior

Critical Thinking Question: How can social workers integrate, if at all, research and practice using human behavior theories?

in field work, social workers often translate these concepts, such as social support and depression. Social workers also may use data gathered from the field to build a conceptual framework that can be helpful for assessment and developmental purposes. For example, Sigmund Freud (1996, 1997) initially developed the psychoanalytic theory based on case studies of his psychotherapy clients. Similarly, Albert Ellis initially developed REBT based on his personal experiences with faulty cognitions that impacted his behavior (Corey, 2008).

Theory in four parts

As illustrated in Figure 4.3, a theory is built on the solid foundation of assumptions, concepts, and a series of interrelated propositions (Chafetz, 1978). Assumptions are a series of underlying premises that are taken as givens and are not subject to empirical verification. For example, an underlying assumption of REBT is that humans have an innate tendency toward the use of rational and irrational thought (Ellis, 2003). An underlying assumption of relational cultural theory is that culture and relationships are agents in relational processes and shape human development (Jordan, 2010).

Concepts "the building blocks of theories"   Every theory also has core concepts or constructs as the building blocks on which it is constructed (Chafetz, 1978). A concept is often described as a "mental image" or "idea" or "understanding" in which objects, relationships, and experiences can be classified (Grinnell & Unrau, 2005).

Proposition   A proposition, or testable hypothesis or prediction, is a statement that illustrates the relationship between two or more concepts. A proposition is a result of placing a concept in relationship to one or more other concepts. Theories are generally made of multiple propositions that are interrelated and often describe pathways of adaption and maladaption; in addition, practice theories outline strategies for facilitating change (Chafetz, 1978).

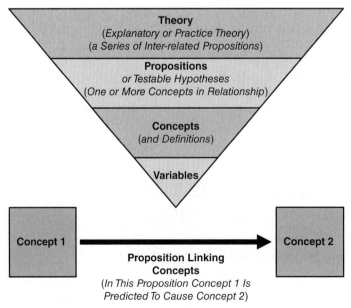

Figure 4.3
Components of a Theory for Theory Testing or Development

Rational emotive behavioral theory (REBT), a practice theory, can be further examined for how it is constructed as a product of interrelated concepts. In the REBT ABC model, there are three concepts, "antecedent," "beliefs," and "consequences" (emotional and behavioral) and two propositions. One proposition states that individuals who experience an antecedent (i.e., an adversity or activating event) may experience adverse consequences (emotional and behavioral responses) to that event. The second proposition states that beliefs (functional or dysfunctional) mediate the relationship between the antecedent and the consequences (adaptive or maladaptive). As in the intervention step, titled dispute (D), the intervention would be to dispute maladaptive beliefs and to restore adaptive emotions and behaviors (Ellis, 1994).

Why is it Important?

It is important to evaluate the explanatory power of theories and the central concepts that drive them. Moving from the world of theories and concepts into real-world practice is a systematic process that translates abstract ideas into variables with measurable and observable operational definitions. Quantitative and qualitative methods begin with a research question that seeks to be answered. The research methods chosen will affect the next steps in the measurement process.

Research Questions

Research questions are derived from the theories or conceptual frameworks that inform the research or practice evaluation processes. For both quantitative and qualitative research approaches, research questions act as a guidepost to identifying the concepts of central interest, identifying the target population, and framing the study. The task may seem ominous for social work students new to the process of developing research questions. This need not be the case because steps can be taken to narrow down the research question.

Narrow the Question

The first step is to move from a broad topic area to narrow down the question. This process will be detailed in chapter 7, but a broad overview is provided here to illustrate the process of moving from the research questions to formulating a hypotheses. Overall, a research question should be specific enough that it identifies the central concepts or variables of central interest, is capable of being answered by observable evidence, and is answerable in more than one way (Monette et al., 2008).

Additional criteria for formulating research questions include (a) consulting the literature for guidance based on an existing theory or a body of empirical support, (b) professional need or obligation to conduct community-based, agency-based, clinical practice evaluation, or a grant-funded project, (c) personal interest in an area, (d) the feasibility (e.g., time, cost, ethics study location limitations) of actually answering the research question, and (e) passing the "so what" test (Engel & Schutt, 2010).

Most importantly, the research question must have direct relevance to your field-based need or contribute to the existing literature for guiding social welfare policy or social work practice (relevance is the most important criterion) (Rubin & Babbie, 2010). For example, Shenickwa, a first-year MSW student, concluded that her proposed research question about the community mental health care needs of family caregivers of adults with early onset

Alzheimer's disease was important because there was lack of empirical literature in this area.

Additional Steps for Confirming Research Questions

In formulating research questions, it is quite useful to evaluate all of the evidence. This includes gaining a thorough background in the literature. It also is useful to obtain feedback from other relevant stakeholders. Depending upon the project, these stakeholders might include colleagues, agency supervisors and other staff members of the targeted population for study (e.g., mental health consumers), and policy makers. When conducting an agency-based evaluation, the social worker must build an alliance with relevant agency personnel, such as the supervisor. Agency consumers also may be involved in all parts of the research design (Friedman, 2008). For example, Shenickwa conducted a thorough review of the available empirical evidence. She had strong alliances with community service providers and consulted with colleagues with expertise in providing services for individuals with early-onset Alzheimer's disease. The agency also linked her with family caregivers so she could learn their views on their mental health needs.

Hypotheses

After crafting a research question, the social worker uses quantitative or qualitative research methods to determine the next steps. Because quantitative research is more strongly guided by an existing knowledge base, it is possible to make predictions or formulate hypotheses. A hypothesis is a tentative statement that predicts relationships between two or more variables (Monette et al., 2008). For example, in her MSW research class, Laudelina asked the following research question: What is the relationship between community violence and mental well-being among a sample of older adult residents living in an urban neighborhood? Based on evidence from the theoretical and empirical literature, Laudelina decided to test the following hypothesis: The higher the level of community violence, the lower the level of psychological well-being among a sample of older adult residents living in an urban neighborhood. Her next step was to clarify the concepts she needed to measure.

Laudelina identified two essential concepts or constructs: community violence and psychological well-being. Her next task was to determine how to translate these "mental images" into observable and measurable terms (Morton, 2002). Behaviors, such as community violence, are more directly observable and are readily identifiable compared to internal thoughts and feelings, such as mental well-being. Some concepts are multidimensional, such as socioeconomic status. Dimensions of socioeconomic status include education, occupation, and family income (Farnworth, Thornberry, Krohn, & Lizotte, 1994; Hollingshead, 1975). See Table 4.4 for examples of concepts, variables, and possible ways to measure them.

Research-Based Practice

Critical Thinking Question: In your view, how do social workers move from the use of conceptual to operational definitions in research and practice?

The Measurement Process

Conceptualization

Community violence, mental well-being, and socioeconomic status are concepts. As noted earlier, concepts are generally abstract and not easily observable and measurable. Concepts are chosen for use in qualitative or quantitative approaches in inductive and deductive research through the process of

Table 4.4	**Examples of Concepts, Variables, and Measurement**	
Concepts	Variables	One item indicators or other measures
Gender	Gender	What is your gender? *(male or female)*
Respect for dignity and worth of every person	Level of agreement with respect for the dignity and worth of all persons	I believe that every person, regardless of his or her race, gender, or ethnicity, deserves to be treated with respect. *(strongly agree to strongly disagree)*
Treatment participation	Treatment participation or not	Yes or no—Participation in 12-week empowerment training
Research-related anxiety	Magnitude or severity of research-related anxiety	On a scale of 0 to 4 (in which 0 = not anxious at all to 4 = completely anxious), how anxious are you today about research?
Social justice activities	Frequency of past month's social justice activities	How many times in the past month would you say you engaged in social justice activities, such as advocating for a client, engaging in public awareness, or political lobbying?
Self-empowerment	Magnitude or severity of perceptions of self-empowerment	On a scale of 0 to 10 in which 0 = not empowered at all to 10 = feel completely empowered, how empowered do you feel right now?
Psychological distress	Duration of symptoms of psychological distress	(After establishing existence of psychological distress) How many days now would you say you experienced psychological distress?
Positive self-talk	Frequency of positive self-talk	How many times today did you make positive self-talk statements?
Socioeconomic status	Education income occupational prestige	Summative score on Hollingshead Index
Community violence	Level of exposure to community violence	Summative score on the ECV Survey (Martinez & Richters, 1993)

"conceptualization." The measurement process involves moving from a more abstract or theoretical level to more specific and concrete terms. Two steps are involved in moving from a conceptual definition to an operational definition (Monette et al., 2008).

Conceptual or Nominal Definitions

Conceptual or *nominal* definitions are similar to the definitions found in a dictionary. For example, a conceptual definition for child physical abuse is the occurrence of severe physical harm during childhood. It is possible to understand the word and its dimensions, but there is still no set of rules for measuring the concept. Therefore, operationalization is another necessary step to more clearly define the measure (see Figure 4.4).

Operational Definitions

Operational definitions indicate the precise procedures or operations to be followed in measuring a concept. Thus, the process of "operationalization" is precisely identifying how we are going to measure the variables that we have

	Vague, Abstract, Imprecise		Observable, Measurable, Variable and Precise	

Concept	Conceptual or Nominal Definition	Operational Definition	Variable
Mental Image	*Dictionary-Like Definition*	*Precise Definition Measurement Rules*	*Varies and Observable*

Figure 4.4
The Process From Conceptual to Operational Definitions

conceptualized. An operational definition includes the precise procedures (or operations) on measuring a concept and the rules for assigning values. Operationalization is important because it can help to increase measurement validity. If a measurement is determined to be reliable and valid, we can be more confident that we are measuring the concept we think we are measuring (Rubin & Babbie, 2010).

Examples   For example, gender is a concept. It can be operationalized as the single question or item: "What is your gender?" Possible response categories are male or female.

Another example of a concept is community violence. Exposure to community violence can be further defined as being a victim or witness to violence in the community. It can be even more precisely defined by measuring the occurrence of being a victim of or witness to violence using the community violence survey (CVS) (Martinez & Richters, 1993). This CVS has been commonly used to measure exposure to community violence with school-age urban children living in a violent neighborhood.

The CVS is a summative 54-item scale that asks children about how they were exposed to various kinds of violence or violence-related activities experienced, seen, or heard within the last 5 years. It includes experiences such as being chased, drug activity, serious accidents, forced entry, police arrests, threats of physical harm, physical aggression (i.e., slapping, hitting, punching, beatings, and muggings), rape and molestation, carrying guns and knives, hearing sounds of gunfire, serious wounding, shootings, dead bodies, suicides, killing, and other types of violence (Richters & Martinez, 1993a, 1993b). Children choose from "never" to "almost every day" to indicate how frequently they experienced each during the past year. Therefore, the operational definition of exposure to community violence is the score on the exposure to community violence (ECV) survey as described earlier.

Multiple Ways to Measure

As illustrated in the examples earlier, it is important to note that many options are available for defining or "operationalizing" a variable from single questions or items or summative scales or indexes. Gender is a relatively straightforward example, whereas other concepts are much more complex. Social workers often look for ideas on how to operationally define central concepts by consulting the empirical literature or other colleagues for options on choosing measures for their research or evaluation activities.

Table 4.5	**Examples of Hypotheses and Variables**				
Hypothesis	Independent variable	Dependent variable	Direction of hypothesis	Population
As the level of social support (low to high) increases the level of mental well-being (poor to excellent) increases among older adults	Level of social support	Level of mental well-being	Positive	Older adults
As the level of self-esteem increases, the level of depression decreases among female adolescents who experienced domestic violence	Level of self-esteem	Level of depression	Negative	Female adolescents
Anxiety disorders are higher in women than in men	Gender	Anxiety disorders	N/A for categorical IV	Men and women
The age of the person predicts physical ability; that is, physical ability is lower for children aged 0 to 17 and adults age 65 and older that adults aged 18 to 64	Age	Physical ability	Curvilinear	Children, adults, and older adults

Variables

In quantitative approaches, it is important to determine a variable with its accompanying operational definition. A variable can be described as a concept that has the two additional properties of being able to "vary" or "change," and when operationally defined, can take on more than one value or attribute (Dudley, 2004). In contrast, a variable that is a constant is a characteristic or property that stays the same in a study or keeps the same value or attribute throughout the duration of the study. An example of a constant in a study on older adults would be "older adults" (defined as adults aged 65 or above), because it is an attribute that all participants in the study have and therefore it does not vary (see Table 4.5).

Types of Variables in Relationship

When describing cause-and-effect relationships such as those often used in quantitative deductive research, the terms *independent* or *dependent variables* are generally used. Similar to propositions, it is helpful to visualize these variables in relationship to one another. A variable, such as racial or gender discrimination, can be viewed as an independent operator that can effect or change a variable that is dependent upon it, such as health disparities or access to social services (Krueger & Neuman, 2006).

As noted earlier, a variable must have a characteristic or property that can vary (take on different values or attributes). However, similar to hypotheses, variables also must be considered in relationship to one another. The term *independent variable* often refers to a variable that can explain or that causes another variable, such as racial or gender discrimination. In contrast, a *dependent variable* is the one being explained or caused, such as health disparities or access to social services.

Social workers often look for causal effects, especially as they relate to the effectiveness of their intervention in regard to improving the lives of the individuals and communities for which the intervention was designed. Another example of an independent variable as a variable that is hypothesized to cause a change or variation on another variable can be seen in a community violence prevention program (i.e., whether the person attended). In this example, the dependent variable (community violence) that is hypothesized to vary is depending on (or under the influence) the independent variable (presence of community violence prevention program). These two variables can be placed in a hypothesized relationship to each other. For example, the independent variable, community violence prevention program (present in community or not), will be hypothesized to reduce levels of community violence (as measured by the CVS).

Mediating Variables

A mediating or intervening variable attempts to further explain the influence of the independent variable on the dependent variable. An independent variable is hypothesized to cause the mediator variable, in turn, the mediator variables causes the dependent variable (MacKinnon, 2008). Albert Ellis's ABC model is a meditational model in which the relationship between an antecedent event and consequence is mediated by beliefs. In other words, the antecedent event influences beliefs about the antecedent event. In turn, beliefs about the antecedent events influence emotional or behavioral consequences. This may be apparent in a practice setting in which a client reports to a clinical social worker. The client was fired from her job, which triggered a belief that she is worthless, which in turn triggered her to relapse by drinking alcohol again.

Variations in Measurement Options

There are many variations in the ways variables can be measured that range from single questions (or items) to summative items and scales.

Sometimes variables are operationalized by a single question, such as, What is your gender? The use of one item (which includes a question with its responses) is commonly referred to as an *indicator* (Monette et al. 2008). Intervention methods or treatments are often measured using a single item, such as participation in treatment (yes or no) or the number of meetings attended over the past 3 months.

Another common way to measure variables is by using scales or indexes. Scales and indexes generally consist of a series of questions in which the sum or average of several questions are used to measure a variable, such as the ECV Scale (Martinez & Richters, 1993). Other examples of scales with measurement validity include the Center for Disease Control Epidemiological Depression Survey (CES-D, Radloff, 1977), the Rosenburg Self Esteem Inventory (Rosenberg, 1989), the Social Justice Advocacy Scale (Van Soest, 1994), or the Reid-Gundlach Social Service Satisfaction Scale (Reid & Gundlach, 1993).

Associations

To understand variables (which vary and change), it is important to think about how they vary and change in relationship to one another. Because a variable must vary, it often is described as either increasing or decreasing. When variables are described in relationship to one another, a change (increase or decrease) in one variable may cause another variable to change in the same or opposite directions (increase or decrease). These relationships are often described as positive, negative, or curvilinear associations (Monette et al., 2008).

Positive Association

A positive association occurs when a variable increases or decreases in the same direction as another. For example, as an independent variable, self-esteem increases, the dependent variable, academic achievement, also increases. Similarly, when an independent variable, such as self esteem, decreases, the dependent variable, academic achievement, also decreases.

Negative Association

In contrast, a negative association occurs when the variables increases or decrease in opposite directions. That is, as the independent variable, community social support, increases, the dependent variable, number of homeless individuals, decreases. As community social support decreases, the number of homeless individuals increases.

Curvilinear Association

Some relationships between variables are not linear but rather curvilinear or U-shaped. For example, let us use the example of physical ability and age. Physical ability is lower for children and older adults and is higher for adults.

"Relational" Association Only

In some cases, such as in descriptive studies, variables demonstrate a relationship to one another but it is not possible to determine whether one variable (e.g., self-esteem) caused another (e.g., physical well-being). These are "relational associations" in which, at best, we can assert only that these variables are associated or correlated.

Dichotomous Variables Caveat

With dichotomous variables (e.g., yes or no variables such as in intervention participation), variables cannot be said to increase or decrease. In social work, variables such as intervention participation (yes or no) or victim of abuse or not (yes or no) are commonly used. In the case of dichotomous variables, the direction of association does not apply (Engel & Schutt, 2010). Therefore, at best only the difference between the two groups (treatment participation or not) or categories can be determined.

SUMMARY

Social work research has historically been influenced by philosophical traditions that range from a postpositivist position on the objective nature of reality to the constructivist position on the subjective nature of reality. In addition, the critical social science position examines structural oppression in an attempt to take action steps for its eradication.

Quantitative and qualitative research approaches offer strategies for knowledge generation and real-world applications. Quantitative methods commonly use numeric data and large sample sizes to test and refine theories for the profession's knowledge base. In contrast, qualitative methods use data to make empirical generalizations and/or build theories. Both types of methods use concepts but use them differently to guide the research and evaluation processes. Studies that use quantitative or qualitative strategies may be classified by study type or purpose, which are exploratory, descriptive, explanatory, evaluation, predictive, and action-oriented.

Quantitative studies use hypotheses based on a theory or other studies' findings. In contrast, qualitative methods commonly use research questions and "sensitizing" concepts to orient the study. Studies that use quantitative methods take an additional step of moving from conceptual or nominal definitions of variables, which are often vague and imprecise, to operational definitions of variables, which are more precise and measurable definitions, and which must vary. Because quantitative approaches often measure cause and effect, it is often important to distinguish between independent variables (which cause another variable to change) and dependent variables (which change due to the influence of another variable).

Inductive and Deductive Orientation Assessment Survey (IDOAS)

Professionals, including social workers and counselors, need to make practice decisions on a regular basis. Practice decision making often involves a problem-solving process that uses deductive reasoning, draws knowledge from existing theories and research, and/or uses inductive reasoning in which data directly from the field is used to build case-level explanations. This anonymous survey was developed to assist professionals in assessing their natural tendencies toward using inductive and deductive approaches to decision making. It should take about 5–7 minutes to complete.

Location: _____   Date : _____   Survey Code: _____

Exhibit 4.1

Inductive and Deductive Orientation Assessment

Source: Maschi, T., Morgen, K., & MacMillan, T. (2010). *The inductive and deductive orientation survey* (IDOS)—unpublished instrument. New York: Fordham University.

Part A: Inductive and Deductive Assessment

Directions: For each of the statements listed below, please complete the statement by placing a check or circling the *one* answer that BEST DESCRIBES your views using the following scale: strongly disagree, disagree, neutral, agree, and strongly agree. After completing the survey please calculate your scores using the right-hand column (labeled score). Using the scoring key, determine whether you lean more toward an inductive, deductive, or mixed approach to decision making. To best ensure your privacy, please do not write your name on the survey. The information provided will help us to gain a better understanding of practice-decision-making processes among professionals.

Statements	Level of Agreement With Following Statements					Score
1. I like to plan ahead about what I do and not deviate from the plan.	Strongly Disagree 1	Disagree 2	Neutral 3	Agree 4	Strongly Agree 5	
2. I see myself as a rational person.	Strongly Disagree 1	Disagree 2	Neutral 3	Agree 4	Strongly Agree 5	
3. I can separate who I am from what I know.	Strongly Disagree 1	Disagree 2	Neutral 3	Agree 4	Strongly Agree 5	
4. I am comfortable using statistics.	Strongly Disagree 1	Disagree 2	Neutral 3	Agree 4	Strongly Agree 5	
5. I believe most people perceive a similar reality that they can agree upon.	Strongly Disagree 1	Disagree 2	Neutral 3	Agree 4	Strongly Agree 5	
6. I see myself as a creative person.	Strongly Disagree 5	Disagree 4	Neutral 3	Agree 2	Strongly Agree 1	
7. I believe that there are multiple subjective realities in which people see the world differently from each other.	Strongly Disagree 5	Disagree 4	Neutral 3	Agree 2	Strongly Agree 1	
8. I prefer to communicate using written or spoken word with others as opposed to numbers and statistics.	Strongly Disagree 5	Disagree 4	Neutral 3	Agree 2	Strongly Agree 1	
9. I am flexible, adaptive, and will initiate changes, when needed.	Strongly Disagree 5	Disagree 4	Neutral 3	Agree 2	Strongly Agree 1	
10. My personal values are an important consideration when I make decisions.	Strongly Disagree 5	Disagree 4	Neutral 3	Agree 2	Strongly Agree 1	
					Total Score	

Scoring: Using the right-hand-side score column, add up your total score. Scores closer to 50 suggest a deductive orientation, whereas scores closer to 10 reflect an inductive orientation. Scores closer to 30 suggest a mixed inductive-deductive orientation.

Exhibit 4.1
Continued

Part B: Background Information

This next section asks about some brief background information. Please answer the following questions by placing an "X" in the box and/or filling in the blanks.

1. What is your gender?
    1. ☐ Male
    2. ☐ Female

2. What is your current age (in years): ————————————

3. What is your race/ethnicity?
    1. ☐ White, not of Hispanic Origin
    2. ☐ African American
    3. ☐ Hispanic
    4. ☐ Asian/Pacific Islander
    5. ☐ American Indian/Alaskan Native
    6. ☐ Inter-racial or Multi-racial
    7. ☐ Other (please list): (3a) ————————————

4. Please check the box that describes your *highest education* degree and major.
    1. ☐ Less than high school diploma
    2. ☐ High school diploma
    3. ☐ BA/BS—criminal justice
    4. ☐ BA/BS—sociology
    5. ☐ BA/BS—psychology
    6. ☐ BA—other major (please list discipline): (4a) ————————————
    7. ☐ MA or MSW—social work (MSW)
    8. ☐ MA/MS/MEd—counseling
    9. ☐ MA/MS—psychology
    10. ☐ MA—criminal justice
    11. ☐ MA—other major (please list discipline) (4b) ————————————
    12. ☐ Psy.D. —clinical/counseling psychology
    13. ☐ DSW
    14. ☐ PhD— (please list discipline) (4c) ————————————

5. Are you currently in professional practice?
    1. ☐ No
    2. ☐ Yes (If yes, please list number of years in practice) ————————————
    3. ☐ (If yes, what is the discipline of your professional license?) ————————————

Exhibit 4.1
Continued

6. Are you currently enrolled as a college or university student?

    4. ☐ Yes (If yes, please answer questions 7 and 10)

    5. ☐ No (If not a student, please go to question 10)

7. What college or university do you attend? —————————————————

8. What year are you in?

    1. ☐ Freshman

    2. ☐ Sophomore

    3. ☐ Junior

    4. ☐ Senior

    5. ☐ Master's Student

    6. ☐ PhD Student

    7. Other: (6b) —————————————

9. What is your major? —————————————————

10. Have you participated in a field placement internship?

    1. ☐ No

    2. ☐ Yes (If yes, please list the number of *months* spent in any internships)

    —————————————————

    —————————————————

    —————————————————

11. Please think about a recent practice (or even personal) decision you have made and that you are willing to share. What was the decision? Then briefly describe how you came to make that decision, including what you were thinking and whom or what you consulted. Please use the back of the paper.

You have successfully completed the survey. We want to thank you for participating.

Exhibit 4.1
Continued

Succeed with PEARSON mysocialworklab

Log onto **www.mysocialworklab.com** and answer the following questions. (*If you did not receive an access code to* **MySocialWorkLab** *with this text and wish to purchase access online, please visit* www.mysocialworklab.com.)

1. **Watch the human behavior video "The Ecological Model Using the Friere Method."** How might this theory be used to inform what specific variables in personal, cultural, and institutional domains influence women's depression?

2. **Read the case study "Community Practice: Golem, Albania."** Consider how a social work research team might engage community members in the different stages of the research and evaluation cycle.

PRACTICE TEST

The following questions will test your knowledge of the content found within this chapter. For additional assessment, including licensing-exam type questions on applying chapter content to practice, visit **MySocialWorkLab**.

1. A social worker who wants to evaluate the effectiveness of cognitive therapy would draw from what type of theory?
   a. Abstract theory
   b. Grand theory
   c. Explanatory theory
   d. Practice theory

2. A social worker who defines a concept that can be observable and measurable has done which of the following?
   a. Conceptualization
   b. Operationalization
   c. Deconstruction
   d. Theory development

3. A social worker who wants to apply methods derived from a research paradigm that addresses root causes of oppression would more than likely choose:
   a. Positivism
   b. Postpositivism
   c. Critical social science
   d. Constructivism

4. A deductive approach using human behavior theories in research and evaluation would more than likely include all but the following:
   a. Testing theories
   b. Refining theories
   c. Operationalizing key theory concepts
   d. Developing theory from the ground up

5. A program coordinator has consulted with you about different ways that the programs can measure depression among its clientele. Provide at least two recommendations.

ASSESS YOUR COMPETENCE

Use the scale below to rate your current level of achievement on the following concepts or skills associated with each competency presented in the chapter:

1	2	3
I can accurately describe the concept or skill	I can consistently identify the concept or skill when observing and analyzing practice activities	I can competently implement the concept or skill in my own practice

_____ can apply diverse research philosophies and paradigms for problem formulation.

_____ can apply human behavior theory in research and practice evaluation.

_____ can develop hypotheses based on an existing theory.

_____ can demonstrate how to move from a concept to operationalizing it as a variable.

5

The Literature as Source Evidence: From Search to Appraisal

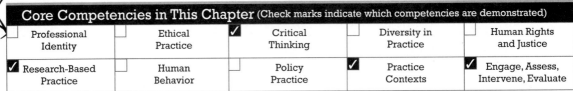

Core Competencies in This Chapter (Check marks indicate which competencies are demonstrated)				
Professional Identity	Ethical Practice	✓ Critical Thinking	Diversity in Practice	Human Rights and Justice
✓ Research-Based Practice	Human Behavior	Policy Practice	✓ Practice Contexts	✓ Engage, Assess, Intervene, Evaluate

INTRODUCTION

Mastering the literature review process, which includes the search for and evaluation of evidence, is a formative task of the consummate social work professional. The nature and quality of the evidence social workers use in their decision-making process has tremendous implications for the quality of life for the individuals, families, and communities they serve. This chapter reviews the literature review process for practice and research purposes from the initial stages of identifying a topic to finding, understanding, and evaluating the literature. As reviewed in this chapter, the term *literature review* may refer to different parts of the literature review process or product, such as: (a) the actual search for scholarly literature, (2) the completed literature review paper or article that is a comprehensive review of a body of literature, or (c) the subsection of a research study entitled "literature review" that commonly proceeds the methods section. This chapter is designed to assist social workers to further develop the skills that foster career-long learning and critical thinking, particularly in the use of practice experience to inform scientific inquiry and the use of research evidence to inform practice.

The Seven Tier Appraise Information Review (STAIR) consists of the following seven steps: (a) question, (b) find, (c) read, (d) appraise, (e) synthesize, (f) write, and (g) share/action and assists with the literature review process.

CASE EXAMPLES

- Jo Ann is a social worker who works as a clinician at a community mental health agency located in the rural Midwest. Recently, she was assigned a case of a 70-year-old Caucasian female named Kasha who emigrated from Russia to the United States about 12 months before. Her client is fluent in English and Russian and is seeking help for major depression. Jo Ann has no prior practice experience working with older adults of Russian descent. Her plan before seeing her client is to consult the scholarly literature for information about effective assessment and intervention strategies with this population.
- Jamal is an assistant director for a New York City agency that serves at-risk youth. He oversees the agency's research and evaluation unit. He works collaboratively with staff practitioners whose case records comprise much of the agency's program evaluation data. The agency wants to add a new program component for an evidence-based after-school arts program. Jamal and his team of researchers and practitioners plan to conduct a comprehensive review of the literature for best practices in an after-school arts program for urban youth. Based on this information, Jamal and his team will decide whether to develop or adopt an after-school program that best meets the needs of their clientele.
- Wanda is a social work researcher and professor at a southeastern U.S. university. Her area of research interest is trauma assessment among incarcerated juveniles. Before designing her study, she plans to conduct a comprehensive literature review to identify a gap from which she can build new knowledge that can help develop or improve trauma-informed assessment and interventions for these youth.

PROFESSIONAL PRACTICE CONTEXTS

In the previous case examples, Jo Ann, Jamal, and Wanda have practice contexts and purposes for consulting the scholarly literature. The scholarly literature is often composed of journal articles and books written by experts in the field. Their research roles and/or activities vary from those of consumer, collaborator, and/or producer of research knowledge. Their purposes vary from a social work practitioner consulting the literature for information for practice to a social work researcher consulting the literature to generate new knowledge to apply to practice.

Jo Ann's professional practice context in a mental health services agency where she is a clinician suggests she will consult the literature as a consumer of research knowledge. Her major purpose for reviewing the literature is to educate herself about interventions most useful to help her client. Jamal, on the other hand, is as an administrator of the youth serving agency's research and evaluation unit. His central research role is as a collaborator. Jamal works in tandem with his frontline practice staff involved in the data collection. His purpose is to review the arts-based after-school program evaluation literature and to use this information to develop or choose a program that best suits his clientele. In contrast, Wanda's practice context is a university where she is an academic researcher and a producer of research knowledge. She will use the information derived from her review to design a research study that builds upon the existing literature on trauma assessment among youth involved in the juvenile justice system. The findings from her study can generate new data about these youth's assessment and services needs and improvement of response.

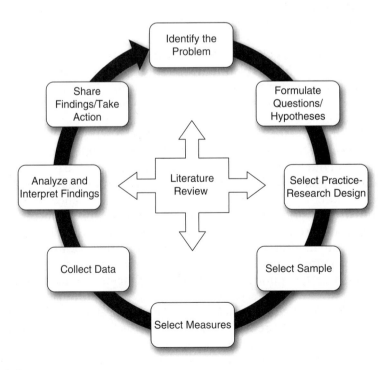

Figure 5.1
The Literature Review as an Ongoing Part of the Research Process

Regardless of the differences in the practice contexts, all three of these social work professionals have one task in common: *to review the scholarly literature*. In fact, the initial and ongoing consultation with the literature is an essential component of effective practice and research as illustrated in Figure 5.1. This ongoing consultation of the literature will enable them to use the most recent theoretical and empirical evidence to implement and monitor their practice and research agendas.

EMPIRICAL LITERACY FOR SOCIAL WORKERS

The commitment to producing empirically literate social workers, that is, social workers who use observable evidence to guide their practice decision making, is underscored by the social work profession's national and international organizations, which include the Council on Social Work Education, the National Association of Social Workers, and the International Federation of Social Workers. In fact, social work practitioners' proficiency in "empirical literacy" is one of the essential pillars of effective social work practice, along with the ongoing use of supervision and consultation in the field.

The CSWE (2008) Educational Policy and Accreditation Standards stipulates that social work professionals develop as one of their ten core competencies the ability to engage in research-informed practice as well as practice-informed research. This two-way "evidence" street enables practitioners the flexibility of using their professional judgment to weigh empirical evidence with evidence from the field to make the informed practice decisions that promote clients' self-determination, well-being, and empowerment.

Perhaps the two core social work values and ethical principles that practitioners' active pursuit of knowledge taps are those of integrity and competence (IFSW, 2004; NASW, 1999). According to both the IFSW and NASW Ethical Codes, social workers should practice with integrity by acting honestly and responsibly and by developing and maintaining the required competence and skills to do their job effectively. Practitioners who are proficient in supplementing their knowledge and skills base with the scholarly literature to guide practice decision making are directly tapping these core social work values and ethical principles.

As reviewed in chapter 2, the NASW Code of Ethics standard about social workers' ethical responsibilities to the profession specifically targets the ongoing use of the social work research knowledge and skills as a core practice behavior (NASW, 1999). Section 5.02 (c) stipulates that practitioners *should* actively incorporate evaluation and research in practice by keeping abreast of social work knowledge, critically appraising it, and fully incorporating evaluation and research evidence in professional practice. Adhering to this standard places social workers—guided by the most up to date practice information—in a position to serve clients.

THE SCHOLARLY LITERATURE AND PEER REVIEW PROCESS

When social workers search for the best quality evidence, they mainly draw resources from a large body of scholarly literature. The term *scholarly literature* most often refers to the writings of academics and researchers who are

The commitment to producing empirically literate social workers, that is, social workers who use observable evidence to guide their practice decision making, is underscored by the social work profession's national and international organizations.

When social workers search for the best quality evidence, they mainly draw their resources from a large body of scholarly literature.

experts in their field. These individuals are often affiliated with higher education institutions, such as colleges and universities, research institutes, or centers.

Scholarly literature goes through a rigorous selection process before it is published in peer-reviewed journals. The process from submission of the manuscript to publication of a journal article often is as follows: Researchers submit manuscripts to journal editors who send the submitted articles through a peer review process. This means that a scholar's work is reviewed by a group of other peers who are experts in that area. The peer reviewers often suggest revisions that would strengthen the manuscript and often determine whether to accept or reject the article for publication with or without revision. If accepted, it would appear as a journal article in the peer-reviewed journal to which it was submitted. Some journals relevant to social work that cover diverse areas of research, education, and practice include *Social Work*, *Social Work Research*, *Social Service Review*, *Research in Social Work Practice*, *Clinical Social Work*, *Journal of Community Practice*, *Journal of Social Work Education*, and the *Journal of Baccalaureate Social Work*.

SOCIAL WORK EDUCATION AND THE LITERATURE REVIEW

Understandably, mastering the literature review process is a formative task of most social work students' education. So what is exactly meant by a *literature review*? As reviewed earlier, the term *literature review* may refer to different parts of the literature review process or the product itself, such as: (a) the actual search for scholarly literature, (b) the completed literature review paper or article that is a comprehensive review of a body of literature, or (3) the subsection of a research study entitled "literature review" that commonly proceeds the methods section. All in all, the literature review process ranges from the initial stages of a project from finding the literature to the final written product and is an important professional developmental task.

The Literature Review as a Search

The *literature review as a search* generally refers to a systematic investigation of available library and electronic resources of published works in a topic area, such as trauma assessment among youth in the juvenile justice system. The published works searched may include peer-reviewed journals, books, dissertations, and other related materials. The literature review search process is an initial and ongoing process that allows for social workers during the course of a practice intervention or research project to inform their practice decisions. The nuts and bolts of how to locate this literature will be reviewed later in this chapter.

Research-Based Practice

Critical Thinking Question: What are the pros and cons of consulting the literature before conducting a research study or meeting with a client?

The Literature Review as a Product

Social workers' interest in being more systematic with literature reviews rose in the early 1970s in response to a growing crisis in the field related to practice effectiveness. As noted in chapter 2, Fischer's (1973) "Is Casework Effective?"

in the journal *Social Work* publicly voiced this concern. In response, the profession has widely adopted the practice of conducting more systematic literature review efforts to synthesize the literature, including content analysis, systematic reviews, and meta-analyses.

These types of reviews are a growing staple of social work practice as their research base expands. The information garnered from these types of reviews, especially systematic reviews, can provide practitioners and policy makers with needed information on a pressing issue, and can inform social policy and social intervention with research findings. As a result of the growing body of research and the demand for professional accountability for their effectiveness, the need for rigorous reviews has significantly grown.

Literature Review

When students first begin research, one of their most common assignments is to conduct a literature review and write a narrative literature review paper. A literature review is described as

> The selection of available documents (both published and unpublished) on the topic which contain information, ideas, data and evidence written from a particular standpoint to fulfill certain aims or express certain views on the nature of the topic and how it is being investigated, and the effective evaluation of these documents in relation to the research being proposed. (Hart, 1998, p. 13)

In general, a literature review can refer to the written paper or "product" that integrates the information found during the search process. Jamal's literature review of the best practices in arts-based after-school programming for urban youth is an example of the product of a literature review. The literature review generally involves mostly a qualitative process and partially structured to unstructured methods. The process involves reading the studies and seeking patterns and themes and/or comparisons across studies in major findings and/or methods used (Videka-Sherman, 1995).

Content Analysis

Although definitions have varied, *content analysis* generally refers to a "systematic, replicable technique for compressing many words of text into fewer content categories based on explicit rules of coding" (Krippendorff, 2004, p. 5). Content analysis can be done on text documents, such as journals, or visual images, such as photographs. A coding scheme is developed to extract information from articles that may involve the frequency counts of how often certain words or images appear, or trends and patterns across the literature (Berg, 2004; Neuendort, 2002).

Systematic Reviews and Meta-Analyses

Systematic review and meta-analysis studies are another important method commonly used to examine the literature. According to Littell, Corcoran, and Pillai (2008), systematic reviews and meta-analyses are complementary approaches to synthesize research in a particular area. Littell and colleagues describe the aims of a systematic review to "comprehensively locate and synthesize research that bears on a particular question, using organized, transparent, and replicable procedures at each step in the process" (p. 4). A systematic review, which follows a carefully planned procedure, is important because it reduces biases and errors, which can accumulate based on biases from the original studies, publication, dissemination, and review methods.

The aims of the review, central concepts under investigation, and the methods used to complete the review are clearly specified in advance. Careful documentation of the decision-making steps is accurately recorded. Published systematic reviews include the details of the methods in order for readers to replicate the study and/or evaluate the methods (Littell, Corcoran, & Pillai, 2008). However, it is important to note that systematic reviews are different from meta-analyses unless a meta-analysis is embedded in a systematic review.

In contrast, a *meta-analysis* studies an area and applies a set of "statistical methods combining quantitative results from multiple studies to produce an overall summary of empirical knowledge on a topic" (Littell et al., 2008, p. 1). A meta-analysis is a systematic review of the literature that statistically combines the results of several studies that share a common research hypothesis. Meta-analyses are particularly important because they are classified as the top of the evidence-based hierarchy as "best evidence" for practitioners to consult to help inform their work (Rubin & Babbie, 2010).

A meta-analysis is situated at the top of the evidence-based hierarchy because it uses statistical analyses of the effect sizes of multiple studies' results to enable the researcher to draw conclusions. Meta-analysis papers are available for review at the Campbell Collaboration: http://www.campbellcollaboration.org/ and at the Cochrane Collaboration: http://www.cochrane.org/ websites.

For example, Petrosino, Turpin-Petrosino, and Buehler (2002) conducted a meta-analysis to examine the impact of the "Scared Straight" prison visitation program on deterring delinquent youths from further delinquent activity and found unexpected results about the intervention's effectiveness. These researchers selected for their meta-analyses only studies that used random or quasi-randomly assignment, had a treatment and no-treatment control group, and used at least one follow-up delinquency outcome measure. Opposite of what was expected, the researchers found that the "Scared Straight" program was more likely to have an adverse effect and increased delinquency, as opposed to reducing delinquency among youth that attended the program. The abstract and full-text article is available online at http://www.cochrane.org/reviews/en/ab002796.html.

The Literature Review as an Assignment

The literature review is often an inevitable part of every social work student's assignments, especially in a social work research course. Generally completed over the course of one or two semesters, the literature review assignment requires that students go through the process of identifying a topic, conducting a library literature search, organizing and synthesizing the literature, and then summarizing their findings. If the literature review is conducted as background for a research study, practice, or program evaluation project, it also requires that social work students craft research questions and/or hypotheses based on the literature review, develop an evaluation or research design, carry out the project (with university or agency IRB approval), and then summarize the final report. Hence, successfully navigating the literature review process is an essential formative step in social work professionals' path toward integrating research knowledge and skills with practice.

THE LITERATURE REVIEW EXPERIENCE

Despite this seemingly straightforward literature review task, evidence suggests students often go through a complex array of thoughts, feelings, and actions about the literature review of an information search process (Kracker, 2002; Kuhlthau, 2005; Maschi et al., 2007). The library science profession offers a theory that describes students' common experiences while conducting a literature search for research papers (Jiao & Onwuegbuzie, 1999; Kracker, 2002; Kuhlthau, 2005). For students who are preparing to conduct a literature review, it might be helpful to be aware of the common thoughts, feelings, and actions that occur while preparing and writing a research report.

The Information Search Process

Carol Kuhlthau (2005) proposed the Information Search Process (ISP) theory of a six-stage process that describes the dynamic process of students' emotions, cognitions, and behaviors from the start of the library information search process to the conclusion of the final paper. As shown in Figure 5.2, a progression of thoughts (cognition), feelings (affect), and actions (physical) is commonly associated with the six steps in the process model, which are (a) initiation, (b) selection, (c) exploration, (d) formulation, (e) collection, and (f) presentation.

Stage One: Initiation

In stage one, *initiation*, most students begin to realize that they have a need for information, such as a need to choose a topic for the research paper. At this stage, for students who do not know much about a topic or how to search the literature, having feelings of anxiety, confusion, uncertainty, and doubt is quite common. Yet at the same time, these thoughts and feelings have a motivating

Tasks	Initiation	Selection	Exploration	Formulation	Collection	Presentation
Feelings (affective)	Uncertainty	Optimism	Confusion/ frustration/ doubt	Clarity	Sense of direction/ confidence	Satisfaction or disappointment
Thoughts (cognitive)	vague ----------------------------->			focused ----------------------------------->		
					increased interest	
Actions (physical)	seeking relevant information, exploring ---------------->				seeking pertinent information, documenting	

Figure 5.2
Information Search Process
Source: Kuhlthau, C. C. (2005). Seeking meaning: A process approach to library and information services (3rd ed.). Norwood, NJ: Ablex.

effect on students to take action and begin the search. Therefore, if you are a student and feel anxious, confused, or doubtful about conducting a literature review, rest assured, this experience is quite common among other students and does not have to immobilize you from moving forward with your project.

Stage Two: Selection

In stage two, *selection*, the majority of students no longer feel anxious or uncertain after having identified or selected a broad topic area for their project (e.g., older adults). In fact, during this stage, students often begin to feel more hopeful and positive. They also commonly engage in actions, such as consulting with others, including professors, agency supervisors, researchers, or librarians about their topics and the search process (Kuhlthau, 2005). Therefore, if you are a student engaged in a research project, the selection of a topic is an important milestone that is often accompanied by positive thoughts, feelings, and actions.

Stage Three: Exploration

In stage three, *exploration*, students often narrow their broad topic to a more specific research paper topic (e.g., cognitive behavioral treatment for older adult women with depression). Students at this stage often learn enough information about a topic to feel a sense of mastery over the material, take concrete actions, such as locating and reading relevant information, and even begin to organize the information gathered for their research paper, though there also might be a return of confusion, uncertainty, doubt, and feeling overwhelmed. Therefore, if you are a student at this stage in the search process, do not be alarmed by negative emotions or thoughts; it is a common and temporary part of the process. If you stay focused on the content of what you have learned, you can begin to make important links and compare the content that was most recently read to content read in the past (Kuhlthau, 2005).

Stage Four: Formulation

Stage four, *formulation*, represents a pivotal turning point in the student's information search process. At this stage, students achieve focus because they significantly narrow their topic even further. This stage is often characterized by students having bouts of sudden or gradual insight, and confidence and clarity of thought while feelings of uncertainty diminish. Therefore, if you are a student, this stage often makes the earlier more "uncomfortable" stages of the process well worth it.

Stage Five: Collection

In stage five, *collection*, students feel a strong sense of direction and confidence. Students at this stage seek relevant information and have an increased interest in their topic. Therefore, if you are a student at this stage, you can search the literature for any important information that you might have overlooked in your initial search or need for the final paper assignment.

Stage Six: Presentation

In stage six, *presentation*, students present or write a paper using the information gathered, documenting their work in the form of a written paper or presentation. During this final stage, students may often either feel satisfied or disappointed about their work. Feelings of satisfaction generally result when students perceive their research and writing process went smoothly. At this final stage, students often are more focused, they have increased interest, and feel a sense of mastery over the material learned. In contrast, students may feel disappointed if they are not satisfied with their search process or if their final papers do not meet their expectations (Kuhlthau, 2005). Therefore, if you are a student at this final stage, evaluate your feelings of satisfaction or disappointment and identify ways to maximize strengths and overcome obstacles to incorporate in future literature search projects.

Empirical Validation

The Kuhlthau's (2005) Information Search Process also has been empirically validated. More than two decades of empirical research on the ISP Model suggests that students' initial feelings of confusion and anxiety at the start of the research assignment (i.e., during the initiation and selection stages) commonly transform to confidence, competence, and satisfaction at project completion and search closure (Kuhlthau, 2005; Kuhlthau & Tama, 2001). Similarly, initial vague thoughts about what and how to research often become more focused as the project progresses and certain action strategies are used (Kuhlthau, 2005). The longitudinal validation of the ISP Model has been conducted with diverse samples, such as high school and college students, legal professionals, and public library users (Kuhlthau, 1983, 1988, 1993; Kuhlthau & Tama, 2001; Kuhlthau, Turock, George, & Belvin, 1990).

Social Work Students and the Research Process

As shown in Figure 5.3, a similar process to the ISP Model has been found among social work students engaged in research coursework (Maschi et al., 2007; Maschi, Probst, & Bradley, 2009). Using a sample of 111 BSW and MSW social work research students and qualitative data collected at two time points, Maschi et al. (2009) examined students' thoughts, feelings, and actions about the research process. They found that for many students their initial feelings of anxiety transformed to greater confidence, increased knowledge and skills, and appreciation of the value of research for social work practice.

More specifically, the findings revealed that although most students did not begin the research project with positive attitudes, look forward to the assignment as a learning experience, or feel excited about a particular topic, the majority of them gave positive comments (59%) toward the end of the process. Approximately 15% of the students connected positive feelings to specific points in the process: selecting a topic, particularly one of personal interest; gathering relevant information and seeing the ideas come together and start to make sense. Thirteen individuals noted that the process became easier as time progressed, and eight individuals noted that the experience was not as bad as they had expected. As illustrated in the following students' quotations, when the task began to seem less overwhelming and more manageable, students' confidence increased.

> *Picking a topic of personal interest helped me look forward to doing it.*
> *When I began to organize my thoughts, the task became more concrete for me.*
> *Drawing an outline/map made the task more manageable and eased my anxiety.*

		Beginning		Middle		Ending
		Starting the Class	**Searching for a Topic**	**Literature Review**	**Writing the Paper**	**Finishing the Project**
Attitudes	Negative	Fear of unknown Overwhelmed Anxiety/apprehension Reluctance/resistance Preconditioned dislike of research	Frustration Confusion/uncertainty More difficult than expected	Stress (demanding/time-consuming) Frustration Confusion Erosion of confidence	Renewed anxiety	Drained/burn-out Self doubt Continued dislike of research
	Positive	Confidence Anticipation Interest Excitement	Selecting topic of personal interest or relevance/pragmatic value enhances motivation	Enhanced understanding Greater confidence as locate relevant material Process easier than expected	Satisfaction as project starts to come together	Sense of accomplishment Relief/survival Increase in knowledge Increase in confidence Increased value of research
	Mixed	Nervous but intrigued Expectation to learn	Uneven process Stress waxes and wanes, eases after topic selection	Difficult to determine if sufficient material Project falling into place yet anxiety continues		Relieved yet still unsure Partial satisfaction Less anxiety about research than at beginning
Obstacles	Professor	Lack of structure Lack of clear explanations Lack of availability				
	Self	Procrastination Lack of experience				
	Other	Competing time commitments	Having to select topic with partner or team	Library shortcomings Gaps in the literature Time constraints	Competing demands APA and formatting requirements	

Figure 5.3

A Matrix Model of Social Work Students and the Research Process

Source: Maschi, T., Probst, B., & Bradley, C. (2009). Mapping social work students' perceptions of the research process: A qualitative exploration. *Journal of Baccalaureate Social Work, 14*(2), 63–78.

Supports	Beginning		Middle		Ending
	Starting the Class	Searching for a Topic	Literature Review	Writing the Paper	Finishing the Project
Professor	Breaking process into steps Providing tools/tips	Enthusiasm Guidance Availability	Feedback clear and thorough explanations	Opportunity to submit draft for feedback	→
Self	Had vision of whole Made a plan Organized tasks Use of past experience	Valuation of topic	Focus on task at hand Time management Stress management	Ability to integrate material Self-confidence	→
Other	Peers learning environment	Other professors			→ →

Figure 5.3
Continued

Breaking it into doable steps, planning how I would accomplish each one, made me more focused and thus less stressed.
You must deal with it in small doses so as not to allow your head to explode.

By the end of the research process, some students who initially felt positive or negative about research reported the following positive feelings: relief and reduction of stress with completion of the project, greater comfort and confidence in their ability to do research, increased knowledge, a sense of accomplishment and satisfaction, and a general sense of enjoyment.

Similar to Kuhlthau's ISP Model, this study also found that it was common for social work research students to experience a dynamic process of thoughts, feelings, and actions about conducting a literature search and writing a research report. Activities that assisted in successfully navigating the process included managing anxiety and self-defeating thoughts, seeking peer and instructor support, and breaking the research tasks into manageable steps.

THE STAIR MODEL FOR CONDUCTING LITERATURE REVIEWS

The STAIR model for conducting literature reviews has seven steps: (a) question, (b) find, (c) read, (d) appraise, (e) synthesize, (f) write, and (g) share/action.

To optimize the successful navigation of the literature review process, we offer the Seven Tier Appraise Information Review to help guide social workers from the initial information search to literature appraisal to the sharing of their findings. As illustrated in Figure 5.4, STAIR consists of the following seven steps: (a) question, (b) find, (c) read, (d) appraise, (e) synthesize, (f) write, and (g) share/action. The three vignettes for Kashka, Jamal, and Tiffany presented are incorporated in the discussion that follows.

Step One: Question

In the first step, *question*, the social worker formulates a guiding review question. The social worker does this before conducting a literature search to help focus the review. For example, if the issue is child maltreatment or substance

Critical Thinking

Critical Thinking Question: Using the STAIR model, how can social workers improve their critical thinking skills to inform professional judgments?

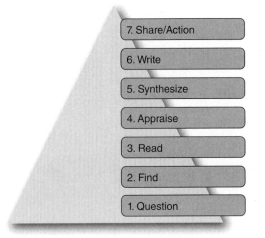

Figure 5.4
The Steps in the "Seven Tier Appraise Information Review" (STAIR)

abuse, a broad guiding review question might be, "What does the scholarly literature report about child maltreatment?" or "What does the scholarly literature report about substance abuse?"

The information search can be further narrowed in three key ways: (a) content area, (b) developmental stage of the population, and (c) characteristic of the population or setting. The first way to classify literature is by content areas, which may include: (a) risk or protective factors, (b) consequences, and (c) assessment or intervention (see Figure 5.5).

For example, for child maltreatment, subsections of this body of literature examine risk or protective factors for child maltreatment (e.g., poverty, parental substance use, and social support), its consequences (e.g., mental health or behavioral problems), and assessment and interventions (e.g., posttraumatic stress disorder assessment and trauma-focused cognitive behavioral treatment). The second central way is to further subclassify the literature by the developmental stage of the population to be studied, for example: (a) children, (b) adolescents, (c) adults, and (d) older adults. The third central way is to subclassify the literature by the characteristics of the setting or population (e.g., foster care, juvenile justice, or immigration status). Figure 5.6 illustrates these categories.

The information search will be shaped based on its intended applied practice or research needs. For example, Tiffany, a social worker, needs to locate literature that targets evidence-based interventions for child maltreatment for a Latina 12-year-old in foster care with a history of physical abuse. She narrows her search to the child maltreatment intervention literature among the population of Latina children in foster care. Focusing her question will assist her in locating the most relevant materials.

Table 5.1 offers guiding review questions to assist social workers with the initial steps of the literature review process. The guiding review template question is: What does the scholarly literature report about [*problem/issue* and/or *interventions*] among [*target population* or a *client system*]? An example of a guiding review question might be What does the scholarly literature report about risk factors for child maltreatment among adolescents in the juvenile justice system?

Positionality

The guiding review question will vary based on the context and whether your review is planned for practice evaluation or research purposes. In other words, is the information sought to guide practice with a specific client in mind?

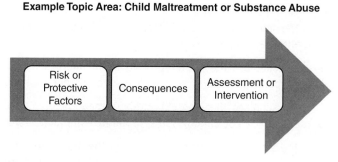

Example Topic Area: Child Maltreatment or Substance Abuse

Risk or Protective Factors   Consequences   Assessment or Intervention

Figure 5.5
Common Content Areas Found in the Scholarly Literature

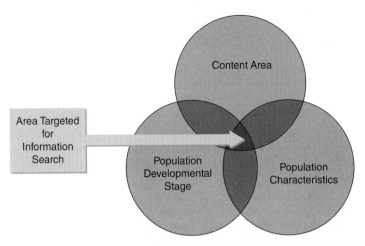

Content Areas	Population Age Group	Population or Setting Characteristics (Examples)
Risk or Protective Factors	Children	Child Welfare
Consequences	Adolescents	Juvenile Justice
Assessment	Adults	Immigration
Intervention	Older Adults	Homeless

Example Broad Topic Areas: Child Maltreatment or Substance Abuse

Guided Review Question Template: What does the empirical literature report about [*problem/issue/* and/or *interventions*] among [*target population*-or for a *client system*]?

Figure 5.6
Common Content Areas and Characteristics Found in the Scholarly Literature

Table 5.1   Examples of "Guided" Questions to Focus the Literature Review Search

Template question	What does the scholarly literature report about _____ and (for) _____ (among _____)?
Risk factors or protective factors	What does the scholarly literature report about risk factors for child maltreatment among children? What does the scholarly literature report about risk (or protective factors) for substance abuse among adolescents?
Consequences	What does the scholarly literature report about the short- and long-term mental health consequences of spousal loss among older adult women?
Assessment	What does the scholarly literature report about the most effective assessment tools for identifying PTSD among youth in the juvenile justice system?
Intervention	What does the scholarly literature report about the most effective interventions for treating trauma symptoms of an 18-year-old Latino male sexual assault victim?

Or is it for the purpose of generating new knowledge for social work practice? It is helpful to know before conducting the information review whether it is for practice or research purposes. It is also beneficial to clearly understand the practice context to make the most relevant decisions.

The Practice Position

The guiding review question for a specific client or client system is practice based. See Table 5.2 for the Evidenced-Based Practice steps. The first three steps that guide the literature review process include (a) formulate a practice-based question, (b) search for evidence, and (c) evaluate the quality of the evidence.

Step 1, formulating a practice-based question, follows the guiding review question format. For example, Jo Ann needs to locate literature about evidence-based interventions for depression for a 70-year-old Caucasian female who emigrated from Russia to the United States 1 year ago. An example of a broad guiding review question is, "What does the scholarly literature report about depression treatment for older women?" Because Jo Ann is searching for a specific issue (e.g., depression) and population (e.g., older adult women and Russian immigrants), her search can be limited for her specific practice needs. Limiting her guiding review question will assist her in locating the most relevant materials to help this specific client. However, if she does not initially find relevant information, she will need to broaden her search to include more general key word search terms, such as *depression treatment* and/or *older adults.*

Similarly, Jamal's evaluation project also will have a narrow guided review question. His guiding review questions might be, What does the scholarly literature report about arts-based after-school programs for adolescent youth (between ages 12 and 17) in urban areas? From the literature he locates, he will be able to identify evidence-based arts programs that have been used with similar populations.

The Research Position

The purpose of seeking information for research is primarily to generate new knowledge that can be used to develop or improve social work practice, policy, or research. A broad review of the literature must be conducted to identify the gaps and plan and implement new studies to fill these gaps. To conduct a

Table 5.2	**Evidence-Based Practice Steps**
Evidence- Based Practice Steps	
Step 1	Formulate a practice-based question
Step 2	Search for evidence
Step 3	Evaluate the quality of relevant studies
Step 4	Select and implement an intervention
Step 5	Monitor progress
Step 6	Evaluate outcomes and document results

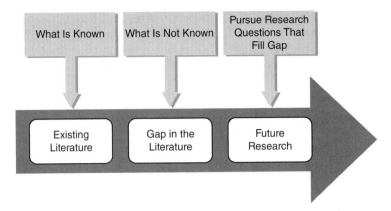

Evidence-Based Research Steps	
Step 1	Formulate a Research-Based Question
Step 2	Search for Evidence
Step 3	Identify Gaps in the Literature
Step 4	Generate Study Research Questions That Fill a Gap
Step 5	Select One or More Feasible Research Question (s)
Step 6	Design and Implement the Study
Step 7	Share and Document the Results

Figure 5.7
Evidence-Based Research Steps

Practice Contexts

Critical Thinking Question:
How do different practice contexts, such as clinical evaluation, agency-based evaluation, or university research, influence how a guiding review question is formulated?

literature review for research purposes, a library search worksheet can assist with the literature search. (See Figure 5.7.)

This guiding review question is refined as the search progresses, often until the gaps in the literature are found from which a new study can be designed. For Wanda, a social work researcher, the initial guided review question (Step 1) was "what does the scholarly literature report about trauma assessment among youth in the juvenile justice system?"

This initial question guided her literature search and became refined as Wanda isolated a gap in the area of trauma assessment among juvenile justice-involved youth. Specifically, her search revealed that a fair amount of published information is available about youth who have histories of child maltreatment in the juvenile justice system. However, there was a dearth of information about witnessing violence and/or other life event stressors experienced among this population. This identified gap influenced Wanda's choice to design a research study to gather data to fill this information gap.

Step Two: Find

In the second step, *find*, literature search is underway. The types of literature that can be consulted can be a range of information sources that are considered more credible than others, with journals from professional peer-reviewed articles high on the hierarchy. The more common sources of published scholarly knowledge include

- Professional peer-review journals (electronic or hard copy)
- Governmental or professional websites, such as those of governmental agencies and/or research institutes
- Academic books
- Research reports and monographs
- Conference proceedings and presentations

Other Information Sources

Other sources of information about a particular content area may include experts in the field, including agency supervisors and academic researchers. Librarians, professors, and peers can be a good reference with regard to the information search process. These sources can help social workers generate practice-based research knowledge that can be used to improve provision of services or refine policies.

Peer-Reviewed Journals

Articles from peer-reviewed journals are an important staple of the literature search. As explained previously, peer-reviewed articles undergo a rigorous review process. Generally, they can be considered a reliable source, although the quality of the journal or articles may vary. Many journals are available in print or electronic form and are available at university or community libraries or by subscription.

Online or electronic database searches   Libraries provide access to electronic databases and indexes. The commonly used electronic databases among social workers include Academic Search Premier, Social Work Abstracts, ProQuest, SocioFile, PsychInfo, MEDLINE, and ScienceDirect. Google Scholar is an Internet search engine available to the general public. These databases or indexes generally are search engines that provide basic and advanced search features to locate key research resources.

The electronic search   The guiding review question is helpful to focus on the initial online search, particularly identifying the key word search terms used. For example, Wanda used her guiding review question to choose key words: "What does the scholarly literature report about *trauma assessment* among *youth* in the *juvenile justice* system?" Her central content area is trauma assessment among the population of youth in the juvenile justice system. Using the advanced search option, the three content or population areas that form the basis of her review are *trauma assessment*, *youth*, and *juvenile justice*. These terms also will be the key word search terms for her initial review (see Figure 5.8).

The "and/or" search option   Similar to a Boolean search, options such as *and* or *or* help to narrow or broaden a search. For example, using *and* narrows a search so that it must combine all the key words, such as *trauma assessment* AND *youth* AND *juvenile justice*. Conversely, *or* broadens the scope of the search to include any article that matches any of the search terms, for example: *trauma assessment* OR *youth* OR *juvenile justice* selects articles that match any of those key word search terms.

Additional search options   As shown in Figure 5.9, additional advanced search options help modify the search results. For example, key words can be used to search full text, author, article title, and journal name. The Academic

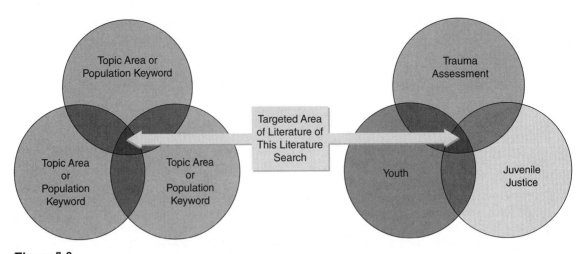

Figure 5.8

Using Keywords Search Terms

Guiding Review Question: What does the scholarly literature report about *trauma assessment* among *youth* in the *juvenile justice* system?

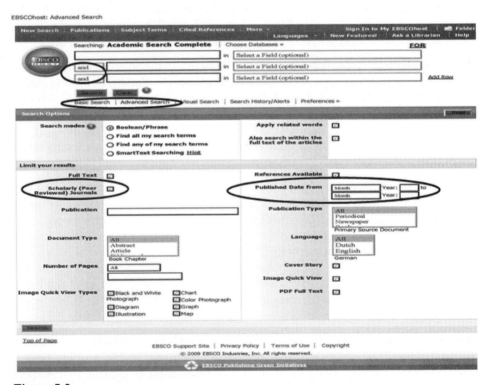

Figure 5.9

EBSCO HOST Search Engine Example

Source: EBSCO host (2010). EBSCO host main frame. Retrieved from http://www.ebscohost.com/

Search Complete/EBSCO host database has other special features in advanced search options in which searches can be limited to include only peer-reviewed articles or limited by the year of publication.

Most university and community libraries offer assistance, including tutorials, on how to use the electronic databases and other library resources. If you are not familiar with these services, contact your library and attend an information session or request a library tour.

Documenting the search   It is often important to track the steps involved in the review process. It is particularly important if your literature review is composed of a systematic review or meta-analysis that the methods section used can be evaluated or replicated by others. As noted earlier, the question may be modified as the search is refined. Table 5.3 shows the Library Search Worksheet that documents the search process.

Many electronic documents also have a digital object identifier, which uniquely identifies an electronic document (e.g., doi: 10.1177/1087057106289725). The digital object identifier has metadata in the electronic document, including a URL where the document can be located.

Table 5.3	**Library Search Worksheet**

Student's Name:	Date:

Directions: Document the search process of scholarly journal articles.

The literature search
1. General topic of interest:
2. Problem (and/or treatment) under investigation:
3. Population under investigation:
4. Date(s) of search:
5. Guiding review question for literature search:
6. Name of library (and location) where search was conducted:
7. What online database(s) was/were searched?
8. What special limiters were used in your search? (e.g., year limits, peer-reviewed articles only):
9. Was a basic or advanced search option used?
10. What key word search terms were used? And in what combinations?
11. How many "hits" did you receive in the initial search?
12. How did you expand or narrow the search?

Selection criteria for sample of articles
13. Is your sample of articles scholarly research studies?
14. What was your decision-making process for including or excluding articles from your sample?
15. Other important notes that other students or research would need to know to replicate your search:
16. List the *APA* references for articles:

Saving the search documents   Articles should be saved as a PDF (as opposed to the HTML version) and downloaded so that the tables and figures also are printed with the article.

Electronic copies of the articles should also be saved using a systematic labeling system. For example, saving each article by the last name of the first author and year of publication can also be useful. All articles can also be saved in a project folder. If hard copies of the articles are printed, they too can be organized in alphabetical order by the last name of the first author and publication year. (Note, if hard copies are made, be sure to copy the entire articles, including the references.). Additionally, bibliographic software, such as EndNote or Refworks, can be used to manage your references.

In Wanda's case, she labeled her electronic literature review folder: "trauma assessment, youth, and juvenile justice literature" and saved the articles in her documents folder. She labeled each article within that folder by the last name of the first author and year of publication. When she began to review her articles, she easily located specific articles for her review. She also used the Endnote bibliographic software to store her growing library of references of peer-reviewed journals, books, book chapters, research reports, including monographs and conference presentations.

Step Three: Read

In the third step, *read*, the researcher selects and reads the relevant journals and other materials available. Identifying the journal article types is particularly important if the goal of the information search is to find peer-reviewed *empirical* articles (e.g., research studies) in a specific topic area (e.g., trauma assessment, youth, and juvenile justice).

As shown in Table 5.4, two central distinctions exist between peer-reviewed empirical journals and those that are not. As illustrated in Figure 5.10, the articles that meet the criteria for peer-reviewed empirical studies are published in peer-reviewed journals and, at a minimum, include the purpose of the study, study methods, findings, and a conclusion or implications sections (American Psychological Association [APA], 2009; Holosko, 2005). A more detailed description is provided in Step Four—Appraise. Figure 5.10 provides an overview of the different sections of a research report.

Articles that are not research studies may include literature reviews, critiques, books, reviews, and editorials and may not include all of the aforementioned sections. This type of article can be classified as a nonempirical article. Table 5.4 provides a checklist for distinguishing peer-reviewed empirical journals from other types of nonempirical articles.

More than one read rule   Once the sample of journals has been selected, we recommend applying "the more than one read rule." In fact, seasoned scholars often recommend reading the article more than once if the goal is to understand and critically analyze it (Asmundson, Norton, & Stein, 2002; Holosko, 2005; Oleson & Arkin, 1996). However, these same scholars vary in their suggestions for how to accomplish this.

Table 5.4   Checklist for Identifying Peer-Reviewed Scholarly Journal Articles

Check Below if Condition Was Met	Essential Component	Description
	Peer reviewed	The article was published in a peer-reviewed scholarly journal.
	Study justification	The article includes an introduction that identifies a rationale or reason for the study being conducted.
	Study purpose	The article has an introduction that clearly states the purpose of the study. It can be in the form of a purpose statement, research question(s), and/or hypothesis(es).
	Methods	The article's method section specifies the sampling strategies, variables and measures, and data collection procedures.
	Results	The article's results section provides a narrative description of the study results. If a quantitative study, it will include statistical analysis and often results in tables and/or graphs. Qualitative results include the use of narrative quotes. Mixed methods includes a combination of both.
	Discussion	The article includes a discussion of the findings, which should include one or more of the following: conclusion, implications, future research directions.
	References	The article includes a list of references that are cited in the body of the text.
		If not a peer-reviewed article, is it one of the following?
	Literature review	A literature review article provides an overview of a body of literature and types of research methods. It can be in the form of a summary and/or analysis of the literature.
	Critiques	Articles that critique theories, methods, laws, programs, policies.
	Book review	An often short article that provides the review of a book that is of interest to the journal readership.
	Editorials	An article published as an editorial piece by an editor or by a reader as a letter to the editor.
	Other	Other types of articles not identified above.

Review Recommendation

We recommend first screening the article by reviewing the title and the abstract to determine if the article meets the criteria (or is relevant) for being included in the review. If relevant, a more detailed initial review should be conducted that includes reading the introduction, the methods, and the discussion sections that review the major findings and implications for practice and policy. The purpose of the initial reading is to comprehend the essential contents as opposed to critiquing them. After the initial reading, write a short summary (300 words or less) to test your comprehension. Paraphrasing or

THE TITLE
Accurate Description of Content

THE ABSTRACT
•Brief general description of study (120 words or less)
•(objective of study, methods, findings, implications)

THE INTRODUCTION
•Statement of the research problem or central issue/s
•Identify gap in literature
•Purpose of study
•Description of research questions and/or hypotheses
•Study rationale
•Significance for social work practice and policy

LITERATURE REVIEW
•Critical review of variables of central interest
•Review of theoretical framework (if applicable)

METHODS
•Description of the methods
•These areas include:
(1) research design
(2) intervention description (if applicable)
(3) variables and measures
(4) data collection procedures
(5) data analysis strategies

FINDINGS
•Review of the research findings
•Connect of research questions to results.

DISCUSSION
•Brief overview of major findings
•A discussion if hypotheses were supported
•Comparison to previous research studies
•Discussion of practice and/or policy implications
•Methodological limitations of current study
•Recommendations for future research directions

REFERENCES
"List references cited in text

Figure 5.10
Organization of a Research Report

summarizing the article's content helps prepare for a more in-depth critical reading and analysis. Table 5.5 provides a worksheet to complete this article paraphrasing and summary task.

More Recommendations

Asmundson, Norton, and Stein (2000) recommend a similar multistep review process: First, carefully read the entire article and refrain from critiquing it or making notes. Second, take a short break (one or two days) from reading the article and review other relevant review material or books (This break can be used to become more familiar with other works in your topic area). Third,

Table 5.5	**Preparing a Journal Article Summary**

Journal Article Worksheet for Preparing a Summary	Article # _____

Directions: Provide a summary of the articles you have selected for review. Cover important aspects while writing succinct and brief summaries (i.e., 300 words or less).

Student's name:	Date:

Purpose of study (noted by author[s]):

Methods of study
Research design (include sampling strategies)
Sample description
Measures used
Data collection procedures

Major findings (one to two major findings):

Implications for practice and/or policy noted by author(s):

APA style reference for this article:

carefully reread the article to determine the strengths, weaknesses, and limitations of the research design and overall report.

In contrast, Oleson and Arkin (1996) recommend two slightly different methods for reviewing a journal. The first method is to read the abstract and the first paragraph of introduction and discussion sections followed by a general scan of the other article sections. The alternative method is to first read the abstract and the first sentence of every paragraph.

Choose a Method that Works

Because there are different options for reviewing articles, choose the strategy that works best for you. In general, the review of journals should result in general understanding of their contents including the study purpose, methods, major findings, and practice and/or policy implications. The in-depth review of the article should result in an increased ability to compare and appraise the contents of the article with research standards and report writing, which is reviewed in the next section.

Step Four: Appraise

Once a clear and succinct summary is written, the next step is to critically review the article contents. In the fourth step, *appraise*, the article should be reviewed to assess how well it meets the criteria for a sound research study and written report. Social workers must be able to critically evaluate the strengths, weaknesses, and limitations of research studies and understand their implications before they consider adapting the study methods or practice recommendations.

Appraising a journal article is critical to assess how well it meets the criteria for a sound research study and written report.

The Research Report

It is also essential that students are able to understand the content and structure of the research report and identify and understand the objectives of the different report sections. Clearly understanding what is expected in a research

Table 5.6   **Critiquing Research Report Worksheet**

Student's Name:

Date Completed:

List *APA* Reference for Article or Book Critiqued:

Directions: Provide your evaluation of the quality (from poor = 1 to excellent = 5). If you believe an item is not applicable to this research article, mark it "not applicable" (N/A). Be prepared to explain your ratings. Add up each response for a total quality score.

Scholarly Journal Article Rating Scale	Poor		Fair		Excellent	N/A
1. The title accurately reflects the article content.	1	2	3	4	5	N/A
2. The abstract provides an overview (e.g., purpose, methods, findings, implications).	1	2	3	4	5	N/A
3. The introduction underscores the purpose and significance of the study.	1	2	3	4	5	N/A
4. The research purpose, question, or hypothesis is clearly stated.	1	2	3	4	5	N/A
5. The literature review provides a background to study variables.	1	2	3	4	5	N/A
6. Research ethics and human subjects protections are adequately addressed.	1	2	3	4	5	N/A
7. Sampling methods are sound and have sampled targeted population.	1	2	3	4	5	N/A
8. Relevant demographics (e.g., age, gender, race or ethnicity) are described.	1	2	3	4	5	N/A
9. Measures chosen for the study variables are reliable and valid.	1	2	3	4	5	N/A
10. Data collection procedures are adequately detailed.	1	2	3	4	5	N/A
11. The results present data for research questions or hypotheses.	1	2	3	4	5	N/A
12. There is a discussion of implications for practice or policy.	1	2	3	4	5	N/A
13. Study limitations are specified by the author(s).	1	2	3	4	5	N/A
14. Future research directions are provided.	1	2	3	4	5	N/A

Total quality score (add numbers 1–14): _____

report can help the reviewer measure whether an article meets the recommended standards and assess whether it is useful for practice. Table 5.6 provides a worksheet that social workers can use to evaluate an article's content.

As shown in Figure 5.10, the common parts of a research report include the title, abstract, introduction, literature review, methods, results, and discussion sections. The report should clearly lead the reader to why the particular study was conducted (i.e., introduction), how it was done (i.e., methods), what results were found (i.e., findings), and how the findings improve practice, policy, or research in this area (i.e., discussion). The different parts of the research report are briefly outlined next. For a more in-depth review, refer to *Publication Manual of the APA* (2009) publication manual or see Bem (2000).

Title   The *Publication Manual of the APA* (2009) guidelines state that the title must accurately reflect the contents and contain no more than 12 words. Social workers who review an article should verify whether the article meets these criteria.

Abstract   The abstract should provide a brief overview of the article. The abstract is often the featured part of the article that is available for review when you search online databases and indexes. If the abstract is for a research study, it should, at a minimum, provide the purpose of the study, the methods, major findings, and practice or policy implications. It also should contain no more than 120 words. Social workers should verify whether the abstract meets these criteria.

Introduction   The introduction of the article "sets the stage" for the population and/or problem issue under investigation. The introduction should provide a background to the central issues and identify the gaps in knowledge that the current study was designed to fill. It should clearly state a purpose for the current study and introduce the research questions and/or hypothesis(es) of the study. The study rationale and the significance of the study for practice, policy, and/or research clearly should be clearly delineated. Reviewers should evaluate the article as to how well these criteria are met.

Social workers should use the following questions to assess the introduction section:

- Do the research questions (or hypotheses) for the study seem important?
- Does the purpose of the study follow logically from the background of the literature and its current gaps?
- Do the study research questions or hypotheses make a new contribution to the literature?
- Does the study have important practice, research, or policy implications?

Literature Review   The literature review section is sometimes combined with the introduction section or presented as its own section. At a minimum, the literature review section provides a background to the central concepts or variables under investigation and their relationship (e.g., depression, older adults, and mental health treatment). For example, Wanda's literature review would surely include what is known about trauma assessment among youth in the juvenile justice system. Social workers should use the following questions to assess the literature review section:

- Does the literature review include the central concepts or variables under investigation and their relationship?
- Does the literature review section give a clear understanding of the available literature for this topic?
- Is there a logical connection to prior literature, and why the current study is being conducted?

Methods   The method section describes the steps that were taken to answer the research question or hypotheses. At a minimum it describes who the study participants were, how they were recruited, what measures were used, and how participants were assessed. Although the names of the subsections of the methods section will vary, common categories may include research design, sample description, variables and measures, study procedures, and data analysis. This section should be detailed enough so that anyone reading the section would have sufficient information to replicate the study.

The methods section should be evaluated as to how appropriate it is for answering the study's research questions or hypotheses. These questions might include the following:

- Did the sample selection, measures, data collection, and analysis seem appropriate based on the purpose of the study?
- If the study tested a causal hypothesis, did it use an experimental design?
- Was the sample representative of the general population from which it was drawn?
- Were the measures reliable and valid?
- Was there any evidence of bias in the study procedures?

Results   The results section explains the type of analysis used and the results obtained. A quantitative analysis generally includes tables of statistical results or numeric data and narrative results. In contrast, a qualitative analysis generally contains verbatim quotes or narrative data. In short, the results section should assess to what extent the statistical procedures were valid or accurate.

Discussion   The discussion section has certain objectives, which include (a) reviewing major findings, (b) comparing the results with prior literature, (c) discussing the implications for findings for practice and/or policy, (d) addressing methodological limitations of current study, (e) outlining future directions for research, and (f) ending with concluding remarks. This section does not provide subheaders, so this section must be carefully reviewed for its organization and content.

The reviewer should assess to what extent the article provides:

- an overview of the major findings,
- a comparison of the current findings compared with the prior literature,
- implications of the findings for practice and policy,
- the current study's methodological limitations,
- future research directions,
- a conclusion.

References   The references section should list only works that are cited in the text. The study should cite the most recent publications available at the time the article was published. The reviewer should assess the following:

- Do all works cited appear in the reference list?
- Do the majority of references fall within 5 years of the article's publication date?

The review is not meant to be exhaustive but to help familiarize students with the types of questions that can be asked when assessing a published research study. Table 5.6 shows a worksheet that social workers can use to critique a preliminary research report. Steps Five to Seven (*synthesize*, *write*, and *share*, respectively) will be reviewed in chapter 12.

Internet Resources for Evidenced-Based Research and Evaluation

Engage, Assess, Intervene, Evaluate

Critical Thinking Question: What are ways in which students can apply the skills to assess and evaluate (appraisal) the literature for clinical and/or policy practice?

As noted earlier, a number of online resources are also a repository for research, including meta-analyses of evidence-based practices. Some of the more well-known resources are the Campbell Collaboration (http://www.campbellcollaboration.org), Cochran Collaboration (http://www.cochrane.org), and Information for Practice (IP) (http://www.nyu.edu/socialwork/ip).

The Campbell Collaboration's (C2) website and international research network focus on health care and provide information to help people make well-informed decisions by preparing, maintaining, and disseminating systematic reviews in education, crime and justice, and social welfare. The Information for Practice website provides information to help social service professionals throughout the world conveniently maintain an awareness of news regarding the profession and emerging scholarship, including meta-analyses in various practice areas. Other useful websites that provide data from reliable sources are reviewed next. However, a cautionary note for social work students is to carefully discern Internet sites that provide scholarly and rigorous research from those that do not.

Internet Resources: Governmental Agencies and Research Institutes

Another reliable and useful Internet resource is the websites of governmental or research institutes, for example, the United States Department of Health and Human Services. Administration for Children and Families (http://www.acf.hhs.gov) houses the Child Maltreatment Report (available at http://www.acf.hhs.gov/programs/cb/pubs/cm07). According to the USDHHS (2008) report, approximately 794,000 children were substantiated victims of abuse or neglect in 2007. The majority (60%) of them experienced neglect, followed by physical abuse (11%), sexual abuse (7.6%), and psychological maltreatment (4.2%).

General population statistics for the United States are also available at sites such as the U.S. Census Bureau (http://www.census.gov). The Child Information Gateway (http://www.childwelfare.gov) provides information related to children and families in the areas such as child welfare, child abuse and neglect, foster care, and adoption. The National Institute of Mental Health (http://www.nimh.nih.gov/index.shtml) provides information on mental health and treatment and publications that include "Mental Health: A Report of the Surgeon General" (http://www.surgeongeneral.gov/library/mentalhealth/home.html).

The Substance Abuse and Mental Health Services Administration (http://www.samhsa.gov/index.aspx) houses information on substance abuse such as the National Survey on Drug Use and Health (http://www.oas.samhsa.gov/nsduh/2k8nsduh/2k8Results.cfm). The Office of Juvenile Justice and Delinquency Prevention (http://www.ojjdp.gov) provides information including the "Juvenile Victims and Offender" report: (http://ojjdp.ncjrs.gov/ojstatbb/nr2006/downloads/NR2006.pdf). The Administration on Aging (AA) provides information on older adults including the report "Older Americans: Key Indicators of Well-Being" (http://www.agingstats.gov/agingstatsdotnet/Main_Site/Data/Data_2008.aspx).

Table 5.7 is a worksheet for gathering population statistics or problem overview. The literature search can continue through the final writing stage.

Table 5.7	**Population Statistics or Problem Overview Statistics Worksheet (from reliable sources, such as governmental or international or established research institutes)**

Student's Name: Date:

Directions: Document governmental or other sources that provide an overview of the population and to which degree they are impacted by the problem under investigation.

1. What population is the center of your investigation?

2. What are the issues or problem(s) with this population under investigation?

3. Government website(s) or international or national institutes that address the problems or needs of your study under investigation.

4. Provide the statistics for the population and/or impact of the "problem" on the population.

5. How helpful was this site toward gathering information about your population interest or topic?

6. What is the *APA* reference for all works cited above?

Online Resources for Evidence-Based Practices and Reviews

A list of resources for evidence-based practices and reviews also can be found on the web and includes

- American Psychological Association (empirically supported treatment): http://www.apa.org/divisions/div12/cppi.html
- OJJDP Prevention Model Programs Guide: http://www.dsgonline.com/mpg2.5/cognitive_behavioral_treatment_prevention.htm
- SAMHSA National Registry of Evidence-Based Programs & Practices: http://www.nrepp.samhsa.gov/
- University of Michigan Library Links: http://www.lib.umich.edu/libraries http://www.icpsr.umich.edu/icpsrweb/ICPSR/

SUMMARY

This chapter looked at the literature review process. This chapter was designed to demystify this process and to help facilitate the use of empirical literature as an essential part of a social worker's career-long learning. Learning how to do a good literature review gives social workers the ability to distinguish, appraise, and integrate multiple sources of knowledge. The commitment to producing empirically literate social workers, that is, social workers who use observable evidence to guide their practice decision making, is underscored by the social work profession's national and international organizations, especially as it relates to the social work values of integrity and competence.

Mastering the literature review process, that is the search for and evaluation of evidence, is a formative task of every consummate social work professional. The term *literature review* may refer to different parts of the literature review process or product, such as (a) the actual search for scholarly literature, (b) the completed literature review paper or article that is comprehensive review of a body of literature, or (c) the subsection of a research study entitled "literature review" that commonly proceeds the methods section. Practitioners can gain information to broaden their knowledge and skills base and be able to demonstrate their synthesis and analysis of the literature through oral and written communication.

Carol Kuhlthau's (2005) Information Search Process theory, which is a six-stage process theory, was reviewed. The theory describes the dynamic process of students' emotions, cognitions, and behaviors from the start of the library information search process to the conclusion of the final paper. A progression of thoughts (cognition), feelings (affect), and actions (physical) are commonly associated with the six steps in the process, which are: (a) initiation, (b) selection, (c) exploration, (d) formulation, (e) collection, and (f) presentation.

To optimize the successful navigation of the literature review and writing process, we offered the Seven Tier Appraise Information Review (STAIR). It consists of the following seven steps: (a) question, (b) find, (c) read, (d) appraise, (e) synthesize, (f) write, and (g) share. In chapter 12, students will learn how to write the literature review and research report. Using these steps can help social workers conduct the literature review assignment efficiently.

Log onto **www.mysocialworklab.com** and answer the following questions. (*If you did not receive an access code to* **MySocialWorkLab** *with this text and wish to purchase access online, please visit* www.mysocialworklab.com.)

1. **Watch the research based practice video "Contracting With the Client to Select an Evidence-Based Therapy."** After listening to the commentary, describe how the social worker used the seven steps of the STAIR model presented in the chapter.

2. **Read the MySocialWork Library case study "Community Practice: Organizing Social Work in the Republic of Armenia, Part I."** As the research assistant, your task is to do the literature review. Using the first two steps of the STAIR model (question, share), identify a guiding review question and steps you took (or would take) to complete the literature search.

PRACTICE TEST

The following questions will test your knowledge of the content found within this chapter. For additional assessment, including licensing-exam type questions on applying chapter content to practice, visit **MySocialWorkLab**.

1. The term *literature review* does not describe which of the following?
   a. The peer review process
   b. The literature review section of a journal article
   c. An article that is a comprehensive review of a topic area
   d. A systematic investigation of publications in a topic area

2. What is the least reliable source of information listed below?
   a. Professional peer-reviewed journals
   b. Publications of governmental research institutes
   c. Newspaper articles
   d. Academic books

3. A social worker who combines quantitative results with multiple studies for an overall empirical summary conducts what type of study?
   a. Survey descriptive
   b. Meta-analysis
   c. Macro-analysis
   d. Exploratory

4. Appraising an empirical journal article generally refers to:
   a. Thorough read and notetaking of the article
   b. Systematic steps taken to locate reliable information
   c. Sound research study and written report assessment
   d. Quoting the article's content

5. Briefly describe one strategy that you would use in appraising the quality of a research report.

ASSESS YOUR COMPETENCE

Use the scale below to rate your current level of achievement on the following concepts or skills associated with each competency presented in the chapter:

1	2	3
I can accurately describe the concept or skill	I can consistently identify the concept or skill when observing and analyzing practice activities	I can competently implement the concept or skill in my own practice

_____ can conduct a library search of the scholarly journal literature.

_____ can conduct a literature review for purposes of a research or practice context.

_____ can apply research findings for use in a practice or research context.

_____ can assess or appraise the quality of the research design and written research report.

6

Sampling in Evidence-Based Practice Research

Core Competencies in This Chapter (Check marks indicate which competencies are demonstrated)				
Professional Identity	✓ Ethical Practice	Critical Thinking	Diversity in Practice	Human Rights and Justice
✓ Research-Based Practice	Human Behavior	Policy Practice	✓ Practice Contexts	Engage, Assess, Intervene, Evaluate

INTRODUCTION

Recently, evidence-based practice (EBP) has become the practice of choice taught in social work education (Fook, 2004; Furmsn & Bender, 2003; Gilgun, 2005). The American Psychological Association defines evidence-based practice as "the integration of the best available research with clinical expertise in the context of patient characteristics, culture, and preferences" ("Evidenced-based practice in psychology: APA presidential task force on evidenced-based practice," 2006). This integration prevents restricted access to services for oppressed groups and provides treatment of choice for persons served (Norcross, Koocher, & Garofalo, 2006). Evidence-based practice helps bridge the gap between expectation and experience by providing evidence-based experiential information to a less experienced clinician or policy maker (Zeithami, Parasuraman, & Berry, 1990; [Figure 6.1]). In addition, EBP is an ethical mandate in social work practice (Gibbs & Gambrill, 2002).

Researchers sample different types of populations. It is highly unlikely that a social work researcher might be interested in a universal population, which literally is everyone, unless he or she is working with census data. More realistically, the researcher wants to study a particular population of interest (target population), details of which may be embedded in census data, or identifiable by a geographic region, or agency setting. Once the target population is identified, the researcher develops a sampling frame, which includes all people who are eligible for the desired sample. Finally, the researcher chooses people to study from the sampling frame using one of the techniques described in this chapter.

GENERALIZABILITY

When choosing samples for a study, the researcher is concerned about the concept of *generalizability*. Generalizability implies that the sample chosen for study represents the population from which it was sampled, allowing the researcher to use the findings discovered in the sample and assume that the findings are consistent with the population from which the sample was drawn and applicable to a target population. This is an ideal concept because in research there is never complete generalizability. All research has some degree of

Evidence-based practice helps bridge the gap between expectation and experience of a social worker by providing evidence-based experiential information to a less experienced clinician or policy maker. In addition, evidence-based practice is an ethical mandate in social work practice.

Practice Contexts

Critical Thinking Question: How do different practice contexts influence the types of sampling strategies used?

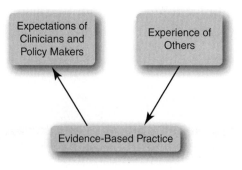

Figure 6.1
Evidence-based practice bridges the gap between expectation and experience by providing the experience of others to the less experienced clinician or policy maker

sampling error. Sampling error occurs when there is a difference in one or more characteristics between the sample being studied and the population from which it was drawn. There are many possibilities for sampling error. For example, the population from which the sample was taken may lack specificity and not clearly represent what the researcher feels he or she is studying. Varying methods (discussed on the following pages) are used to select the sample that may introduce sampling error. In addition, the larger the sampling error, the further the researcher moves from being able to generalize the research findings to the target population.

HOMOGENEITY

Homogeneity is a concept that approximates the idea that the sample chosen has identical characteristics to the population from which it was drawn. In social work research there is never a complete match between the target population and the sample. This is because the elements of study in evidence-based social work are people. People are differentiated by many variables, for example, age, ethnicity, gender, health status, religious beliefs or nonbelief, height, weight, and so on. It would be ideal if a target population was homogeneous, but in human research the population is skewed toward being heterogeneous, requiring larger sample sizes and replication of research findings by other researchers studying the same target population. This provides an empirical gauge for supporting the generalization of findings. Another complication of homogeneity is that the population studied by one researcher may differ from the same type of population studied by another researcher. That researcher's population could differ by geography, cultural variability, seasonal variability, and cohort variability (a time variable) making generalization to a common target population difficult, and at the worst, impossible.

> *Generalizability implies that the sample chosen for study represents the population from which it was sampled, allowing the researcher to use the findings discovered in the sample and assume that the findings are consistent with the population from which the sample was drawn and applicable to a target population. This is an ideal concept because in research there is never complete generalizability. All research has some degree of sampling error.*

REPRESENTATIVENESS

A researcher wants the sample being studied to be representative of the target population from which it is drawn. Therefore, the researcher must carefully define the population of interest, set up a sampling frame that represents the population of interest, and ideally create a sample that represents the population of interest. *Sampling bias* is a type of sampling error that can prevent a true representativeness of the target population. Sampling bias is a systematic distortion of a research sample. It prevents the sample from being representative of the population from which it is drawn. This creates a *biased sample*. A biased sample is either an overrepresentation or an underrepresentation of certain variables relative to the population being studied. This condition presents ethical concerns because a biased sample may make false conclusions about the target population that may lead to interventions that oppress vulnerable populations. This occurs when these populations are underserviced because they are not adequately represented in the sampling frame. In addition, when soliciting subjects for the study, the researcher must fully inform the subjects of any risks or possible damage from participating in the study and provide an option for subject debriefing. This debriefing is important to eliminate potential harm to any vulnerable population, such as the vulnerable African American population used in the unethical Tuskegee Syphilis

Study between 1932 and 1972, which is discussed in detail in chapter 2. During this study, African American subjects were not fully informed of the risks and harms involved in the study and they were denied proper medical care for syphilis.

An example of sampling bias that can distort representativeness can be seen in an exploratory study recently conducted by Youdin (2010). The target population for this study was mental health professionals defined as social workers, psychologists, psychiatric nurses, and psychiatrists in psychiatric emergency screening services, in-patient units, and out-patient centers in the New York/ New Jersey metropolitan area. Several centers and units were chosen randomly. These mental health centers and units are called *enumeration units*, and they contain the subjects (mental health professionals) of the study. This study focused on the diagnostic accuracy of social workers, psychologists, psychiatric nurses, and psychiatrists when diagnosing older adults (age 65 and over).

After the results were obtained, Youdin consulted with colleagues about the findings. During the discussion of the findings, another colleague pointed out that an outpatient treatment center, in the catchment area from where the samples were drawn was not studied but had a unique characteristic that differentiated it from the other centers and units studied. This mental health treatment center employed Russian-speaking social workers, psychologists, psychiatric nurses, and psychiatrists who diagnosed and treated Russian-speaking older adults. This setting introduced a cultural variable that needed to be accounted for in order to generalize findings to the target population. When the data were analyzed, Youdin found that this additional population that was sampled differed significantly in their degree of diagnostic accuracy from African American, Latino, and White mental health professionals in the original sample. Therefore, when using due diligence, Youdin discovered this sampling error. Whether using due diligence during the research processes, or having other researchers replicate the study by studying similar populations, by understanding that the elements being studied are clear representations of the target population studied, the specificity of homogeneity increases.

SAMPLING METHODS

Sampling is a group of techniques that enable the evidence-based researcher to study small samples of a population and make assumptions that are generalizable to the target population from which the samples are selected. This section will examine two types of sampling methods: probability sampling methods and nonprobability sampling methods.

PROBABILITY SAMPLING METHODS

Probability sampling is the most common technique used when a researcher wants to generalize the results of a study to the population sampled. Based on probability theory, the central assumption is that there is a mathematical likelihood that an event will occur.

Probability sampling is the most common technique used when a researcher wants to generalize the results of a study to the population sampled. Based on probability theory, the central assumption is that there is a mathematical likelihood that an event will occur. The typical example of this assumption that is used in most research texts is tossing a coin. The probability of the coin landing on heads is 50%. It also has an equal probability of 50% of landing on tails. However, if one tosses a coin three or four times these results may not occur. The law of averages states that over time results will balance out and the event (coin toss) will occur, as it theoretically should. Therefore, the larger the sample, the greater probability that the results observed in the study did not occur by chance.

Sampling error is another way of saying that there is a certain chance that the sample may vary from the population as a natural occurrence. Sampling error is also referred to as the *null hypothesis*. The null hypothesis states that the relationship found between variables within a sample being studied is an error representing the tendency of a sample to differ from the population from which it is drawn. Therefore, the finding is based on a natural occurrence rather than a predicted relationship.

Probability sampling is based on the concept that the probability of selecting an element is not zero so there is some likelihood of selecting each element. In social work research, an element is a person. In probability sampling, a technique of *random sampling* is used. Random sampling is a systematic method that ensures a purely random (chance) process occurs. The four types of random sampling are simple random sampling, systematic random sampling, stratified random sampling, and cluster sampling.

Simple Random Sampling

Simple random sampling is commonly used in evidence-based social work research. Simple random sampling is based on a clearly defined procedure that theoretically generates a sample on the basis of probability. The probability of an element being chosen must be equal, meaning that each element has an equal probability of being selected. When working with a relatively small population, the researcher may use a random numbers table to assure that the selection of the sample is performed on a random basis. The list of people being studied is all encompassing and is known as the *sampling frame*.

Each person in the sampling frame is assigned a number. Using a random numbers table, people are selected for the sample to be studied based on the order their number appears on the random numbers table. When the sample size is achieved, the remaining people are not included in the study. When the population being studied is too large to assign numbers to each person and to manually select a sample using a random numbers table, the researcher uses a computer program that will generate a random selection of the elements (people) for the study. In nonreplacement sampling, once a person is selected for the study he or she is not returned to the sampling frame. In replacement sampling, each element selected is returned to the sample frame so that it may be sampled again. The majority of social work studies use non-replacement sampling.

Figure 6.2 shows a section of a random numbers table that was used to select five people from a 30-person sampling frame. Each subject in the target population was assigned a number from 1 through 30. A computer generated a random numbers table consisting of a column of five-digit numbers. The researcher then used the random numbers table by selecting two-digit numbers from the last two columns (in bold print for this example). When any number between 01 and 30 appeared, a person with that preassigned number was chosen. This process was repeated five times until the sample of five people was chosen from the target population of 30 people.

If a researcher wants to replicate the study with a *matched sample*, the sample used in the initial study needs to be defined by key variables such as

```
09117
10402
34764
16877
39885
85247
28709
20344
93433
24201
40610
76493
```

Figure 6.2

A section of a computer-generated random numbers table for selecting five people from
a target population of 30. People chosen had numbers (in bold for this illustration)
17, 02, 09, 01, 10.

gender, socioeconomic status, age, or other factors that clearly define the original sample frame. Next, the researcher must draw another sample from
the target frame and choose the elements (people) that match the criteria of the
original sample. From this new sampling pool of matched participants, the
researcher can randomly choose subjects to replicate the study.

Systematic Random Sampling

Systematic random sampling is rarely used in evidence-based social work research because of its complexity and labor-intensive nature. Systematic random sampling is a technique used for creating a small random sample from a
large target group. For example, a researcher wants to study the experience of
all patients who had been hospitalized in a psychiatric hospital for the past 3
years. The total number of patients in this target group is 4,800. Given time
and budget constraints, sampling 10% of the target population proves to be not
feasible. A 10% sampling would require locating 480 patients, most of whom
were discharged from the hospital. In this case the *sampling ratio* is 0.1, which
means that the researcher must choose 10 patients for every 100 patients in the
target population.

A more feasible alternative method of sampling would be to decide on a
5% sample of 240 patients. This would give the researcher a sampling rate of
0.05, which means that the researcher must choose 5 patients out of every 100
patients in the target population.

Stratified Random Sampling

Using the previous example of studying 4,800 patients, the researcher may
be interested in experiences of these patients by their gender characteristics.
Because patient records contain the exact percentage of men, women, and
transgender patients, exact proportions can be obtained by dividing the sample into subgroups called *strata* and then sampling the appropriate proportion from each stratum. In this study the researcher would obtain patients for
each strata—men, women, and transgender and then choose randomly from
each stratum.

Cluster Sampling

When a researcher is not able to obtain a sampling frame (a complete list of all people in the target population to be studied), an alternative strategy is to use a cluster sampling. For example, if the researcher wants to study the attitudes of social workers toward older adult clients, the researcher contacts the National Association of Social Workers and asks for names and contact information for all social workers by state chapters. Therefore, the researcher divides the total population of social workers into state chapter members and then takes a random sample of state chapters and then random samples the members in each sampled cluster (state chapter) to obtain data. This is called a *one-stage cluster sampling*. A *two-stage cluster sampling* would be dividing the social workers into state chapters (clusters) and then sampling members from each selected state chapter.

Suppose a researcher wants to study the attitudes of older adults toward social workers who render psychotherapy to older adults in social work agencies in California and New York, which is a more specific population than the study discussed earlier. To find the population to study, a *multistage cluster sampling design* is employed. In this type of sampling, the researcher must engage in several steps of the sampling process.

First, the researcher must identify all mid- to large-size (staff of 40 workers or more) social service agencies in California and New York that have treatment programs for older adults. From this cluster of agencies, the researcher must identify the cities in which these social service agencies are located. From that cluster of cities, specific agencies must then be identified. Then agencies within the city clusters must be randomly sampled.

NONPROBABILITY SAMPLING

Availability or Convenience Sampling

Availability sampling is the most cost-effective method used in evidence-based social work research. The researcher using this type of sampling finds a convenient population using methods such as stopping people at a busy intersection to interview them, or choosing people in a shopping mall who pass a certain location. This type of accidental sampling has its problems. The researcher must be cautious about generalizing this sample to a target population due to the lack of specificity in the sample. For example, if the research study is on how people feel about the federal government cutting Medicare benefits to older people and the available sample is taken in a shopping mall outside a popular store for younger people, the results may be biased by the age of the people coming or leaving the store; the degree of ageism in the sample; the possible lack of knowledge about Medicare; and certainly, the lack of experience with Medicare.

Many social work researchers conduct survey studies with students in their classes. Although the data may produce interesting findings, it would be unwise to generalize these findings to students in the university or college setting. However, a case could be made for generalizing to social work students at the particular institution if the study was specific for students in a social work administration, social policy, or clinical track. Then the researcher may generalize the results to social work students.

Availability sampling is the most cost-effective method used in evidence-based social work research. The researcher using this type of sampling finds a convenient population using methods such as stopping people at a busy intersection to interview them, or choosing people in a shopping mall who pass a certain location.

Purposive Sampling

Purposive sampling is also called judgmental sampling. This type of sampling is used in preliminary studies that are exploratory, or might be used for testing a uniquely constructed questionnaire. In purposive sampling the researcher chooses subjects based on his or her knowledge of the target population for the study. Though this research does not create a true representative sample, it is still useful as a pilot or pretest study. For example, if a researcher wants to study runaway adolescents, he or she might solicit safe houses where these adolescents reside and have the staff members choose a certain number of adolescents in each house based on their knowledge of the adolescent residents.

Another variation on this study would be the researcher soliciting social work professionals who service runaway adolescents in safe houses or other community settings. The researcher then picks what he or she feels are those professionals who are most knowledgeable about the needs of these adolescents. Then an exploratory study can be made assessing the service needs of runaway adolescents based on the expertise of this purposeful sample of social work professionals. Another type of purposeful sampling is paradoxical. A researcher interested in the etiology of spousal domestic violence might study the children in families where there is spousal domestic violence and compare them to children from families where there is no spousal domestic violence. The children would be followed into adulthood and an assessment would be made on whether children who witnessed spousal domestic violence in turn commit spousal domestic violence.

Quota Sampling

When collecting a quota sample, the researcher begins by constructing a matrix that describes the target population with the greatest specificity to increase the likelihood of a true representation of the target population. Examples of the cells in the matrix would be gender, ethnicity, age, socioeconomic status, geographic (urban, suburban, rural), and so on.

Once the matrix is established, the researcher tries to identify what proportion of each of the cells is found in the target population. Once the proportion is determined, the researcher collects data from people who have the characteristics for each cell in the matrix. The researcher then applies a technique called *weighting*. Weighting is a method where people are assigned weights in such a manner as to make the sample representative of the target population from which it is drawn. The mathematical weight is based on unequal probability contained in each person for meeting the criteria for each cell when sampled. This weighting enables the researcher to adjust the sample to be representative of the target population.

Quota sampling is vulnerable to errors. If the researcher's diligence is lax in determining the proportions of the target population for each cell in the matrix, then true representativeness is not achieved. The number of cells in the matrix that describes the composition of the target population may be limited and not fully represent the target population. Therefore, when selecting subjects, the researcher may miss vital characteristics of the target population by being guided by a limited matrix, for example, not addressing the political affiliation of a research subject, or not addressing the type of housing he or she lives in. The final type of problem that may contaminate the quota sample is poor training of interviewers employed by the researcher to obtain the sample data. If not properly supervised, the interviewers may neglect certain subjects because it is inconvenient for them or they are difficult to interview, or an interviewer rushed to finish his or her task and may neglect to strictly follow the matrix for the sample.

Snowball Sampling

Imagine making a snowball using readily available snow while standing at the top of a steep snow-covered hill. Next, you let the snowball roll down the hill where it gathers additional snow, becoming larger and larger. This is a metaphor for how snowball sampling works. Snowball sampling is usually employed when the target population to be sampled from is difficult to locate. Many social work researchers use this technique when studying the homeless population in a geographic area. In this sampling, the researcher first locates a few homeless individuals representing the target population of homeless people, and then asks them to identify other homeless people they know so that the researcher may add them to the study. This is considered an *interactive sampling process* where the researcher interacts with the subjects to find new subjects. This process continues, gathering more and more homeless people until the desired sample size is reached. Unfortunately, this procedure may lack specificity of representativeness of the target population, is usually reserved for exploratory research studies, and is often used in qualitative research studies.

BIAS IN SAMPLING

Research-Based Practice

Critical Thinking Question: What are the benefits and drawbacks to using probability and nonprobability sampling methods for clinical or agency-based practices?

Sampling bias takes many forms. If a sampling frame is selected that is less inclusive than the researcher has anticipated, many types of people may have been excluded from the sampling frame. For example, when sampling a list of clients in a hospital setting, the list provided by the administrator may include only inpatients, and not include outpatients, or day surgery patients.

Many times a researcher may decide to use a survey method to derive data, which rely on respondents to provide answers to questions. Ideally, the respondent would answer the questions truthfully. However, many respondents may give false information out of fear of self-identifying, may rush through the survey not responding to some questions or making up answers, or may resent how the interviewer instructs them and consequently become uncooperative.

In research where interviewers are used to collect data from a sample, interviewers may have biases, false information, or stereotypes that affect the way in which they interact with the sample subjects. This is called *interviewer bias*. Interviewers may also make errors when collecting data. The risk of this occurring can be reduced somewhat by rigorous interviewer training. A most repugnant form of *interviewer error* occurs when an interviewer, who is under the pressure to publish or perish, makes up data to avoid the hard work of finding and interviewing subjects, or produces false data.

Respondents may cause *respondent error*. Respondents may want to please or annoy the researcher and consequently skew their responses to achieve their goal. These responses could include refusing to respond to the study in whole or part.

The instrument may also cause a sampling bias called *instrument error*. For example, a survey questionnaire may appear to be too long, causing some respondents to refuse to participate, which in turn produces a lower response rate. The survey questionnaire may be written in an unclear style or have ambiguous terms that will cause respondents to give misleading data. The language in the questionnaire may be confusing or not understandable to people from other cultures who employ different words or terms for the same meaning (Boynton, Wood, & Greenhalgh, 2004). In addition, the questionnaire may be littered with professional jargon that is not understood by the respondents, producing unreliable data.

DETERMINING SAMPLE SIZE

Most social work research is conducted with meager financial resources. Therefore, the size of the sample is determined by the number of people that can be sampled within the constraints of the research budget. Many research textbooks suggest using sampling tables that specify permissible errors. These permissible errors are, called the *margin of error*. The margin of error is the amount of sampling error that the researcher is willing to endure. The typical margin of error in research studies is 5%, meaning that the data may vary five points either positively or negatively. The margin of error is related to the *confidence level*. The confidence level indicates how often you can expect to replicate similar results when the study is repeated. For example, with a 95% confidence level a researcher can predict that if the study were repeated 100 times, the repeated studies would deviate from the findings only in 5 of the 100 repetitions. This 95% level is the most common confidence level used in social work research.

Rubin and Babbie (2010) suggest another method for determining the sample size for probability sampling. They indicate that the researcher should consider the minimum number of subjects needed to mathematically satisfy the statistical tests used in the data analysis. They suggest "multiplying the number of variables to be simultaneously analyzed by the minimum number of cases per variable required by the appropriate statistical procedure" (p. 352). Therefore, as an example, for multiple regression analysis 10 subjects are needed for each variable being studied. If the researcher were studying social work students by specialty, then 10 students would be needed for the administration track, 10 students for the policy track, 10 students for the clinical track, and 10 students for the gerontology track. Therefore, a minimum number of students for this study would be a total of 40 students.

Galtung (1967) suggests the following formula for determining sample size:

$$r^n \times 20 = \text{sample size}$$

In this equation, r equals the number of values in each predictor variable and n refers to the number of variables.

An example of this would be a study of social workers' attitudes toward psychiatric clients. The independent variable, social workers, would have three values—BSW, MSW, and PhD. The antecedent variable, gender, would have three values—male, female, and transgender. Therefore, $r = 6$ and $n = 2$. $6^2 \times 20 = 36 \times 20 = 720$. Galtung (1967) finds that this formula works when each of the variables has the same number of values. This study with 720 subjects is ideal. However, due to financial and logistical constraints in social work research, most studies have a minimum of 100 subjects in the sample.

HUMAN RIGHTS AND SOCIAL JUSTICE CONSIDERATIONS

Ethical Practice

Critical Thinking Question: In what ways can social workers use research ethics and human rights and social justice to choose a study sample?

Many concerns regarding EBP must be considered when a social worker selects a sample. Furman (2006) feels that quantitative evidence-based studies do not give the insights that qualitative research provides. Therefore, the nosology of quantitative research using concepts such as reliability and validity may give a false perception of the clinical or administrative reality being studied. The argument is that qualitative studies bring depth of insight and are *metaphorically generalizable* (Stein, 2004). Furman and Bender (2003) caution that quantitative EBP is skewed by the research to favor individual treatment diluting social work mezzo and macro practice skills, and corresponding insights in the social work curriculum. Butler, Ford, and Tregaskis (2007) express concern that samples in evidence-based research focus on the persons receiving service, or the programs administrated by agencies, leaving little emphasis on social workers' conscious use of self, which is a fundamental concept in the social worker–client relationship. This fact may lead to maltreatment or underservice of many multicultural populations due to the practitioners' lack of multicultural knowledge, stereotypic biases, and use of inappropriate treatment approaches for some multicultural populations (La Roche & Christopher, 2009). Because this dyad is a primary interpersonal vehicle for change, a greater emphasis in EBP is needed when selecting social workers as the *target population* for study. A target population is "a set of elements (people) larger than or different from the population that was sampled and to which the researcher would like to somewhat generalize any study findings" (Engel & Schutt, 2005, p. 106). Therefore, the basic assumption of sampling is that a small set of elements (*sampling units*) can lend information about a larger population (target population).

Sampling bias often leads a social worker to study clinical techniques or create social policy that leads to underservicing of vulnerable populations. For example, most intake interviews in social service organizations indicate clients' gender as male or female. Often this decision is made by the social worker based on whether clients look like a man or woman. Very few social workers ask clients how they perceive their gender, or indicate if some clients identify themselves as transgender.

Identification of transgender individuals is essential because this population is consistently underserved and understudied by health care providers (Bockting, Robinson, & Rosser, 1998). Kenagy (2005) finds from a survey administered to 113 male-to-female individuals and 69 female-to-male individuals that about three-fifths of respondents had engaged in unprotected sex during the past 12 months, that the risk for HIV infection from unprotected sex was significantly higher among respondents of color than among white respondents, and that 30.1% of respondents had attempted suicide. More than half of respondents had been forced to have sex, 56.3% had experienced violence in their homes, and 51.3% had been physically abused. Twenty-six percent of respondents had been denied medical care because they were transgender (pp. 22–24). These findings suggest that screening for transgender individuals as a gender category is essential because of the vulnerability that appears in this population.

Therefore, there is an ethical imperative for social workers engaging in research and evaluation activities to question how samples are drawn and how such samples lead to the promotion of human rights in vulnerable populations (Gruskin & Ferguson, 2009). In addition to questioning the composition of a research sample, colleges and universities and organizations must consider including ongoing training for all students and staff members in the importance of being sensitive to human rights issues. Particularly, students and staff members should be trained in the importance of understanding that any study should be oriented to identifying when the concept of equal values for all people is not upheld and how some vulnerable populations are maltreated or underserved (Hall, Backman, & Fitchett, 2010).

Research-Based Practice

Critical Thinking Question:
In what ways can social work practice be informed by social work research?

SUMMARY

Evidence-based research bridges the gap between expectation and experience of a social worker by providing evidence based experiential information to a less experienced clinician or policy maker. It is the practice of choice taught in social work education. To construct a research study, the researcher needs to sample a population of interest. A sample is a subset of the population of interest (target population). Many methods are used in selecting a sample, each with the goal of generalizing findings to the population from which the sample was drawn.

There are many concerns about generalizing in quantitative research. Using concepts such as reliability and validity may give a false perception of the findings. The counterargument is that qualitative research brings a depth of insight that is metaphorically generalizable. In addition, quantitative evidence-based research is mostly skewed in favor of individual treatment, which ultimately neglects mezzo and macro practice knowledge. In addition, most studies are on clients, or programs serving clients, with little emphasis on social workers and their experience working with clients.

Different types of populations are used for sampling in social work research. Universal populations, which include everyone, are not often used in social work research unless the researcher is using census data. Most research uses populations of interest (target populations), the details of which may be embedded in census data or agency setting. Once the target population is identified, the researcher chooses people by constructing a sampling frame using one of the techniques discussed in this chapter.

Generalizability is an important concept in sampling. This concept implies that the sample chosen for study represents the population from which it was sampled, allowing the researcher to use the findings discovered in the sample and assume that these findings are consistent with the population from which it is drawn.

All sampling techniques contain some form of sampling error, which occurs when a difference exists in one or more characteristics between the sample being studied and the target population from which it is drawn. The larger the sampling error, the further the researcher moves from being able to generalize the research findings to the target population.

Homogeneity is a concept that approximates the idea that the sample chosen has identical characteristics to the population from which it is drawn. In social work research the elements of study are people. Because people are differentiated by many variables such as gender, age, socioeconomic status, health status, and so on, human research is somewhat skewed to being heterogeneous requiring the researcher to draw larger samples and to have the research replicated to support the generalization of his or her findings.

Representativeness implies that the sample being studied is representative of the target population from which it is drawn. Sampling bias is a systematic distortion of a research sample that prevents it from being fully representative of the population from which it is drawn. A biased sample is either an over-representation or an underrepresentation of certain variables relative to the population being studied.

Probability sampling methods are the most common techniques used when a researcher wants to generalize the results of a study to the population sampled. Based on probability theory, the central assumption is that there is a mathematical likelihood that an event will occur. Each member of the target population must have the same known, nonzero probability of being selected into the sample.

Nonprobability sampling methods are considered less reliable and are fraught with sampling errors. However, because these sampling methods are cost-effective and less labor intensive, they are often used in evidence-based social work research. The four nonprobability sampling methods are availability (convenience) sampling, purposive sampling, quota sampling, and snowball sampling.

There are many types of bias in sampling. For example, the sampling frame may be less inclusive than the researcher anticipated. When responding to a survey, respondents may give false information, make up answers, or be uncooperative. Research interviewers may have bias, false information, or stereotypes that affect the way they interact with the sample subjects, further compounding the flaws in the sampling method. The worst form of error is where the interviewer, when being under pressure to publish or perish, makes up data to avoid work, or produces false data results. The instrument used to question respondents may be too long, have unclear or ambiguous terms, be filled with professional jargon, or be culturally confusing.

Sample size determination is difficult because the ideal sample sizes are often large and therefore unavailable to social work researchers who have meager financial resources or find the data collection from large sample sizes too labor-intensive. Two direct methods for determining sample size were discussed.

Succeed with PEARSON mysocialworklab

Log onto **www.mysocialworklab.com** to access a wealth of case studies, videos, and assessment. (*If you did not receive an access code to* **MySocialWorkLab** *with this text and wish to purchase access online, please visit* www.mysocialworklab.com.)

1. **Watch the engage in research-informed practice and practice-informed research video "Engaging in Research Informed Practice."** Describe three

sampling methods and how they can contribute to a social worker's assessment of an appropriate evidence-based therapy.

2. **Watch the practice context video "Keeping Up With Shifting Contexts."** After you have viewed this video, has your awareness about changing practice concepts influenced your approach to developing a research sample?

PRACTICE TEST The following questions will test your knowledge of the content found within this chapter. For additional assessment, including licensing-exam type questions on applying chapter content to practice, visit **MySocialWorkLab**.

1. Handpicking elements to represent a population is used in which kind of sampling?
   a. Quota
   b. Snowball
   c. Random
   d. Purposive

2. A practitioner who is interested in studying the relationship between gender and depression chooses clients who happen to be in the treatment center that day. This is an example of a:
   a. Random sample
   b. Accidental or convenience sample
   c. Cluster sample
   d. Disproportionate sample

3. When a practitioner is concerned that an insufficient number of persons in a particular subgroup of the population will be included in the survey, the best kind of sample to use would be:
   a. Simple random
   b. Accidental
   c. Stratified random
   d. Systematic random

4. Every *k*th element in a list is chosen for inclusion in the sample in
   a. Disproportionate sampling
   b. Cluster sampling
   c. Systematic sampling
   d. Convenience sampling

5. A social work practitioner wishes to study the effects of cognitive behavior therapy on clients suffering from depression. Unfortunately, the mental health center he is working at has a majority of clients who are White and from a middle-income population. To generalize the results from his study to the population in general, what must he do to increase multicultural representation in his study sample to be consistent with current practice standards?

ASSESS YOUR COMPETENCE Use the scale below to rate your current level of achievement on the following concepts or skills associated with each competency presented in the chapter:

1	2	3
I can accurately describe the concept or skill	I can consistently identify the concept or skill when observing and analyzing practice activities	I can competently implement the concept or skill in my own practice

_____ can demonstrate knowledge of research sampling in designing studies to inform practice.

_____ can apply strategies of research sampling from studies to inform my research practice.

_____ can provide leadership in promoting multicultural sensitivity in research sampling.

_____ can employ social justice principles when constructing research samples.

7

Tapping the Scientist Within: Quantitative Research Methods for Social Work

CHAPTER OUTLINE

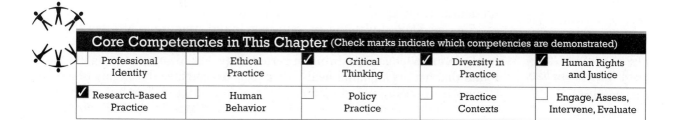

	Core Competencies in This Chapter (Check marks indicate which competencies are demonstrated)								
	Professional Identity		Ethical Practice	✓	Critical Thinking	✓	Diversity in Practice	✓	Human Rights and Justice
✓	Research-Based Practice		Human Behavior		Policy Practice		Practice Contexts		Engage, Assess, Intervene, Evaluate

INTRODUCTION

Quantitative research is a research process that converts data into a numerical form so that observations and results can be analyzed statistically. This type of research is based on deductive reasoning, which causes the researcher to develop testable hypotheses and operational definitions of concepts derived from theories that contain a variety of concepts and propositions. Once testable hypotheses are determined, the practitioner tests the hypotheses by making observations and statistically determines whether the hypotheses are true (significant), or not (null hypothesis). Deductive reasoning is the opposite approach to inductive reasoning used in qualitative research. In inductive reasoning, theory emerges from the data. As more data are collected, the theory that emerges is continuously shaped and redefined. This type of reasoning is called *grounded theory*.

In order for social workers to understand the quantitative research process, this chapter uses a research study to demonstrate the various aspects and principles of this type of research. In this study, the practitioner identified that, after reading in numerous evidence based research articles, mental health professionals who treat older adults have little knowledge or training in gerontology. Therefore, the practitioner decided to study the various types of mental health professionals—social workers, psychologists, psychiatrists, and psychiatric nurses—to understand their degree of knowledge of older adults. We will illustrate the various steps a practitioner takes to prepare a quantitative research study, to execute the study, and to statistically test the research hypotheses using a recently completed study that explored mental health practitioners' knowledge of older adults (Youdin, 2010).

THE ANATOMY OF A QUANTITATIVE STUDY

Many aspects of a quantitative study are discussed in detail in other chapters. The following are brief descriptions of the many parts and procedures of a quantitative study.

The Literature Review

The literature review is a critical first step in establishing what research questions the practitioner should ask. By searching the literature, the practitioner determines whether other researchers have already answered the research questions he or she has in mind. In addition, the practitioner learns from this review how others have approached similar research questions, which, in turn, aids him or her in constructing a research design that provides answers to the research questions he or she generates. The techniques for conducting a literature review are covered in detail in chapter 5.

For the KOP study, the practitioner found numerous articles that addressed different aspects of the problem of mental health professionals having little knowledge or training in gerontology. For example, Corrigan (2007) found that having a mental health diagnosis exacerbates the stigma of mental illness in the diagnosed client. This type of stigma further oppresses an older adult who, because of age, is already stigmatized. Williams (2007)

Research-Based Practice

Critical Thinking Question: How does quantitative research bridge the gap between research and practice, and how does practice inform the quantitative researcher?

The literature review is a critical first step in establishing what research questions the practitioner should ask. By searching the literature, the practitioner determines whether other researchers have already answered the research questions he or she has in mind. In addition, the practitioner learns from this review how others have approached similar research questions, which, in turn, aids him or her in constructing a research design that provides answers to the research questions he or she generates.

indicates that clinicians need to challenge the stereotype of aging, as perceived by most, of a very old-aged adult by understanding the inner experience of an older adult, and his or her social environment and cultural context. Komiti, Judd, and Jackson (2006) describe the many problems that arise when an older adult seeks mental health services from a general practitioner who is biased by stereotypes of older adults, which consequently influence his or her attitude toward the older adult patient. Jopling (2007) advocates for equal treatment for older adults who can be discriminated against in a hospital setting because of age, without the same protections people have against discrimination because of gender, disability, religion, or sexual orientation, to name a few. Cummings and Galambos (2002) studied social work students who more often than not are reluctant to work with older adults after graduation from their social work programs.

These examples of the information are unearthed in a literature review. In the KOP study, the practitioner did an extensive literature review, which set the stage for the identification of the research questions for the study.

Choosing a Scale

A scale is designed to measure one or more concepts of the relationship between variables. Some researchers use preexisting scales that have a high degree of validity and reliability. Researchers who construct their own scales must establish the validity and reliability of their scale. The advantage of using a scale is that the practitioner may ask several questions that measure a single concept.

For example, in the KOP study the Knowledge of Older People (KOP) scale contains 20 statements that define mental health professionals' degree of accuracy in assessing whether empirical statements about older people are true or false. For example, most old people are really no different from anybody else. They are as easy to understand as younger people. The majority of old people feel miserable most of the time. Normative statements are from a Revised Facts on Aging Quiz developed by Palmore (1988), and statements from a questionnaire developed by Kogan (1961) for studying negative attitudes toward the elderly. Respondents in this study achieved a "knowledge of older people" total score (KOP) ranging from 20 through 120, with 120 indicating the highest degree of accuracy in correctly determining whether normative statements are true or false and 20 indicating a complete failure to make such discriminations. Scores were derived from a six-item Likert scale. Responses were measured by asking respondents to check whether they felt a statement was definitely false, most likely false, possibly false, possibly true, most likely true, and definitely true. Scores for each statement ranged from 1 through 6. Scores for correctly identifying a false statement about older people were reversed, making positive and negative scores consistent. Scores for each respondent represent the total points scored.

If a scale, whether preexisting or constructed by the practitioner, is found to have statements that measure more than one concept, it is considered a *multidimensional scale*. When the practitioner detects a multidimensional scale, he or she must start again from the original concept and revise the target of the study. In some cases, a multidimensional scale may be constructed to measure more than one concept until consensus is reached on a single concept.

Reliability and Validity

Reliability is a measurement procedure that yields consistent scores when the concept being measured remains the same. Reliability may also occur when the measurement procedure yields a change in scores that is consistent with the change in the concept over time. In order to test for validity, reliability must be established in the measurement.

Reliability is a measurement procedure that yields consistent scores when the concept being measured remains the same. Reliability may also occur when the measurement procedure yields a change in scores that is consistent with the change in the concept over time. To test for validity (discussed on the following pages), reliability must be established in the measurement. If a measurement procedure is not significantly affected by chance variation or random error, it is reliable. The five basic types of reliability are alternate-forms reliability, internal consistency reliability, interobserver reliability, intraobserver reliability, and test-retest reliability.

Alternate-forms reliability occurs when the practitioner compares a subject's response to different survey questions addressing the same concept. Another strategy is to reverse the order of questions, reverse the order of the scale, or change the wording of questions given to different subjects while keeping the concept the same. In the KOP study, subjects were given one of four different versions of the same survey in order to compare response patterns, which indicated that the KOP scale was reliable.

Internal consistency reliability occurs when the practitioner constructs a survey that has multiple measures measuring the same concept. In this design, the practitioner is able to ascertain whether statements measuring the same concept are highly associated with one another. In the KOP study, responses were evaluated for empirical statements measuring positive or negative statements about older people. Positive statements were found to be highly associated with one another, as were negative statements. However, positive statements were not highly associated with negative statements as they were two distinct concepts.

Interobserver reliability occurs when more than one observer measures the same event using the same measuring instrument. If the measurements across the observers are relatively the same, then the practitioner has a good degree of confidence that the measurement instrument is reliable. This technique for assessing reliability is used primarily where the measurement instrument being used is looking at complex phenomena that require many levels of judgment. For example, if a social worker wants to study the social interaction of several children and requires measurements of physical interaction, verbal interaction, and eye contact, the rater is involved in a complex task. This requires diligent training of the raters to ensure reliability of the measurements. If several raters observing the same children have similar results, then the practitioner can presume that the measurement instrument is reliable.

Intraobserver reliability occurs when the same observer measures the same concept at two different points in time. Clinicians who make clinical judgments at different points in time using one or more measurements often use this type of reliability testing. For example, a clinical social worker may assess a client at two points in time using an Axis IV determination for psychosocial stressors and a global assessment of functioning. If repeated in a relatively short period, the ratings should be highly associated which would indicate intraobserver reliability.

Test-retest reliability occurs when a researcher administers a scale to the same group on more than one occasion over a specified period of time. If the instrument used produces consistent results, then the researcher considers the instrument reliable. While there may be some individuals within the group tested that have non-consistent changes in their test scores, the majority of the group tested should show consistent scores.

A practitioner must consider many types of validity indicators when designing a study. A concept measured in a quantitative design must be related to other valid concepts of the same measurement. This is called *measurement validity*. To test measurement validity, a practitioner employs one or more of four different validation subtypes: content validity, construct validity, criterion validity, and face validity.

Content validity occurs when the practitioner establishes that he or she is measuring a concept that has a meaning that is all encompassing. To assess content validity the practitioner relies on a comprehensive literature review of the same concept in conjunction with gathering opinions about the content validity from colleagues expert in the same content area. The KOP study used an extensive literature review and the questionnaire was pretested on 10 colleagues, two each, representing the five mental health professional subgroups studied. These colleagues were not participants in the KOP study. Each colleague indicated that the KOP scale was all encompassing in its measurement of knowledge of factual statements about older people.

Construct validity requires the practitioner to demonstrate that the measure used is related to other measures as specified in a theory, in this case, grounded in social work theory. These measures must be from deductive research so that comparisons can be made between the measurements in the practitioner's study and measurements from other studies under the same theoretical umbrella. Construct validity may also be tested by comparing a similar measurement in other studies measuring the same concept, and measuring different concepts. If the measure correlates highly with the same concept, and has a low correlation with different concepts, the practitioner may use achievement of construct validity. For example, if the KOP scale was compared to other scales that predict knowledge of older people with similar results (convergent validity), and if compared to scales that measure knowledge of children, adolescents, or young adults that do not show similar results, then construct validity was achieved.

Criterion validity occurs when scores of one measurement are compared to already validated measurements of the same concept and the results are the same. For example, scores from a test predicting future success in law school can be compared to the degree of success in law school as evidenced by academic grades. This is called *predictive validity*. If two measurements are taken at the same period of time and the same results occur, this is called *concurrent validity*. For example, if a client who admits to abusing cannabis and at the same time is immediately administered a urine test that indicates recent cannabis use, concurrent validity is achieved.

Face validity is a less formal measurement of validity. It relies on the practitioner's ability to evaluate the measure and, through careful observation, feel that it is appropriate on face value. For example, if a practitioner chooses to observe (i.e., count) how many women and men purchase gerontology books at certain designated book stores, the face observation would be the direct count of the number of gerontology books purchased by women and men. However, although the practitioner is confident about the measure, the conclusions of face validity may be false because many people purchase gerontology books through Internet retailers, which may produce different results.

A concept measured in a quantitative design must be related to other valid concepts of the same measurement.

Identifying Variables to Study

In order for the practitioner to explain concepts that are being studied, he or she must identify many different types of variables that represent these concepts. Once the concepts have been represented as variables, the practitioner will develop research questions and hypotheses about the relationships between the variables.

In order for the practitioner to explain concepts that are being studied, he or she must identify many different types of variables that represent these concepts (Figure 7.1). Once the concepts have been represented as variables, the practitioner will develop research questions and hypotheses about the relationships between the variables. The first task for the practitioner is to identify the independent and dependent variables. This is the most basic relationship between variables found in a quantitative study. The *independent variable* explains or makes changes in another variable. The variable that the independent variable changes or explains is called the *dependent variable.*

In the KOP study, the independent variable is a mental health professional. This is based on the concept of a mental health professional. Within the concept of a mental health professional are *attributes*. These attributes are social worker, psychologist, psychiatrist, and psychiatric nurse. The dependent variable is the KOP scale. Therefore, the type or different attributes of a mental health professional determine scores on the KOP scale, which measures mental health professionals' knowledge of older people.

In addition to ascertaining the independent and dependent variables, social workers must consider other variables. These antecedent variables and intervening variables are important because they may have a predictable effect on the independent variable by creating possible subattributes of the attributes of the independent variable. For example, if the independent variable's concept is a social work student, the attributes of the independent variable may be a BSW student, an MSW student, or a PhD student. Subattributes may be created when considering gender. A BSW student may be a man, woman, or transgender. The same subattributes may be found significant for MSW and/or PhD students.

Antecedent variables are concepts that one brings to the event, task, or situation being measured. For example, many studies are interested in the effect age, ethnicity, and gender have on the independent variable. In the KOP study, the age variable had attributes of 18–25 years, 25–40 years, 40–65 years, 65–75 years, and 75+ years. The ethnicity variable had attributes of African American, Asian American or Pacific Islander, White, Latino, Native American or Alaska Native, Russian-speaking, and others. The gender variable had attributes of male, female, and transgender.

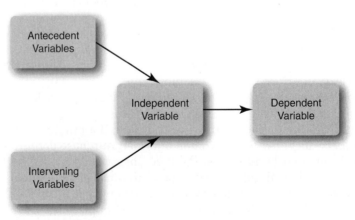

Figure 7.1
Types of Variables Found in a Quantitative Research Study

Intervening variables are variables that influence the independent variable at the time of the study. In the KOP study, the intervening variables were the type of agency the mental health professionals work in and the type of gerontology training the mental health professionals may have had. The attributes of the agency type were inpatient, outpatient, and psychiatric emergency screening center. The attributes of gerontology training were undergraduate course; graduate course; postgraduate workshop; supervision, less than 3 hours; supervision, more than 3 hours; and others.

Research Questions

The basic task for a practitioner in developing research questions is to take a broad topic of interest and to dissect it into specific questions that address the aspects of the broad topic to be researched (Figure 7.2). The broad topic of interest in the KOP study is the knowledge that mental health professionals have about the older adults they serve. However, this topic is too broad and does not illustrate its specific aspects that the practitioner wants to study. The practitioner derives research questions from the literature review, anecdotal experience, suggestions from colleagues expert in the broad topic of interest, and from social work theory.

The following are the research questions that the practitioner generated after considerations derived from the literature review, discussions with colleagues, and gerontological theories of ageism:

1. How do socio-demographic aspects of mental health professionals contribute to their degree of accuracy in assessing true and false empirical statements about older people?

2. Is there a difference in degree of accuracy in assessing true and false empirical statements about older people among counseling psychologists, psychiatric nurses, psychiatrists, psychologists, and social workers?

3. Does agency setting influence mental health professionals' degree of accuracy in assessing true and false empirical statements about older people?

4. How does prior professional training and specialized education in gerontology influence mental health professionals' degree of accuracy in assessing true and false empirical statements about older people?

Creating Hypotheses

Hypotheses are predictive statements the practitioner makes before collecting data for the study. These statements are derived from the theoretical ideas discovered in the comprehensive literature review. Each hypothesis predicts a

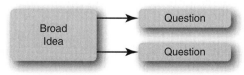

Figure 7.2
Research Questions—From a Broad Idea to Specific Questions

relationship between two or more variables. The content of the hypothesis might predict that when one variable increases then the other decreases. Alternatively, the relationship between the variables may be curvilinear, or increase or decrease together. Once the data for the study are analyzed, the practitioner determines whether to accept or reject each hypothesis.

The following are the hypotheses for the KOP study:

1. Mental health professionals who have specialized training in gerontology will have higher KOP scores than those without such training.

2. Psychiatric nurses and social workers will have higher KOP scores than psychologists and psychiatrists.

3. Older mental health professionals will have higher KOP scores than younger mental health professionals.

4. Mental health professionals working in psychiatric emergency screening centers will have higher KOP scores than mental health professionals working in inpatient and outpatient agencies.

5. Female mental health professionals will have higher KOP scores than male or transgender mental health professionals.

6. White mental health professionals will have higher KOP scores than African American, Asian American or Pacific Islander, Latino, Native American or Alaska Native, or Russian-speaking mental health professionals.

Determining the Type of Study

There are many types of research studies that the practitioner must consider: descriptive research, exploratory research, explanatory research, and evaluation research. In *descriptive research,* the practitioner first observes an event, a clinical situation, or a social circumstance. Then, the practitioner describes what he or she observed. In quantitative research, descriptive research is often conducted by taking a poll. An example would be studying what types of social work students enroll in gerontology courses nationwide. Many points of description—such as gender, age, prior experience with older adults, the fluctuation in the rate of enrollment in gerontology courses from year to year, percentage of social work faculty members who teach gerontology courses—are collected about the students. The data for this type of research can be quantitative by reducing observations to numbers for statistical evaluation, or it can be qualitative by producing a deep narration of the experience of faculty members and students taking gerontology courses.

A practitioner may be interested in collecting data on a topic to identify new information about it that has not been extensively studied; this type of research is called *exploratory research.* The information collected is relatively unstructured and is used to learn about what is happening in the phenomena being studied. Exploratory research sets a foundation for other practitioners to undertake comprehensive follow-up studies on the findings from the initial exploratory study.

When a practitioner is interested in studying what causes phenomena and what subsequent social effects are produced by these phenomena, this type of research is called *explanatory research.* The KOP study is an explanatory research study. This study is designed to define the influence that socio-demographic aspects, personal and professional characteristics, and false information about older people have on mental health professionals' knowledge about the older adults they serve. The purpose is to analyze the causal relationship among variables that were not manipulated by this researcher and their subsequent effect on mental health professionals' knowledge of older people.

Another important type of social work research is evaluation research. Many practitioners call this type of research *practice evaluation*. This type of social research focuses on social policies and/or agency programs, and interventions. When using this type of research, the practitioner often simultaneously explores, describes, and explains the effects of a social policy or program on target populations. In addition, this type of research is predictive when it attempts to explain how a change in one phenomenon in a policy or program will affect other phenomena. A detailed description of program evaluation research is found in chapter 11.

Creating a Model of the Study

Once the type of research study is determined, it is helpful to diagram the various elements of the research study (Figure 7.3). This diagram should represent the variables to be studied.

Figure 7.3 represents an exploratory model of the potential contributing factors that influence mental health professionals when assessing whether empirical statements about older people are true or false. Mental health professionals were subdivided into the particular type of mental health professional by type of mental health practice. Age, ethnicity, and gender represent personal characteristics that mental health professionals bring to their professional training. Gerontology training and agency setting represent the environmental influence

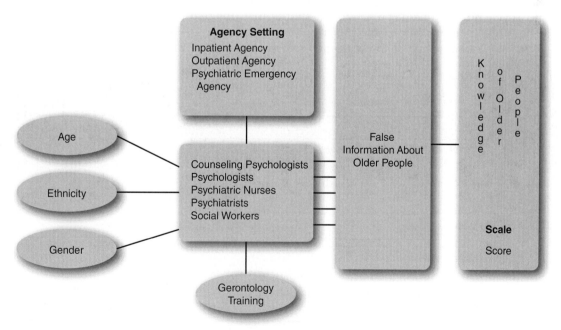

Figure 7.3

Degree of Accuracy in Assessing Whether Empirical Statements About Older People Are True or False on the type of mental health professional. The KOP scale measures the degree of accuracy in mental health professionals' assessments of whether empirical statements about older people are true or false. Employment of false information causes lower KOP accuracy scores.

Creating the Sampling Plan

The creation of a sampling plan is an essential element in the construction of a research study. Because people are the basic *units of analysis* in social work research, a clear plan must be articulated on which people will be studied, and how they will be located for the study. In the KOP study, the people being studied (target population) are mental health professionals. The *study population* of mental health professional is psychiatric nurses, psychiatrists, psychologists, and social workers.

Mental health professionals are defined as:

1. Psychiatric nurses holding a BSN or an MSN
2. Psychiatrists holding a DO, MD, or MD-PhD
3. Psychologists holding a PhD or PsyD
4. Social workers holding a BSW, an MSW, a DSW, or PhD

The next task in making a sample to study is to identify where the sample is located. In the KOP study, the psychiatric nurses, psychiatrists, psychologists, and social workers were sampled from three types of agencies. The agency types were inpatient psychiatric, outpatient mental health, and psychiatric emergency screening agencies located in New Jersey and New York.

There are many types of samples used in research. These types of sampling were explained in detail in chapter 6. In the KOP study, a stratified, disproportional sample was studied. This sample was stratified by the type of mental health professional (psychologist, social worker, etc.). Sampling by mental health professional type produced subpopulations that differed in size. The size of the samples reflects the different population sizes of mental health professional subtypes in the agency settings studied (Figure 7.4).

	f	%	Cumulative (%)
Subtype			
Counseling Psychologist	15	10.6	10.6
Psychiatric Nurse	25	17.7	28.4
Psychiatrist	16	11.3	39.7
Psychologist	13	9.2	48.9
Social Worker	72	51.1	100.0
Agency			
Inpatient	44	31.2	31.2
Outpatient	78	55.3	86.5
Psychiatric Emergency Screening Center	19	13.5	100.0

Figure 7.4
Different Population Sizes of Mental Health Professional Subtypes in Agency Settings

Schedule, Data Collection Plan, Assurance of Confidentiality, and Debriefing Plan

Before initiating the study, the practitioner must have a clear plan indicating the schedule for all the events of the study, a data collection plan, safeguards to assure all subjects of their confidentiality and that no harm is intended to occur as a result of the study, and debriefing.

The following is the schedule, data collection plan, assurance of confidentiality, and a plan for debriefing:

1. *Data collection*—Data were collected over a period of 2 months; questionnaires were administered at a rate of 13–25 per agency. The respondents took approximately 45 minutes to complete the questionnaires.

2. *Distribution and collection of questionnaires*—All questionnaires were distributed and collected by a designated agency representative at each agency to control biases that may result from the distribution and collection of questionnaires by the practitioner.

3. *Anonymity assurance*—Only summary data were used, and subject names were not required. Upon completion of the questionnaire, the respondent placed it in a self-seal envelope, provided during distribution, to ensure anonymity.

4. *Debriefing*—Subjects were told that when the study is completed they have the option to be debriefed by the practitioner who will tell them the purpose of the study, the methods used, and the findings of the study. In addition, the practitioner told the subjects he would ask the subject to describe their experience with the study. In the case of a subject having a negative experience, the practitioner told the subject that he or she might be referred for appropriate counseling.

Response Rate

Rubin and Babbie (2010) indicate that a response rate of 74% is *very good*, significantly reducing the problem of response bias. A poor rate of return would produce the possibility of a biased sample that is not representative of the target population for the research study. In the KOP study, 160 questionnaires were distributed to inpatient, outpatient, and psychiatric emergency screening agencies in New Jersey and New York. Designated representatives at each agency studied collected all questionnaires, complete or not completed. Eligibility was determined by initial qualifying questions in the questionnaire that identify whether a subject is a counseling psychologist, psychiatric nurse, psychiatrist, psychologist, or social worker.

The researcher received 141 questionnaires from the agencies, for a response rate of 88%.

Instrumentation

The practitioner must decide on the measurement instrument to use for the research study. Because of the comprehensive literature on instrumentation, the practitioner may choose to use an instrument that is well established in the literature and has precise indications of its reliability and validity.

162

Alternatively, the practitioner may want to develop his or her own measurement instrument for the dependent variable. In either case, the practitioner must assess the feasibility of administration of the instrument and should ask the following questions before using it. Is the instrument too cumbersome, causing a poor response rate? If the instrument is not a survey instrument, and requires direct observation by the researcher, is there adequate time available to conduct the observations? Is the instrument sensitive enough to adequately measure the dependent variable? Does the instrument contain clear instructions that are also sensitive to the culture and age of the respondents? Does the instrument cause no harm? Is client confidentiality protected? Is the instrument cost-effective? Is the instrument compatible with the staff members assisting the practitioner?

Developing a Code Book

A *codebook* is a collection of instructions on how each variable's attributes are coded with a number, producing a recognizable category for statistical analysis of the collected data. In addition, instructions are given for the numerical coding of the responses in the survey instrument. Most statistical programs have their own spreadsheets that are, in effect, the codebook. Most statistics programs also have the ability to import data from popular spreadsheet programs. Once set-up, data are entered directly into the spreadsheet or statistics program.

An example from the KOP study of a codebook entry for the variable gender with the attributes male, female, and transgender is shown in Figure 7.5.

Figure 7.6 shows a codebook entry for a survey response to a narrative statement about older people.

Variable	Gender
1	Male
2	Female
3	Transgender

Figure 7.5
Codebook Entry for the Variable *Gender*

Variable		
1. The Majority of Old People Are Socially Isolated and Lonely	1	Definitely agree
	2	Most likely agree
	3	Possible agree
	4	Possible disagree
	5	Most likely disagree
	6	Definitely disagree

Figure 7.6
Codebook Entry for a Statement in the Questionnaire

Preparing the Data

Once the data are collected, the practitioner must review each questionnaire to determine that all demographic questions (e.g., age, gender, ethnicity) and questionnaire responses have been completed. Sometimes, respondents do not answer all questions or respond to certain aspects of the questionnaire. The practitioner must develop a set of rules on how to deal with missing data, data that were ambiguously marked (e.g., not clear which box was checked or circled). A plan must also be made for open-ended questions, the traditional *other* on a questionnaire. The practitioner must develop a set of rules for these *other* answers. Are they coded if the respondent gives multiple answers? Should the respondent be limited to one answer? Whatever the rules, they should be followed consistently from respondent to respondent.

Critical Thinking

Critical Thinking Question: How does quantitative research help the practitioner to communicate professional judgments?

Presenting the Findings

The first step in data analysis is a visual presentation of graphs and frequency distributions of each variable of interest in the study. For example, frequency distributions may be displayed in tabular form (Figure 7.7), or as a graph that would show central tendency, the extent of variability in the distribution, and the degree of skewness of the distribution (Figure 7.8).

Data at a nominal level are often displayed in bar charts. Figure 7.9 shows the data for the gerontology training variable in the KOP study.

Data may also be displayed in a cross tabulation. This method, often called *crosstab*, is used to display the distribution of one variable for each category of another variable. Another term for this type of distribution is a *bivariate distribution*. Figure 7.10 shows a crosstab for mental health professional subtype by age.

Testing Hypotheses

Once univariate and bivariate distributions are represented in a figure, line graph, or bar chart, the data are ready for statistical analysis. Statistical analysis will either confirm a hypothesis or deny it (null hypothesis). For each hypothesis that has been developed before data collection, an appropriate statistical evaluation is performed to determine whether the finding is significant ($p < 0.05$). The following is an example of a significant finding where the hypothesis was accepted, and a nonsignificant finding where the hypothesis was rejected.

Hypothesis

Psychiatric nurses and social workers have higher KOP scores than psychologists and psychiatrists.

This hypothesis was derived from research question 2: Is there a difference in degree of accuracy in assessing true and false empirical statements about older people between psychiatric nurses, psychiatrists, psychologists, and social workers?

The mental health professional variable was studied because the subtypes of psychiatric nurse, psychiatrist, psychologist, and social worker were thought to contribute to a mental health professionals' degree of accuracy in assessing true and false empirical statements about older people. The KOP Score is the dependent variable.

KOP Score	f	Valid Percentage	Cumulative Percentage
56	1	0.7	0.7
61	2	1.4	2.1
63	1	0.7	2.8
64	1	0.7	3.5
65	3	2.1	5.7
66	6	4.3	9.9
67	2	1.4	11.3
68	2	1.4	12.8
69	4	2.8	15.6
70	3	2.1	17.7
71	4	2.8	20.6
72	4	2.8	23.4
73	2	1.4	24.8
74	5	3.5	28.4
75	5	3.5	31.9
76	5	3.5	35.5
77	5	3.5	39.0
78	3	2.1	41.1
79	5	3.5	44.7
80	6	4.3	48.9
81	2	1.4	50.4
82	6	4.3	54.6
83	6	4.3	58.9
84	3	2.1	61.0
85	2	1.4	62.4
86	2	1.4	63.8
87	5	3.5	67.4
88	3	2.1	69.5
89	6	4.3	73.8
90	3	2.1	75.9
91	6	4.3	80.1
92	6	4.3	84.4
94	4	2.8	87.2
95	3	2.1	89.4
96	4	2.8	92.2
97	3	2.1	94.3
98	2	1.4	95.7
100	1	0.7	96.5
102	2	1.4	97.9
106	1	0.7	98.6
107	1	0.7	99.3
108	1	0.7	100.0
Total	141	100.0	

Figure 7.7
Frequency Distribution for KOP Scores

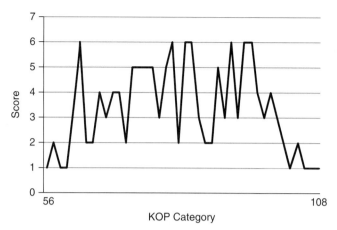

Figure 7.8
A Line Graph Showing the Number of Respondents Scoring in Each KOP Category From 56–108

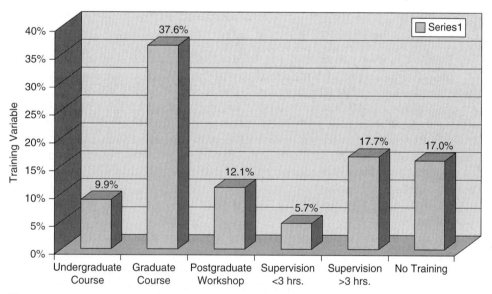

Figure 7.9
A Bar Chart Represents the Gerontology Training Variable From the KOP Study

	Counseling Psychologist	Psychiatric Nurse	Psychiatrist	Psychologist	Social Worker
Age					
18–25	2		4	2	5
25–40	4	4	12	5	28
40–65	9	21		6	38
65–70					1

Figure 7.10
Crosstab of Mental Health Worker Subtypes by Age

	Mean	N	Standard Deviation
Mental Health Professional Subtype			
Psychiatric Nurse	87.40	25	11.02
Psychiatrist	79.62	16	10.09
Psychologist	80.07	28	11.12
Social Worker	80.44	72	10.40

Figure 7.11
Mean KOP Scores for Mental Health Professional Subtypes

	Sum of Squares	df	Mean Square	F	Significance
Between Groups	1063.849	3	354.616	3.142	0.027
Within Groups	15461.385	137	112.857		
Total	16525.234	140			

Figure 7.12
One-Way Analysis of Variance of Mental Health Professional Subtypes; Dependent Variable Is KOP Score.

Figure 7.11 shows the mental health professional suptypes' mean KOP scores.

One-Way Analysis of Variance was performed to discover the association between the four subgroups of mental health professionals (Figure 7.12). The findings were significant, $p \leq .05$. Psychiatric nurses had the highest mean KOP score (87.40), followed by social workers (80.44), and psychologists (80.07). Psychiatrists had the lowest KOP score (79.63). Psychiatrists had the lowest degree of accuracy. This hypothesis was supported by the findings. Psychiatric nurses and social workers had significantly higher KOP scores than psychologists and psychiatrists.

Hypothesis

Female mental health professionals will have higher KOP scores than male or transgender mental health professionals.

This hypothesis was derived from the research question: How do socio-demographic aspects of mental health professionals contribute to their degree of accuracy assessing true and false empirical statements about older people?

The gender of mental health professionals was studied for contributions to mental health professionals' ability to assess true and false empirical statements about older people. Because there were no respondents who indicated being transgendered, the gender attributes were collapsed from 3 to 2 showing data for female and male. Knowledge of Older People Score is the dependent variable. Figure 7.13 shows the mean KOP scores for female and male mental health professionals.

A *t*-test was performed to discover the association between female and male mental health professionals and KOP scores. Figure 7.13 shows females scored 82.23 and males scored 79.34. This comparison of mean scores suggested that female mental health professionals were more accurate when evaluating empirical statements about older people than were male mental health professionals. However, no statistical significance was

	Mean	N	Standard Deviation
Gender			
Female	82.23	106	10.92
Male	79.34	35	10.54

Figure 7.13
Mean KOP Scores for Gender

	N	Mean	Standard Deviation	t	df	Significance (Two-Tailed)
Gender						
Female	106	82.23	10.92	1.366	139	0.174
Male	35	79.34	10.54			

Figure 7.14
T-Test on Mental Health Professional Gender, Dependent Variable Is KOP Score

found. Figure 7.14 shows the *t*-test results. This hypothesis was not supported by the findings and was therefore rejected.

HUMAN RIGHTS ISSUES IN QUANTITATIVE RESEARCH

A practitioner who completes a study and has several significant findings may cause harm to a vulnerable population because that population may be excluded from the findings because the relationship category they were in was found to be not significant. The practitioner must follow up on data that are not significant to determine whether the original research questions need to be modified to test other relationships the vulnerable population in question might have to the dependent variable, or to test other variables that would prove to be significant. A researcher can easily check many variable relationships with the mission to find significance. Oftentimes, this causes an intellectual blindness to findings that are not significant that consequently are ignored for future research.

For example, in the KOP study, gender was not found to be a significant predictor of mental health professionals' knowledge of older people. The variable gender had three attributes—female, male, and transgender. Because no individuals indicated a transgender status, the attribute category was collapsed to two attributes—female and male. Even though the research sample of 141 was acceptable for a quantitative study, by rejecting gender as a significant predictor of mental health professionals' knowledge of older people, the practitioner may miss an opportunity to run another study with a larger population that captures more people indicating a transgender status. A significant finding for gender may occur in a larger study. Most contemporary social work research studies ignore transgender as a gender attribute. This cultural pattern of ignoring transgendered people extends to the clinical arena. When surveying the literature, one can discover the fact that transgender people are often underserved (Bockting, Robinson, & Rosser, 1998; Kenagy, 2005).

Diversity in Practice

Critical Thinking Question: What are three examples of how quantitative research may result in oppressing, or helping vulnerable populations?

Human Rights and Justice

Critical Thinking Question: Explain how quantitative research may advance or hinder human rights and social justice.

SUMMARY

This chapter detailed the anatomy of a quantitative study. This chapter is a roadmap of all the steps ranging from conducting a literature review, to developing research questions and hypotheses, to creating a study model, to developing a sampling plan, to preparing the data, to presenting the findings. The importance of identifying relationships between variables was emphasized as a statistical tool for understanding social problems and social phenomena. However, an illusion can be created by quantitative research. The practitioner tends to limit the understanding of social phenomena to a collection of significant statistical findings. Contemporary researchers advocate for combining quantitative and qualitative techniques in a research study. This gives the practitioner the ability to drill down under the numbers to understand the human experience of the phenomena studied.

Succeed with PEARSON mysocialworklab

Log onto **www.mysocialworklab.com** to access a wealth of case studies, videos, and assessment. (*If you did not receive an access code to* **MySocialWorkLab** *with this text and wish to purchase access online, please visit* www.mysocialworklab.com.)

1. **Watch the research-based practice video "Engaging in Research Informed Practice."** Indicate how quantitative research studies are effective in informing social work practice.

2. **Watch the human rights and justice video "Advocating for Human Rights and Social and Economic Justice."** Indicate how each component of a quantitative research study addresses human rights and social and economic justice issues.

PRACTICE TEST The following questions will test your knowledge of the content found within this chapter. For additional assessment, including licensing-exam type questions on applying chapter content to practice, visit **MySocialWorkLab**.

1. The literature review should:
   a. Not include articles more than 8 years old.
   b. Give a brief description of each article
   c. Focus on recent articles, but include classic studies
   d. Include all articles published on the subject

2. Which of the following is a usable hypothesis?
   a. Social workers should be sensitive to the poor.
   b. Attending class is related to good grades.
   c. More money should be given to agencies.
   d. Research is needed in social work.

3. A practitioner uses an exploratory study because it:
   a. Gives an accurate representation of a situation being studied
   b. Demonstrates how frequently one variable is related to another
   c. Discovers ideas, concepts, and insights that can be used for future studies
   d. Tests the causal relationships in the different hypotheses

4. Reliability in a study implies:
   a. Accuracy of the study
   b. Whether a procedure applied repeatedly yields the same results each time
   c. That what the practitioner is measuring what he or she thinks he or she is measuring
   d. That the study is comprehensive

5. Use a social work journal quantitative research study from a literature review you recently wrote for class. Did the researcher address all the subcategories outlined in this chapter? Did the researcher consider social justice issues in the study?

ASSESS YOUR COMPETENCE Use the scale below to rate your current level of achievement on the following concepts or skills associated with each competency presented in the chapter:

1	2	3
I can accurately describe the concept or skill	I can consistently identify the concept or skill when observing and analyzing practice activities	I can competently implement the concept or skill in my own practice

_____ can communicate the knowledge discovered in quantitative research.

_____ can use quantitative research studies to inform my practice.

_____ can use a quantitative research study to inform other practitioners.

_____ can infuse multiculturalism and social justice concepts in a quantitative research study.

8

Causation—Experimental, Quasi-Experimental, and Nonexperimental Designs

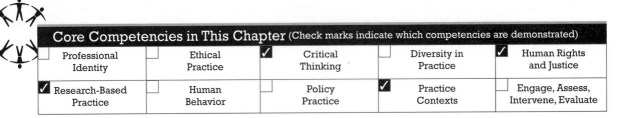

Core Competencies in This Chapter (Check marks indicate which competencies are demonstrated)				
☐ Professional Identity	☐ Ethical Practice	✔ Critical Thinking	☐ Diversity in Practice	✔ Human Rights and Justice
✔ Research-Based Practice	☐ Human Behavior	☐ Policy Practice	✔ Practice Contexts	☐ Engage, Assess, Intervene, Evaluate

INTRODUCTION

Practitioners of social work research are in the business of explaining and/or changing aspects of clients, organizations, social policies, and social conditions. In social work practice, a practitioner identifies a client's specific behavior or problem by assessing numerous reasons to explain how the behavior or problem was caused. This type of reasoning is called *idiographic explanation*. In contrast, when a practitioner studies a general phenomenon that applies to many individuals, he or she employs a different type of causal reasoning. This phenomenon is called *nomothetic causal explanation*. As learned in chapter 10 on qualitative research, causation implies that some variation in the independent variable will have a consequent effect on the dependent variable. In an ideal world, this is a clear-cut cause-and-effect relationship. However, in the research world many considerations have to be taken into effect before the practitioner can declare causation with confidence. In addition, the practitioner deals with different considerations when engaged in research based on experimental group designs, quasi-experimental designs, or nonexperimental designs.

Critical Thinking

Critical Thinking Question: Articulate at least three ways that knowledge of causation and group experimental and non-experimental designs inform practice decision-making.

PRACTITIONER CONSIDERATIONS FOR CAUSATION

Before a practitioner can choose an experimental, quasi-experimental, or non-experimental design as described on the following pages, he or she must consider many influences that determine the degree of confidence in determining a causal relationship between the independent and dependent variables. These considerations help support the notion that the research study achieved internal validity (Campbell & Stanley, 1963).

Practice Contexts

Critical Thinking Question: How does a social work researcher engaging in research-informed practice or practice-informed research choose which experimental design would be appropriate for his or her study? Provide at least two examples.

Association

Association occurs when a practitioner observes an association between the independent and dependent variables. In traditional pharmacological studies where one group of patients receive drug X and another group of patients do not receive drug X, any change that the practitioner observes in the patients taking drug X, and not in the patients not taking drug X, is associated with drug X. This type of association study is called an experimental group study, which uses an experimental group (those taking drug X) and a control group (those not taking drug X). Experimental group data are analyzed using statistical tests in order to prove that the differences between the experimental group and the control group were not caused by chance. This model may be extended to multiple experimental groups to assess different attributes of an independent variable or combinations of values of more than one independent variable. For example, the independent variable of social work student may be broken down into three groups—BSW, MSW, and PhD. These groups can further be divided into: male BSW, female BSW, transgender BSW, and so on. These variables may be used to predict social work students' desire to work with older clients.

Causal Means

In a clinical setting, the social work practitioner looks for an explanation as to what enabled a problem that brought a client to counseling. In this case, a practitioner relies on a clinical theory to explain the cause of a problem. The practitioner's explanatory analysis may be based on psychoanalytic, cognitive behavior, existential, person-in-environment, or any other social work theory. In this case, the theory explains the causal means of the client's problem.

In a clinical setting, the social work practitioner looks for an explanation as to what enabled a problem that brought a client to counseling. In this case, a practitioner relies on a clinical theory to explain the cause of a problem. The practitioner's explanatory analysis may be based on psychoanalytic, cognitive behavior, existential, person-in-environment, or any other social work theory. In this case, the theory explains the *causal means* of the client's problem. In an experimental setting, assessing the means that enabled the causal relationship between the independent and dependent variables is necessary to support a nomothetic causal relationship.

Contamination

A practitioner must be careful to prevent the experimental group from having awareness of the control group. In most studies, this is accomplished by the random assignment of subjects to either the control or experimental group and by not revealing to the subjects which group they belong to. In addition, researchers or observers participating in measurement activities in the study are unaware of whether a subject is in a control or experimental group. This is called a *blind study*.

Context

A practitioner often tries to put a causal relationship into a greater context defined by other variables to test under what condition (context) the phenomenon of the relationship between the independent and the dependent variables exists. In the example of the practitioner studying social work students' desire to work with older adults, the practitioner may explore different regions the schools are located in, or may determine whether the schools are public or private. This gives the practitioner the ability to see whether the causal relationship between the independent variable (social work student) and the dependent variable (desire to work with older adults) exists across these concepts.

Experimental Mortality

When a practitioner runs a study over time, there is the potential for loss of subjects either in the experimental group or in the control group. Any loss of subjects threatens the internal validity of the study because the internal dynamic of each subject group changes with subject loss.

History

Another threat to internal validity is any event or events that may occur when the practitioner is taking measurements over time. Obviously, it is almost impossible to control for a historical event, but in order to support causation a practitioner must consider any significant event that might bias internal validity over the time course of the study.

Instrumentation

If a practitioner makes any change in the measuring instrument, and/or makes changes in multiple observers that collect data, these changes may in turn have their own causal effect on the relationship between the independent and dependent variables.

Maturation

Maturation is another potential threat to internal validity. The fact is, subjects age over time. Aging of subjects has its own causal effect on the relationship between the independent and dependent variables.

Fatigue

If respondents are filling out a questionnaire that requires several hours of concentration, fatigue may bias the causal relationship between the variables. The respondents may rush through questions, guess answers to finish fast, or just put false answers.

Time Order

A practitioner must make sure all subjects involved in a study start at the same status and are measured at the same time. An example of status is studying the effects of cognitive behavior therapy in alcohol dependency treatment. All subjects in the study start at the same status—admission to the rehabilitation facility and are measured at the same time—on admission, after withdrawal, and after one month and six months of treatment.

Third Variable Causality (Selection Causality)

A practitioner must be certain that the causal relationship effects between the independent and dependent variables are not biased or caused by a third variable. For example, a practitioner runs a study on the hair color of social workers and its effect on diagnostic ability. The results of the study indicate that social workers with gray hair have more accurate diagnostic abilities than social workers with brown or black hair. This is not a true conclusion, because the type of agency in which social workers practice, is shown to have a positive effect on diagnostic accuracy levels, not the age of the social workers (Youdin, 2010). Obviously, there is a high probability of social workers with many years of experience having gray hair. However, the type of agency they worked in was not controlled for the study. Many experimental designs discussed on the following pages try to control for third variable influence by random assignment to groups, controlling for as many extraneous variables as possible.

EXPERIMENTAL DESIGNS

In social work research, experimental designs are a precise means of verifying clinical, organizational, or policy interventions in practice settings. Using experimental designs enables the practitioner to establish a temporal perspective

In social work research, experimental designs are a precise means of verifying clinical, organizational, or policy interventions in practice settings. Using experimental designs enables the practitioner to establish a temporal perspective on the effectiveness of new interventions without excluding previously established interventions.

on the effectiveness of new interventions without excluding previously established interventions. It is human nature to embrace the new and novel and to disregard the old and well-worn. Many experimental designs help the practitioner test new interventions and develop new causal explanations, by adding to a cumulative knowledge that keeps past interventions and causal concepts that remain effective, and help discern past interventions and causal concepts that are no longer valid.

Experimental Comparison Groups

Most social work research students think of experimental group research as an *experimental group* compared to a *control group*. A group that receives an intervention is the experimental group, and a group that does not receive the intervention is called the control group (Figure 8.1). However, in some cases, the control group may be receiving an intervention that is common practice in the agency, or some other clinical intervention(s). In this case, the group is called the *comparison group* (Figure 8.2) or *multiple comparison groups* (Figure 8.3). Some researchers study multiple independent variables and their causal effects on the dependent variable (outcome measure) (Figure 8.4). An example of multiple independent variables is the classic study of schizophrenia treatment (May, 1968) in which schizophrenic patients who had not had treatment prior to admission to a psychiatric hospital were assigned to five treatment groups: antipsychotic medications only, individual psychotherapy only, individual psychotherapy plus antipsychotic medications, electroconvulsive treatment only, and milieu therapy only. The outcome (dependent measure) was rate of

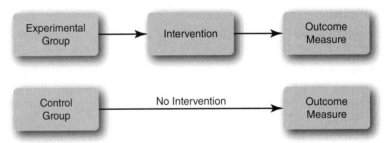

Figure 8.1
Experimental Group–Control Group Design

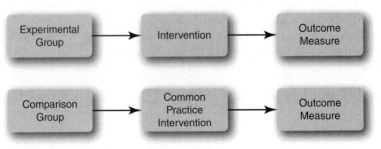

Figure 8.2
Experimental Group–Comparison Group Design

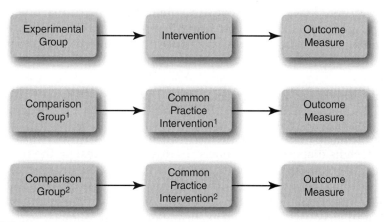

Figure 8.3
Experimental Group–Multicomparison Groups Design

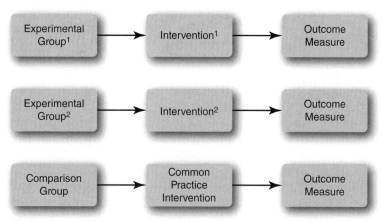

Figure 8.4
Multiexperimental groups–Comparison Group Design

release from the hospital. The control group did not receive treatment during the time of the experiment. The findings were that the group receiving antipsychotic medications only had the highest rate of release from the hospital, followed by the groups having psychotherapy and antipsychotic medications.

Most social work researchers use comparison groups rather than control groups for ethical reasons. Clients coming to an agency for service need to be provided with a service. By putting clients in a control group, the practitioner is denying these clients services, or at best, delaying services to these clients.

Random Assignment of Subjects

Simple random sampling is used to ensure that the experimental group(s) and comparison group(s) are chosen on a clearly defined procedure that theoretically generates a sample based on probability. The probability of an element (subject) being chosen must be equal, meaning that each element has an equal probability of being selected. The list of people being studied in the experimental and comparison group(s) is all encompassing and is known as the

Most social work researchers use comparison groups rather than control groups for ethical reasons. Clients coming to an agency for service need to be provided with a service. By putting clients in a control group, the practitioner is denying these clients services, or at best, delaying services to these clients.

sampling frame. The same random assignment is used to place people in a control group. Randomization increases the probability that the changes made by the independent variable on the dependent variable are true experimental findings.

QUASI-EXPERIMENTAL DESIGNS

Quasi-experimental designs lack the full experimental control found in experimental designs discussed previously. In this type of design, the practitioner does not use the random assignment of subjects that is key to experimental designs. Instead, he or she may take periodic measurements on a group or an individual before and after an intervention, or may use a comparative group that is thought to be equivalent to the experimental group. In quasi-experimental design, the practitioner may achieve only one or two aspects of internal validity. Therefore, the practitioner must be aware of all the internal validity criteria in order to be aware of how residual imperfections in the design may lead to multiple interpretations of the data. Nevertheless, quasi-experimental designs are cost-effective, are not time consuming, and are viable evidence-based outcome measures for practice accountability.

Time Series Design

The basic tenet of a time series design is that the practitioner is able to make periodic measurements on a group or an individual, introduce an intervention, and then continue to make periodic measurements without the necessity of having a comparison or control group (Figure 8.5). Comparison or multiple comparison groups may be used but are not necessary. Results are significant when there is a discontinuity in the measurements when observations after the intervention differ from those taken before the intervention. In addition, by continuing to observe for a significant period after the intervention, the practitioner is able to see if the causal relationship of the intervention persists.

A time series design is useful when a practitioner is evaluating changes resulting from a clinical intervention, a new policy, a change in administrative

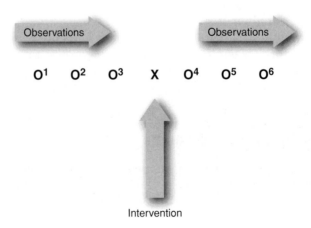

Figure 8.5
Time Series Design

practice, or new agency program initiative. Many threats to internal validity that are not controlled for may cloud the practitioner's ability to determine causality. The most significant threat to internal validity in a time series design is history. As discussed earlier, there can be a possible contamination of the study from some external event to the study converging at a particular point in time.

Nonequivalent Control Group Designs

The nonequivalent control group designs are similar to the pretest–posttest designs described later in this chapter. In this design, an observation is made on the experimental group and the control group, then an intervention is introduced to the experimental group, and finally, observations are once again made on the experimental group and the control group. Alternatively, when an intervention is introduced to the experimental group, a second intervention may be introduced to the control group. The practitioner chooses this approach when he or she wants to compare two interventions (Figure 8.6).

Being a quasi-experimental design, the nonequivalent control group design does not assign subjects randomly to the groups. Instead, the practitioner attempts to match individual subjects in the treatment group with similar individual subjects in the control group. This type of matching is called *individual matching*. Alternatively, the practitioner may choose to match groups of people with attributes that match the important variables of the study. This is called *aggregate matching*. The practitioner chooses one group for the experimental group and one group for the control group. To maintain some level of internal validity, subjects assigned to either group should not be identified to each other, and they should not know whether they are in the experimental or control group. This type of design greatly eliminates problems of instrumentation, maturation, and history. In addition, if the practitioner is confident in the matching of subjects, he or she can attest to the comparability of the experimental and control groups though they were not randomly selected.

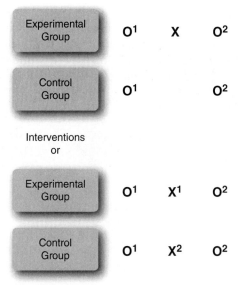

Figure 8.6
Nonequivalent Control Group Designs

Ex Post Facto Control Group Design

An ex post facto group design is a way for a practitioner to study an intervention effect retrospectively. This type of a design appears to be the same as a nonequivalent group design. However, instead of assigning subjects to the experimental and control groups before initiating the study, and instead of performing a pretest before implementing an intervention, the practitioner approximates this model retrospectively. Posttest observations are made on the experimental group and control group similar to the nonequivalent group design. The difference in designs is that the ex post facto design has the practitioner hypothesizing the effect the intervention had on the experimental group without the knowledge of a pretest. Alternatively, the practitioner may embed pretest questions in the posttest instrument to ascertain a retrospective history from the subjects of their perceptions of their pretest status. This type of design does not carry the same level of confidence in equivalence of groups that the nonequivalent group design achieves. Instead of assigning subjects to a group before implementing the intervention, the practitioner forms groups based on whether subjects received or did not receive the intervention. This type of group assignment may introduce bias from how subjects initially were chosen for the intervention. Did the subjects choose to receive the intervention? If so, are they fundamentally different from subjects who did not choose to receive the intervention?

NONEXPERIMENTAL DESIGNS

Nonexperimental designs are groups of designs that do not provide comprehensive mechanisms for control over potential sources of bias to internal validity. However, these designs are cost-effective, are easy to administer, and are often used for program evaluation.

Pretest–Posttest Design

Researchers administer a pretest to all subjects before introducing the independent variable being studied. A posttest is administered to ascertain the causal effects the independent variable has on the dependent variable. Is the posttest's result significantly different from the pretest's result (Figure 8.7)?

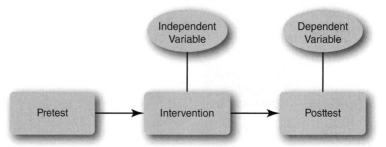

Figure 8.7
Pretest–Posttest Design.

This type of design does not have a control group to allow comparison between an experimental and a control group. In most studies, the pretest and posttest instruments are the same. In some studies, a posttest that is not the same as the pretest may be administered, if the practitioner is confident that the new posttest measurement is measuring the same phenomenon. Maschi, Bradley, Youdin, Killian, Cleaveland, and Barbera (2007) used a pretest–posttest design to measure students' anxiety about taking a research course (does this sound familiar?). Students were administered an anxiety scale prior to taking a social work research course, and measured again after taking the research course. Results indicated that taking the course significantly reduced students' anxiety about social work research. Some practitioners prefer to study the effects of the independent variable over time. In order to do this, they administer several posttests over an extended period.

One-Shot Case Study and Static Group Comparison Designs

A one-shot case study design is chosen by a practitioner when he or she decides to study a single group only once by observing the group subsequent to an intervention or independent variable that may have an effect on the observation instrument (Figure 8.8). For example, Youdin and Cleaveland (2006) studied how religious affiliation affects the attitude of social work undergraduate and graduate students toward old poor people. The attributes of the independent variable were no affiliation, Christian Catholic affiliation, Christian Protestant affiliation, and Jewish affiliation. The attitude toward old poor people scale (KOPP) administered (dependent variable) indicated that social work students with the most positive attitude toward old poor people were those self-identifying as nonaffiliated. They were followed by Jewish affiliation, and Christian Catholic affiliation. Christian Protestant affiliation showed the most negative attitude toward old poor people.

In the case where a practitioner is administrating a clinical intervention, he or she may choose a *static group comparison design.* For example, similar to the one-shot design, the static group design would have one group of subjects who are given a cognitive behavior intervention, such as reframing, to lessen anxiety in the subject. Subsequent to the subjects practicing reframing of their anxiety thoughts, they are administered an anxiety scale instrument. In the static group comparison design another equivalent group would be administered the same anxiety scale at the same time without experiencing the cognitive therapy intervention (Figure 8.9).

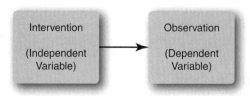

Figure 8.8
One-Shot Case Study Design

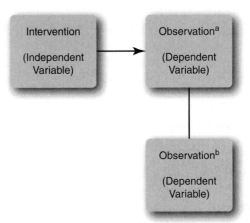

Figure 8.9
Static Group Comparison Design

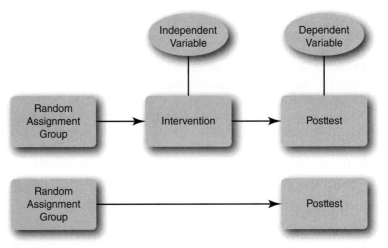

Figure 8.10
Posttest-Only Control Group Design

Posttest-Only Control Group Design

The posttest-only control group design looks like an experimental design but is considered nonexperimental where true randomization may be questioned because of the absence of a pretest, even though subjects are assigned to the groups randomly (Figure 8.10). Therefore, the practitioner is not completely certain that the effects of the independent variable on the dependent variable are solely due to the intervention. If a pretest was administered, the practitioner would have a greater degree of confidence that there is equivalence between the experimental and control groups.

Cross-Sectional Designs

A cross-sectional study occurs at one point in time. Data collected analyze all the elements of the cross-section. For example, at an agency that has both inpatient and outpatient services, a practitioner may conduct an open-ended (unstructured) interview of all clients, at one point in time, who completed their treatment, or who left the agency before treatment was completed. The cross-section would be inpatient clients who completed treatment, inpatient clients who did not complete treatment, outpatient clients who completed treatment, and outpatient clients who did not complete treatment. This study would give the practitioner the ability to run an exploratory study on what causes an inpatient or outpatient client to complete, or not complete treatment. Alternatively, if the practitioner wanted to test the hypothesis that social workers' attitude toward clients is a cause for completion or noncompletion of treatment, then the cross-sectional study would be explanatory. The major criticism of cross-sectional studies is that they occur at one time rather than across time, which may introduce historical bias from some unique phenomena that happened at the time of the study.

Repeated Cross-Sectional Designs

Repeated cross-sectional designs give the practitioner the ability to assess changes that might occur in a population over time. A weakness in this design is that each time a population is sampled, participants may or may not be from a prior group and new participants may be added. This change in the sample may cause bias due to population mortality (people leaving the study) and new members may bias the data due to intervening variables not yet identified.

Event-Based Designs

Event-based designs sample a population from the same cohort. Age group, level of education, vocational groups, and so on are examples of cohorts. In event-based designs, data are collected over two or more times from the original cohort. A criticism of event-based designs is that even though the subjects are from the same cohort, this does not ensure that subjects within the cohort are equivalent across intervening variables. For example, if a practitioner studies the baby boomers and assesses the percentage of baby boomers who access mental health services and samples them at community mental health centers, the practitioner would not be including those who are able to afford mental health practitioners in private practice. Therefore, if the practitioner were making some conclusion about the rate of mental health service needs of baby boomers over time, the data would be distorted.

Fixed-Sample Panel Designs

Fixed-sample panel designs collect data from a group identified at one point in time, and then follow the same individuals to collect data at two or more different points in time. Because the sample is fixed, new individuals are not allowed to join the study later. Some practitioners feel that because the sample is fixed, the design has an advantage over repeated cross-sectional studies. However, in fixed-sample panel designs, individuals more often than not leave the study sample at some point in time. This introduces experimental mortality, which may produce effects confounded with the effect of the independent variable of the study.

Human Rights and Justice

Critical Thinking Question:
In what ways can the group experimental design facilitate or hinder the advancement of human rights and social and economic justice?

Many research designs involve preventing subjects from knowing whether they are in an experimental or control group. This is called deception and it enables the practitioner to bypass giving subjects informed consent. Many practitioners argue that deception enables a real life simulation that avoids any bias from a subject's preknowledge of the purpose of the experiment. This is a significant ethical dilemma for social work practitioners engaged in research.

Longitudinal Designs

Longitudinal designs give the practitioner the advantage to collect data that can be precisely time-ordered. For example, a practitioner might want to study a group of children diagnosed with attention deficit hyperactivity disorder (ADHD) at age 7 and test them at different developmental stages to learn how ADHD is expressed with increase in age. This would be useful evidence-based knowledge for practitioners because the study would identify problems that occur in ADHD children as they age. Study results may lead to early intervention strategies that would help clients with an ADHD diagnosis avoid consequent problems at later developmental stages in their lives. Longitudinal studies are subject to experimental mortality, which may confound the effects of the independent variable, in this case an ADHD diagnosis before age 7.

SOCIAL JUSTICE ISSUES IN RESEARCH DESIGNS

Many research designs involve preventing subjects from knowing whether they are in an experimental or control group. This is called deception, and it enables the practitioner to bypass giving subjects informed consent. Many practitioners argue that deception enables a real-life simulation that avoids any bias from a subject's preknowledge of the purpose of the experiment. This is a significant ethical dilemma for social work practitioners engaged in research. As a means of addressing this ethical dilemma, most institutions have an institutional review board that insists that the practitioner researcher prove that no harm will come to any subject because of the experimental research. In the case where there is some degree of deception, the practitioner must provide a means of debriefing the subjects. This would entail a detailed review of the purpose of the study and a comprehensive report of the findings of the study. In addition, the practitioner is required to provide a means of counseling if any subject feels that he or she may have been harmed or is conflicted by his or her participation. In rare occasions, this may entail referral to a mental health practitioner. Debriefing usually elicits a positive response from subjects because it provides a forum to answer their questions, validates the participatory relationship between practitioner and subject, and acknowledges their valuable contribution to the study.

Another ethical dilemma is, the opposite of potential harm, that subjects in the experimental group may receive benefits that those assigned to the control group do not receive. A remedy for this is that the practitioner makes available the same benefit, when possible, to the control group members. In addition, in the preliminary instructions given to all subjects before an experiment, the practitioner is obligated to explain the risks and benefits that may occur to the experimental group. This enables subjects to leave the study before it begins if they are not in agreement with the concept that they may not derive a benefit from the study.

SUMMARY

This chapter describes the many types of research designs available to the practitioner or researcher. The most valuable types of designs are experimental designs. These designs give the most precise ability to the practitioner for testing nomothetic causal hypotheses. Experimental designs enable the practitioner to control for extraneous variables that may be confounded with the effect of the experimental stimulus (independent variable).

When not practical to administer an experimental design, the practitioner may resort to using quasi-experimental designs or nonexperimental designs. These designs are employed when the practitioner is unable to have full control over the independent variable, or does not have the ability to randomize subjects into groups, or simply does not have the funding or time to conduct experimental designs. Whichever design is chosen, be it experimental, quasi-experimental, or nonexperimental, the practitioner as researcher is always on an exciting journey to assess causation and add to the ever-growing body of evidence-based knowledge.

Research-Based Practice

Critical Thinking Question: How does knowledge of causation and research design impact context that shape practice? What are the risk and benefits?

Succeed with PEARSON **mysocialworklab**

Log onto **www.mysocialworklab.com** to access a wealth of case studies, videos, and assessment. (*If you did not receive an access code to* **MySocialWorkLab** *with this text and wish to purchase access online, please visit* www.mysocialworklab.com.)

1. Watch the human rights and justice video "Advocating for Human Rights and Social and Economic Justice."

Indicate three types of research designs you would use to develop findings as a form of advocacy for human rights and social and economic justice.

2. **Watch the research based practice video "Engaging in Research Informed Practice."** Indicate three of the most effective research designs for informing practice.

PRACTICE TEST The following questions will test your knowledge of the content found within this chapter. For additional assessment, including licensing-exam type questions on applying chapter content to practice, visit **MySocialWorkLab**.

1. The function of an experimental research design is:
   a. To identify key concepts
   b. To develop hypotheses
   c. Describe a social phenomenon
   d. Identify causation

2. The essential difference between an experimental design and a quasi-experimental design is:
   a. All quasi-experimental designs use a pretest.
   b. Practitioners find quasi-experimental designs too complicated.
   c. Experimental designs use random assignment of subjects.
   d. Quasi-experimental designs use a control group.

3. A questionnaire given to clients measures their levels of depression. Then instructions are given on reframing depressed thoughts, followed by the same questionnaire. Which type of design do the above statements refer to?
   a. One-shot case design
   b. One group pretest–posttest design
   c. Static group comparison design
   d. Longitudinal design

4. Most social work researchers use comparison groups rather than control groups because:
   a. Comparison groups do not delay service to clients.
   b. Comparison groups clearly show experimental effects.
   c. Comparison groups are more accurate than control groups.
   d. Comparison groups are more humanistic.

5. A social worker is interested in studying variables that affect a client's ability to benefit from treatment with cognitive behavior therapy. What antecedent, intervening, and independent variables do you feel should be used for this study? What dependent variable should be used to measure the effectiveness of treatment?

ASSESS YOUR COMPETENCE Use the scale below to rate your current level of achievement on the following concepts or skills associated with each competency presented in the chapter:

1	2	3
I can accurately describe the concept or skill	I can consistently identify the concept or skill when observing and analyzing practice activities	I can competently implement the concept or skill in my own practice

_____ can design experimental and quasi-experimental studies to inform other practitioners.

_____ can apply practice concepts when designing a study.

_____ can design studies based on knowledge derived from other studies.

_____ can design studies that are sensitive to human rights and social justice issues.

9

Tapping the Evidence-Based Practitioner Within: Single-Subject Design

CHAPTER OUTLINE

Core Competencies in This Chapter (Check marks indicate which competencies are demonstrated)				
Professional Identity	✔ Ethical Practice	Critical Thinking	Diversity in Practice	✔ Human Rights and Justice
✔ Research-Based Practice	Human Behavior	Policy Practice	Practice Contexts	✔ Engage, Assess, Intervene, Evaluate

INTRODUCTION

Single-subject design is an ideal way to evaluate changes in an individual or organizational policy over time, due to purposeful interventions by the social worker. Some practitioners prefer to use the terms *single case design* when referring to work with families or small groups. *Single system design* refers to working with communities or large organizational groups. For the purpose of simplicity, this chapter prefers to use the term *single-subject design*.

The fundamental principle of any time-series design is the ability of the social worker to take periodic measurements of a process on an individual's designated target behavior, or an organization's target problem, and to evaluate if change occurs with the introduction of an intervention or experimental change into the ongoing temporal measurements (Figure 9.1). In addition, these time-series measurements allow the social worker to test the effectiveness of an intervention, or a combination of interventions, by discontinuing the intervention(s) and continuing to monitor the target behavior or organizational problem target to ascertain sustained change. This is called reversal.

Contemporary single-subject research is an extension of an experimental design that was developed by 19th century scientists pursuing studies in biology and the various physical sciences. For social work, the foundation for single-subject design was laid by Skinner (1938) in the Law of Chaining and the design was formalized for psychological research by Sidman (1960). Skinner proposed that responses are capable of producing an eliciting or discriminative stimuli for subsequent responses. All responses in an observable chain of behaviors are maintained by the reinforcement derived by the terminal response. Therefore, if one intervenes on the chain of behaviors, a new set of responses may arise, changing the original target behavior and its consequent terminal response. For example, if a client is depressed and the social worker has the client monitor his or her depressed feelings over time, without intervention, the client's terminal response would be a major depression. However, if at some point in time a therapeutic intervention is introduced, the social worker has the ability to determine if the therapeutic intervention is effective in reducing or

> *The fundamental principle of any time-series design is the ability of the social worker to take periodic measurements of a process on an individual's designated target behavior, or an organization's target problem, and to evaluate if change occurs with the introduction of an intervention or experimental change into the ongoing temporal measurements.*

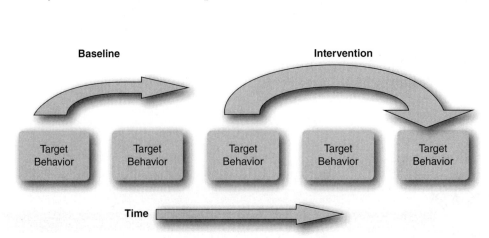

Figure 9.1

The Basic Process of a Single-Subject (Case) Design Showing a Baseline of a Target Behavior and the Introduction of an Intervention eliminating the client's depressed feelings, which, in turn, changes the terminal response of major depression to normal mood. If not, the social worker has the ability to change the intervention, add an intervention or interventions to the original intervention, and then evaluate the effect over time. Therefore, single-subject design is an effective tool for evidence-based practice and/or program outcome measurement.

ELEMENTS OF SINGLE-SUBJECT DESIGN

Baseline

Research-Based Practice

Critical Thinking Question: Describe how the social worker can use the single-subject design to engage in research-informed practice and practice-informed research.

A *baseline* is a period of many observations taken over time by either the social worker or client. A target must be identified to make these observations. This target can be a behavior, a thought, a measure of a program, or anything else agreed upon by the social worker and client (individual or organization) that is problematic or where there is a perceived need for change. The target that is measured is the dependent variable, which must be operationalized.

To operationalize the target of interest, the social worker must understand how the target is measured and what rules are assigned to the value of the target, and how to interpret the measurement (Figure 9.2). For example, a single-subject design can be useful when a client presents a problem of "being angry all the time." When the social worker carefully parses with the client what he or she means by *angry*, they reach a common definition. In this case, the client and social worker agreed that *anger* meant an event when the client looks at another person and becomes angry at one or more attributes of that person. The person's attributes may be that he or she is obese, is dressed in a manner not approved by the client, or is talking to another person about something the client feels is ridiculous. Even though the client understands that the person in question is not interacting with him or her, nevertheless, the client generates a feeling of anger and is unable to enjoy interacting with others while angry.

Once agreed upon, the client and social worker begin measuring each time the client feels angry as previously operationalized. The client makes a tick mark on a pad for each angry thought and continues to do so throughout the day. The next day, the client contacts the social worker and reports the previous day's counts. The social worker next generates a graph, showing the client's anger level per day (number of tick marks each day). This procedure

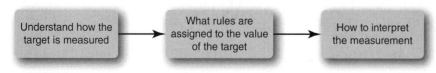

Figure 9.2
The Process of Operationalization

continues until the social worker feels that a relatively stable baseline is achieved. Figure 9.3 shows the baseline data for this client.

Baseline data may take many forms. The most basic form is a *stable pattern* (Figure 9.3), where the scores or counts form a relatively horizontal pattern (in the case of the angry client), a relatively ascending or descending pattern, a cyclic pattern, or relatively curvilinear pattern with little variability. When any of these patterns forms a narrow band of responses, as seen in Figure 9.3, these data lend themselves to visual analysis making changes to the baseline in subsequent phases of intervention(s) and removal of intervention(s) obvious. However, when the same type of pattern shows significant variability, forming a wide band of responses, interpretation of findings becomes more problematic. Figure 9.4 shows examples of variability for a horizontal pattern with significant variability.

A baseline may reflect a trend in the target behavior (dependent variable). The trend may show a progressive increase (ascending trend) or decrease (descending trend) in target behaviors. The baselines in Figure 9.5 show a progressive trend with little variability.

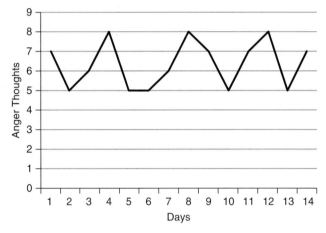

Figure 9.3

Baseline Data of the Number of Anger Thoughts the Client Has Each Day for a 14-Day Period

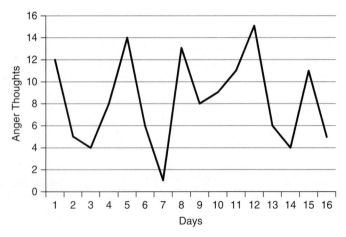

Figure 9.4

Significant Variability From a Wide Band of Responses Makes This Baseline Data Problematic to Interpret

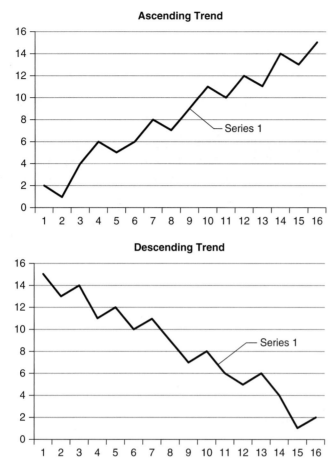

Figure 9.5
Baselines Showing Ascending and Descending Progressive Trends

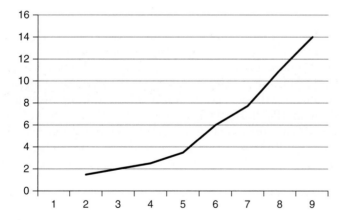

Figure 9.6
A Curvilinear Baseline

The last type of baseline data that may be observed is cyclic data. These data may represent environmental changes. The data might vary due to the day of the week; may be seasonal; may occur during academic semesters, during payroll periods, or any other type of cyclic phenomena (Figures 9.6 and 9.7).

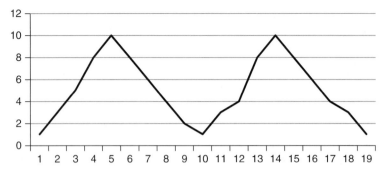

Figure 9.7
Example of Cyclic Data

Intervention

Once a baseline of repeated temporal measurements is established, next an intervention is introduced. This may take the form of a cognitive behavioral therapy (CBT) technique, any other clinical technique, or may be a change in organizational policy. A change in organizational policy is equivalent to changing a clinical technique in social work counseling practice. A social worker must evaluate policy changes in order to understand their degree of effectiveness.

In either case, the task is to evaluate whether there is a significant change in the target behavior from the baseline period (designated as A) to the intervention period (designated as B, or in other designs as subsequent letters after B—C, D, etc.).

SINGLE-SUBJECT DESIGNS

Traditional A-B Design

The A-B design is the traditional design used by most single-subject researchers. This method of research is used extensively in educational, scientific, and psychological research (Gast, 2010). In this design, A is the baseline, and B is the intervention. Client R is a 47-year-old Asian American woman who has been recently diagnosed with diabetes and hypertension by her primary care physician (PCP). Her PCP warned her to stop overeating and comply with a diet specifically designed for diabetics. However, her PCP did not give her any guidance on how to accomplish this goal. Fortunately, Client R had enough insight and strength to seek help from her local community mental health center.

Client R presented herself for treatment at a community mental health agency because she was "out of control with her eating." Client R and her social worker agreed that they would work together to bring Client R's overeating under control so that she would be able to comply with a diabetic diet that was a medical necessity for her. The first step in their work together was to operationalize Client R's overeating behavior. After numerous discussions, they agreed that the target behavior to be observed and treated was Client R's urges to overeat. Therefore, urges to overeat was the dependent variable, and any intervention used to modify this behavior was considered the independent variable.

Ethical Practice

Critical Thinking Question: How might social work ethical principles facilitate or create obstacles to using single-subject design research in practice?

The A-B design is the traditional design used by most single-subject researchers. This method of research is used extensively in educational, scientific, and psychological research (Gast, 2010).

To ensure that Client R and her social worker perceived the target behavior the same way, urges to overeat had to be operationalized. Urges to overeat was operationalized by the following three rules:

1. The urge or desire to eat any food not allowed by Client R's diabetic diet
2. The urge or desire to eat too much of a food allowed by Client R's diabetic diet
3. The urge or desire to eat a food allowed by Client R's diabetic diet, but at the wrong time (e.g., a breakfast for dinner or a snack)

Using this definition of urges to overeat, Client R was instructed to keep track of the number of urges to overeat she had each day for a baseline period of 27 days. Each time Client R had an urge to overeat, she was instructed to make a tick mark on a pad and then she may choose to overeat or not to overeat. She was instructed not to indicate whether she overate, because the target behavior was her urges to overeat. The belief was that if Client R no longer experienced urges to overeat, her subsequent overeating behavior would be eliminated. In Figure 9.8 the baseline data for Client R's urges to overeat are represented. Visual inspection determines that her urges to overeat per day ranged from two urges to eight urges to overeat per day. Client R's mean urges to overeat was 4.67 per day. These data indicate a consistent overeating urge rate per day with little variability. This type of baseline data is satisfactory to continue Client R's treatment with the introduction of a CBT.

Client R and her social worker agreed that because the urge to overeat was the first cognitive moment Client R experienced before making subsequent decisions that would enable her to overeat, an intervention was needed to disrupt her normal pattern of thinking. This would create a choice for the client rather than the automatic behavior of overeating. If successful, Client R would find that she no longer would have urges to overeat, which would enable her to stick to her diabetic diet without the overeating behavior that was present before treatment.

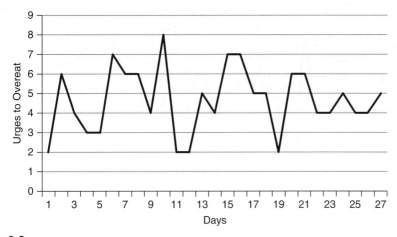

Figure 9.8
Baseline Data for Client R Showing the Number of Overeating Urges Occurring Each Day for 27 Days

Once again, Client R and her social worker had to operationalize the next step in her treatment, which is the intervention that would be used to attempt to eliminate her urges to overeat. The social worker decided to use a cognitive intervention that would interrupt the chain of thoughts Client R would engage in that would lead her to overeat. Client R was instructed to write the following questions on a pad each time she had an urge to overeat:

1. Why do I want to eat this food when I am participating in this program to stop overeating?
2. Do I want to jeopardize my health by overeating?
3. Do I want to continue to hurt myself by overeating?

Client R was instructed to write the three questions on her pad and make a tick mark indicating an urge to overeat; then she may or may not choose to overeat. The social worker explained to Client R that it was unnecessary to write an answer to each question because she would be automatically having an internal dialogue during which she would ask and answer each question. At times, she may be aware of this dialogue, and at times, she may have no awareness of this dialogue.

Figure 9.9 shows Client R's baseline and intervention data. The baseline intervention mean was 4.67 overeating urges per day. The intervention mean was 0.43 overeating urges per day. The intervention period was 16 days. Midway through the intervention period, Client R reported no longer overeating although she was experiencing between zero and one overeating urge per day. This suggests that the correct focus for Client R's overeating problem was on her urges to overeat, which continued after cessation of her overeating behavior. Because of short-term limitations placed on therapy by her agency, the social worker had to terminate Client R's treatment at the end of 33 days.

A-B-A and A-B-A-B Follow-Up Designs

A weakness in the A-B design leaves the clinician and client wondering whether the therapeutic effect of virtually eliminating the target behavior is long lasting, or occurs only while being treated.

A weakness in the A-B design discussed earlier leaves the clinician and client wondering whether the therapeutic effect of virtually eliminating Client R's urges to overeat is long lasting, or occurs only while being treated.

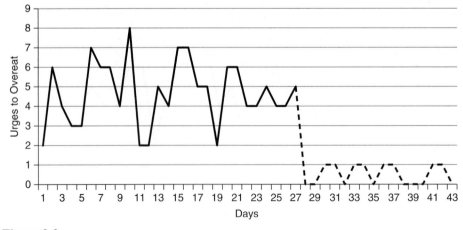

Figure 9.9
Data for Client R Showing Daily Urges to Overeat Rate for Baseline (A, Solid Line) and Intervention (B, Dashed Line) Phases

A way to overcome this uncertainty is to have the client return to the agency for a follow-up visit to determine whether therapeutic change occurred on a sustained basis. In this case, Client R returned to the mental health agency for a 6-month follow-up visit. On her return, the social worker instructed Client R to monitor her urges to overeat once again. She was told to follow the same procedure and make a tick mark on a pad each time she had an urge to overeat. She was told to return to the agency after a 2-week period for a reevaluation. In effect, the social worker was employing an A-B-A design. The A-B (baseline-intervention) occurred during the time Client R presented for treatment. The additional A in this new A-B-A design is the follow-up baseline monitoring 6-months after treatment was terminated.

Figure 9.10 shows the original baseline (A), the intervention phase (B), and a separate graph of the 6-month follow-up baseline. The 6-month follow-up baseline mean was 0.57. This value indicates that Client R had a sustained therapeutic effect 6-months after treatment. Client R indicated that she did not return to overeating, has been compliant with her diabetic diet, and automatically asks herself the three intervention questions anytime she thinks she might want to overeat.

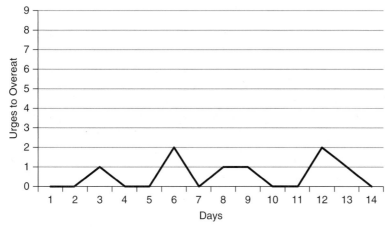

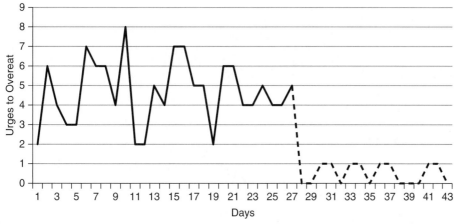

Figure 9.10
Baseline (A) and Intervention (B) Data for Client R in Bottom Graph. Baseline (A) 6-Month Follow-Up Data in Top Graph

However, if Client R did not show the significant removal of urges to overeat, then the social worker would employ an A-B-A-B design. In this case, the follow-up baseline would indicate that Client R showed a return of urges to overeat and was in need of another intervention phase (B). If this subsequent intervention phase proved successful, then further follow-up may be initiated at another 6-month interval, which would extend the A-B-A-B design to an A-B-A-B-A design.

Concurrent Multiple Baseline Designs

Not all cases using the A-B-A or A-B-A-B design show a desired outcome on the target behavior. Rather than withdrawing intervention to a client or organizational policy, the social worker has an option to employ a concurrent multiple baseline design to rule out the possible influence of external events that may have skewed results when looking at a single case. This procedure is also useful when an intervention is successful and the social worker wants some assurance that the intervention was not the result of some external influence. It may be difficult to have multiple clients with the same target behavior in the same agency. For this reason, concurrent multiple baseline designs usually have a minimum of three cases.

In the case of Client R, the social worker used an A-B design. If the social worker decided to do a more rigorous study, she would choose two additional cases with the same target behavior—urges to overeat. In this design, all three cases would begin monitoring their urges to overeat at the same time (Figure 9.11). To control for external events that may affect the outcome of the intervention phase (B), the social worker would not introduce the intervention phase to the second client until the first client's intervention phase stabilizes. Once the first client's intervention phase stabilizes, the second client would enter his or her intervention phase. Once the second client's intervention phase stabilizes, the third client would enter his or her intervention phase. If the social worker is using an A-B-A-B design, the second A-B phases would be introduced on the same staggered schedule.

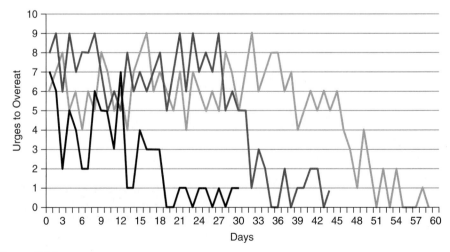

Figure 9.11

A Concurrent Multiple Baseline A-B Design Showing Three Subjects Monitoring Urges to Overeat and Subsequent Effects of Interventions for Each Subject

Multiple Intervention Designs

Multiple intervention designs are used when a social worker decides to use an intervention that increases in intensity over time, or interventions that are different and are applied at different times. In either case, the client or organization tracks a target behavior to establish a baseline level, and then assesses any change in the baseline due to each intervention, whether different in intensity, or different in kind.

The nomenclature for an intervention that increases in intensity over time is A-B^1-B^2-B^3 . . . . The nomenclature for interventions that differ in kind over time is A-B-C-D- . . . . In both cases, A is the baseline, and the other designations are the interventions. Another variation is combining a previous intervention with a subsequent intervention. The nomenclature is A-B-BC. This combination is used when no satisfactory change results from an intervention, so another intervention is added to increase the probability of desired change. In addition, this model may extend itself the same way for the model in which the intervention differs in kind. The nomenclature is: A-B-BC-D-E-EF, or any other variation of combinations.

Another variation is the A-B-A-C design. In this design, the social worker has the ability to test more than one intervention after each baseline phase. A limitation of this design is concluding what the effect of each intervention is. Is the C intervention an effect that is cumulative from the B intervention? Alternatively, does the C intervention have its own unique effect?

In some cases, determining a baseline is not possible. This situation may occur when a client presents for treatment, is in considerable distress, and a clinical decision is made to immediately perform an intervention. When a change is observed in the target behavior, a baseline can be initiated to determine if the intervention successfully reduced or eliminated the target behavior after withdrawal of the intervention. The nomenclature for this design is B-A. B is the intervention, and A is a baseline measurement after withdrawal of the intervention. An alternative approach is to retrospectively create a baseline from a client's record or an organizational record.

DIFFICULTIES WITH SINGLE-SUBJECT DATA ANALYSIS

Although many methods have been tried to interpret change in single-subject data, the most reliable approach is visual analysis (Kahng et al., 2010). However, visual analysis requires a high level of training if several raters are used to evaluate findings from different subjects. Several certified academic programs have been established nationwide to train behavioral analysts in the visual analysis of behavioral data (Shook, 2006).

Complications of data analysis occur in each phase of single-subject designs. Baseline data are not necessarily true baseline data. By having a client track a target behavior, the baseline may be an intervention. Because the client is developing a heightened awareness of a target problem during the baseline phase, variability in the baseline data may be a result of focusing on the target behavior. In addition, if there is a wide variability in the baseline data, making it impossible to see a clear trend in the data, judging any change in the data

*No matter which design
the social worker
chooses, he or she must
structure all design decisions and interactions
with the client by considering the culture of the
client, and causing no
harm to the client by ad-
hering to the National
Association of Social
Workers Code of Ethics.*

because of the introduction of an intervention becomes difficult. Was the change in the data applicable to all points on the baseline? Alternatively, did the intervention affect the data only at certain levels?

Scale differences in graphed data can bias the interpretation by the degree to which the data are compressed or exaggerated. During the intervention phase the exaggeration of data can be used in itself as an intervention. In a single-subject study of five women undergoing treatment of urges to overeat (Youdin & Hemmes, 1978), a logarithmic scale was used to grossly exaggerate the target behavior. If the client reported zero urges/day and returned to 1 or 2 urges/day, the logarithmic scale distorts the scale making the return look very serious. Subjects in this study reported feeling "alarmed" at the change from zero urges/day to 1 or 2 urges/day, a consequent perception that would not have occurred if a normal scale was used. Therefore, the choice of scale can distort data to the interpreter, or to the client.

SINGLE-SUBJECT DESIGNS AND HUMAN RIGHTS

When a social worker decides to use a single-subject design as part of a treatment plan for a client or an organization, he or she must determine if the resultant data are only for treatment purposes, or will be used for subsequent publication. If they are used only for treatment purposes, the client needs to be briefed on the confidentiality of the data, the problems of delaying treatment while determining a baseline, issues involved with early termination of an intervention that occurs in an A-B-A design. When possible, preference should be for A-B-A-B, A-B-C-D, A-B-BC, or $A\text{-}B^1\text{-}B^2\text{-}B^3$ designs. No matter which design the social worker chooses, he or she must structure all design decisions and interactions with the client by considering the culture of the client, and causing no harm to the client by adhering to the National Association of Social Workers Code of Ethics.

In the case of a social worker working for an institution that requires an Institutional Review Board approval, such approval must be given to assure safety of the client, and to protect the confidentiality of the client if the results of the single-subject study are published. In addition, the client must be presented with a mechanism for debriefing that includes explanation of the results of the study and availability of counseling if the client feels that any harm occurred because of the study.

SUMMARY

Single-subject design is a valuable tool for social work as it enables the social worker to use it as a method for evidence-based practice. Whether working in an agency, in private practice, or as a consultant, the social worker can gather information on practice effectiveness without using large sample sizes, control groups, or sophisticated data analysis. From an ethical point of view, the social worker has a tool for examining practice effectiveness, giving the client or organization an individualized rapid assessment of the effectiveness of chosen interventions, and if found ineffective, the ability to quickly employ more effective interventions.

However, many environmental influences often hinder the social worker's ability to employ single-subject design. In many acute settings, a client is seen on a short-term basis, making it impossible for the social worker to take baseline data before using an intervention. In many agencies, a social worker's caseload is considerably high, requiring an extraordinary amount of paperwork, and leaving little time for him or her to engage in the activities required for single-subject design.

Most social workers implementing single-subject design as an everyday tool require a change in orientation from research to practice. Social workers need to see single-subject design as a critical tool for evidence-based practice rather than a research technique. Although single-subject design is a valid tool for publishable research, social workers need to see single-subject design as one of the techniques in the armamentarium of clinical or organizational practice. Evidence-based practice implies the ability of the social worker to self-inform whether practice techniques are effective, and in addition, to make such information available to other social workers.

Succeed with PEARSON mysocialworklab

Log onto **www.mysocialworklab.com** to access a wealth of case studies, videos, and assessment. (*If you did not receive an access code to* **MySocialWorkLab** *with this text and wish to purchase access online, please visit* www.mysocialworklab.com.)

1. **Watch the ethical practice video "Managing Personal Values: The Code of Ethics."** Using the example from this video on recognizing and managing personal

values and consulting with a supervisor, determine how you would consult a professor or colleague to ensure your single-subject research design adheres to the Code of Ethics.

2. **Watch the research based practice video "Engaging in Research Informed Practice."** Indicate how you would use single-subject research designs to inform and develop evidence-based practice.

PRACTICE TEST The following questions will test your knowledge of the content found within this chapter. For additional assessment, including licensing-exam type questions on applying chapter content to practice, visit **MySocialWorkLab.**

1. The length of the baseline in single-subjects designs is usually:
   a. Extended until a stable trend appears
   b. No longer than 7 days
   c. Determined by the subject
   d. Never longer than the intervention phase

2. The one aspect that is not valid for a target problem in single-subject design is:
   a. Frequency
   b. Ratio to baseline
   c. Duration
   d. Magnitude

3. Single-subject design was formalized for psychological research by:
   a. Freud
   b. Ellis
   c. Sidman
   d. Richmond

4. The traditional single-subject design used by social workers is:
   a. Experimental design
   b. Longitudinal design
   c. A-B design
   d. Pretest–posttest design

5. A social worker has a client who wants to stop smoking. The client indicates that every time she thinks about smoking she has to smoke a cigarette. She has tried numerous times to quit smoking but was never successful. Recently, she suffered from a bad case of pneumonia that scared her and motivated her to stop smoking. How would you design a single-subject study that would determine whether cognitive behavior therapy is an effective intervention for this client to stop smoking?

ASSESS YOUR COMPETENCE Use the scale below to rate your current level of achievement on the following concepts or skills associated with each competency presented in the chapter:

1	2	3
I can accurately describe the concept or skill	I can consistently identify the concept or skill when observing and analyzing practice activities	I can competently implement the concept or skill in my own practice

_____ can apply social work ethical principles when designing a single-subject study.

_____ can infuse human rights and social justice principles to protect a client participating in a single-subject study.

_____ can use single-subject study research done by others to inform my practice.

_____ can use a single-subject study to facilitate the treatment and evaluation of my clients.

10

The Qualitative Approach: Tapping the Artist and Scientist Within

Core Competencies in This Chapter (Check marks indicate which competencies are demonstrated)				
☐ Professional Identity	☐ Ethical Practice	☐ Critical Thinking	✓ Diversity in Practice	☐ Human Rights and Justice
✓ Research-Based Practice	☐ Human Behavior	☐ Policy Practice	✓ Practice Contexts	✓ Engage, Assess, Intervene, Evaluate

INTRODUCTION

Case Study: Qualitative Research Example

Alice is an 80-year-old grassroots activist whose story was gathered as part of a qualitative narrative or life history interview conducted in 2005. The purpose of the study was to explore what factors motivated and sustained her grassroots activism, especially for peace during a century of world wars. Alice reminisced about her life journey over four decades of social and political change efforts. She reflected:

> My whole thinking about how change comes about is different. Now I think of everything as energy. And I think peace cannot be imposed. I think something has to happen to people's hearts.

The in-depth life history interview took place in Alice's home on a dead-end street in a northeastern suburban home in the United States. She shared photos and newspaper clippings that spanned four decades of her local and national activist efforts. Analysis of the qualitative data revealed three themes related to spirituality, relationships, and empowerment. Table 10.1 presents a timeline of significant life events that highlights the personal, social, political, and historical events of her life that she discussed during her interview.

Table 10.1   Significant Life Events Timeline of Alice, an 80-Year-Old Grassroots Activist

Year	Age	Family	Religion	School	Historical Event	Friends	Description
1925	0	Alice born on Nov 11					Learned values
1929	4		Evangelical Church		Great Depression		Learned values
1933	8		Evangelical Church		FDR President Great Depression		Learned values
1935	10	Mother dies Moves to aunt's home		Changes schools	Great Depression		Learned values
1936	11	Aunt dies Moves to conservative uncle		Changes schools	Great Depression		Learned values
1939	14		Methodist Church	Graduates grammar school	Depression ending	Teacher role model	Learned values
1940	15		Methodist Church	Enters high school	Europe at War	Teacher role model	Learned values

Table 10.1   **Significant Life Events Timeline of Alice, an 80-Year-Old Grassroots Activist (Continued)**

Year	Age	Family	Religion	School	Historical Event	Friends	Description
1941	16		Methodist Church		US enters WWII	Teacher role model	Learned values
1942	17		Methodist Church	Graduates high school		Teacher role model	Learned values
1943	18			Enters college			Learned values
1945	20				WWII ends		Learned values
1946	21			Graduates college in 3 years		Exchange trip to Mexico	Learned values
1947	22	Married Moves to California					Learned values
1948	23					Travels to Mexico with friends	Learned values
1950	25	Divorced first marriage Returns to Illinois		Begins graduate school	McCarthy Era	Involved with political man	Angry about social and political conditions
1952	27				Eisenhower runs against Adlai Stevenson and wins		Angry about social and political conditions
1954	29	Father dies		Finishes graduate school	McCarthyism ending Desegregation illegal		Angry about social and political conditions
1955	30	Marries second husband			Rosa Parks refuses to move to the back of the bus		Angry about social and political conditions
1956	31	Has first child					Angry about social and political conditions
1958	33	Moves to New Jersey					Angry about social and political conditions

(continued)

Table 10.1   Significant Life Events Timeline of Alice, an 80-Year-Old Grassroots Activist (Continued)

Year	Age	Family	Religion	School	Historical Event	Friends	Description
1960	35	Second child born, daughter			Strontium-90 scare Kennedy president	Significant female friends' support	Takes social action
1961	36	Third child born, daughter				Collective organization	Action and affiliation
1962	37	Fourth child born, daughter				Collective organization	Action and affiliation
1963	38	Husband supports political involvement		Learns Marxism and Socialism	Kennedy assassinated Buddhist monks set themselves on fire Betty Friedan publishes the *Feminine Mystique*	Collective organization Support of female friends in movement	Personal integration: Individual and social transformation
1964	39	Fifth child born, daughter; Husband supports political involvement		Learns Marxism and Socialism	Congress passes civil rights act	Grassroots Community Organizing	Personal integration: Individual and social transformation
1965	40	Husband supports political involvement		Learns Marxism and Socialism	Malcolm X shot, American troops in Viet Nam	Grassroots Community Organizing	Personal integration: Individual and social transformation
1966	41	Diagnosed breast cancer Husband supports political involvement		Learns Marxism and Socialism		Grassroots Community Organizing	Personal integration: Individual and social transformation
1967	42	Husband supports political involvement		Learns Marxism and Socialism	"Race" riots in Newark, NJ	Grassroots Community Organizing	Personal integration: Individual and social transformation
1968	43	Husband supports political involvement		Learns Marxism and Socialism	Martin Luther King shot	Grassroots Community Organizing	Personal integration: Individual and social transformation

Table 10.1   Significant Life Events Timeline of Alice, an 80-Year-Old Grassroots Activist (Continued)

Year	Age	Family	Religion	School	Historical Event	Friends	Description
1973	48	Husband supports political involvement		Learns Marxism and Socialism	Vietnam War ends	Grassroots Community Organizing	Personal integration: Individual and social transformation
1974	49	Husband supports political involvement		Back to school for second master's degree		Grassroots Community Organizing	Personal integration: Individual and social transformation
1975	50	Husband supports political involvement		Teacher		Active in Teacher's Union, Parent/Teacher Alliance	Personal integration: Individual and social transformation
1983	58	Husband wants to end marriage	Begins Yoga, Therapy, Spiritual quest	Teacher		Grassroots Community Organizing	Personal integration: Individual and social transformation
1988	63	Divorced	Spiritual Path	Retired	Bush president	Grassroots Community Organizing	Personal integration: Individual and social transformation
1991	66		Spiritual Path	Teaches yoga, attends spiritual classes	Desert Storm War	Grassroots Community Organizing	Personal integration: Individual and social transformation
1992	67	Makes amends with ex-husband	Spiritual Path	Teaches yoga, attends spiritual classes	Clinton president	Grassroots Community Organizing	Personal integration: Individual and social transformation
1993	68	First grandchild born	Spiritual Path	Teaches yoga, attends spiritual classes		Grassroots Community Organizing	Personal integration: Individual and social transformation

(continued)

Table 10.1　**Significant Life Events Timeline of Alice, an 80-Year-Old Grassroots Activist (Continued)**

Year	Age	Family	Religion	School	Historical Event	Friends	Description
1997	72	Second grandchild born	Spiritual Path	Teaches yoga, attends spiritual classes		Grassroots Community Organizing	Personal integration: Individual and social transformation
2000	75	Close with family	Spiritual Path	Teaches yoga, attends spiritual classes	Bush president	Grassroots Community Organizing	Personal integration: Individual and social transformation
2001	76	Close with family	Spiritual Path	Teaches yoga, attends spiritual classes	WTC attacks	Grassroots Community Organizing	Personal integration: Individual and social transformation
2002	77	Close with family	Spiritual Path	Teaches yoga, attends spiritual classes	War on Terror Afghanistan	Grassroots Community Organizing	Personal integration: Individual and social transformation
2003	78	Close with family	Spiritual Path	Teaches yoga, attends spiritual classes	War on Terror Iraq	Grassroots Community Organizing	Personal integration: Individual and social transformation
2005	80	Close with family	Spiritual Path	Teaches yoga, attends spiritual classes	War on Terror Iraq	Grassroots Community Organizing	Personal integration: Individual and social transformation

Alice's Story

Alice was born on November 11, 1925, to Abe and Mary English in America in the Midwestern state of Illinois. She was the only child of impoverished working-class parents during the Great Depression (1929–1933). As a child she remembered having a distant father and fearful mother. Alice also shared her memorable spiritual experiences as a child, such as being Methodist but attending an Evangelical church where she attended Bible schools and services in which "any time things would start really getting emotional and people would start giving themselves over and people would start fainting, my mother would then take me by the hand and march me home."

Alice was sensitized to class differences and emotional and financial insecurity at a very early age. As a child, she viewed social injustice as the "seeping in of class differences." She also talked about society like it had a voice with an attitude when she recounted, "I heard the message loud and clear that there is something wrong with being poor." Alice shared that the *Great Depression* was much harder on the other middle-class families in her neighborhood compared to her family. She said, "we were already poor with not much more to lose."

Alice also experienced a traumatic loss that she reported as having reverberating spiritual and emotional impact. Between the ages of 10 and 11, the unexpected loss of both her mother, from a brain aneurism, and her favorite aunt, who was hit by a car while crossing a street, signified the loss of two significant female relationships in her life. During the interview, Alice stumbled over her words as she talked about the aftermath of "feeling outside the pale, that something was not right." Alice explained: "I think that the death of my mother and my aunt pretty much . . . uh . . . I think that I left my body. I was just so traumatized . . . it was mostly just emotional and reacting to things."

Despite her personal losses during her adolescence, Alice remained spiritual and class-conscious. Alice reported that the unequal distribution of wealth became even more blaringly obvious to her in grammar school after she transferred from her working-class school to the upper-class district school. Alice elaborated, "I had this, I guess, this thing of justice and injustice. And there was a big difference in the way people lived and in their education." Alice described important mentoring relationships, such as a female teacher who ran a community service program entitled the Sunshine Club. Alice recounted about the positive impact that this woman had on her emotional life and her aspirations to help others.

In her adult years, Alice was married, received advanced degrees in education, and became an elementary school teacher. She recollected that the McCarthy Hearings of the 1950s were a "wake-up call" to her. She said at the time she felt "angry and indignant" over societal injustice. In the 1960s, Alice gave birth to three children. Her shift into motherhood during a time of great societal transition became an important shift of thoughts into action. Soon afterward she became politically active in response to the Strontium 90 (radiation) scare and the Vietnam War. She said, "I vividly remember when the Buddhist monks burned themselves and the sacrifice they were willing to make for peace. I just felt I had to do something about the growing radiation scare and what seemed like a needless war." She began to hand out fliers at local doctors' offices that contained information about how radiation could adversely affect young children. Other acts soon followed, such as participating in a spontaneous sit-in at a Memorial Day parade in protest of the Vietnam War.

Alice's entry into activism affiliated her with other women activists. Support from female activist friends and her family was an important source of Alice's spiritual and emotional sustenance as she advocated for social change. This lifelong process led to Alice's current views on change. At the time of the interview, Alice saw individual and social change as indivisible. Her perspective shifted from seeking peace as solely an inward experience to seeing it as an outward experience as well.

QUALITATIVE APPROACH: THE JOURNEY AS THE REWARD

The Chinese proverb, "the journey is the reward," emphasizes the importance of the process of using a qualitative approach to understanding human experience.

The Chinese proverb, "the journey is the reward," emphasizes the importance of the process of using a qualitative approach to understanding human experience. As illustrated in the previous example, qualitative methods provided a mechanism for Alice to reconstruct 80 years of memorable events, the meaning she ascribed to these events, and reflection upon the life process that help shaped her current worldview.

But What of Qualitative Research?

So, has your curiosity been piqued as to what it is about a qualitative approach that could elicit such an in-depth response? Cresswell (2006) described qualitative research as an "inquiry process of understanding based on distinct traditions of inquiry that explores a social or human problem. The researcher builds a complex, holistic picture, analyzes worlds, reports detailed views of information and conducts the study in a natural setting" (p. 15). Similarly, in their groundbreaking text, *Naturalist Inquiry*, Lincoln and Guba (1985) underscored the "discovery oriented" nature of qualitative research. It is a flexible, as opposed to rigid, design that most often occurs in the natural setting of participants. As previously reviewed (see Figure 10.1), a qualitative inductive

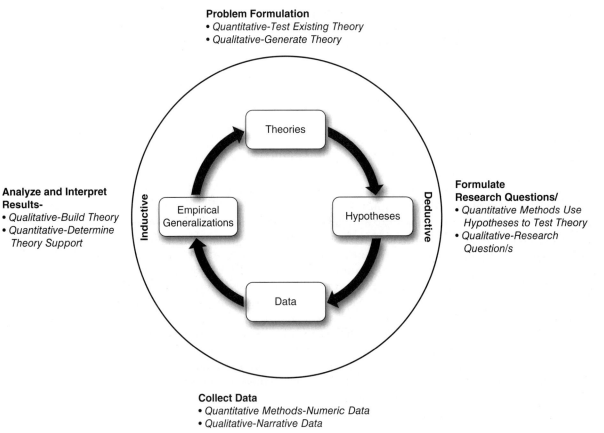

Problem Formulation
• *Quantitative-Test Existing Theory*
• *Qualitative-Generate Theory*

Theories

Inductive

Deductive

Empirical Generalizations

Hypotheses

Data

Analyze and Interpret Results-
• *Qualitative-Build Theory*
• *Quantitative-Determine Theory Support*

Formulate Research Questions/
• *Quantitative Methods Use Hypotheses to Test Theory*
• *Qualitative-Research Question/s*

Collect Data
• *Quantitative Methods-Numeric Data*
• *Qualitative-Narrative Data*

Figure 10.1
The Cycle of Inductive and Deductive Processes for Research and Practice Evaluation

approach is well positioned to capture the authenticity of individuals and cultures from the individuals' point of view.

The methods used also can help create ideal conditions for participants to share their world. Qualitative research most often uses narrative data (i.e., words) gathered during in-person or focus group interviews and visual observations, and/or reviews of existing documents (written or visual, such as photo albums, case records). These narrative data are then sifted and sorted to identify patterns and themes to develop empirical generalization or theories (Padgett, 2008). As illustrated with Alice, the findings often include verbatim quotes from participants to best represent individuals using their own words.

This chapter introduces the important phases and methods used in a qualitative approach to research. It begins with a comparison of qualitative and quantitative approaches, followed by a discussion of the purpose of qualitative inquiry and the different phases and methods choices related to sampling, data sources, data analysis, strategies for rigor, and dissemination.

Complementary Relationship: Quantitative and Qualitative

Qualitative research may be a powerful source of evidence as a solo method or complementary to quantitative methods (see Table 10.2). As noted in previous chapters, quantitative studies most often start with deductive processes in

Diversity in Practice

Critical Thinking Question: Diversity in practice also may refer to diversity in thought. How do qualitative methods differ from quantitative methods in diversity in thought and practice?

Table 10.2	**Comparison of Qualitative and Quantitative Designs**	
	Qualitative Design	Quantitative: Experimental Design
Objective	To explore or describe internal or external experiences	To determine cause and effects
Setting or conditions	Natural setting, minimal manipulation	Manipulated conditions and external influences
Logic	Inductive (specific to general)	Deductive (general to specific)
Worldview	Constructivism, holistic and subjective	Postpositivism, linear mechanistic, objective
Use of theory	Generate theory, use data to make empirical generalizations	Test hypotheses based on existing theory or prior empirical support
Conceptualization	Use sensitizing concepts	Use operational definition of key concepts
Research design	Dynamic	Fixed
Focus	Process oriented	Outcome oriented
Researcher role	Collaborator	Expert
Values	Value-laden/subjective	Values influenced but controlled/objective
Data	Narrative data (words) and qualitative data analysis	Numeric data and statistical analysis
Sampling	Nonprobability/purposeful sampling	Probability, random sampling

which their hypotheses are firmly grounded in existing theories or existing literature. In contrast, qualitative methods commonly use an inductive process to answering research questions and analyzing findings. This method includes using data to generate theory or empirical findings from the ground up. Similar to a quantitative approach, both consult the existing literature and use existing theoretical and empirical literature to inform and/or frame a study. However, in a qualitative study this information does not dictate the study direction as compared to a quantitative study that is directed by hypothesis testing. In contrast, a qualitative approach is known for its flexible and emergent design and is commonly guided by open-ended and nondirective research questions (Krueger & Neuman, 2006; Marshall & Rossman, 2010; McLeod & Thomson, 2009).

Whereas quantitative approaches often use large random samples, experimental designs, and valid measures, qualitative approaches often use in-depth interviews, descriptive notes from field observations, and document reviews (Creswell, 2009). See Table 10.2 for a comparison of approaches.

Examples

There are strengths and weaknesses of using either a quantitative or qualitative approach, especially in relation to the breadth and depth of the findings. On the one hand, quantitative methods can generate generalizable findings by analyzing the responses of a large number of people. This method might include gathering data on the frequency of binge drinking among adults aged 50 and older (Creswell, 2009). For example, using a nationally representative sample, the National Survey on Drug Use and Health found that about 30% of individuals aged 50 to 64 reported binge drinking (i.e., five or more drinks at one sitting during the past month [Substance Abuse and Mental Health Services Administration, 2006]). Whereas this information is useful in identifying at-risk populations, we have little information as to why this pattern exists, or how other factors, such as cultural background, may influence drinking patterns. This is where qualitative methods might help to fill in knowledge gaps.

Qualitative methods can help gather the story behind adaptive and maladaptive patterns of drinking. This can occur when conducting a study by purposefully asking a select number of information-rich cases about their drinking patterns and the meaning they ascribe to drinking.

For example, Wooksoo (2009) explored patterns of drinking among older adult Korean immigrants in Canada. She conducted focus group interviews with 19 older adults of Korean descent who emigrated from Korea to Canada. She analyzed her data using a grounded theory analysis method (using constant comparison to identify unique categories in the data). She found that relocation to a new country only minimally changed their understanding of drinking or their drinking patterns. However, the factors that did influence the respondents' drinking behavior were related to structural and legal factors. Sociolegal factors that helped to impede binge or excessive drinking included strict governmental alcohol policies that include high price of alcohol, lack of venues to purchase alcohol, and the strict oversight and enforcement of alcohol policies by Canadian law enforcement personnel (Wooksoo, 2009).

Because qualitative and quantitative methods involve differing strengths and weaknesses, they constitute alternative, but not mutually exclusive, strategies for research. This comparison was meant to weigh the benefits of approaches for answering different research questions. Some social workers opt for mixed methods (both qualitative and quantitative methods) to reap the benefits of both approaches (Creswell, 2009; Tashakkori & Teddlie, 1998). Therefore, when choosing methods, social workers must weigh the difference between needing to know "how much" and "how meaningful" or both (Patton, 2002).

Purpose of Qualitative Research

One of the major purposes of qualitative research is to capture the authentic lived experiences of humans and their social environment (Strauss & Corbin, 1998). Qualitative research attempts to do so by conducting research and evaluation projects in a natural setting and by providing a flexible framework for naturalist inquiry (Lincoln & Guba, 1985).

One of the major purposes of qualitative research is to capture the authentic lived experiences of humans and their social environment.

"Becoming the Instrument"

Perhaps one of the most important aspects of qualitative approach is delving into the artistic as well as scientific aspects that give it form (Denzin & Lincoln, 2005). In quantitative research, validity and reliability hinge on the quality of a measurement instrument, such as a survey or questionnaire with predetermined questions administered using fixed standardized procedures (Krueger & Neuman, 2006). In contrast, when using a qualitative approach the researcher is the instrument (Patton, 2002).

Critical Self-Reflection

The old adage "physician know thyself" (Veysman, 2005) is apropos when a qualitative research is used. Similarly, use of a qualitative approach demands "social worker know thyself." Therefore, in "being the measurement instrument" social workers have a continuous gaze on their internal "mirror" of self and use what they see for critical self-reflection and awareness.

Awareness includes an in-depth attunement to oneself, others, and the dynamic interactions of the social and physical environment that is often unnoticed in everyday living (Glesne, 1999; Patton, 2002). In fact, the credibility or believability of qualitative research results often hinges on the skill, competence, and rigor of the person doing the research. It is very important, therefore, to be aware of one's *positionality*, which refers to understanding one's position in the context of race, gender, age, socioeconomic status, and culture and how it impacts interactions with other individuals who may be similar to or different from oneself. In a qualitative approach, the validity (or trustworthiness and credibility) is literally the internal experiences of the person conducting the research who is minimally influenced by biases so that he or she is best able to capture the authentic experiences of the individuals or culture under investigation (Shaw & Gould, 2001).

Practice Awareness

A qualitative approach is well suited for social workers because of their direct contact with clients and constituents in the field and their prolonged engagement in many practice and community settings (Merriam & Associates, 2005). The combined rise of evidence-based practice and action research makes it an imperative for social workers to have a strong sense of awareness of self, others, and the environmental context. Table 10.3 presents a list of common values and practices of a qualitative approach.

Table 10.3	Qualitative Methods: Awareness and Practices
Awareness (internal and external)	Practices
Internal (self) • Curious • Respectful • Open • Humanistic • Sensitive • Pragmatic • Creative • Flexible • Perceptive • Owns one's perspective • High tolerance for ambiguity • Well-developed relationship orientation • Self-analytical • Awareness of inner voice • Aware of personal biases (positionality) • Self-reflective • Mindfulness (e.g., being fully present) • Neutral (balances subjectivity and objectivity) • Trustworthy • Open to diversity of perspectives • Strives for credibility of the inquirer *External (other)* • Holistic perspective • Social, political, cultural consciousness • Relational awareness • Context awareness • Sensitivity to immediate and larger contextual environments • Responsive • Capable of in-depth immersion	*Internal (self)* • Articulates ownership of one's own voice and perspective • Mindfulness • Regular use of active reflection • Ability to understand others without being judgmental • Ability to correct sources of personal biases and errors • Practices heightened awareness of senses (e.g., sight and hearing) • Sensitive to nuances in verbal and nonverbal communication • Attuned to interpersonal and environmental dynamics • Practices trustworthiness • Actively strives for credibility *External (other)* • Careful attention to interviewer–interviewee relationship • Uses advanced interviewing and observational skills (verbal and nonverbal) • Advanced communication skills (formal and informal discussions) • Engages in careful and diligent effort in designing and implementing research • Engages in precision in thoughts • Writes detailed descriptive field notes • Documents narrative data in verbatim form

Social workers, who have strong grounding in awareness of self, others, and the environment, are in an ideal position to excel in qualitative fieldwork, including evidence-based practice decision-making. Arguably, these characteristics are consistent with social work practice expectations, which are to be self-aware and empathic (Fox, Martin, & Green, 2007; Jarvis, 1999). Qualitative approaches can help reinforce these characteristics.

As illustrated in Table 10.3, awareness of internal and external values involves careful calibration of an internal and external value orientation (Patton, 2002). As the term *calibration* suggests, social work involves continual checking of the self as a "measuring instrument" to correct for potential biases or inaccuracies in perception.

Self-Awareness

Essential qualities that help foster a qualitative approach emphasize self and other awareness. Common characteristics noted by scholars of qualitative methods include authenticity, humanism, trustworthiness, respectfulness, open-mindedness, sensitivity, and creativity. These humanistic qualities are balanced with precision and accuracy in thought, attention to detail, diligence, consistency, pragmatism, and high tolerance for uncertainty.

Another essential qualitative quality is to take complete ownership of one's perspective. In fact, a strong awareness of one's inner voice can silence inner ramblings and falsehoods that might cloud accurate interpretations of self and the world. Reflexivity, or the use of critical self-reflection, suggests being aware of oneself and personal biases (e.g., Cresswell, 2006; Padgett, 2008; Patton, 2002).

Other Awareness

A qualitative approach also necessitates a well-developed "other" orientation. Qualitative qualities in the relational realm include an internal worldview that includes mindfulness (i.e., being fully present with others and/or in a situation); a holistic perspective (e.g., seeing the dynamics of the entire picture); neutrality (e.g., balancing subjective and objective realms); and social, political, and cultural consciousness (e.g., internalized mezzo and macro-level awareness). Relational awareness (i.e., awareness of others and contexts) consists of externalized sensitivity (i.e., sensitivity to immediate and larger contextual environments) and openness to a diversity of perspectives (Guba & Lincoln, 1994).

Qualitative Practices

However, it is not enough to only have an internal values orientation only; it also has to be practiced. These values must also be translated into observable practices (see Table 10.3). For example, using a qualitative approach to research and evaluation, a social worker should be able to demonstrate the ability to express ownership of his or her own voice and perspective in verbal or written work. Other practice behaviors include the demonstrated use of active reflection, responsiveness and empathy toward others, and demonstration of trustworthiness and credibility. The behaviors also include the ability to recognize and correct sources of personal biases and errors in thinking, using advanced interviewing and observational skills (verbal and nonverbal), and engaging in formal and informal discussions. As for documentation, the behaviors include the ability to write detailed descriptive field notes and to document narrative data in verbatim form. (e.g., Cresswell, 2006 Moustakas, 1990; Padgett, 2008; Patton, 2002). Having a strong foundation in qualitative values and practices is useful across a diversity of qualitative perspectives, which will be reviewed next.

Diversity in Perspective: Qualitative Approaches to Inquiry

Currently, a diverse array of theoretical traditions or approaches from many professional disciplines with early roots in late 19th-century ethnography (Madden, 2010) are classified as a part of qualitative theoretical traditions or approaches. This diversity in perspectives across methods provides in-depth insights that range from an individual's lived experience (e.g., psychology) to a community's experience of culture (e.g., anthropology) at both local and

Currently, a diverse array of theoretical traditions or approaches from many professional disciplines are classified as a part of qualitative theoretical traditions or approaches.

global settings. Some scholars have classified upward of 16 to 19 different types of qualitative theoretical traditions (e.g., Patton, 2002); other scholars have classified fewer than three to five categories (e.g., Cresswell, 2006; Marshall & Rossman, 2010; Padgett, 2008).

Three-Genre Classification Scheme

For example, Marshall and Rossman (2010) classified qualitative methods into three main "genres" or approaches. These include the individual or societal-level or communication processes: individual lived experiences, society and culture, and language and communication. For example, qualitative approaches that explore individual lived experiences often use in-depth interviews of individuals to gather their "internal" lived experiences (e.g., phenomenology). A second category of qualitative approaches focuses on studying societies and cultures. This macro-level focus often uses observations and interviews of group members of the culture, group, agency, or organizations to capture the diversity of the culture and setting (e.g., ethnography and action research). In contrast with the other two methods, a third category of qualitative approaches focuses on language and communication as opposed to the individual or group culture. This includes text analysis of speeches, interactions, and written and visual documentation (e.g., discourse analysis).

Other Qualitative Classification Schemes

Cresswell (2006) identified five central qualitative approaches to inquiry that have relevance to social work. These approaches include (a) narrative (biography, life history), (b) phenomenology, (c) case study, (d) grounded theory, and, (e) ethnography. Padgett (2008) added the additional category for action-oriented approaches, such as action research, participatory action research, and community-based participatory action research. Oftentimes, social workers planning a research or evaluation project must weigh out among these options which approach might best answer their research questions. These core approaches that range from an individual focus to social/cultural focus are briefly reviewed next.

Individual Focus Approaches

Narrative Approach

A narrative approach (or narratology) explores people's narratives or stories about their world (Atkinson, 1998; Reissman, 2008). The narrative approach is rooted in the humanities and social sciences and involves gathering the stories of one or more individuals, gathering and reporting their experiences, including organizing them chronologically, thematically, or according to a story line that includes plots (Reissman, 2008). Narrative studies may be in the form of a biography, autobiography, life history, or oral history of one or more individuals. A biographical study is an account of a person's life written by another person. In contrast, individuals themselves write an autobiography.

Similarly, an oral history interview consists of gathering personal reflections of events and their causes and effects from one or more individuals (Hoopes, 1979; Poll, 2002; Ritchie, 1995). In the oral family history, oral tradition, which is practiced by many indigenous populations, such as Native Americans, and oral history are in the form of stories handed down across multiple generations. These stories also may contain human and nonhuman characters, such as animals (Hesse-Biber & Leavy, 2011).

Oral History Exercise   The oral history exercise involves practicing how to conduct an oral history interview with older adults who have personal or family histories of immigration. Exhibit 10.1 of "Conducting a Literature Review" section provides an example of an oral history interview that can be conducted with adults (aged 50 and older) who have personal or family histories of immigration. The oral history questionnaire contains open-ended questions that attempt to capture the individual's personal or family history of life before, during, and after the immigration experience. This exercise can be practiced with classmates. Some instructors may choose to officially implement the project. A detailed guide (Maschi, Jardim, & Georas, 2009) on how to conduct an oral history project, including how to obtain IRB approval, can be found on the Moving Stories website (http://www.fordham.edu/movingstories).

Phenomenological Approach

Phenomenology, based in psychology, focuses on the individual. It attempts to describe the meaning behind common experiences, such as the stigmatization of individuals with mental health problems (Moustakas, 1990; Smith, Flowers, & Larkin, 2009). For example, Davidson (2003) used a phenomenological approach to explore the lived experiences of individuals with schizophrenia using in-depth interviews. Participants described a significant turning point after developing a self-identity that existed outside of being "a person with an illness."

Mixed Individual or Social or Cultural Focus Approaches

Grounded Theory Approach

Initially derived from sociology, grounded theory is a qualitative approach that seeks to develop a theory, especially related to understanding processes that are related to individual, social, or cultural factors (Glaser & Straus, 1967). Using an inductive analysis, theory is generated from data gathered from many participants who share an experience under investigation (Charmaz, 2006).

Merighi and Grimes (2000) conducted a grounded theory study of the coming-out experience for an ethnically diverse group of gay men. The sample consisted of 57 gay men with a mean age of 21.6. The data were collected during 1.5-hour semi-structured interviews and were analyzed using grounded theory strategies (see Table 10.4). The results of the grounded theory analysis revealed the varying dynamics with family related to the coming-out process. These variations were classified as follows: (a) types of disclosure (i.e., direct or indirect), (b) cultural factors that hampered or facilitated disclosure (i.e., hamper—family preservation and perception of family, facilitate—family unity and unconditional love), (c) familial response to the initial disclosure (i.e., support through action, support that preserves the kinship bond, avoidance, distancing, and disengagement), and (d) turning points in the initial disclosure (e.g., accessing gay supportive resources, establishing distance to foster self-reflection and resolution, letting go of heterosexual assumptions and ideals) (Merighi & Grimes, 2000).

Table 10.4   Example of Grounded Theory Findings

Coming Out to Families in a Multicultural Context

Study purpose: The purpose of this qualitative research study was to explore the coming out experiences of young men of diverse ethnic backgrounds

Sample size: 57 gay males

Sample characteristics: 18 African American, 25 European American, 8 Mexican American, 6 Vietnamese Americans; mean age 21.6, Disclosed sexual identity between ages 16 and 19

Data sources: 1.5 hour semi-structured interviews

Data analysis: Data analyzed using grounded theory methodology

---

Grounded theory results: Overview of findings

A) Types of Disclosure

   1. Direct

   2. Indirect

B) Cultural factors that hamper or facilitate disclosure

   1. Hamper: Family preservation and perception of family

   2. Facilitate: Family unity and unconditional love

C) Familial responses to initial self-disclosure

   1. Support through action

   2. Support that preserves the kinship bond

   3. Avoidance

   4. Distancing and disengagement

D) Turning points in initial disclosure

   1. Accessing gay supportive resources

   2. Establishing distance to foster self-reflection and resolution

   3. Letting go of heterosexual assumptions and ideals

Source: Adapted from Merighi, J. R., & Grimes, M. D. (2000). Coming out to families in a multicultural context. *Families in Society, 81*(1), 32–41.

Social or Cultural Focus Approaches

Ethnographic Approach

Based in anthropology, ethnography explores the culture of a group of people (Fetterman, 2010). Participants in an ethnographic study are generally located in the same place and share a culture of shared values, behaviors, and language. The observer adopts both an emic (insider perspective) and an etic (outsider perspective) perspective, attempts to gain a better understanding of the culture by becoming immersed in it (immersion) over a long period of time (prolonged engagement), engages actively with and observes members of the culture (participant observation), and conducts in-depth interviews (Madden, 2010).

For example, in the classic ethnographic study, *Number Our Days*, anthropologist Barbara Myerhoff (1978) used participant observation and in-depth interviews to explore the culture of older adults of Jewish descent in Venice, California. She embedded herself in the culture, including the local senior centers, for a prolonged period of time. In her examination of the culture, she found the stories of culture and accompanying rituals were a source of resilience for the participants, despite their struggles, such as ongoing poverty, loneliness, and health and housing problems.

Case Study Approach

A case study approach explores one or more cases that are part of a bound system, setting, or context (Stake, 1995). Using a case study approach, a social worker explores a case system, such as an agency, or multiple bounded systems (more than one agency) through multiple data sources that include in-depth interviews, observation, and case record reviews (e.g., observations, interviews, visuals, documents, and reports) (Denzin & Lincoln, 2005; Yin, 2008). For example, Streets of Hope is a case study of an inner-city neighborhood, referred to as Dudley Street in Massachusetts, that transformed itself (Medoff & Sklar, 1994). Mutual respect and a shared vision of change brought neighborhood residents of diverse cultures together to create a better community environment.

Action-Oriented Research Approach

An action-oriented research approach represents several methods with common features, such as action research, participatory action research, and community-based participatory action. There is a democratic nature among stakeholders represented by collaboration that takes place from formulating the initial problem through selecting and implementing research methods to taking action with the findings to help improve the community.

For example, Alice McIntyre (2000) conducted a participatory action research project that incorporated activism with research with inner-city minority youth. Using data collection methods, such as community photography, the youth identified problem areas, such as lack of educational opportunities and community violence that included the presence of trash, pollution, and abandoned houses. McIntyre's use of participatory action methods helped enable the youth to empower themselves to participate in proactive activities and create programs within their community to address their concerns, including picking up the trash. The outcome of the study resulted in youth becoming community social change agents (McIntyre, 2000).

Common Themes Across Approaches

Despite these different approaches, there are many common themes across these approaches related to attitudes and practices (Patton, 2002). In general, qualitative methods have a well-developed strategy and most often involve inductive processes of gathering data in which data are analyzed for common patterns and themes. For example, the Merighi's and Grimes's study (2000) reviewed under the grounded theory section is an example of building a theory from the ground up.

Research-Based Practice

Critical Thinking Question: In what ways can qualitative methods be used to inform research? And why?

RESEARCH CYCLE

The following steps guiding the investigation involve problem formulations (as reviewed in chapters 3 and 4). These steps included deciding on the problem for investigation, the study purpose, and the guiding research questions. Because the qualitative design has an open and flexible design, it does not use predetermined hypotheses and operational definitions for variables (Cresswell, 2006). However, a qualitative approach may use "sensitizing concepts" as a frame serving to remind us that social workers using a qualitative framework do not enter the field with a completely blank slate (Patton, 2002). There are some "sensitizing concepts," such as "juveniles," "schizophrenia," "alcohol use," and "community violence" that might be used to guide a research or evaluation project.

The next section reviews research and evaluation design options that can be used to answer qualitative research questions. The design options highlighted are research design and sampling strategies, data sources, data analysis, and strategies for rigor.

QUALITATIVE RESEARCH DESIGN CHOICES

A study is structured in what is referred to as a research design. Similar to the frame of a house, a research design provides the overall structure in which to construct a research and evaluation plan. In general, the overall structure of a qualitative research design should be flexible and be minimally intrusive to the natural setting (Marshall & Rossman, 2010). In early 20th-century qualitative research, the anthropologist Margaret Mead traveled to remote global locations, such as Samoa, to study other cultures (Fetterman, 2010). In the 21st century, social workers have extended these efforts to both local and global locations with diverse cultures.

On a local level, the field settings may be in agencies or institutions. A social worker may be employed as an administrator or a staff evaluator and use evaluation methods to ensure accountability. Additionally, a social worker may be hired as an outside evaluator for a community or an organization (Shaw, 1999). Overall, the design is often flexible and, if it is an action-based project, should take into account the views of interested stakeholders in conceptualizing the problem and planning and implementing solutions (Stringer, 2007). The research design should be flexible enough to be open to capture the natural world in process. However, for an action research project, a more active participation role engages the social work researcher in a collaborative change effort (Stringer & Dwyer, 2005; Healey, 2001).

Fieldwork: Entering to Exiting the Field

In qualitative research, moving from planning a project to implementing it is often referred to as going into the field to do fieldwork. During the course of fieldwork, a social worker participates and observes with the purpose of gathering descriptions of activities, behaviors, actions, conversations, interpersonal interactions, organization or community processes, or any other aspect of observable human experience. Similar to the phases of generalist practice, there is a beginning, a middle, and an end phase. This process is often referred to in qualitative research as *entering and exiting the field* (Cresswell, 2006).

Timelines

The timeline for qualitative projects may vary. On one end of the continuum are long-term longitudinal studies that may last 1 year or more, and on the other end are short-term or cross-sectional studies that may last as little as an hour. The rule of thumb most qualitative researchers recommend is to conduct fieldwork "long enough" to answer the research or evaluation questions and fulfill the purpose of the investigation (Padgett, 2008; Stringer, 2007).

Evaluation and action research (and their more modest aims) typically involve shorter time periods to generate useful information for action and/or for timelines (Stringer, 2007). Other types of qualitative studies may necessitate prolonged engagement in the field to capture the complexities of a social situation or culture. (Madden, 2010; Padgett, 2008; Yin, 2008).

Beginning or entry stage   The beginning or entry stage involves gaining access and building rapport. If a study location has not already been located, the first step is to locate a site and gain access to interested stakeholders or the population of central interest. This stage requires that social workers actively use their relational skills to build and sustain partnerships. These partnerships may be with a community and/or agency or organizational leaders and constituents (Cresswell, 2006).

Middle phase or working phase   Once the social worker locates and enters the setting, the project moves to middle phase or working stage. The social worker moves beyond initial adjustment to see what is really happening in a setting. The social worker's tasks include selecting the purposive sample, collecting the data (including recording interviews), managing the data (storing the data), and attending to unexpected issues that arise (e.g., ethical issues) (Cresswell, 2006).

The routinization of fieldwork requires a concentrated effort and immersion in gathering data. It is an arduous task. Discipline is needed to maintain high-quality, up-to-date field notes, follow emergent possibilities, and build on what is observed and learned each step along the way. A feeling of connection with people being studied may emerge. Key informants are people who are knowledgeable about a topic. Their insights can prove particularly useful in helping an observer understand what is happening and why. Key informants are critical to providing information about what the observer has not experienced or cannot experience, as well as explaining events the observer has actually experienced (Emerson, Fretz, & Shaw, 1995; Madden, 2010).

Ending or exit phase   As fieldwork comes to an end, a researcher needs an exit or disengagement strategy. The researcher becomes increasingly concerned with the verification of data and less concerned about generating new data. If conducting evaluation, the observer must begin to consider what feedback is to be given to whom and how, including deliverables such as evaluation reports that present the research or evaluation results (Cresswell, 2006).

DESIGN CHOICES

Another important design choice decision involves sampling strategies, data sources, and, qualitative data analysis. An overview of these options follows.

Sampling Strategies

Essential design choices involve sample size and sampling strategies. As reviewed in chapter 8 on sampling, random probability sampling, often used in quantitative research, involves obtaining a large sample to generate

Practice Contexts

Critical Thinking Question: How do different practice contexts, such as clinical evaluation, agency-based evaluation, and university research, influence the decision to use qualitative methods in research and practice evaluation?

representative and generalizable results (Krueger & Neuman, 2005). In contrast, purposeful sampling in qualitative research and evaluation involves purposefully selecting information from central stakeholders or key informants about the topic of interest (Creswell, 2009).

Generally, there are no standard rules for sample size in qualitative inquiry. However, experienced qualitative researchers offer some recommendations.

Lincoln and Guba (1985) recommended sample selection to the point of redundancy. That is, continue to include participants until no new information is obtained, to the point of saturation. Patton (2002) noted that sample size often depends on the purpose of the inquiry, usefulness, credibility, time, and resource availability. In the end, this decision must be made by the social worker and/or team conducting the project.

Cresswell (2006) provides some ball park sample-size figures based on the type of study. For example, biographical studies, in which researchers study the life of an individual, justifiably can be a sample of one. Phenomenological studies, with which researchers attempt to capture the lived experience of a phenomenon, generally have a sample size of 8–10. A grounded theory approach, which seeks to generate a theory, generally involves a larger sample size of 20 to 30 participants to capture the maximum variation in a phenomenon and to capture confirming and disconfirming evidence. The sample size of case studies may range from one to four cases depending upon whether a single case or multiple case study design is used. The sample size of ethnographic studies varies depending upon the nature of the culture or setting under investigation.

Data Sources

Another design option is a choice of one or more data sources. The three central kinds of qualitative data used are observations, interviews, and documents (written and visual) (Coffey & Atkinson, 1996; Rose, 2010). These methods can be used individually or in combination. Combining the use of different data sources can be a powerful source of triangulation, that is, establishing data from different angles to see if evidence is corroborated. For example, interview data, that is, what people say (in verbal, written, or visual form), are a major source of qualitative data. However, to avoid the limitations of pure interview data and to more fully understand complex situations, observation or review of documents may offer supplementary materials not captured in the interview process (Marshall & Rossman, 2010; Rose, 2010).

Interviews

Interviews are another essential data source using a qualitative approach. As interviewing is an essential practice task, this method is very familiar for many social workers at all levels of practice. Using a qualitative approach, the social worker can gather direct quotations from participants, which provide the raw data in qualitative inquiry. Interview data can capture an individual's internal world—including past experiences, thoughts, emotions, values, and behaviors—subjective viewpoints and experiences not readily observable by others. The data can provide insight into how an individual constructs meaning to his or her experiences (Kvale & Brinkman, 2008; Patton, 2002; Rubin & Rubin, 2010; Seidman, 2006; Weiss, 1995). However, interview data generally represent only one subjective viewpoint, unless interviews are conducted with multiple stakeholders found in a study setting.

Interviewing approaches   Qualitative interviews most often include open-ended questions and probes that yield in-depth responses about people's experiences, perceptions, feelings, and knowledge. The three basic approaches to collecting qualitative data using open-ended interviews are (a) the informal conversational interview, (b) the general interview guide approach, and (c) the standardized open-ended interview. These approaches differ to the extent in which interview questions are determined and standardized before the interview is conducted (Marshall & Rossman, 2010; Merton, Fiske, & Kendall, 1990).

Informal conversational interview   In the informal conversational interview, questions are generally not prepared in advance. This type of interview is generally conducted as a part of spontaneous discussion. For example, an evaluator attends a community advisory board meeting and has a discussion with a board member. Although this method has the benefit of being unstructured and spontaneous, its use is limited because it may be difficult to compare data across respondents (Patton, 2002).

General interview guide approach   The general interview guide is slightly more structured compared to the informal conversational interview. Generally in outline form, it summarizes topics to be covered without providing specific questions or their sequencing. For example, a general interview guide approach to the immigration narrative of older adults could provide four broad categories that cover experiences related to: (a) life in the homeland, (b) the immigration journey, (c) arrival to the new country, and (d) subsequent experiences in the new country. Although this approach is flexible, it also may compromise consistency and comparison across different respondents.

Standardized open-ended interview   Standardized open-ended interviews use preset wording and sequencing of questions. Interviewers are generally trained and administer the survey uniformly, including the order and the wording of questions. Questions are in open-ended format. This strategy increases the ability to compare responses, but lacks flexibility. For example, see Exhibit 10.1 of "Conducting a Literature Review" section for the Culturally Competent Oral History Interview that includes standardized questions. The next section provides recommendations on how to word questions for use in in-depth qualitative interviewing.

Qualitative interviewing 101   Similar to psychosocial assessments, qualitative methods use questions that are generally asked about one or more areas, which include life experiences, values (beliefs and opinions), cognitions (thoughts), emotions (feelings), actions (behaviors), knowledge, relationships, sensory perceptions, and personal background questions. Questions can be asked in the present, past, and/or future tense (Kvale & Brinkman, 2008; Patton, 2002; Rubin & Rubin, 2010; Seidman, 2006; Weiss, 1995). For example, people can be asked about what they do now, what they did in the past, and what they plan to do in the future. Table 10.5 presents a description and sample questions for each question type. Table 10.5 is provided in a checklist format for use in developing interview questions and can also be used as a worksheet to determine what domains need to be covered to answer the research questions.

Table 10.5   Common Question Types and Objectives in Qualitative Interviewing

Guiding Research Questions				
Directions: Based on your research questions, what question types and time frame you wish to gather information for? Please check all that apply.		Areas for inquiry (check all that apply)		
Question Types and Objectives	Sample Questions	Past	Present	Future
Life experience questions Aim to elicit data about life experiences	Please tell me about a memorable experience of your childhood. What was your experience like?			
Values (beliefs, opinion) questions Aim to elicit data about values, beliefs, opinions	What values would you say you learned from your parents? What is your opinion about immigration?			
Cognition (thoughts) questions Aim to elicit information about cognitive processes	What was your first thought after you found out? How did your thoughts, if at all, change?			
Feeling questions Aim to elicit data about emotions and feelings	What were your feelings about it? What do you mean when you say you are "sad turned angry"?			
Action (behavior) questions Aim to elicit data on observable actions, behaviors, and activities	What kinds of activities did you participate in this week? Thinking back over the past 3 months, how would you describe your behavior in detention?			
Knowledge questions Aim to elicit factual data	For what reasons do you take psychotropic medication? What does it help do?			
Relationship questions Aim to elicit data about interpersonal relationships	Currently, how would you describe relationships in your life?			
Sensory questions Aim to elicit data about the senses (e.g., sight, sound, touch, taste, smell)	What do you remember seeing? What do you remember hearing?			
Background questions Aim to elicit background data (i.e., age, ethnicity, relational status, education)	What is your age? What is the highest grade you completed?			

Source: Adapted from Patton, M. Q. (2002). *Qualitative research and evaluation methods* (3rd ed.), p. 352. Thousand Oaks, CA: Sage Publications, Inc.

Suggestions for sequencing and use of probes   Most qualitative texts recommend that interviews be structured with a beginning (introductory) phase, a middle phase, and an end phase that influence the sequencing of questions that are incorporated in the following recommendations.

It is quite common to begin the interview with a short introduction followed by noncontroversial straightforward questions related to behaviors, activities, and experiences, for example, questions such as "What kinds of music do you enjoy listening to?" or "What brought you to this program?" Questions related to opinions and feelings are more likely to be elicited once the respondent has relived the "experience."

Follow-up probes or follow-up questions can be used to elicit more details related to description. For example, once general life or relationship experiences have been gathered, the researcher follows up with probes related to thoughts, feelings, or opinions about those experiences. Probes help social workers to build on the interpretations or aid in understanding how individuals construct meaning of their experiences. For an example of follow-up probes see Exhibit 10.1 of "Conducting a Literature Review" section.

Background and demographic questions also should be asked. These questions can be short-answer questions, such as What is your age? These questions also can be worded in a way to capture how the participants ascribe meaning, such as How do you describe your social class? Most recommend that questions about demographic information be asked at the end of the interview because questions asked about age, income, education, and so on, may be considered private information and elicit a defensive response if asked first.

Ending the interview on the participant's terms is important. Generally, interviews should provide participants with an opportunity to fill in any gaps not captured in the questions asked. For example, "We have now finished the interview, are there any questions that I should have asked? Is there anything else you would like to share about your experience?"

Data Collection

Interviews can be conducted face-to-face, by phone, or using web-based questionnaires. Regardless of the method chosen, the social worker should capture the exact wording of the participants. The interviewee's actual quotations are the raw data. Therefore, a good digital recorder and meticulous note taking are indispensable to fieldwork (Patton, 2002). Contemporary social workers can use a number of technological devices to make their research and evaluation fieldwork considerably more efficient. For example, battery-operated digital recorders or laptop computers can be used to take field notes or record interviews. Additionally, video or digital cameras can be used to capture both verbal and nonverbal interactions (Marshall & Rossman, 2010; Patton, 2008). However, the use of digital recording devices may make some participants uncomfortable or influence them to respond differently. Therefore, social workers should ask for permission from their participants to record an interview or other types of activities.

Focus Groups

In addition to one-on-one interviews, interviews can be conducted in groups. Focus groups are a form of "research group work" designed to gather information related to the social worker's research questions. Usually organized and led by a member of the research and evaluation team, a focus group is generally composed of unrelated individuals who participate in a facilitated group discussion of a topic for 1 to 2 hours. The approximate size of a group is 6–10 people. The focus group leader reviews rules and creates expectations for participation. Similar to one-on-one interviews, qualitative data are collected through the use of open-ended questions, using an interview format with a beginning phase, a middle phase, and an end phase. Usually several focus groups are conducted to check for consistency of responses across participants (Krueger & Casey, 2000; Morgan, 1997).

Archival Records, Documents, and Other Artifacts Review

Other essential sources of qualitative data collection are from archival records, documents, and other artifacts. These are unobtrusive (nonreactive) sources of data that include documents, such as governmental or community agency records, newspapers, clinical case records, program files, personal memoranda and correspondence, official publications and reports, personal diaries, letters, artistic works, photographs and memorabilia, and written responses to open-ended surveys (Neuendorf, 2002; Richards, 2009; Rose, 2010).

Because they are unobtrusive and are nonreactive sources of data, they can be useful sources for triangulating or checking for consistency with interview or observational data.

Observation

Another essential source of qualitative activity and data is observation (Fetterman, 2010). Because human perceptions are highly subjective and variable, the use of participant observation in qualitative research is a learned skill that must go beyond "seeing as usual" (Madden, 2010). In fact, a skilled qualitative observer generally has undergone intensive physical, emotional, and psychological training to become more proficient in recording accurate and authentic observations of other people's experiences (Patton, 2002). Additionally, depending upon the type of study, the level of participation will range from passive to active.

Focus on observational skills   Observational skills are an important component of participant observation. According to Patton (2002), training to become a skilled observer includes (a) learning to pay attention to seeing and hearing what is actually there, (b) practice in qualitative descriptive writing, (c) being disciplined with regular field note writing, (d) learning to distinguish necessary detail from trivial events, (e) using rigorous and multiple strategies to validate and triangulate observations, and (f) recognizing and documenting one's own perspective, including the use of self-knowledge and self-disclosure to identify and address potential biases (Patton, 2002).

Field notes   The fundamental work of the social worker conducting an observation is taking field notes. Field notes include information with rich and detailed descriptions of social interactions, environmental contexts, and the internal perceptions of the observer (Madden, 2010). The quality of field notes has been linked to the quality of data analysis. Lofland (1971) asserted that if field notes are not recorded, "the observer might as well not be in the setting" (p. 102).

Use of vivid description   In field notes, observers strive for vivid description. The use of detail is a key factor in description (Patton, 2002). Vivid description should provide sufficient information so that the reader does not have to speculate what is meant. That is, the description of the setting should be sufficiently detailed so that the readers feel as if they can see the setting. Social workers should use words that are as close to factual as possible. Vague words, such as *lovely* or *gargantuan* should be avoided. Avoid interpretive or subjective adjectives (e.g., well-dressed, poorly groomed, comfortable) except if they are used by the participants in describing their reactions to and perceptions of that environment (Fetterman, 2010; Madden, 2010; Patton, 2008).

Writing vivid descriptions requires careful attention to detail. The social worker as observer must be disciplined to avoid vague, inaccurate, or broad phrases that can be interpreted differently by others. For example, what if a description of the main room of a shelter in the South states that it was "too big and had no color." Let us consider the next statement, which accurately describes the same room: The room was 75 feet long, 60 feet wide, with a ceiling 20 feet high. The grey-painted concrete walls were lackluster in a room with one small window on the north end of the room that appeared to let one large beam of light shine on a southwest corner.

Directions for an observational exercise   This exercise is designed to assist students in refining their observation skills. Students are asked to observe a public setting and write a vivid description of that setting. The exercise can be done individually or in groups of two to four people who observe the same sight. After following the directions below for observing a participant, students can share their writings about a descriptive setting with one another and ask several people if they can visualize the setting and compare it with their subjective impression of the setting.

Directions for an observational (only) exercise:

1. Observe a public environment for 15–30 minutes. If there are two or more people, observe the same environment and exchange descriptions.

2. Because observational notes often involve describing a setting, begin with observing the larger physical environment. Drawing the layout of the setting may even be helpful. Next, describe the social environment (the people in the environment). Look for how people organize themselves into dyads or groups. If the setting is large, focus the observation on a particular section of the room. Pay particular attention to both verbal and nonverbal (e.g., mannerisms, posture, type of dress) communication patterns. The vivid description may include descriptions of individuals (e.g., age, race or ethnicity, and gender), types of interactions (verbal and nonverbal), frequency of interactions (e.g., number of people participating in conversation), and the direction of communication patterns (e.g., who is talking and who is listening).

3. When sharing their work, students can offer constructive feedback to help one another discern between the use of clear and accurate descriptive language and the use of interpretive (vague) adjectives.

Participant Observation

Participation is the other essential component of participant observation and varies depending upon the type of research project. This can range from observation only (with no participation) to complete participant observation. As illustrated in the previous exercise example, participation involved solely being a spectator in the social setting. At the opposite end of the continuum is complete immersion. Full participant observation commonly uses multiple data sources that constitute a collection of field strategies including direct participation and observation, interviews, document analysis, and critical self-reflection (Denzin & Lincoln, 2005; Healy, 2001; Patton, 2002). Because qualitative projects often involve prolonged engagement in a setting, the level of participation also may change during the course of a project based on the different phases of the project or study setting (Padgett, 2008; Patton, 2008).

Disclosure and participant observation   Participant observation also may vary on the level of disclosure from covert (hidden) to overt (obvious) participation. It ranges from overt or full disclosure to no (covert) disclosure. Because they involve observation of people's private behaviors, without explicitly and fully receiving their informed consent, covert methods often raise concerns and debates regarding ethical conduct. However, the use of covert observation is generally monitored by institutional review boards that set guidelines for informed consent procedures that often limit the use of covert methods (Padgett, 2008; Patton, 2002).

From Solo Effort to Collaboration

The nature and degree of participation also varies along a continuum. A social worker may be conducting the project solo or be involved as part of a research team in a research-driven project. On the opposite side of the collaboration continuum, a qualitative investigation may involve collaborations with interested stakeholders in the setting (Minkler, Wallerstein, & Hall, 2010; Mostes & Hess, 2007; Suarez-Balcazar & Harper, 2003). Other variations in between may be partial or intermittent collaboration (Patton, 2002). As equal partners in the project, stakeholders collaborate with researcher(s) in formulating the research and evaluation questions, choosing a research and evaluation design, and implementing the design (locating a sampling, collecting data, and analyzing the results). Based on these results, they would formulate and implement an action-based plan (McIntyre, 2008).

The action-oriented approach has many benefits for clients. Participants may use the findings and gain an increased sense of being in control of, deliberative about, and reflective on their own lives and situations (Suarez-Balcazar & Harper, 2003). Qualitative approaches such as participatory action research and empowerment approaches can also be used as collaborative approaches (McIntyre, 2008). As illustrated in the example of the McIntyre (2000) participatory action research study, the researcher becomes a facilitator, collaborator, and teacher in support of those engaging in inquiry.

Engage, Assess, Intervene, Evaluate

Critical Thinking Question: How does a qualitative approach incorporate the phases of practice (engage, assess, intervene, and evaluate)?

QUALITATIVE DATA ANALYSIS STRATEGIES

After data are collected using interview, observation, and/or documents, the next stage is data analysis. Qualitative data analysis is an inductive and creative process. Mounds of qualitative data go through a careful process of coding and categorizing into readable narrative descriptions with major themes, categories, and illustrative case examples. The themes, patterns, and insights that emerge during field work comprise grist for the mill in qualitative inquiry (Bernard & Ryan, 2010; Coffey & Atkinson, 1996; Miles & Huberman, 1994; Richards, 2009).

Qualitative data analysis, sometimes referred to as *inductive analysis*, moves from organizing interview and observational data from the field into general patterns and themes. The data analyzed can be from one or more participants. Theories developed are firmly supported by the data gathered from the field. It is critical at the data analysis stage to let patterns emerge naturally and to not impose personal views on interpretation (Coffey & Atkinson, 1996; Richards, 2009).

Because the type of data analysis depends upon the type of qualitative approach chosen, such as narrative, phenomenology, ethnography, grounded theory, case study, or action research (Bernard & Ryan, 2010), and is beyond the scope of this chapter, a "common elements" qualitative data analysis approach to coding and identifying categories is reviewed in this chapter. It consists of four stages, preparation, literal coding, cluster coding, and visual coding. A sample qualitative data that can be used with this coding scheme is shown in Table 10.6.

Table 10.6	Qualitative Data Sample of 18 Social Work Students

2009 Social Work Students' Values Survey Qualitative Results

Directions: Here are qualitative results in response to the following survey question: Please share some of your thoughts, feelings, and experiences about significant life relationships and/or events that you believe influenced your current value system. Search for patterns and themes in the data. Please be prepared to write up at least three major patterns or themes.

MFU001: "God, my parents, and other family members have a big influence on my current value system; I learn from them that life is about the choices you made."

MFU002: Since I've discovered sobriety and life w/AA, many values have changed such as the importance of relationships, living an honest life, and the importance of helping others.

MFU003: I think that I've had a strong support system over the years. However, I feel that my turning point was when my first daughter was born. Although, there were many individuals that influenced me over the years to become the person that I was up to that point, having her made me look at life from a completely different perspective which contributed to the value system that I have now and have taught my other two daughters. This experience and value system is what drives me to help and make positive contributions to our communities."

MFU004: "My family and friends have assisted in shaping my thoughts and feelings in relation to my value system. I have had many experiences such as marrying out of my race, ethnic and religious background. I grew up in a rural setting near Canada and moved to New York City for college. I have lived in New York City for 8 years which has opened and expanded my knowledge and competence of other backgrounds. I value life and helping others who are less fortunate; this belief in helping others transpired when I was younger. My father was a teacher and he always reached out to the community. I believe when you give you begin to live."

MFU005: "Since I was adopted into a family that comes from a different background than I am, it has taught me to be open minded and accepting of others that are different than I am."

MFU006: "I believe that environment has a lot to do with the person you are and who you become and what you believe. If you grow up in a stable environment, you have more of a chance of becoming a stable person. What you live you learn."

MFU007: "I believe that, whether negatively or positively I am not sure, my upbringing and my religion that I was raised in have most profoundly influenced my current value system."

(continued)

Table 10.6	**Qualitative Data Sample of 18 Social Work Students (Continued)**

MFU008: "My family experiences have helped to shape my value system. They emphasize being spiritual and having high morals. They also had a strictness to them, but also allowed me to be open minded, which will be helpful to me in my practice."

MFU009: "My significant life relationships have been rewarding, pleasurable, difficult, loving, and hurtful. They have therefore contributed to my current value system by helping to shape what I value, what I thought I valued and what I need to value. My values have gone through a metamorphisis of shallowness to deep value of life itself."

MFU010: "My father's views are fairly conservative, and, my mother's views would be considered liberal. I find that this dichotemy has contributed and influenced my current value system."

MFU011: "I believe that my work and personal life are influenced by my values. The way my parents raised me regarding how I should treat others and respect others reflects my behavior at work and to my friends."

MFU012: "I believe that most of my value system is influenced by my family upbringing. However, my values are also from personal choices meaning the decisions are based upon my own judgment or from what I have learned from previous experiences."

MFU013: "My parents have influenced my value system a great deal. My life experience has contributed as well. I think that life experience has a lot to do with how a person internalizes their values."

MFU014: "My current value system has been influenced heavily by my family and friends around me."

MFU015: "I feel that immigrating to the USA at an early age, somehow helped me in seeing life and the world different from what is define as the 'normal' in my culture and society.'"

MFU016: "There are many things that influence my current value system; being raised by parents who came to America for a better life, being the sister of someone who has dealt with numerous health issues and remained strong and positive in the process, being surrounded by faces of diversity and most of all being someone who believes in God and knows that I am not entitled to judge."

MFU017: "I was raised in a spiritual grounded family. We are also a very close family; aunts, uncles and extended family were always at our house. I think one of the most important events that changed my life was watching my grandmother and mother help people. My grandmother who lived in the south was the one everyone came to when there were problems. I think watching them inspired me to want to also make a difference in someone's life."

MFU018: "The teachings of my parents have had a significant influence on my value system and how I view relationships. My exposure to social work have also influenced my values."

Source: Maschi, T. (2010). Social work students' values. Unpublished manuscript.

Stage 1: Preparation

Transcription

Before analyzing the data, the social worker must prepare them in transcript form. Narrative data may need to be transcribed from written or audio or videotape files. Transcripts can be in the form of a hard copy, Microsoft Word file, or as a document from a qualitative data analysis software package. It also is important to determine who will transcribe the data; common choices include a member of the research team or a transcription service. Therefore, confidentiality issues must be addressed in advance to keep private the identity of participants. Transcribed raw data should always be verbatim (Richards, 2009).

Transcripts should also be formatted. Printed or electronic documents should have wide margins and numbered lines. This allows for ample space for coding and ease in documenting the line number in which specific codes appear.

Establishing Rules

In the process of data analysis, the analyst commonly develops definitions for emerging concepts and establishes rules for coding. The development of rules often flows naturally when the analyst has largely determined how the patterns begin to cluster into similar codes and/or categories. Because inductive analysis is an emerging process, it is quite common that rules, like a working definition of identified concepts, such as family values, are modified based on new evidence that emerges. Near the end of the analysis stage it is quite common for the data to be sufficiently organized and categories defined so that the social worker can consistently apply rules (Miles & Huberman, 1994; Richards, 2009).

Memoing

It is important to use memos to document the decision-making process during analysis. Memos may be described as notes to oneself about the analysis process. Because these memos are written for the purposes of analysis, they are often referred to as *analytic memos*. Formatting strategies and necessary content include (a) date the memo, (b) label memos with headings that describe the primary category or concept being earmarked, (c) identify the particular code(s) the note addresses, (d) note when you think a category has been sufficiently defined, and (e) provide documentation of references or other sources of information used for the memo. Content to include in the analytic memo includes (a) documentation of the free flow of ideas, including brainstorming, (b) the use of visual diagrams to draw out relationships among concepts, and (c) documentation of the analysts' thinking and feeling process to assist with description and interpretation (Bernard & Ryan, 2010; Miles & Huberman, 1994; Richards, 2009).

Examining the Whole and Its Parts

In the preparation phase, it is best to review the individual transcripts before beginning the coding process. Consistent with a holistic perspective, it is strongly recommended that the social worker read each individual transcript to understand the whole person. The next step of data analysis begins with making cross-case comparisons, which result in "partialization" of individuals to examine some common characteristics or processes, such as "parental involvement" or "substance use patterns" (Richards, 2009).

Stage 2: Literal Coding

Be Literal, Code Literally

In stage 2, literal coding, the analyst should approach the transcript data as literal or "authentic" coding: within the context of the person interviewed. As the word *literal* coding suggests, the analysis should concretely identify the "conceptual items" by coding data using the exact words and phrases (verbatim) or by using specific words that validly represent participants' words and meaning. For example, a participant who referred to his or her substance-using days as "dazed and confused" was assigned a code, "dazed and confused." The challenge for the analyst is to remain literal and not jump unduly to inferences not suggested by the data (Coffey & Atkinson, 1996).

Code Assignment Suggestions

Assign shorthand codes to conceptual items. Shorthand codes can consist of one word (e.g., *sad*) or letter codes (e.g., DC = depression-child). It is important to keep a record of assigned codes and their meaning. For example, a conceptual item code for grassroots activism might be labeled GA and should be documented in a code book.

Identifying categories or families

During the literal stage, it also is useful to begin to identify how codes for conceptual items are related or fit together with other items into categories or families. A constant comparison approach among conceptual items of data helps to discern similarities and differences. For example, conceptual items coded "sad," "angry," and "depressed" suggest a category for emotions. In contrast, conceptual items, such as playing basketball and running a marathon, are distinct from emotions and suggest a common category of engagement in sport activities (Coffey & Atkinson, 1996; Richards, 2009).

Sifting, sorting, and categorizing

As noted by the previous examples, sifting and sorting conceptual items into common categories or families helps the analyst to discern what conceptual items can be compared with other conceptual items according to similarities and differences. Conceptual items that have similar characteristics are placed in the same category. At this stage the analyst should also create and record preliminary definitions for categories. These notes are kept in analytical memos that comprise part of the audit trail (Bernard & Ryan, 2010).

Category saturation

However, conceptual item codes, categories, and definitions may change based on new evidence found during the data analysis mining process. Therefore, the analyst must remain open and continue to refine and reorganize. Eventually, category saturation will be reached where items seem unified and complete and represent the overarching category themes, such as in Rational Emotive Behavior Therapy (REBT) with categories for antecedent events, emotions, cognitions, and behaviors (Richards, 2009).

Stage 3: Cluster Coding

At the next stage of data analysis, cluster coding, the social worker moves from literal and begins to make more abstract inferences or interpretations of the data within conceptual categories. At this stage, the large chunks of narrative data are reduced to the codes that represent them. This process is often referred to as *data reduction*. The conceptual items (e.g., angry, sad) are classified into categories (e.g., emotions) (Richards, 2009).

The next step is to look for pattern recognition within each category among the conceptual items clustered into their respective categories. Common relationships within categories may include nested categories or subcategories (e.g., positive or negative emotions), temporal processes (how time influences the relationships), reactions to stimuli (emotional, cognitive, behavioral), and context influences (such as social or environmental conditions). For example, the category of emotions may include conceptual items that are subcategorized as positive or negative emotions. Temporal processes may reflect a point in a process where things shift, such as different points in the process where negative versus positive emotions were salient. Response to stimuli may reflect different emotions in response to a situation. Contextual influences may be represented by conditions in the environment, including actions of other persons that may have influenced feelings (Patton, 2002).

The next step is to compare across categories to discover relationships between them. This comparison consists of locating patterns, themes, and relationships. Using a cross category comparison, the analyst should examine for potential temporal processes that suggest the relationship among categories is part of a process, a causal relationship where one category proceeds another, such as temporal (parts of a process), causal, one contained within the other, or possibly a typology of characteristics. For example, results of an analysis with thought, feelings, and actions suggest a causal process that thought led to feeling, which led to behaviors that were acted upon.

Stage 4: Visual Coding

The next step is to develop a diagram or conceptual classification scheme. The use of a diagram, matrix (i.e., table), or metaphor to describe the results is common. Shown in chapter 5 was Kuhlthau's (2005) visual diagram of the common thoughts, feeling, and actions of students during the information search process. Visualizing the findings assists in identifying the individual conceptual categories and how they are related. Scholars also recommend that researchers search for potential alternative explanations to evaluate contrary information (Glaser & Strauss, 1967; Miles & Huberman, 1994).

Rigor in Qualitative Research

Rigor in qualitative research generally refers to being self-disciplined and vigilant during each stage of the qualitative research process, including data analysis. These strategies include an audit trail and trustworthiness. Additional strategies for rigor include triangulation, prolonged engagement, member checking, peer debriefing and support, negative case analysis, and reflexivity.

Audit Trail

An audit trail is an essential part of the entire research process, including the qualitative data analysis process. Journal or field notes and analytical memos provide an ongoing record of the decision-making processes and subjective impressions. Without careful documentation, the trustworthiness of the researcher and credibility of the study can be undermined. Considerations to address throughout the research process include keeping checks and balances on potential flaws, which include losing one's subjective view due to personal biases or taking on the views of participants (going native). The analyst should attempt to reduce biases that might affect interpretation by avoiding making premature conclusions and intentionally disregarding contradictory evidence.

Trustworthiness

Guba and Lincoln (1994) asserted that trustworthiness must be established such that ethical and fair practices and the results accurately represent the participants' actual experiences. Strategies that enhance believability of your findings include establishing credibility or consistency (or dependability).

Credibility

Credibility is providing evidence and reasons to your audience as to why you are credible. Demonstrating credibility includes sharing information about your relevant training experiences, and keeping a detailed journal that documents the decision-making processes during the data collection and analysis stages. This documentation includes keeping meticulous records to create an audit trail so that the steps that resulted in the final interpretations can be retraced.

Consistency

Consistency, also referred to as *dependability*, is also a factor in establishing trustworthiness and believability. Although the research design is flexible, it is quite feasible that it also be consistent. Consistent strategies include conducting rigorous interviews, establishing and following results for coding, keeping detailed journal and analytic memos, developing rules for coding, and having written detailed records (include context of study) of decision-making processes (for an audit trail or for use in study replication).

Triangulation

Triangulation is a strategy for rigor, which refers to using two or more sources of evidence to confirm conclusions. Patton (2002) refers to theory triangulation (using more than one theory to explain results), data triangulation (using multiple data sources such as interviews, documents, and observations), methodological triangulation (using more than one method, such as quantitative and qualitative methods), and observer triangulation (using more than one observer or informants to check for intersubjective agreement or disagreement) (Padgett, 2008; Patton, 2002).

Prolonged Engagement

Prolonged engagement is when fieldwork occurs over an extended period of time. A possible benefit is that it reduces reactivity of participants to a research outsider in their setting. However, prolonged engagement must be balanced by remaining neutral in the setting and resisting "going native" (Padgett, 2008; Patton, 2002).

Member Checking

Member checking is a strategy for rigor in which participants have a say in the research process. Member checking involves obtaining feedback about the results and conclusions drawn directly from the research participants. Member checking commonly occurs during the data analysis and interpretation stages and allows participants to confirm or refute interpretations.

Peer Debriefing and Support

Padgett (2008) noted peer debriefing and support as a strategy for ensuring rigor. In peer debriefing, research and evaluation team members meet regularly to provide feedback and be a sounding board for processing insights from the field or processing biases.

Negative Case Analysis

Negative case analysis is another strategy to ensure rigor. Negative case analysis resembles constant comparison, looking for outliers and using extreme cases that provide contradictory evidence. Negative case analysis is especially useful during the preliminary data analysis stage when conclusions are made to see if any data contradict or are inconsistent with interpretations drawn.

Reflexivity

Reflexivity involves engaging in critical self-reflection. It is important to document in field notes and journal writing biases that were uncovered and what was done to control them, especially in the data analysis stage. Keeping a memo or log can serve as a reminder to keep potential biases in check. Part of the reflexive process involves conducting an ongoing assessment of one's positionality: A social worker using a qualitative approach should carefully evaluate his or her position (positionality) to the participants. Common questions to self-reflect upon include "what is relevant and important about *me* and which might impact on *me* when carrying out research?" This includes carefully assessing one's age, gender, sexual orientation, religious beliefs, political views, personal experiences, relationship status, socioeconomic status, and occupational background.

Recommendations for Writing Qualitative Research

The social worker must be aware of the effects of self-awareness and self-expression when writing up qualitative results. It is important to know one's own voice and creative writing skills, and conduct a critical self-analysis. Use the active voice and factual and authentic descriptions. The reader should feel like a part of the setting being described. The writing also must reflect the depth, breadth, and detail of the settings, their inhabitants, and their interactions. Appealing to the multiple senses, such as sight, sound, and smell, helps recreate the setting for readers.

The social worker must be aware of the effects self-awareness and self-expression when writing up qualitative results.

Application of Findings

Qualitative studies that make empirical generalizations or build theories form the foundation of an important next step, which is applying the findings to practice or taking action. For example, let us revisit the Merighi and Grimes (2000) study. As the findings illustrated, coming out is an ongoing family affair impacting gay youth, their family members, and society. So what is next? Because the findings suggest that coming-out (or keeping homosexuality a secret) can be stressful and cause psychological and emotional distress in young gay people and their family members, social workers can help make this process smoother for family members as well as temper potential negative consequences.

Social workers can work with gay youth and/or their family members about the coming-out process by using education, linkages to peer support systems, and empowerment strategies. For example, strategies may involve educating family members about typical reactions that occur from disclosure, mediating conflicts that may arise from differing family viewpoints, and dispelling myths and stereotypes about homosexuality. Social workers can help by providing linkage to gay youth and/or family members with similar experiences. For example, social workers can refer families to organizations such as

Parents, Families and Friends of Lesbians and Gays (PFLAG, 2009). PFLAG is a national nonprofit organization and grassroots network with local chapters. Families can be linked with local groups for peer support networks at http://community.pflag.org/Page.aspx?pid=194&srcid=-2.

Social workers also can refer gay youth to organizations, such as the National Youth Advocacy Coalition (NYAC, n.d.). The NYAC promotes social justice by advocating for and with young people who are lesbian, gay, bisexual, transgender, or questioning (LGBTQ). The organization also combats discrimination and promotes well-being among these youth. For more information about the organization visit its website at http://www.nyacyouth.org/#.

SUMMARY

A qualitative approach to research and evaluation is flexible and occurs in a natural setting. Despite the diversity of traditions, many common methods are used. The qualitative method commonly uses purposive sampling and data sources include interviews, participant observation, and documents. The data obtained should best represent individuals and their cultures' authentic experiences. Qualitative data analysis involves a process of data reduction and organizing data into patterns and themes to make empirical generalizations or build theories. Trustworthiness includes credibility and dependability and strategies for rigor.

Baccalaureate Experiential Learning (BEL) Project

The "Moving Stories" Project

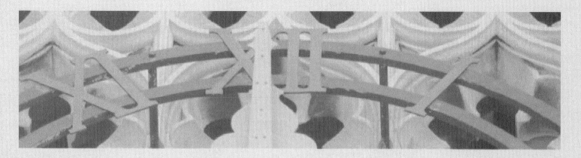

Culturally Competent Oral History Interview Schedule
For Older Adults With Personal and/or Family Histories of Immigration

Tina Maschi, PhD, LCSW, ACSW
Ana Jardim Messenger
Marina Coleman

September 2008

Fordham University Lincoln Center Campus
113 West 60th Street
New York, NY 10023

(212) 636-6633
Email: collab@fordham.edu
Website: http://www.fordham.edu/movingstories

Baccalaureate Experiential Learning (BEL) Project (2008)
Moving Stories: Older Adults Talk about their Experiences Before, During, and After Immigration

Exhibit 10.1
Moving Stories Project Interview Schedule

ORAL HISTORY INTERVIEW SCHEDULE

This section is to be completed by interviewer:
Time and Date of Interview:
Interview Place:
List People Present at Interview:

INTRODUCTION

Hello and thank you for taking part in this interview. During our talk, I am going to ask you questions about your past and present experience, including your family, friends as well as your immigration experience. This interview will take about ½ to 2 hours. I am interested to hear your life story in your own words, including your personal or family history of immigration. I would like you to talk freely and spontaneously about your life experiences. If we don't finish today, we can schedule another follow-up interview.

If there are any questions that you would rather not answer, just let me know and we can skip those questions. If you want to take a break at any time, let me know. Also, if you want me to repeat or explain any of the questions, I will be happy to do that. Any questions before we start? If yes: What might they be? If no or after the question is answered: Okay we are ready to begin.

NOTE TO INTERVIEWERS

If your interviewee is 55 years old or above and is a first-generation immigrant (i.e., personally immigrated to the United States), use *Interview Schedule I*. If your interviewee is 55 years or older and was born in the United States and is a descendant of immigrants (second generation or later immigrant), use *Interview Schedule II*.

Exhibit 10.1
Continued

INTERVIEW SCHEDULE I: PART 1: SHORT

The Past: Oral History Interview for First-Generation Immigrants

(Note: Bold print represent the central questions. The Part I Long Version provides additional examples of optional probes if you want to stimulate additional discussion about the topic.)
This series of questions ask about your life before, during, and after immigration.

First-Generation Immigration Questions
The Homeland: Country of Origin
1. Tell me about the country that you came from? What about your experiences there?

The Journey
2. What was the actual journey to this country like?

The Arrival
3. What was it like when you first reached these shores?

4. What is it like for you now?

5. What does your culture mean to you? And your family's country of origin?

6. Is there anything else you would like to add about yourself, your family, or your culture?
   [Interviewer: There is an optional Part 2 Life History Interview Questions that you can draw from if you seek additional information.]

CLOSURE
1. Is there anything we left out of your life story that you would like to share?
2. Overall, what has the interview experience been like for you?

FINAL COMMENTS
Thank you so much for sharing your story with me. I will be back in touch with you to provide a copy of the interview and to plan the next steps of the project. If you have any questions, feel free to contact me at (fill in your contact information for telephone number and e-mail).

Exhibit 10.1
Continued

INTERVIEW SCHEDULE II: PART 1: SHORT VERSION

The Past: Oral History Interview for Second or Later Generation Immigrant

(Note: Bold print represent the central questions. The long version on the next page has optional probes for each question if you find you would like more information on one of the topic areas.)

Second- or Later Generation Immigration Questions
This first set of questions asks about your ancestors' immigration experience, that is, before, during, and after their arrival to the United States.

The Homeland: Country of Origin
1. **Tell me about the country your family came from? What about their experiences there?**

The Journey
2. **What was their actual journey like to this country?**

The Arrival
3. **What was it like when your family first reached these shores?**
4. **What is it like for you and your family now?**
5. **What does your culture mean to you? And your family's country of origin?**
6. **Is there anything else you would like to add about yourself, your family, or your culture?**

CLOSURE
Is there anything we left out of your life story that you would like to share? Overall, what has the interview experience been like for you?

FINAL COMMENTS
Thank you so much for sharing your story with me. I will be back in touch with you to provide a copy of the interview and to plan the next steps of the project. If you have any questions, feel free to contact me at (fill in your contact information for telephone number and e-mail).

Exhibit 10.1
Continued

Succeed with PEARSON mysocialworklab

Log onto **www.mysocialworklab.com** and answer the following questions. (*If you did not receive an access code to* **MySocialWorkLab** *with this text and wish to purchase access online, please visit* www.mysocialworklab.com.)

1. **Watch the diversity in practice video "Engaging the Client to Share Their Experiences of Alienation, Marginalization."** After listening to the commentary, apply it to qualitative research as it relates to interviewing strategies and positionality.

2. **Watch the engagement, assessment, intervention, evaluation video, "Assessment."** After listening to the commentary, describe how it is similar to or different from the engagement process described for qualitative research. How would you do things differently (if at all) for a qualitative study?

PRACTICE TEST

The following questions will test your knowledge of the content found within this chapter. For additional assessment, including licensing-exam type questions on applying chapter content to practice, visit **MySocialWorkLab**.

1. A social worker wants to conduct a qualitative study to generate a theory. What qualitative theoretical approach seems most suited?
   a. Narrative
   b. Phenomenology
   c. Ethnography
   d. Grounded theory

2. A social worker engaging in an action research study generally includes all but the following:
   a. Collaboration with central stakeholders
   b. Researcher-defined problem to investigate
   c. Feedback about the findings from participants
   d. Formulation and implementation of an action-based plan

3. The middle or working phase in a qualiative study generally includes all but the following:
   a. Collecting data
   b. Selecting the sample
   c. Managing data
   d. Gaining access

4. Qualitative methods can inform scientific inquiry mostly because they use:
   a. Positionality
   b. Qualitative data analysis techniques
   c. Inductive processes to gather data to make empirical generalizations
   d. Multiple theoretical traditions

5. Identify at least one way qualitative data from the practice field can be used to inform scientific inquiry.

ASSESS YOUR COMPETENCE

Use the scale below to rate your current level of achievement on the following concepts or skills associated with each competency presented in the chapter:

1	2	3
I can accurately describe the concept or skill	I can consistently identify the concept or skill when observing and analyzing practice activities	I can competently implement the concept or skill in my own practice

_____ can design a qualitative research study.

_____ can apply qualitative interviewing techniques.

_____ can apply qualitative fieldwork strategies (e.g., gaining entry, sampling, and collecting data).

_____ can analyze qualitative data and make empirical generalizations.

11

Evaluation as a Theory of Change

Core Competencies in This Chapter (Check marks indicate which competencies are demonstrated)				
☐ Professional Identity	☐ Ethical Practice	☐ Critical Thinking	☑ Diversity in Practice	☐ Human Rights and Justice
☐ Research-Based Practice	☑ Human Behavior	☑ Policy Practice	☐ Practice Contexts	☑ Engage, Assess, Intervene, Evaluate

INTRODUCTION

Social work has historically used social interventions for individual and social change (Mullen, Dumpson, & Associates, 1972). As shown in Figure 11.1, most social work activities are based on a "theory of change" that posits change in a situation or problem area in a desired direction as a result of the intervention (Richards, Taylor, Ramasamy, & Richards, 1999; Rossi, Freeman, & Lipsey, 2004). On an individual level, a social worker may use an evidence-based cognitive behavior intervention to reduce symptoms of depression among youth with a history of trauma. Similarly, a foster care agency may offer a family reunification program designed to increase the numbers of children reunited with their birth families. A community organization may offer support services to adult ex-offenders to reduce recidivism. A countywide public awareness nutrition campaign may be designed to increase community members' knowledge of nutrition and healthy eating habits, which, in turn, are predicted to lead to long-term improved health status among community members.

A common theme among all of these intervention types is a focus on the outcome of the intervention (Chinman, Imm, & Wandersman, 2010). In an era focused on outcome-based evidence and accountability, everyone from case-level practitioners to agency administrators are increasingly accountable to multiple stakeholders (Bamberger, Rugh, & Mabry, 2006). These stakeholders include clients or constituents, executive board members, policy makers, public and private funders, and the general public. Clients or constituents may ask, "Can your agency provide us with quality service?" Executive board members may ask, "How did we do? Did we have an impact?" Policy makers may ask, "What is the impact of legislative changes and mandates on addressing a targeted issue?" Public and private funders may ask, "How effective are your programs? Are the social benefits worth the financial cost?" The general public might ask, "Are our tax dollars worth the cost of this intervention?" or "How will this program contribute to community well-being and safety?"

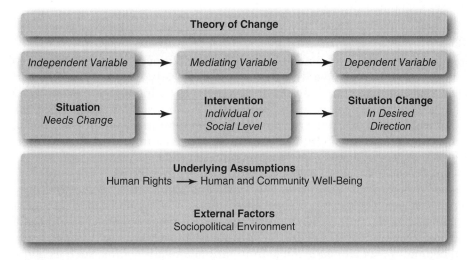

Figure 11.1
Social Work Intervention Theory of Change

Social workers can arm themselves with reliable answers to stakeholders' questions using sound evidence from research and evaluation results. In this era of increased accountability and service effectiveness, integrating evaluation as a routine activity is a practice imperative. Agency funding is often dependent upon some demonstration of service effectiveness (Boulmetis & Dutwin, 2000).

The purpose of this chapter is to prepare social workers with basic competencies in understanding the language and practice of the evaluation of social work interventions, particularly program evaluation. The chapter frames evaluation in the context of a "theory of change" and "impact theory" and is illustrated by using the logic model that predicts the change process that is expected to occur as a result of an intervention. Although this chapter focuses on program-level evaluation, a theory of change framework can be applied to individual- and community-level social work practice with individuals, families, groups, programs, organizations, or communities. Various evaluation methods, such as needs assessment and process and outcome evaluation, and empowerment and culturally competent practice, also are discussed in this chapter.

Needs, Rights, and Social Work Intervention

Social Problems

Social workers who intervene using a human rights and social justice framework foster human rights and social justice aims.

Social workers who intervene using a human rights and social justice framework foster human rights and social justice aims. If social justice is an ideal social condition in which every person has equal rights and opportunities (Barker, 2003; UN, 1948), interventions must be devised to help achieve that overarching desired result. However, a major obstacle to achieving social justice aims are societal conditions that create social problems, which often involve *adverse societal conditions* that can cause emotional, social, or economic suffering (Wronka, 2008). Examples of social problems include crime, social inequality, poverty, racism, drug abuse, family problems, and unfair distribution of limited resources. Since the birth of the social work profession, social work interventions have attempted to combat these issues (Day, 2008). Despite some progress, social workers need to do much more to combat adverse social conditions.

Needs

Traditionally, social work interventions have been designed to promote optimal human and community well-being based on a "needs" perspective (Reichert, 2001, 2003). As shown in Table 11.1, Maslow's (1943) hierarchy of needs represents needs as physical, security, social, esteem, and self-actualization. Many social work settings, such as social services, community mental health agencies, homeless shelters, child protective services, battered women's shelters, and prisons, are designed to help address these needs.

According to Maslow (1943), the most primary and basic needs are physical needs. Physical needs are critical to survival and include food, water, and sleep. Security needs, the second highest level, include safety and security, such as freedom from violence in the home or community, shelter, and access to health and employment. Social needs, the third highest level, refer to the need for social belonging. Social needs range from intimate relationships, such as family and friends, to participation in social and spiritual communities. The fourth highest level is esteem needs. Esteem needs include self worth endeavors, such

Table 11.1	**Maslow's Hierarchy of Needs and Common Social Work Practice**		
Level of Needs	Characteristics of Needs	Human Rights	Common Social Work Services That Address These Needs or Rights
5. Self-actualization	Self-awareness, personal growth, self-assertiveness and fulfilling one's potential	Mental well-being rights, the right to education	Education, mental health services, politics, advocacy work
4. Esteem	Personal worth and recognition for achievements	Mental well-being rights, freedom of thought and conscience	Education, mental health services, community programs, politics
3. Social	Important social relationships (family, friends, and social groups)	Social and cultural rights, the right to relationships, and freedom of associations	Community child and family agencies, mental health services, community prevention program
2. Safety and security	Freedom from violence in the home or community, shelter, access to health, education, and work	Safety and security rights, right to education and work, freedom from arbitrary arrest, detention, or exile, and the right to fair and public hearing by an impartial tribunal	Child welfare agencies, domestic violence shelters, medical hospitals, social services, education, correctional settings, family and community violence victims services, unemployment service, victim advocate programs, community organizing
1. Physical	Bodily needs, food, water, sleep	Economic rights, right to social security, shelter, life, and liberty	Social services, homeless shelters, hospitals, case management agencies, advocacy organizations, legal aid

Source: Adapted from Maslow, A. H. (1943). A theory of human motivation, *Psychological Review 50*(4), 370–396.

as personal worth and social recognition for achievements. The highest level in the hierarchy of needs is self-actualizing needs, which represent self-awareness, personal growth, self-assertiveness, and fulfilling one's potential (Maslow, 1943, 1954). Social work interventions are designed to help individuals and communities obtain optimal well-being related to health, education, housing, economics, justice and public safety (Wronka, 2007, 2008).

Rights

The current trend in social work is to shift from a needs perspective to a rights perspective (Riechert, 2003; United Nations [UN], 1994). Similar to Maslow's hierarchy of needs, the Universal Declaration of Human Rights (UN, 1948) espouses physical, security, social, esteem, and self-actualization not just as needs but as inalienable rights. These rights relate to economic, and social and cultural rights, such as the right to social security, shelter, education, work, and social participation in community cultural life, scientific advancement, and the arts. Human rights also don't discriminate. These rights are guaranteed to all individuals regardless of age, race, gender, language, or religion.

More specifically, each individual is accorded basic civil rights (e.g., life and liberty), safety and security rights (e.g., personal security, freedom from arbitrary arrest, detention, or exile, and the right to a fair and public hearing by an impartial tribunal), and self-esteem and self-actualization rights (e.g., the right to freedom of thought and conscience, the right to work and education), and social rights (e.g., the right to relationships and freedom of associations). Social workers and social service agencies are well positioned to engage in intervention efforts to improve the peoples' economic and social conditions because of the existing social service agency networks whose mission is to address issues related to social security, shelter, education, work, and social participation (UN, 1948, 1994; Wronka, 2008).

CONCEPTUALIZING CHANGE

Historically, social work interventions were designed with the distinct purpose of influencing change or having an impact in a desired direction.

Historically, social work interventions were designed with the distinct purpose of influencing change or having an impact in a desired direction (Addams, 1910; DuBois & Miley, 2010; Ely, 1895; Richmond, 1917). For example, social work interventions or programs have been created for purposes such as reducing poverty, improving mental health, or decreasing family and community violence. Therefore, it is helpful to understand the change process using a lens of change or impact theory. As illustrated in these examples, a social work intervention or program predicts that change will occur in a desired direction as a direct result of the impact of its intervention activities.

Intervention and Impact Theories

Human Behavior

Critical Thinking Question: Explain how program and practice evaluation as a theory of change are used to effect human behavior in the social environment.

As illustrated in Figure 11.1, intervention and impact theories can be used to illustrate the change process and cause-and-effect sequence of interventions. An intervention or program theory can be described as a set of assumptions that clarifies how a program or an intervention will produce the expected level of individual and social benefits and the strategies used to achieve the projected goals and objectives (Rossi et al., 2004). Similarly, impact theory is a causal theory for programs or other interventions. Impact theory posits a cause-and-effect chain in which program or intervention activities facilitate a positive change in individual and social benefits. Therefore, similar to a theory of change, impact theory refers to the beliefs, assumptions, and expectations inherent in a program or an intervention about the nature of the change brought about by program action and how it results in the intended improvement in social conditions (Rossi et al., 2004).

What Is an Intervention?

So what is meant by the terms *intervention* and *community organization* or agency in social work? A *social work intervention* often refers to an interception, or intervening with individual, groups, communities, or events (Barker, 2003). When used in social work, the term *intervention* has been viewed as similar to the term *treatment* in the medical profession. However, in social work, the term *intervention* is much broader in scope than a mere medical prescription and includes an array of activities from case level (micro level) to an agency or community level (macro level).

Types of intervention strategies   Intervention strategies may include but are not limited to individual, group, or family counseling; case management services; advocacy; mediation; social planning; community organizing; lobbying; policy practice; community development; finding and developing resources; media awareness programming; and psychoeducation (CSWE, 2008; National Association of Social Workers, 1999).

Common process   Despite the variety of intervention methods, they commonly follow a problem-solving process. The steps involved include identifying assets and problem areas, developing an intervention plan, implementing the plan, which may include mobilizing resources, engaging community leaders, policy makers, and potential consumers, and encouraging collaborations (Marlow, 2010; Unrau, Gabor, & Grinnell, 2006). This common problem-solving process makes it feasible to apply a broad framework for understanding and evaluating the change process and the impact of interventions.

Community Organization or Agency

The establishment of a community organization or agency is to use a large-scale organized and sustained intervention effort that uses collective action to help a community (i.e., people with a common interest and/or from the same geographic areas) to ameliorate social problems and enhance community well-being (Schram, 1997). A historical example is the establishment of Hull House in 1898. Perhaps the most well-known settlement house, it was founded in Chicago in 1889 by Jane Addams and Ellen Gates Starr. Hull House was designed to address poverty and the poor living and working conditions of the rapidly growing immigrant population. It was a community center for poor and disadvantaged people from the neighborhood. The agency also initiated various social reform efforts related to working conditions, poverty, immigration, and at-risk youth (Ehrenreich, 1985; Ely, 1895).

Types of organizations   Social services organizations or agencies are often part of the community. They can be public or private organizations that target the local, state, and/or federal levels (Weinbach, 2005). Grassroots organizations, in which social work may be involved, are citizen-led change efforts, such as the National Alliance for the Mentally Ill. Sources of funding for the organization can include any combination of the following: public or private funding at the local, state, and/or federal levels. In addition to governmental funding, other sources of revenue may include client or member fees, charity funds, and private donations (Schram, 1997; Unrau et al., 2006).

Activities and change   The activities of the social work staff in collaboration with clients foster the change process and the achievement of desired goals. The activities may include helping individuals become more self-sufficient, strengthening family bonds, and mobilizing community groups to increase community safety. An essential next step is to evaluate the effectiveness of these change efforts by using research and evaluation strategies.

Engage, Assess, Intervene, Evaluate

Critical Thinking Question: What are some ways you can use the logic model to plan an evaluation at your agency setting to improve case- and program-level practice?

THE NATURE OF EVALUATION

In social work, policies of organizations, programs, or other types of interventions can be evaluated for their effectiveness. Evaluation has been defined as "the systematic collection of information about the activities, characteristics, and outcomes of a program or other intervention to make judgments about the intervention, improve intervention effectiveness, and/or inform decisions about future intervention efforts" (Patton, 2002, p. 10). The purpose of evaluation is to systematically determine whether an intervention works and the process by which it works.

Evaluation Context: From Case- to Organizational-Level Intervention

As described in an intervention change theory, a social organization's activities are expected to improve outcomes for those individuals and communities affected (Rossi et al., 2004). As illustrated in Figure 11.2, there is a direct connection between the case level (i.e., micro-level practice with individuals and families) and organizational level (i.e., macro-level practice with organizations and communities) (Smith, 2010; Unrau et al., 2006). Social workers conducting case-level evaluation evaluate services with one client at a time. These combined case-level evaluations contribute to program evaluation. Similarly, program-level decisions can influence social workers' case-level evaluation

Figure 11.2

The Organization in the Environment: From Case Level to Organizational Evaluation efforts. Therefore, no matter where a social worker is positioned in an agency, he or she must understand the connection between case-level and program-level interventions.

Therefore, to be the most effective agents of change, social workers are best served by understanding how agencies are organized to bring about and measure change. Agencies are generally organized by an overarching mission statement from which the agency goals and objectives are established. The agency staff is to carry out these goals and activities in their daily practices and activities.

Mission, Goals, Objectives of Social Work Organizations

Mission Statements

An organization's mission statement, including the mission statement of a social service organization, articulates its vision. The mission statement declares to the public the organization's purpose and projected outcomes. It usually addresses the targeted clientele and services offered (Schram, 1997; York, 2009).

A social service organization's mission statement articulates its vision.

As a document, organizations' mission statements may vary in length from 1 paragraph to 10 to 20 pages. Their contents are used to help make planning decisions and to provide a broad conceptual framework from which programs within that organization are constructed. The grand vision advanced in the mission statement influences the directive goals that flow from it (Schram, 1997; Unrau et al., 2006).

Agency Goals

The mission statement guides how agency goals are formulated. Unrau, Gabor, and Grinnell (2006) identified four components of goals: (a) the nature of the targeted social condition that the organization will address, (b) the targeted clientele for the services, (c) the direction of proposed change effort among clientele, and (d) the strategies used to bring about the desired change.

Goals can range from broad to narrow, depending on the geographical reach of an organization. The larger the organizational setting, such as at the national or state level, the broader the goal statements (Unrau et al., 2006). On a national level, a program goal may be to enhance the lives of juvenile offenders and their families by providing block funding to states that offer evidence-based programming related to reducing youth recidivism. More specific goals on a local level may include improving educational outcomes from county youth by providing remedial educational services for at-risk youth. These goals are further clarified or operationalized in the form of observable and measureable objectives (Neuman, 2002; Westerfelt & Deitz, 2010).

Agency to Program Objectives

Moving from goals to objectives in evaluation is similar to the process of moving from a conceptual to an operational definition in research (see chapter 4). That is, an agency objective that is derived from a goal must be specific, measurable, and variable. The agency objective should clearly identify an activity or service that is directly linked to agency goals (Chinman et al., 2010; Coley & Scheinberg, 2008). For example, to help improve academic performance, an agency may offer an after-school tutoring program for middle and high school students who are at risk or who have failed a class.

Programs within agencies   It is important to understand the structure of community organizations and the programs within them. An organization may offer one program, such as a self-standing "Meals on Wheels" for older adults. However, many organizations offer several programs housed under one umbrella. For example, the National Alliance of Mentally Ill offers a host of programs, including programs that provide support services for mental health consumers and family members. Therefore, each program component must be directly related to the organization's mission statement, organizational goal, and at least one organizational objective. Similarly, a program objective should be specific and measurable and must clearly identify the desired direction of the change (Merinko, Novotney, Baker, & Lange, 2000; Unrau et al. 2006).

Program goals   According to Unrau and colleagues (2006), a program goal must have four characteristics. A program goal must identify (a) a specific social problem, (b) the population affected by the target social problem area that the program will serve, (c) the projected change or desired state, and (d) the methods used to achieve the projected change or desired state. The next step is to derive program objectives from these goals.

Program objectives   Program objectives offer a clearer direction as to the specific targeted change or projected results for program participants or clientele. Program objectives generally relate to knowledge (thoughts), affect (values and feelings), and actions (behaviors) (Unrau et al., 2006). For example, a knowledge-based program objective often aims to increase knowledge about a specific content or topic area. For example, an anger management program objective may be to increase participants' knowledge of the physiological signs of anger by having them complete a 12-week anger management program. In contrast, an affect-based objective generally targets a change in feelings, values, and/or attitudes. An anger management program may want to reduce participants' feelings of hostile anger upon completion of a 12-week program. Action-based objectives commonly aim to change the behavior or conduct of program participants. For example, a behavioral (action) objective may be to reduce the number of fights and hostile angry outbursts to zero within 3 months of completion of the program.

SMART Objectives

Some evaluation projects use "SMART" objectives. SMART is an acronym for specific (S), measurable (M), attainable (A), results-oriented (R), and timed (T). SMART objectives must identify the person(s) or situations that are the target of change (who/what). They must indicate the desired change and the direction of the desired effect (what change and what direction) and be achievable (possible to change), within a certain time frame (when).

Example 1   The Senior Center executive board will revise organizational policies designed to improve nutrition and increase available programming for physical exercise activities by January 2012.

Example 2   Families participating in the child welfare-based program (who) will increase their knowledge of community resources (what directional change) by the completion of 4-week courses (attainable and timed). Families participating in the child welfare-based program (who) will increase their use of community resources (what directional change) within 6 months of program completion (attainable and timed).

The Logic Model and the Change Process

The logic model is a useful tool for identifying and evaluating the change process in a program and its link to the evaluation. As illustrated in Figure 11.3, a logic model tells the story of an organization and its theory of change. The logic model is commonly used in evaluation to plan decision making based on program development and refinement. The model describes the situation that led to the creation of a program and inputs or resources that went into developing the organizations and the activities of staff and other stakeholders that are used to facilitate the project-desired outcomes (Taylor-Powell & Henert, 2008; W.K. Kellogg Foundation [WKKF], 2004). Figure 11.4 provides an example of a logic model for an after-school program for at-risk youth aged 7 to 11.

The logic model is a useful tool for identifying and evaluating the change process in a program and its link to the evaluation.

The logic model is a versatile diagram that traces the change process. A logic model can be devised for just about any intervention, including a 1-hour psychoeducation program or a long-standing complex organization that houses multiple programs. The logic model generally presents the most salient details that are essential to the change process and of interest to stakeholders. Different shapes, such as boxes, circles, and arrows, are used to indicate the direction of the change process and the outcomes. The diagram can be simple or complex and can use nested models to illustrate multiple programs in context (Taylor-Powell & Henert, 2008; WKKF, 2004). The next section provides an overview of the different parts of the logic model and how it can be linked to evaluation.

The Parts of the Logic Model

The logic model illustrates the change process from the initial problem to its projected intended results (see Figure 11.4). The first chain in the logic model often identifies the situation and needs, the target population, and the key stakeholders. The next chain in the causal sequence illustrates intervention planning and implementation in the form of input or resources, activities, and output. The final chain in the causal sequence shows the outcomes of the intervention. Other influential factors are underlying assumptions and external factors (Neuman, 2002; WKKF, 2004). These concepts in the context of the change process are described next.

Problem or situation   The *problem* or *situation* refers to an assessment of the adverse situations or problems and the priorities that need to be addressed. A short situation statement often includes a description of the problem (and assets) and the impact of social, economic, and/or environmental factors on the target population, and what might happen if the problem is not addressed.

Target population   The *target population* refers to the population impacted by the problem, and who the agency and/or program were designed to serve. Organizations generally specify the target population they serve, such as children with cancer residing in X county.

Stakeholders   Stakeholders involve the individuals, groups, organizations, or governmental agencies that have some interest in the target populations or intervention. These individuals may be members of the target population, staff, policy makers, and the general public. The organization is accountable to all of these stakeholders. Stakeholders are generally involved in the early stages of the process of identifying the situation (Neuman, 2002; Taylor-Powell & Henert, 2008; WKKF, 2004).

Agency/Organization/Program Name:

Situation Statement:

Assumptions:

External Factors:

Inputs	Process		Outcomes		
	Activities	Participation	Short Term	Medium Term	Long Term
What Is Invested?	*What Is Done?*	*Who Is Reached?*	*Changes Expected*	*Changes Expected*	*Changes Expected*

Figure 11.3

Logic Model Template

Source: Based on W.K. Kellogg Foundation (2004). *Logic Model Development Guide.* Battle Creek, MI : Author. Retrieved from http://www.wkkf.org/knowledge-center/resources/2010/Logic-Model-Development-Guide.aspx

Agency/Program Name: After-School Music Program for Local Youth (children age 7 to 11)

Brief Situation Statement: Low-income neighborhood comprised of mostly new immigrant Latino families with young children, who lack access to affordable arts training and after-school programs.

Assumptions: Positive youth development can be facilitated by participation in the arts.

External Factors: Lack of school and community access to music lessons and instruments.

Inputs	Process		Outcomes		
	Activities	Participation	Short Term	Medium Term	Long Term
What Is Invested?	*What Is Done?*	*Who Is Reached?*	*Changes Expected*	*Changes Expected*	*Changes Expected*
Financial Resources (Grants and donors)	Musical Instruction	Students (Children)	• Music Knowledge	• Positive Self-Esteem	• Academic Achievement
In-Kind Contributions	Mentoring	Parents	• Music Appreciation	• Creativity	• Sustained Music Involvement
Client Fees	Community Events	Teacher Volunteers	• Musical Skills	• Social Competence	
Staff		Parent Volunteers			
Volunteers		Community Members			
Equipment					
Space for Lessons and Public Performances		*Outputs:*			
Community Support		Number of Teacher Volunteers Recruited per Month			
		Number of Children Who Attend 80% of Lessons			

Figure 11.4

Logic Model Example

Source: Based on W.K. Kellogg Foundation (2004). *Logic Model Development Guide.* Battle Creek, MI : Author. Retrieved from http://www.wkkf.org/knowledge-center/resources/2010/Logic-Model-Development-Guide.aspx

Inputs or resources   *Inputs* commonly refer to investments (assets) or the human and material resources that are put into the program. Human resources generally refer to staff, volunteers, and community stakeholders. In contrast, material resources include funding, training items, and equipment. Inputs are an essential investment that provide a mechanism for an agency to achieve desired outputs and outcomes.

Activities   *Activities* refer to what the program does to achieve its required outputs and outcomes. Activities of a program may include individual, group, or family counseling; intake assessment; discharge planning; psychoeducational classes; advocacy and lobbying; and staff meetings. Program clientele also engage in program activities. *Participation* refers to the individuals or groups reached by the program and what program activities they participate in. Examples might include mental health consumers who participate in individual and group counseling or children who participate in play therapy services.

Outputs   *Outputs* generally refer to the concrete end products of agency activities and client participation. Outputs are activities conducted or products created that reach targeted participants or populations. For example, an output might be the number of individuals who completed the 12-week stress management program and workbook activities. Outputs also can be described as intermediate and final outputs. Examples of intermediate outputs can be the number of volunteers recruited per month. Final output could be the number of clients who attended 75% of scheduled medication management sessions.

Outcome or Impact Factors

Outcomes, or impact factors, are the projected results of a program. They represent the changes or benefits for individuals, families, or communities that are the target of the intervention. Outcomes are generally described in terms of short-, medium-, or long-term outcomes (Neuman, 2002; Taylor-Powell & Henert, 2008; WKKF, 2004). For example, a group educational program for families teaches budgeting skills to increase their financial literacy, which, in turn, will assist families in controlling their spending, which, in turn, assists them in maintaining long-term financial stability.

Assumptions   Assumptions are the undergirding beliefs as to why the problem exists and what intervention is projected to achieve.

External factors   *External factors* refer to environmental conditions that may impact the problem or the program intervention. Generally out of a program's control, these factors may influence the success level of a program. For example, public policies, economic factors, or community factors may have a positive or negative effect on the program.

Exercise-Logic Model Worksheet

One key value of a logic model is that it displays the chain of connections showing how a program is expected to work to achieve desired outcomes. Before completing this exercise (Figure 11.3), students are encouraged to view the 30-minute online tutorial from the University of Wisconsin–Extension at http://www.uwex.edu/ces/lmcourse/.

Policy Practice

Critical Thinking Question:
What are three major ways that policy practice helps inform program- and case-level evaluation?

Figure 11.3 can be used as a worksheet to complete a logic model of a program. Working alone or as part of a group, choose a familiar agency program to complete the logic model worksheet. When completed, the logic model should explicitly illustrate the connection among the situation, input, activities, and outcomes. Share your results with the larger group.

EVALUATION AND THE LOGIC MODEL

The age-old social work question is, How do we know it works? The research and evaluation processes involve asking questions and answering them and can address the need for the program, its design, implementation, impact, and efficiency. Evaluation assists with accountability to central stakeholders, which is an important consideration for decision making in program development and evaluation (Unrau et al., 2006). The common types of evaluation in social work include needs assessment and process, outcome, or efficiency evaluations. Figure 11.5 illustrates how these types of evaluation fit within the logic model sequence. Table 11.2 is a worksheet to gather evaluation information.

Assets and Needs Assessment

An assets and needs assessment is an evaluation study that seeks to find answers about social and environmental conditions (Rossi et al., 2004) and to determine the situation or problem, individuals or groups affected, and the need for an intervention or to develop a program to ameliorate the problem and foster assets (Goldman & Schmalz, 2005). Oftentimes in the needs assessment phase, multiple stakeholders are involved in the process and information is obtained from all angles about the problem (Percy-Smith, 1996; Soriani, 1995).

General questions that may be answered by a needs assessment might include, What are the characteristics of the problem (magnitude and severity)? What population segments does it impact? Of the identified problems, what are the priorities that need to be addressed? What are potential barriers to resolving the problem? What are the assets or facilitators that might help resolve the problem? Is there a need for a program to address this problem? What seems to work? What doesn't seem to work? (Rossi et al., 2004).

Process Evaluation

If a need is established, a blueprint or plan for a program is commonly developed and then implemented. A program must move from an idea on paper to an actual dynamic structure composed of program activities that are expected to have an impact on improving outcomes for its program clientele. A process evaluation is a type of study that serves to examine the program's process or course of action that leads its projected outcomes. It does so by examining program operations, implementation, and service delivery. A process evaluation is useful when a social worker wants to know the degree in which the program being offered is consistent with the original program plan (i.e., program fidelity). It also often involves obtaining feedback from participants about their experience in the program. A satisfaction survey is a common tool used with consumers. A formative evaluation to a process evaluation goes one step further and actively applies the evaluation results to improve the program so that it

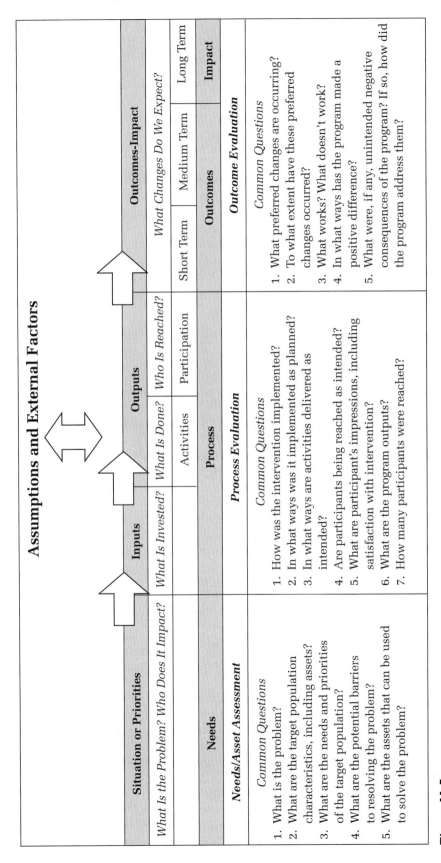

Figure 11.5

The Logic Model with Evaluation Stages

Source: Based on W.K. Kellogg Foundation (2004). *Logic Model Development Guide.* Battle Creek, MI : Author. Retrieved from http://www.wkkf.org/knowledge-center/resources/2010/Logic-Model-Development-Guide.aspx

Table 11.2   Evaluation Exercise

Directions: Please document the sources of data that were used to gather information for this exercise. They can include information obtained during interviews with agency supervisors, official agency reports, and/or agency official websites, etc . . . *If information for any of the questions was not available, please document for that question that information was not available).*

Description of agency and organization

1. What is the history of the organization? What was the reason it was formed?
2. Who are the key stakeholders of the agency or organization?
3. What is the mission statement, goals and objectives of the agency?
4. Is cultural competence, human rights, or social justice part of the mission statement?

Program services

1. What is the history of at least one program offered by the agency or organization?
2. What is the situation or "problem" that the program addresses?
3. What are the target population characteristics?
4. How were needs or rights assessed or identified for this target population?
5. What needs or rights are addressed by the current services?
6. What needs or rights are not addressed by the current services?
7. In what ways is cultural competence addressed in program services?

Program operations

1. Does the agency (or program) have a research and evaluation staff or unit?
2. How does administration or evaluation staff monitor how the program objectives are being met?
3. Does this agency monitor improvement in providing cultural competent services?
4. How are the program services being delivered to the target population?
5. Are there unserved individuals or groups that the program is not reaching? If so, why?
6. Do sufficient numbers of program participants successfully complete the program? Explain.
7. What is the program participants' level of satisfaction with the program? Explain.

Program outcomes

1. What are the stated goals and objectives of the program under investigation?
2. What, if any, are the beneficial effects of the program participation on its participants?
3. What, if any, are the adverse effects of program participation on the participants?
4. Are services distributed fairly among the subgroups that attend (age, race/ethnicity, gender, and/or other)?
5. Does it appear that the problem(s) targeted by the program are adequately addressed given the design of the services and interventions?

Program cost and efficiency

1. How is this program funded? Have the funding sources changed over time?
2. What is the cost of this program?
3. What is the yearly budget for this program? Does the cost exceed the budget?
4. What policies and procedures are there to ensure that agency resources are used efficiently?
5. Does the cost of the program outweigh its benefits to participants and the community?

(continued)

Table 11.2	**Evaluation Exercise (Continued)**

Integration of social work ethics and human rights principles

1. In what ways does the agency adhere to the NASW Code of Ethics?
2. What are common ethical issues that arise in this agency setting?
3. Overall, in what ways is the agency sensitive to issues of diversity and cultural competence?
4. What articles of the Universal Declaration of Human Rights (1948) does this program directly address?
5. In general, in what ways does the agency support human rights and social justice in their program design and service delivery systems? Please explain.

Source: Based on Rossi, P. H., Freeman, H. E., & Lipsey, M. (2006). *Evaluation: A systematic approach* (7th ed., pp. 87–88). Thousand Oaks, CA: Sage Publications.

can best reach projected outcomes (Maschi & MacMillan, 2009; Royse, Thyer, Padgett, & Logan, 2006; Unrau et al., 2006; York, 2009).

Some general questions that may be answered by a process evaluation include, What services or activities are delivered by the program? Does the program do what it was intended to do? To what extent are program participants satisfied with the program activities? To what extent was the program implemented according to the original program plan (i.e., fidelity)? Were the interventions delivered as planned (i.e., fidelity of the program implementation)? How many people attended the program? How many people completed the program? (Rossi et al., 2004).

An example of an agency satisfaction survey using both closed-ended and open-ended questions can be found in Table 11.3. Similarly, Table 11.4 presents the results of a student research project. It presents the descriptive results of how 17 juvenile correctional officers perceived the helpfulness of program services for detained youth.

Outcome Evaluation

An outcome evaluation is conducted to determine if a program has met its specific goals and objectives. Also referred to as a *summative evaluation* and an *impact assessment*, an outcome evaluation provides information on the extent to which change occurred among program participants (e.g., prosocial attitudes, reduced criminal activities) and the targeted larger or social environmental conditions (community crime reduction). Outcomes are often described in achievable increments that range from short-term (1 year or less) to medium-term (3 year) to long-term (10 year) impact (Dudley, 2008; Engel & Schutt, 2010).

Generally, outcomes represent important milestones in the change process for individuals and communities. The outcomes often result in some type of improvements, such as improved mental well-being or reduced community crime, that are meaningful to key stakeholders. The progression of outcomes from short- to medium- to long-term outcomes must be directly connected to the program activities. Most of all, the outcomes must be achievable given the resources and the situation (Taylor-Powell & Henert, 2008; WKKF, 2004).

Some general questions that might guide an outcome evaluation are, To what extent are desired changes occurring (short term, medium term, long term)?

Table 11.3   Satisfaction Survey Sample

After-School Music Program for Youth Satisfaction Survey

Parent/Caretaker Survey

We are interested in knowing how satisfied you are with your child's (or children's) experience with the After-School Music Program for Youth. Note: Please respond to the following statements using the scale below. For each statement, please circle the response that best represents your views.

1 = Strongly Disagree
2 = Disagree
3 = Neutral
4 = Agree
5 = Strongly Agree

	5	4	3	2	1
1. How much do you agree or disagree with the following statements:	5	4	3	2	1
2. I am satisfied with the musical training provided for my child here.	SA	A	N	D	SD
3. This program makes good use of my child's time.	SA	A	N	D	SD
4. My child's musical skills have improved.	SA	A	N	D	SD
5. My child has improved at public performance because of this training.	SA	A	N	D	SD
6. The teacher always keeps me informed of my child's progress.	SA	A	N	D	SD
7. The teachers are well prepared and know what they are doing.	SA	A	N	D	SD
8. Overall, the teachers at this program are very helpful.	SA	A	N	D	SD
9. Other staff members are well prepared and know what they are doing.	SA	A	N	D	SD
10. The other staff members at this program are very helpful.	SA	A	N	D	SD
11. Everyone at the program treats each other with mutual respect.	SA	A	N	D	SD
12. My child received a lot of positive attention at this program.	SA	A	N	D	SD
13. My child is happy at this program.	SA	A	N	D	SD
14. My child feels a sense of belonging at this program.	SA	A	N	D	SD
15. This program has a calming environment.	SA	A	N	D	SD
16. This program teaches children about mutual respect of one another.	SA	A	N	D	SD
17. This program offers my child a strong sense of community.	SA	A	N	D	SD
18. Overall, this program has a positive influence on my child.	SA	A	N	D	SD
19. Overall, my child would love to come back to this program.	SA	A	N	D	SD
20. This program has many opportunities for me to see my child perform.	SA	A	N	D	SD
21. This program has many opportunities for me to volunteer.	SA	A	N	D	SD
22. I would recommend this program to my family and friends.	SA	A	N	D	SD
23. Overall, I am very satisfied with this program.	SA	A	N	D	SD

(continued)

Table 11.3   Satisfaction Survey Sample (Continued)

After-School Music Program for Youth Satisfaction Survey

24. How would you describe the atmosphere here?

25. How has your child changed as a result of participating in this program?

26. Is there anything else you would like to share about your child's experience in the program?

Thank you very much for sharing your views. Your opinions help make a difference toward improving our program.

Source: Maschi & MacMillan (2009).

Table 11.4   Descriptive Statistics for Juvenile Correctional Officers' Perceptions of the Helpfulness of Detention Program Services for Detained Youth

Service Kind	Percentage of Services and Their Level of Helpfulness				
	Not Helpful	Kind of Helpful	Helpful	Very Helpful	N/A
Interaction time with staff	5.6 ($n=1$)	5.6 ($n=4$)	33.3 ($n=6$)	27.8 ($n=5$)	5.6 ($n=1$)
Individual counseling	11.1 ($n=2$)	27.8 ($n=5$)	27.8 ($n=5$)	22.2 ($n=4$)	0.0 ($n=0$)
Group counseling	16.7 ($n=3$)	33.3 ($n=6$)	27.8 ($n=5$)	5.6 ($n=1$)	11.1 ($n=2$)
Family therapy	5.6 ($n=1$)	5.6 ($n=1$)	77.8 ($n=14$)	88.9 ($n=16$)	11.1 ($n=2$)
Psychiatric help	22.2 ($n=4$)	27.8 ($n=5$)	5.6 ($n=1$)	5.6 ($n=1$)	22.2 ($n=4$)
Medical services	0.0 ($n=0$)	22.2 ($n=4$)	44.4 ($n=8$)	22.2 ($n=4$)	5.6 ($n=1$)
Psychiatric services	11.1 ($n=2$)	11.1 ($n=2$)	16.7 ($n=3$)	5.6 ($n=1$)	22.2 ($n=4$)
Substance abuse counseling	22.2 ($n=4$)	16.7 ($n=2$)	27.8 ($n=5$)	11.1 ($n=2$)	16.7 ($n=3$)
Case management services	16.7 ($n=3$)	22.2 ($n=4$)	33.3 ($n=6$)	16.7 ($n=3$)	5.6 ($n=1$)
Classroom instruction	16.7 ($n=3$)	16.7 ($n=3$)	44.4 ($n=8$)	11.1 ($n=2$)	0.0 ($n=0$)
Tutoring	5.6 ($n=1$)	11.1 ($n=2$)	11.1 ($n=2$)	16.7 ($n=3$)	50.0 ($n=9$)
Gang training	22.2 ($n=4$)	33.3 ($n=6$)	11.1 ($n=2$)	0.0 ($n=0$)	27.8 ($n=5$)

Table 11.4 **Descriptive Statistics for Juvenile Correctional Officers' Perceptions of the Helpfulness of Detention Program Services for Detained Youth (Continued)**

| Service Kind | Percentage of Services and Their Level of Helpfulness | | | | |
	Not Helpful	Kind of Helpful	Helpful	Very Helpful	N/A
Job or vocational training	16.7 ($n = 3$)	5.6 ($n = 1$)	11.1 ($n = 2$)	5.6 ($n = 1$)	55.6 ($n = 10$)
Life skills training	22.2 ($n = 4$)	22.2 ($n = 4$)	27.8 ($n = 5$)	11.1 ($n = 2$)	11.1 ($n = 2$)
Social skills training	16.7 ($n = 3$)	22.2 ($n = 4$)	27.8 ($n = 5$)	11.1 ($n = 2$)	11.1 ($n = 2$)
Recreational activities	16.7 ($n = 3$)	22.2 ($n = 4$)	22.2 ($n = 4$)	22.2 ($n = 4$)	5.6 ($n = 1$)
Community service work	5.6 ($n = 1$)	16.7 ($n = 3$)	16.7 ($n = 3$)	0.0 ($n = 0$)	50.0 ($n = 9$)
Faith-based volunteers	5.6 ($n = 1$)	22.2 ($n = 4$)	38.9 ($n = 7$)	27.8 ($n = 5$)	0.0 ($n = 0$)
Mentors	5.6 ($n = 1$)	5.6 ($n = 1$)	44.4 ($n = 8$)	16.7 ($n = 3$)	22.2 ($n = 4$)
Transportation	0.0 ($n = 0$)	0.0 ($n = 0$)	38.9 ($n = 7$)	44.4 ($n = 8$)	5.6 ($n = 1$)
Aftercare services	22.2 ($n = 4$)	11.1 ($n = 2$)	5.6 ($n = 1$)	5.6 ($n = 1$)	44.4 ($n = 8$)

For what individuals or groups does the program work? Is the program making a difference in the intended direction it expected? What are unintended outcomes or consequences of the program for participants, other stakeholders, and the community? (Rossi et al., 2004).

Efficiency Evaluation

As noted earlier, key stakeholders, particularly public officials, policy makers, and funders, are most interested in fiscal issues related to community programming. Therefore, the costs of starting and maintaining an agency are an important area in which ongoing assessments are conducted. In order to address this concern, most programs conduct efficiency evaluations. An efficiency evaluation compares the effects of a program to its cost. It is an approach to making economic decisions of any kind and is often a requirement of program funding (Levin, 2001).

The two types of efficiency evaluations commonly used in social work program evaluation are cost-benefit analysis and cost-effectiveness analysis.

Cost-benefit analysis is an evaluation weighing the total expected costs against the total expected benefits of one or more actions in order to choose the best financial option. A cost-benefit ratio is determined by dividing the projected benefits of a program by the projected costs. A wide range of projected benefits, such as well-being or quality of life, are measured because of their potential indirect and long-term cost-saving benefits. In contrast, cost-effectiveness analysis analyzes costs related to a single, common effect (crime reduction), usually in terms of cost expended per outcome achieved (Levin, 2001).

General questions that an efficiency evaluation may answer about a program include, What are the program costs in comparison to the monetary value of its benefits? How much does it cost to run? Does the total cost exceed the budget? Do the social benefits outweigh the fiscal costs? (Rossi et al., 2004).

Stakeholder Collaboration

Engaging interested stakeholders who have direct or indirect interests in the formation of a program, its progress, and its results is important. Social workers are well served before they undertake an evaluation project to understand who the stakeholders are and the motives for their interest so that collaborative relationships can be fostered. For example, most often, policy makers are concerned about financial resources, community safety, or political ramifications in the decision-making process. Similarly, agency clientele, frontline social workers, program administrators, agency executives, and private and public funders often have a voice in the process.

Evaluation Exercise

It is recommended that students complete the evaluation program information worksheet found in Table 11.2. It provides questions related to the common types of evaluation in social work, which include a needs assessment and process, outcome, or efficiency evaluations. Students are encouraged to consult multiple data sources including publicly available agency information, the program or county or state websites or agency report, and interviews with agency administrators or other identified key stakeholders. When conducting an interview, get permission from participants to record the interview or be prepared to write copious verbatim notes. If possible, create a logic model of at least one program. Based on your findings, write a 5–6 page report that highlights major findings and provides recommendations to the organization for improved service provision. Share a copy of the report with the interviewee(s) upon request.

ADDITIONAL EVALUATION STRATEGIES

Additional evaluation strategies relevant to social work include community asset mapping, empowerment evaluation, and action-oriented research.

Community Asset Mapping

Community asset mapping is another form of visual narrative of a neighborhood or community that can be used for social and economic development (Hillier, 2007). It can be used to document community assets, socioeconomic conditions, and housing patterns (Emery & Flora, 2006). Mapping is a user-friendly visual representation of socio-demographic data by geographical location.

Community maps can range from simple to complex and display a few variables over a wide geographical area (context map) to multiple variables. A context map is used to represent a few variables of interest over a wider geographic level to many variables over smaller geographic areas (e.g., display map) or a combination of both (analytical maps). Community mapping is a useful tool because it can visually map community well-being in an easy-to-understand manner (Jasek-Rysdahl, 2001). The maps can be used to support participatory decision-making and program and intervention planning (Kretzman & McNight, 1993).

Empowerment Evaluation

Empowerment evaluation is an evidence-based evaluation strategy that uses an empowerment approach that fosters self-determination. Empowerment evaluation is defined as an evaluation approach that aims to increase the probability of achieving program success by building the capacity of stakeholders to conduct evaluation from initial planning, implementation, and evaluation and by streamlining the process to make evaluation manageable. This process involves mainstreaming evaluation as part of the planning and management of the program or organization (Fetterman & Wandersman, 2004).

The 10 empowerment principles that guide the process are (a) improvement, (b) community ownership, (c) inclusion, (d) democratic participation, (e) social justice, (f) community knowledge, (g) evidence-based strategies, (h) capacity building, (i) organizational learning, and (j) accountability.

Empowerment evaluation shifts the traditional evaluation methods of the external expert to the internal program experts who know their program. It fosters internal expertise, self-determination, capacity building, and collaborative decision-making. Empowerment evaluation has been used in a variety of settings from community-based programs to government agencies to business, educational and religious settings. Populations include youth and adults and diverse racial ethnic groups, such as African Americans, Latinos, Caucasians, and Native Americans (Fetterman & Wandersman, 2004).

Action-Oriented Research

Action research, including participatory action research, is a collaborative research and evaluation framework in which creating positive social change is the driving force. There are several common themes across action-oriented research methods. The methods used are highly rigorous and reflective; they actively engage participants and contributors in the research process and offer the participants practical outcomes; and they use a spiraling of steps composed of collaborative planning, action, and evaluation (Stringer, 2007; Suarez-Balcazar & Harper, 2003).

Action research differs from traditional research and evaluation approaches in several ways. The action research approach is heavily reflective, experiential, and participatory. All individuals participating in the study, including research team members and participants alike, take part in all stages of the research process from formulating problems, gathering data, analyzing the results, and taking action. An action research project also generates information directly for the individuals or agencies that need it. The strategies used often merge research, education, and sociopolitical action. The method also educates and empowers the individuals involved in the project to use the information gained to take sociopolitical action (McIntyre, 2000, 2008).

Action research uses methods that suggest parity in the research process, consistent with human rights and social justice philosophies. An action-oriented research approach democratizes knowledge production and use. It is ethical in that the participants take part in the process and can reap the benefits of the knowledge gained. It uses an ecological and strengths perspective and assumes a holistic view of a human being's ability to reflect, learn, and transform (Stringer, 2007; Stringer & Dwyer, 2005).

MIXED METHODS DESIGNS AND EVALUATION

As the term *mixed methods* suggests, it denotes mixing both quantitative and qualitative methods. This combination is commonly used in practice and program evaluation where gathering narrative and numeric data is a routine part of practice, for example, quantitative evidence in the form of test scores and census data. Qualitative evidence, such as the use of participant interviews, may provide useful insights that can better explain how well the program worked (Creswell, 2009).

Creswell (2009) described two types of mixed methods designs that can be useful to consider for evaluation: sequential and concurrent designs using quantitative and qualitative approaches. A sequential mixed method design is to use one approach first, followed the other method (quantitative followed by qualitative or qualitative followed by quantitative). If quantitative methods are used, they can provide representative data in which results can be explored in more detail, especially if an unexpected result is found. Qualitative methods can be used to explore issues from which the information can guide a quantitative study that could generate generalizable information useful to the target population. A concurrent design is a research design that uses both quantitative (e.g., sociodemographic characteristics, standardized measure scores on program outcomes, satisfaction surveys) and qualitative methods (e.g., open-ended interviews) to understand and explain a program's process or outcomes. A concurrent design is able to capture both the breadth and depth of an issue under investigation.

As reviewed in chapter 8, the use of an experimental or quasi-experimental design for quantitative research helps to increase confidence in the results that the program intervention has had a significant causal effect on the predicted outcomes and in the intended direction (e.g., increased self-esteem and decreased antisocial attitudes).

COMMON DATA SOURCES FOR EVALUATION

Also reviewed in chapter 7 were common measures used in practice evaluation, including graphic rating scales, self-anchored rating scales, test scores, and standardized summative scales (Richards et al., 1999). Graphic rating scales often represent an attribute on a numeric continuum, such as 0 to 10. For example, a rating scale for depression may consist of 0 = not depressed at all, 5 = moderately depressed, and 10 = completely depressed. A self-anchored rating scale differs from a graphic rating scale in that participants use their own words to describe what makes sense to them about their experience on a continuum. Using a program participant's words to describe his or her depression may consist of 0 = "feeling like frozen zombie," 5 = "cloudy thoughts but little chance of crying," and 10 = "feeling groovy!"

Test scores may be based on pre and posttest knowledge quiz results, for example, comparing what such participants knew about the physiological signs of anger before and after 12 weeks of psychoeducational training. Standardized measuring scales often are used in evaluation because they represent a valid measurement instrument, especially for outcomes, such as self-esteem, anger, prosocial attitudes, and/or behaviors. Many standardized measures use a summative or additive score in which the individual scale items are added together for a total score. Standardized measures are valid and reliable. Uniform administration and scoring generates normative data that can be used to compare results with different populations or with the same program participants to compare their scores before and after their participation. Common qualitative data sources include structured and semi-structured interviewing of central stakeholders, including participants, program staff, public officials, policy makers, and community members (Creswell, 2009; Engel & Schutt, 2010). Review of program documents and observation also may be used.

EVALUATION AND CULTURAL COMPETENCE

Diversity in Practice

Critical Thinking Question: Provide at least two or three ways in which the Assessment of Organizational Cultural Competence can be used to improve service delivery.

In this rapidly growing diverse society, social workers must make every effort to design programs with culturally competent policies and practice (Rothman, 2008). Organizations, programs, or individuals can evaluate their level of cultural competence by using such tools as the Cultural Competence Continuum (Cross, Baron, Dennis, & Isaacs, 1989). As shown in Figure 11.6, these stages are as follows: cultural destructiveness, cultural incapacity, cultural blindness, cultural precompetence, cultural competence, and cultural proficiency.

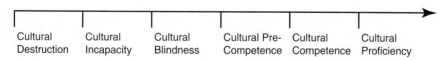

Figure 11.6

The Cultural Competence Continuum

Source: Adapted from Cross, T., Bazron, B., Dennis, K., & Isaacs, M. (1989). *Towards a culturally competent system of care, Volume 1.* Washington, DC: CASSP Technical Assistance Center, Center for Child Health and Mental Health Policy, Georgetown University Child Development Center.

Cultural Competence Continuum

Cultural Destructiveness

Cultural destructiveness is at the negative end of the continuum. This stage is characterized by the presence of adverse attitudes, policies, structures, and practices within a system or organization that are destructive to a cultural group or groups. For example, some programs may not offer culturally competent services for the cultural groups in their geographic location.

Cultural Incapacity

Cultural incapacity is the next stage and is represented by the organization's inability to respond effectively to diverse cultural group needs, interests, and preferences. Examples of cultural incapacity include the use of discriminatory practices in hiring and promoting staff and the unequal allocation of resources of one cultural group over another.

Cultural Blindness

Cultural blindness is the next stage of cultural competence. The organization's philosophy is to treat all cultures the same as opposed to honoring diversity. For example, organizational policies may expect assimilation with the dominant cultural group. This includes when a program lacks a culturally diverse workforce, has minimal to no training available on cultural competence, and its services do not adequately reflect cultural sensitivity to the diverse cultural groups served.

Cultural Precompetence

Cultural precompetence reflects the beginning of culturally competent practice. The program has a realistic awareness of the agency's areas of strengths and areas where it needs to grow to respond effectively to the cultural groups it serves. Examples include the organization's overt commitment to human and civil rights and high-quality culturally competent practices. There is a visibly culturally diverse staff. The organization has the capacity to conduct culturally competent asset and needs assessments. However, a lack of cultural diversity exists in staff holding executive positions. There also is no clear plan on how to make the organization more culturally competent.

Cultural Competence

Cultural competence is the next stage on the cultural competence continuum. At this stage, the acceptance and respect of differences is evident in the organization. The organization's mission statement clearly articulates cultural diversity and the organization evaluates its progress regarding the mission statement among individual staff members and the agency. It has targeted areas of providing cultural competent practices to some cultural groups. There is evidence of program clientele participating in the planning, implementation, and evaluation of agency programs. The staff of the organization actively seeks advice and consultation to improve in culturally competent service provision, including allocating financial resources to diversity training. The organization begins to develop the capacity to conduct agency-based research and evaluation to monitor progress in providing culturally competent services.

Cultural Proficiency

Cultural proficiency is the final stage of the cultural competence continuum. It represents the positive end of the spectrum. The organization's commitment to cultural diversity is a central organizing concept of service provision. The organization is able to recruit and maintain a diverse staff. The agency is recognized by the community as having expertise in the development and provision of culturally sensitive practices. The organization engages in active outreach to community members for their feedback and participation. The organization has a well-developed research and evaluation unit that develops, evaluates, and disseminates its findings related to culturally competent best practices (Cross et al., 1989).

Organizational Assessment of Cultural Competence

Social workers working within organizations can assist with assessing an organization's level of cultural competence. For example, the Association of University Centers on Disabilities (AUCD, 2004) offers suggestions on how to assess cultural competence. Central cultural competence areas to assess include organizational commitment, administration, clinical services, research and evaluation programs, education and training, and community training.

Organizational Commitment

Some specific areas to assess whether an organization has achieved cultural competence are (a) cultural competence is included in the mission statement, policies, and procedures; (b) a committee/task force/program area addresses issues of cultural competence; (c) partnerships with representatives of ethnic communities actively incorporate their knowledge and experience in organizational planning; and (d) the organization supports involvement with and/or utilization of the resources of regional and/or national forums that promote cultural competence.

Service Provision

As illustrated in Table 11.5, central services areas to assess include administration, clinical services, research and evaluation programs, education and training, and community training. An assessment includes whether the organization almost always has the following practices and procedures in place. The Association of University Centers on Disabilities (AUCD, 2004) has an Assessment of Organizational Cultural Competence available for download on MySocialWorkLab.

Table 11.5   Organization Assessment for Cultural Competences

---

Administration

1. Personnel recruitment, hiring, and retention practices reflect the goal to achieve ethnic diversity and cultural competence.
2. Resources are in place to support initial and ongoing training for personnel to develop cultural competence.
3. Position descriptions and personnel performance measures include skills related to cultural competence.
4. Participants for all advisory committees and councils are recruited and supported to ensure the diverse cultural representation of the organization's geographic area.
5. Personnel are respected and supported for their desire to honor and participate in cultural celebrations.
6. Fiscal resources are available to support translation and interpretation services.
7. Agencies can respond.

Clinical services

1. Clinical services are routinely and systematically reviewed for methods, strategies, and ways of serving consumers and their families in culturally competent ways.
2. Cultural bias of assessment tools is considered when interpreting of the results and making recommendations.
3. Translation and interpretation assistance is available and utilized when needed.
4. Forms of communication (reports, appointment notices, telephone message greetings, etc.) are culturally and linguistically appropriate for the populations served.
5. Pictures, posters, printed materials and toys reflect the culture and ethnic backgrounds of the consumers and families served.
6. When food is discussed or used in assessment or treatment, the cultural and ethnic background of the consumer and family is considered.

Research and program evaluation

1. Input on research priorities is sought from consumers and/or their families representing diverse cultures.
2. Research projects include subjects of diverse cultures representative of the targeted research population.
3. The researchers include members of the racial/ethnic groups to be studied and/or individuals who have acquired knowledge and skills to work with subjects from those specific groups.
4. Consumers and families representing diverse cultures provide input regarding the design, methods, and outcome measures of research and program evaluation projects.

Education

1. Trainees/students are actively recruited from diverse cultures.
2. Trainees/students from diverse cultures are mentored.
3. Representatives of the diverse cultures are actively sought to participate in the planning and presentation of training activities.
4. The training curriculum and activities incorporate content for the development of cultural competence.
5. The training curriculum, materials and activities are systemically evaluated to determine if they achieve cultural competence.

Table 11.5	**Organization Assessment for Cultural Competences (Continued)**

Community/continuing education

1. Participants are actively recruited from diverse cultures.
2. Representatives of diverse cultures are actively sought to participate in the planning and presentation of these activities.
3. The content and activities are culturally and linguistically appropriate.
4. Participant evaluation of community/continuing education activities includes components of cultural competence.

Source: Association of University Centers on Disabilities. (2004). *Assessment of Organizational Cultural Competence.* AUCD Multicultural Council.

SUMMARY

Social work has historically used social interventions for individual and social change. Using a human rights and social justice lens for evaluation efforts underscores providing services that are a right as opposed to a need. The logic model can illustrate a theory of change, and by illustrating a cause-and-effect sequence, program activities can ameliorate targeted social conditions. Using a conceptual diagram format, it identifies the social conditions that led to program development, implementation, and results. Common types of evaluation used in social work include assets and needs assessments and process, outcome, and efficiency evaluations. The information garnered during the evaluation process can be used to develop or refine service provision that is most relevant to the populations served. The use of a cultural competence continuum provides guidelines for fostering a culturally proficient organization that can become an ongoing aspect of agency and program evaluation.

Succeed with PEARSON mysocialworklab

Log onto **www.mysocialworklab.com** and answer the following questions. *(If you did not receive an access code to **MySocialWorkLab** with this text and wish to purchase access online, please visit* www.mysocialworklab.com.*)*

1. **Watch the engagement, assessment, intervention, evaluation video "Intervention."** After listening to the commentary, describe what connections you can make to case-level intervention and how it relates to the program's mission and objectives.

2. **Watch the engagement, assessment, intervention, evaluation video "Evaluation."** After listening to the commentary, describe what connections you can make between case-level and program-level evaluation.

PRACTICE TEST
The following questions will test your knowledge of the content found within this chapter. For additional assessment, including licensing-exam type questions on applying chapter content to practice, visit **MySocialWorkLab**.

1. An evaluation theory that describes a cause-and-effect chain in which a program facilitates positive change is:
   a. Behavior theory
   b. Rational choice theory
   c. Impact theory
   d. Positive change theory

2. A social worker will conduct what type of evaluation to examine the results of a substance abuse program on reducing drug use among his or her clientele?
   a. Needs or resource assessment
   b. Outcome evaluation
   c. Process evaluation
   d. Efficiency evaluation

3. Case-level or program level objectives generally indicate all of the following except:
   a. Prior history
   b. The person or situation
   c. Desired change
   d. Achievable change within a certain time frame

4. An organization that demonstrates cultural proficiency will more than likely do which of the following?
   a. Treat all cultures similarly
   b. Be unaware of cultural differences
   c. Have research and evaluation units for culturally competent best practices
   d. Unequally allocate resources of one cultural group over another

5. You were hired as a consultant to conduct an evaluation of a prisoner reentry program that targets reducing recidivism among ex-prisoners with mental health problems that serves 150 clients. What type of evaluation plan would you recommend?

ASSESS YOUR COMPETENCE
Use the scale below to rate your current level of achievement on the following concepts or skills associated with each competency presented in the chapter:

1	2	3
I can accurately describe the concept or skill	I can consistently identify the concept or skill when observing and analyzing practice activities	I can competently implement the concept or skill in my own practice

_____ can assess an agency or a program for level of cultural competence.

_____ can apply a theory of change to case-level or program-level evaluation.

_____ can complete a logic model of a program.

_____ can develop an evaluation plan.

Writing for a Change and Other Advocacy Tips

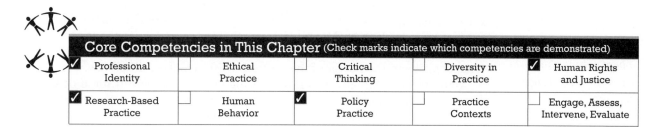

Core Competencies in This Chapter (Check marks indicate which competencies are demonstrated)				
✓ Professional Identity	Ethical Practice	Critical Thinking	Diversity in Practice	✓ Human Rights and Justice
✓ Research-Based Practice	Human Behavior	✓ Policy Practice	Practice Contexts	Engage, Assess, Intervene, Evaluate

INTRODUCTION

In the following passage, Clifford Beers (1908) writes about the sense of responsibility he felt to share his story in the book *A Mind That Found Itself: A Memoir of Madness and Recovery*.

> I am not telling the story of my life just to write a book. I tell it because it seems my plain duty to do so. A narrow escape from death and a seemingly miraculous turn to health after an apparently fatal illness are enough to make a man ask himself: For what purpose was my life spared? The question I have asked myself, and this book is, in part an answer. (Beers, 1908, p. 1)

Published in 1908 and unbeknownst to Beers, his gripping autobiographic account of his struggle with mental illness would become a pivotal force that launched the mental hygiene movement in the United States. The mental hygiene movement has evolved into the contemporary mental health consumer movement. His story was much like others who experienced mental illness and treatment, except that he wrote his down.

In his book, Beers chronicled his life as a recent Yale graduate who became depressed and was admitted to a psychiatric hospital in which he spent several years battling bipolar disorders with psychotic features. However, his story doesn't end there. Beers provides detailed ethnographic accounts of being a victim of and witness to brutal and inhumane treatment by hospital staff as his ongoing struggle with serious mental illness and psychiatric hospital placements continued. In the following passage, Beers (1908) described "a detestable form of restraint that amounted to torture" (p. 40). He wrote

> To guard me at night while the remaining attendant slept, my hands were imprisoned in what is known as a "muff." A muff, innocent enough to the eyes of those who have never worn one, is in reality a relic of the Inquisition. It is an instrument of restraint which has been in use for centuries and even in many of our public and private institutions is still in use. The muff I wore was made of canvas, and differed in construction from a muff designed for the hands of fashion only in the inner partition, also of canvas, which separated my hands, but allowed them to overlap. At either end was a strap which buckled tightly around the wrist and was locked. . . .The putting on of the muff was the most humiliating incident of my life. (pp. 40–41)

However, despite these restraints, Beers' autobiography is one of triumph in which he learns to manage his mental illness and becomes an advocate for the just and fair treatment of individuals with mental illness. What initially appeared as the lone voice of one man became the symbolic voice of an entire mental health consumer social movement. Beers, the writer, also became a committed reformer. His lifelong work with mental health consumer movement organizations, such as the National Committee for Mental Hygiene and the American Foundation for Mental Hygiene, helped to transform the treatment of individuals with mental illness. Beers' story is a testament to the triumph of the human spirit and the power of the written word to make a difference.

Many writers can attest to how writing can be a powerful force of social change.

Many writers can attest to how writing can be a powerful force of social change. Writing is also a skill that many people approach with trepidation. However, initial trepidation can be transformed by challenging and overcoming self-defeating thoughts about writing and practicing the craft. As illustrated in the case of Clifford Beers, whose mind was continually challenged and whose hands were restrained, he was able to write. And his writing made a difference.

Similar to Beers (1908), other writers express an obligation to share their knowledge and experience. For example, Williams (2004) described writing as using the art of language and the story to witness the positive and negative of the world. As social workers, bearing witness to the positive and negative of the world is a large part of the work we do. Social workers continually share the beauty and pain experienced by individuals, families, and communities. They also are often witnesses to healing and transformation. An important part of the process is asking what do they do with what they know and with the evidence that they have accrued with their research and practice experience? Do social workers also feel compelled to share what they know and do? If the answer to both of these questions is *yes*, it is consistent with the National Association of Social Workers (NASW, 1999) ethical standards about social workers' ethical responsibilities to the profession and the broader society, as outlined next.

Professional Identity

Critical Thinking Question: How important to a social worker's professional identity is engaging in research and evaluation, including writing or presenting his or her work, and why?

In the NASW (1999) Code of Ethics (section 5), social workers' ethical responsibilities to the social work profession provide the mandate to share what they do in a variety of ways, including writing, teaching, research, and public presentations. For example, section 5.01 on the integrity of the profession states:

> (d) Social workers should contribute to the knowledge base of social work and share with colleagues their knowledge related to practice, research, and ethics. Social workers should seek to contribute to the profession's literature and to share their knowledge at professional meetings and conferences. (p. 10)

Similarly, this section of the Code underscores the high value placed on social workers sharing their knowledge and experiences to help improve the profession:

> (c) Social workers should contribute time and professional expertise to activities that promote respect for the value, integrity, and competence of the social work profession. These activities may include teaching, research, consultation, service, legislative testimony, presentations in the community, and participation in their professional organizations. (p. 10)

The NASW (1999) Code also underscores social workers' ethical responsibilities to the broader society (section 6). For example, section 6.04 on social and political action states:

> (a) Social workers should engage in social and political action that seeks to ensure that all people have equal access to the resources, employment, services, and opportunities they require to meet their basic human needs and to develop fully. Social workers should be aware of the impact of the political arena on practice and should advocate for changes in policy and legislation to improve social conditions in order to meet basic human needs and promote social justice. (para. 1)

These combined responsibilities provide social workers with the profession's encouragement and permission to share their knowledge and experiences and to take action to help change the profession and the world for the better.

DISSEMINATION AND HUMAN RIGHTS

As reviewed in chapter 1, the research cycle is a process in which the final phase is to share research and evaluation findings and take action with these findings. For social workers to advance human rights and social and economic justice, it is imperative that evidence generated from research, practice, and program evaluation be used and shared. This includes writing and disseminating findings to an academic as well as community audience (see Figure 12.1). Social workers commonly communicate research findings through writing and speaking. Getting the message out includes publishing reports and journal articles, making public presentations, and using the media (Ife, 2001a, 2001b; United Nations [UN], 1994; Reichert, 2003; Wronka, 2007). These activities are detailed throughout this chapter.

As social workers, part of our position is to motivate or to persuade some type of change, whether it is at the individual or community level. As reviewed in chapter 1, effective written or oral communication and the combined effect of ethos, logos, and pathos were essential in promoting a human rights agenda (Wronka, 2007). The example reviewed here will be applied to writing. Ethos represents a writer's recognized authority to write on a particular topic. Logos often reinforces ethos with their use of evidence and reason, such as factual data and statistics, for the purpose of persuading others. For example, logos mostly describes the use of evidence to support an important point, such as the national statistics of maltreated children. Pathos, on the other hand, represents an appeal to emotions, in the form of passionate delivery, including the assertion that an issue concerns human rights. The combined effect of making a connection with an underlying value, such as fairness and equity, and coordinating it with ethos and logos is a key factor for succeeding at making persuasive arguments (Aristotle, 350 B.C./2000; Wisse, 1989). This, in turn, may lead to using research findings to advocate agency- or governmental-level policy reform and improve social conditions for individuals and families (Thomas & Mohan, 2007).

Human Rights and Justice

Critical Thinking Question: What are the pros and cons of different ways of disseminating research (e.g., writing journal articles, newspapers, presentations) to help advance human rights and social justice?

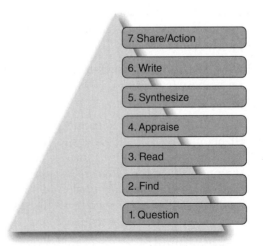

7. Share/Action

6. Write

5. Synthesize

4. Appraise

3. Read

2. Find

1. Question

Figure 12.1
The Seven Tier Appraisal Information Review (STAIR) Model

WRITING: START WITH A COMMITMENT AND A PURPOSE

To be a good writer with the potential to make a difference takes commitment, reflection, and practice. Singer (2006) underscores that critical awareness begins with strong reading and writing habits. Moreover, she refers to writing and reading to change the world as "stirring up justice" (p. 1).

Writing in research involves several common types of written formats. Perhaps the most common are the research report, proposal, evaluation report, and literature review. Social workers need to be proficient in understanding the content and format of these reports in order to read or write them.

The Research Report: Empirical Journal

The research report provides an organized structure that documents a research project and uses a consistent reader-friendly format (Szuchman & Thomlinson, 2008). Social workers commonly consult empirical literature in search of the best evidence to use for practice or research (Rubin, 2008). However, within the confines of the report structure, there are opportunities to be creative (Bem, 2000). Most academics would agree that most good writing tells a story. This also is true in empirical research reports. The writer's goal is to effectively and succinctly convey details about the study, for example, "why the study was done, how it was done, what was found, and what it possibly means" (Asmundson, Norton, & Stein, 2002, p. 170).

Overview

As shown in Figure 12.2, a research report of an empirical research study generally consists of four sections represented by the acronym IMRAD: introduction, method, results, and discussion. The "I," or "introduction" section, alerts the reader to what problem was studied, why it was studied, and how the current study fills the gap in the literature. The "M," or "methods" section, details what methods or strategies were used to conduct the study. The "R," or "results" section, reports the result(s) of the investigation. The "D," or "discussion" section, interprets what these findings mean (Bem, 2000; Szuchman & Thomlinson, 2008).

Hourglass shape   Bem (2002) described a research report as written in the shape of an hourglass. As shown in Figure 12.3, the beginning or introduction starts with a broad overview of a general topic area, such as domestic violence. It narrows its focus to describe the rationale for your current study. At the narrowest center point, the report specifies the current study's methods and findings. The discussion section begins anchoring the reader with a quick review of the current study's major findings. The discussion begins to broaden by comparing the current findings to the existing literature. It broadens even further by discussing the findings and implications for practice and policy, followed by recommendations for future research in the area.

Empathy for the reader   Research reports should be written in clear and plain language. Most important, they should be free of jargon. If technical terms are used, define them. If abstract theoretical concepts are used, explain

---

TITLE
- Accurate description of content

ABSTRACT
- Brief general description of study (120 words or fewer) (objective of study, methods, findings, implications)

INTRODUCTION
- Statement of the research problem or central issue(s)
- Identify gap in literature
- Purpose of study
- Description of research questions and/or hypotheses
- Study rationale
- Significance for social work practice and policy

LITERATURE REVIEW
- Critical review of variables of central interest
- Review of theoretical framework (if applicable)

METHODS
Description of the methods, including
1. research design
2. intervention description (if applicable)
3. variables and measures
4. data collection procedures
5. data analysis strategies

FINDINGS
- Review of the research findings
- Connection between research questions to results

DISCUSSION
- Brief overview of major findings
- Discussion if hypotheses were supported
- Comparison to previous research studies
- Discussion of practice and/or policy implications
- Methodological limitations of current study
- Recommendations for future research directions

REFERENCES
- References cited in text

Figure 12.2
The Research Report Map: Section of an Empirical Report

them. A research report should be written in a reader friendly manner so someone who knows very little about a topic area can understand it. Remember you have an important message to share and you want your reader to understand it. We recommend practicing reader empathy, or putting yourself in the reader's shoes. Try to engage the reader and help him or her understand your important message. The next section reviews the tasks you must accomplish in each section of the research report. Apply this material to writing your own research report or critiquing other research reports.

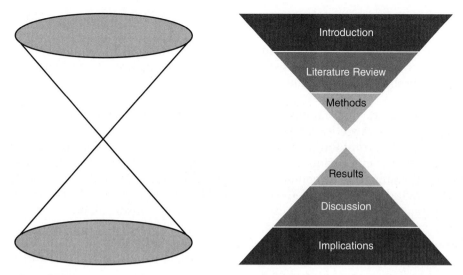

Figure 12.3
Writing the Research Report in the Shape of an Hourglass
Source: Bem (2000).

Introduction   The purpose of the introduction is to situate your study in context. The opening introductory statement is most effective when it sets the stage for readers and engages them. As the writer who has a growing command of the subject topic area, lead readers through an overview of the problem, and a brief background of the related literature, and clarify the gap in the literature that your current study fills. These gaps may include moving research into a new area or with new populations, improving upon prior research methods, or testing or developing a theory. Then state the rationale or purpose of your study. Again, define terms that are unfamiliar to the reader. In fact, if any content is vague, use definitions or examples to guarantee the reader understands (American Psychological Association [APA], 2009; Szuchman & Thomlinson, 2008).

Literature Review

The purpose of the literature review section of the empirical report is to provide a background of prior works in the topic area (see Figure 12.1). This section is not an exhaustive review but highlights the selected studies that inform the current study. The literature review should lead logically to the research questions and/or hypotheses used in the study. There should be no question in the readers' minds as to how the current study builds on the literature review. The hypothesis (or hypotheses) and research questions generally appear at the end of the literature review, signifying the transition to a discussion of the current study. Literature reviews commonly have an introductory paragraph that provides an overview of contents. Headers notify readers about transitions in topics and subtopics (APA, 2009; Belcher, 2009; Szuchman & Thomlinson, 2008).

From information search process to results   As shown in Figure 12.3, the literature review is a culmination of the information search process that results in a written end product. Writing the literature review is a challenging, but surmountable task that requires the writer to assess, organize, and synthesize a broad range of gathered information; sort for relevant information; and sift out irrelevant information. The writer's task is to convey that he or she has read, understood, and integrated the relevant research in the problem area and understands the concepts or constructs under investigation (Kuhlthau, 2005; Maschi, Probst, & Bradley, 2009).

Content covered   The content covered in the literature review is the result of careful analysis. A well-written literature review cites only studies that have relevance to the current topic. This can be achieved by carefully considering only the most important previous relevant research and theoretical perspectives. Generally a literature review contains studies that include empirical literature with scientific findings and theoretical literature that describe the concepts and constructs related to the current study (Szuchman & Thomlinson, 2008).

Organize and synthesize   A well-written literature review is the result of organizing and synthesizing the literature before writing. Articles in the literature review are often grouped according to similar purposes, results, or methods used. The writer must use creativity and critical thinking skills to organize the literature in a unique way. Similar to a qualitative data analysis, writers often identify patterns and connections, which include similarities and differences, across the studies. Many writers construct tables to organize their findings (Belcher, 2009).

Housekeeping issues   Keep in mind the *Publication Manual of the American Psychological Association* and good writing practices when writing the literature review. Use the past tense to discuss findings of a study that already occurred. Use headings and subheaders, as in this section, to provide signposts so readers know where you are taking them. If this section was completed without an outline, try constructing an outline now to see if it makes sense. If you don't write your paper from an outline, outline your paper after it is written. Make sure the literature review is in essay form, not an annotated bibliography that just summarizes study after study. Cite all of your sources. Alphabetize references with more than one author by the first author's last name (APA, 2009).

Methods

The methods section is very straightforward because it simply documents the methods or practical steps taken to conduct the study. This section is at the center of the hourglass because it is specific to the current study. The *Publication Manual of the American Psychological Association* spells out in detail what subsections need to be included in the methods section of an article. These subsections include research design, sample description, variables and measures, data collection procedures, and data analysis methods. An effectively written methods section should take the readers through the process as if they were there. Begin with an overview of the study, including the description of participants, setting, and measures or data sources used. Each section that follows should provide enough detail so that anyone could replicate the study by following the same process (APA, 2009; Bem, 2000).

Research design   The type of research design and sampling strategies should be described in the research design section. For a quantitative study, include details as to whether the study was an experimental, quasi-experimental, or preexperimental design. The temporal design, that is, whether cross-sectional or longitudinal, should also be specified (APA, 2009).

Other aspects of the research design should also be described. For example, the description of the study setting should include important details such as the year the study was conducted, a description of the surrounding geographic location (e.g., urban low-income community), and the actual study settings (e.g., community mental health agency). Next, the sampling strategies should be clarified. How were the participants selected for the study? Important characteristics include the type of probability or nonprobability sampling used. If there were inclusion and/or exclusion criteria for the sample selection, make this clear to the reader (APA, 2009; Bem, 2000).

Sample description   The subsection on sample description includes the overall sample size and a sociodemographic description of age, gender, race, and ethnicity, all of which are often presented as statistics in tables. Other relevant characteristics of importance to the study should be highlighted as well. For example, if the study compares adults with or without depression, the percentages of these subgroups are relevant. Note that this sample description section may be presented in the results section as opposed to the methods section (APA, 2009).

Measures or data sources   The measures (or data sources section) should detail the instruments that were used to measure the concepts or construct under investigation. For a quantitative study, each of the variables in the study hypotheses should have a corresponding measure (or measures) that appear(s) in this section (APA, 2009).

Social workers should provide an overall description of any survey or questionnaire used. Questions or items from the questionnaire used also help to orient readers. For example, "Participants then filled out Consumer Satisfaction Survey, which is a 30-item survey that uses a 5-point Likert to measure the level of agreement ranging from 'totally disagree' to 'agree,' about their satisfaction with the program (e.g., 'The staff is helpful here')." Also, social workers should indicate how the instruments were scored. They should describe any steps in which raw scores were converted for the purposes of analysis. If instruments used belong to other authors, cite references in the text and include a reference list. If there are psychometric properties for an instrument, such as reliability and validity information, provide that information. If using an unpublished instrument, social workers should include a copy in the appendix (Bem, 2000; Pyrczak & Bruce, 2007).

Data collection procedures   The data collection procedures section clarifies how the measures were administered. The section also details how the data were collected. Potential options include in-person interviews, observations, mailed surveys or questionnaires, telephone interviews, and online surveys. The section also details the process of how the instruments were distributed and characteristics of the setting where the study was conducted. Also important to address are ethical issues, including informed consent, privacy, and confidentiality (APA, 2009).

Data analysis   The data analysis subsection of the report simply details the data analysis method used. This is relevant to both quantitative and qualitative studies. If a software package, such as SPSS 18.0 or Atlas.ti, was used, document that information here. Social workers should refrain from reporting results in this section. Study results or findings go into the results section (APA, 2009; Pyrczak & Bruce, 2007).

Results   The purpose of the results section is to inform the reader of the study findings. Because it is specific to the current study, this section is also at the center of the hourglass. The introduction, literature review, and methods sections must be carefully organized to lead the reader to this point. Most readers want to know what happened! The results section provides answers by presenting the actual study findings. Organize qualitative results so they make sense to the reader. In quantitative studies, it is common to organize the results section around the hypothesis, purposes, or questions used across studies. If hypotheses are used, organize the results in the order the hypotheses were proposed. Generally, with quantitative findings, descriptive statistics are presented before inferential statistical results of the hypothesis testing (APA, 2009).

The results of statistical tests are presented in tables that are referred to in the narrative text (e.g., as shown in Table 1). Because the tables give an overview of the data, it is common to highlight the most important details. General statements that are made about the findings should be supported with data. For example, the mean of the group that received the treatment was significantly higher than the mean of the group that did not receive the treatment, $t(6) = 4.5$, $p < 0.05$. The *Publication Manual of the American Psychological Association* provides details on how to present findings.

It also is important to avoid the common mistake of interpreting the data in this section. The interpretation of the data belongs in the discussion section.

Discussion   The discussion section begins to broaden from specific content about the current study to more general applications of the findings. In terms of the hourglass, the discussion is in the bottom of the hourglass shape. Here the writer must help the reader understand what the findings mean (APA, 2009).

The first paragraph of the discussion section generally summarizes the major findings of the study. Writers often use layperson language in this section, especially if the text of the findings section presents complicated statistical results. If hypotheses were used, clarify whether the hypotheses were supported. If not, offer potential explanations as to why (Bem, 2000).

The next paragraph places the current study findings in the broader context of the existing literature for a comparison. The writer must indicate to what extent the study confirms or disconfirms the findings in the existing literature (the existing literature has often already been cited in the earlier literature review). The writer explains how the current findings support, contradict, or build upon the existing literature (APA, 2009).

This section reviews the implications of the study for social work practice, policy, and research and draws inferences from the findings. Conclusions that are drawn should be based on the data. The implications section is perhaps the most creative part of the discussion section. This is the chance for the social worker to pull together all of his or her expert knowledge on the topic and make sense of the study findings (APA, 2009). Writers can make good use of this section by providing social workers in the field with practical suggestions on how these findings can be applied to one or more of the following: clinical practice, administration, leadership and policy practice, education, and professional development.

Before describing the implications or future directions for research, an acknowledgment of the methodological limitations of the study is warranted. A section that reviews the methods decisions while designing the study usually pinpoints areas where research rigor was compromised. For example, the use of a small, nonrepresentative sample in a quantitative study comprises its generalizability. In the discussion of future directions for research, the recommendations should build upon the limitations. For example, future studies should use larger, more representative samples. The writer can offer recommendations that improve methods or expand to new content areas (e.g., how gender influences the stress response among children) in this section (APA, 2009; Pyrczak & Bruce, 2007).

Conclusion   Last but not least is the conclusion. The conclusion is the end point of the report and perhaps the hardest for the writer. The reader should feel as if the discussion is finished. Generally a conclusion has a short summary statement of the central premise of the research study. A final thought based on the study should leave a lasting imprint on the reader (Bem, 2000).

Title

The title of the paper helps readers to obtain a quick overview of the study. The title should accurately represent the contents of the study and make sense when read alone. Because the recommended length for a title is 10 to 12 words, the writer must prioritize the most essential details. Most writers draft several versions of a title before choosing the final one. The title appears on the title page and then again at the top of the first page of the manuscript (APA, 2009).

Abstract

The abstract falls directly after the title (or title page). The abstract is a compact summary of the study. It often includes the background and purpose of the study, methods, results, implications, highlights of methods, and discussion. It should define the problem under investigation (in one sentence if possible). According to the *Publication Manual of the American Psychological Association*, the abstract generally should not exceed 120 words. Therefore, the writer must include only essential information and edit out unnecessary words. The abstract is effective when it clarifies the problem under investigation and includes only the most pertinent details of the methods and results (APA, 2009).

Reference List

The reference list, a critical component of the manuscript, documents all works cited in the narrative text and thus enables the reader to locate studies of interest. The reference list appears on a separate page with the heading *References*. Only the references that appear in this list should be cited in the text. Similarly, references that are cited in the text should appear in the reference list. Each reference should be carefully reviewed for punctuation, capitalization, italics, spacing, and paragraph indents for consistency with the style format used, such as the *Publication Manual of the American Psychological Association* style (APA, 2009). Visit the American Psychological Association website for tutorials on using APA style. (http://www.apastyle.org/).

Write, Revise, Review, and Revise

Importance of Revision

Revising the paper is as important as writing the first draft. Most experienced writers are aware that there is more than one way to write a statement. Conscientious writers go the extra yard to make their ideas optimally clear to their audience. The two types of revisions are macro revising and micro revising (Belcher, 2009). Macro revising involves revising a paper for large sweeping changes. Macro-level revising is perhaps harder because it involves reorganizing

Revising is as important as writing the first draft. Most experienced writers are aware that there is more than one way to write a statement.

contents, deleting sections, and rewriting sections, if needed. In contrast, micro-level revision involves small-scale changes, mostly editing or proofreading for grammar, punctuation, spelling, and formatting. The following section discusses areas to review for micro-level revision.

Avoid Bias in Writing

From a human rights and social justice perspective, the use of language is very important (Ife, 2001a). Words can reflect hidden biases. The conscientious writer carefully proofreads his or her work for biased language, especially related to gender, race, and other vulnerable groups. The sixth edition of the *Publication Manual of the American Psychological Association* (chapter 3 on writing concisely) offers guidelines on writing about gender and race. It also recommends avoiding the use of *minority* for *non-White*. (APA, 2009).

APA Heading Styles

Heading styles are an important area often overlooked by social workers new to the research writing process (see Table 12.1). Headings are important because they function like an outline of the paper's organization. Therefore, if a writer wants to ensure that a reader follows his or her work, the use of header styles acts as road signs to help guide the reader. *APA*'s heading style has five levels of headers in which level 1 is the highest and level 5 is the lowest. As shown in Table 12.1, in a topic outline, a level-1 header corresponds with the main topic usually represented by a Roman numeral (I, II, III, etc.) (APA, 2009, p. 43).

Most research reports use two- or three-level heading styles. Starting with level 1, headings always are used consecutively. In a research report, the main sections use level-1 headers (e.g., introduction, literature review, methods, results, and discussion). Subsequent subsections within each level-1 header use level-2 headers. For example, the common subsections of the methods section

Table 12.1   Level of Heading Styles Compared to Levels of a Topic Outline

Heading Level		Corresponding Topic Outline Levels
1	**Centered, Boldface, Upper and Lowercase** Start paragraph here (indented).	I. **Main Topic 1 (Introduction)** II. **Main Topic 2 (Literature Review)** III. **Main Topic 3 (Methods)** IV. **Main Topic 4 (Results)** V. **Main Topic 5 (Discussion)**
2	**Flush Left, Boldface, Uppers and Lowercase** Start paragraph here (indented).	A. **Subtopic 1 of Level 1 Heading** B. **Subtopic 2 of Level 1 Heading**
3	**Indented, boldface, lowercase paragraph heading that ends with a period.** Start paragraph here.	1. **Subtopic of level 2 heading** 2. **Subtopic of level 2 heading**
4	***Indented, boldface, italicized, lowercase paragraph heading that ends with a period.*** Start paragraph here.	a. ***Subtopic of level 3 heading*** b. ***Subtopic of level 3 heading***
5	*Indented, italicized, lowercase paragraph heading that ends with a period*. Start paragraph here.	(1) Subtopic of level 4 heading (2) Subtopic of level 4 heading

Source: APA (2009, pp. 62–63).

correspond with a level-2 header (e.g., research design, sample description, measures, data collection, and data analysis). Any subsections within any of these sections are a level-3 header. For example, it is common in the measures subsection to have a level-3 header that distinguishes between the different measures used (APA, 2009; Szuchman & Thomlinson, 2008).

Title Page

In *APA* style, the use of a title page is important to identify the title, the authors, and the characteristics of the manuscript (APA, 2009). The title page represents the cover page of the manuscript and enhances its professional presentation. Important elements of the title page include

- *Title:* The title should be set in uppercase and lowercase letters and centered on the page. The title should be concise (no more than 12 words and capitalize only significant words and any words of four letters or more).
- *Author(s):* The author's name (first and last name) appears a double space below the title in uppercase and lowercase letters, centered. If there are additional authors, list each one on their own additional line, double-spaced below.
- *Institutional affiliation:* The institutional affiliation is set in uppercase and lowercase letters, centered, and double-spaced on the line following the author(s).
- *Running head:* The running head is an abbreviated title that should be no longer than 50 characters (including spaces and punctuation). The running head is typed flush left (all uppercase) following the words *Running head*: (e.g., Running head: BULLYING PREVENTION PROGRAM). It appears in the header (left, opposite the page number).
- *Pagination:* The title page is assigned the page number 1.
- *Line spacing:* Similar to the main part of the paper, the cover page content is double-spaced.

General Formatting

Other general formatting aspects covered in the *Publication Manual of the American Psychological Association* include the following:

- *Typeface (Font):* Use Times New Roman, 12-point for text and 12-point sans-serif (e.g., Arial) for tables.
- *Line-Spacing:* The entire paper is double-spaced.
- *Margins:* Margins are 1-inch by 1-inch (i.e., the top, bottom, right, and left of every page).
- *Alignment:* The report sets flush left (do not justify the right margin).

Having a copy of the *Publication Manual of the American Psychological Association* is helpful while preparing a report (APA, 2009). Social workers can access the American Psychological Association website (http://www.apastyle.org/index.aspx) where they can explore video tutorials to find a wealth of helpful information.

WRITING A REVIEW OF THE LITERATURE

Common Social Work Research Course Assignment

A journal article also can be a self-standing literature review. Because this type of paper is often an assignment in social work research classes, it is reviewed in this chapter. As shown in the stair model, writing the literature review involves finding an area of interest, and reading and appraising the literature in a topic area. For a review of these steps, see chapter 5 on conducting the literature search. The final step is writing the paper.

A literature review as part of a bachelor's or master's level social work course may include between 10 and 20 articles and require a 10–15 page paper. These details can be clarified by the course instructor. It is important to note, however, that a peer-reviewed literature review is often an exhaustive review of the literature and may include a review of 50 or more articles. Sample literature reviews, especially if they are in your topic area, are helpful to use as a model.

Purpose

The purpose of a literature review is to describe and critique an area of knowledge. Generally the three major sections for a literature review paper are the introduction, the literature review, and the conclusion (Pan, 2008; Szuchman & Thomlison, 2008).

Introduction   Similar to the empirical research report, the introduction describes the topic area or problem under investigation. It provides a brief overview of the trends in the literature reviewed. Trends may include areas of agreement or disagreement, methods used, or literature gaps. The introduction also should include a clear rationale or purpose for the review and its significance.

Literature review   The literature review section is the main body of the report. This section demonstrates the writer's ability to organize and synthesize the literature. The use of tables or diagrams can assist with the organization and synthesis of the literature. For example, studies may be grouped according to patterns or themes identified in the literature (Pan, 2008; Szuchman & Thomlison, 2008).

To reinforce the themes, social workers should begin paragraphs with broad topic sentences to help organize the brief discussion of related studies. For example, a paragraph may begin with the topic sentence: Depression among older adults has been shown to be related to social isolation. Directly following the topic sentence, the essential studies that reiterate this point are reviewed. Present the related major findings of the study but discuss the details of the study sparingly (Belcher, 2009; Pan, 2008).

Conclusion   Similar to the discussion section, the literature review conclusion section provides a review of major themes, critique, and future directions for research. An evaluation of the research is appropriate for this section. It begins with an overview of the major themes of findings. It is followed by a critique of the methods, major findings, and/or theoretical perspectives reviewed. The implications for future research are delineated as a guide for future research and evaluation studies (Hart, 1998; Pan, 2008).

Student Samples of Literature Review Materials

Examples of how students organized their literature review materials are provided in this section. The students used a variety of creative and organizational techniques to help gain a better understanding of their literature review articles.

Example One   Example one is based on a literature review on immigrants and mental health conducted by Kristen, a student. As shown in Table 12.2,

Table 12.2	Descriptive Statistics of Journal Articles on Immigrants and Mental Health (*n* = 52)
Type of study	Quantitative (*n* = 27, 51.9%)
	Qualitative (*n* = 17, 32.7%)
	Mixed methods (*n* = 1, 1.9%)
	Theoretical (*n* = 7, 13.5)
Years of publications	1979–2006
Study locations	United States = 40 (76.9%)
	Canada = 4 (7.7%)
	Hong Kong = 2 (3.8%)
	Australia = 1 (1.9%)
	Israel = 1 (1.9%)
	Mexico = 1 (1.9%)
	The Netherlands = 1 (1.9%)
	South Africa = 1 (1.9%)
	Other = 1 (1.9%)

Kristen located 52 articles from the Social Work Research abstract database that were published in peer review journals between 1979 and 2006. The majority of the studies were conducted in the United States (76.9%) and slightly over half (51.9%) were quantitative studies. To help her organize the results, Kristen drew a conceptual diagram. As illustrated in Figure 12.4, Kristen used her qualitative data analysis skills to identify three categories or themes that she could use to classify the literature. She found that the three threads in the literature on immigrants and mental health fell within three categories: stressors, resources, and cultural influences. She identified both micro-level (e.g., stressful life events, coping skills, cultural identity) and macro-level (e.g., employment, family support, language barriers) factors for each of these categories. Kristen organized the outline and writing of her literature review using the conceptual and organizational framework she developed.

Example two   Kristen was able to organize the methods and major findings of her studies using an article extraction tool. The directions and template can be found in Exhibits 12.1 and 12.2 of "Conducting a Literature Review" section. After she completed the extraction form, she was able to use the study purpose and major findings to extract her major category themes.

Similarly, another social work student, Shantia, conducted a review of the literature on stigma reduction programs. The first extraction she completed was of a research study by Wood and Wahl (2006) that evaluated the effectiveness of the In Our Own Voice Program developed by the National Alliance on the Mentally Ill. Shantia's results can be found in Figure 12.5.

Exercise   Readers are encouraged to locate the Wood and Wahl's study (2006) via their university electronic databases and extract the article. Compare your results with Shantia's results as part of an inter-rater reliability check.

Conceptual Model of Major Findings

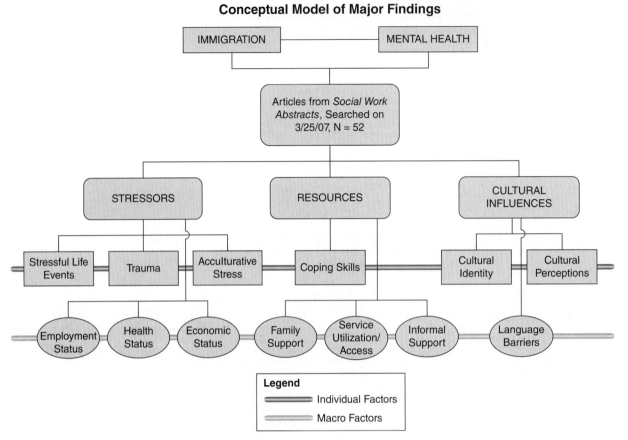

Figure 12.4
Conceptual Model of Major Findings on Immigration and Mental Health

Example three In this example, two social work students, Amy and MaryAnn, were research assistants on a social work professor's research project. They were conducting a literature review to determine the methods and major findings that examined trauma and posttraumatic stress disorder among incarcerated youth. Using these criteria, they located 12 peer reviewed journal articles published between 1994 and 2009. To organize the information, they created tables for the methods and major findings (see Tables 12.3 and 12.4). They identified the correlates associated with trauma and PTSD among incarcerated youth, which include life events stressors, such as family dysfunction, and psychological and behavioral well-being.

Exercise Readers are encouraged to review the tables and identify the different types of research methods used and then critique them. After reviewing Table 12.5, what patterns and themes can you identify? How might you organize a literature review of the methods and major findings using the literature review format of introduction, review, and conclusion reviewed earlier?

Table 12.3   **Major Findings of Empirical Studies That Examined Trauma and PTSD Among Youth in the Juvenile Justice System (1994–2009)**

Author/s (Year)*	Research Design	Study Setting	Trauma (%)	PTSD (%)	Sample Size	Sample Description	Measures	Data Collection	Data Analysis
Abram et al. (2004)	Cross-sectional single-group design, probability (stratified random) sampling	Detention center, Cook County, Illinois, data from epidemiological longitudinal study (1995–1998)	92.5	11.2	898	Juvenile detainees aged 10–18, 59% males, 41% females, African American (n = 247), Hispanic (n = 177), Caucasian (n = 107)	Diagnostic Interview Schedule for Children-IV (DISC-IV)	Structured clinical interviews	Poisson regression models
Ariga et al. (2008)	Cross-sectional single-group design, probability random sampling of 181 juvenile offenders	Juvenile detention center in Japan (2004–2006)	77	33	64	Japanese female juvenile detainees aged 16 to 19 (M = 17.2%, sd = 1.0)	Mini-International Neuropsychiatric Interview (MINI-KID) (Japanese version); Traumatic Event Checklist-Clinician-Administered PTSD Scale for DSM-IV (CAPS)	Structured clinical interviews (raters were trained to administer measures)	ANOVA, logistic and multiple regression
Brosky and Lally (2004)	Cross-sectional comparison group design, nonprobability sampling	Child Guidance Clinic of Superior Court, District of Columbia (1998)	75 (females) 51.3 (males)	21.1 (females) 7.9 (males)	152	Juvenile victims and offenders aged 12–18; referred by court for a psychiatric evaluation (76 = females, 76 = males), 91% (n = 69) African American; 2.6% (n = 2) Hispanic, 6.6% (n = 5) unknown	Compiled checklist for the incidence of trauma, PTSD (using DSM-IV criteria), and dissociative symptoms	Case record review (archival records)	Chi-square

(continued)

Table 12.3 Major Findings of Empirical Studies That Examined Trauma and PTSD Among Youth in the Juvenile Justice System (1994–2009) (Continued)

Author/s (Year)*	Research Design	Study Setting	Trauma (%)	PTSD (%)	Sample Size	Sample Description	Measures	Data Collection	Data Analysis
Burton et al. (1994)	Cross-sectional single-group design, non-probability sampling	Secure camp setting in Los Angeles County, Probation Department (year not reported)	75	24	91	Adjudicated juvenile offenders with serious offenses; 100% males, aged 13–18 ($M = 16$, $sd = 1.0$); 40% -African American, 40% Hispanic, 10% Caucasian, 7% Asian, and 3% other	Trauma questionnaire and PTSD symptom checklist (self report measure)	Self-report questionnaire, case record review (arrest records and probation reports)	ANOVA, stepwise multiple regression analysis
Cauffman et al. (1998)	Cross-sectional comparison group design, nonprobability sampling	California Youth Authority (CYA) school setting (1996 and 1997)	76	65.3	189	96 incarcerated female offenders, aged 13–22, ($M = 17.2$, $sd = 1.8$) (23.3% Caucasian, 21.% African American, 28.9% Hispanic, 12.2% Asian, 20.2% other); comparison group–93 incarcerated adolescent males aged 13–18 ($M = 16.6$%, $sd = 1.2$); 37.6% African American, 26.9% Hispanic; 30.2% Caucasian, 5.4% other	Traumatic experiences questionnaire; PTSD module of the Revised Diagnostic Psychiatric Interview-*DSM-III-R* criteria	Semi-structured clinical interviews (15–45 minutes) (used two independent raters)	ANOVA

	Setting				Sample	Measures	Data collection	Analysis
Dixon et al. (2004)	Cross-sectional comparison group design matched on age and SES, nonprobability sampling	State female juvenile detention center and five public schools (Sydney, Australia) (year not reported)	70	37	200	100 female juvenile offenders, average age 16.5 (sd = 1.2); Aboriginal (48%) or White (33%), other (19%); comparison—100 female high school students mean age 16.4 (sd = 1.2); Aboriginal (5%) or White (63%), other (32%)	The PTSD Traumatic Events component of the K-SADS-PL (self report measures)	Juvenile justice files; assessment interview and self reports.	Chi-square, t-tests, logistic regression
Erwin et al. (2000)	Cross-sectional single-group design, non-probability sampling	Seven secure care facilities near Boston, MA, area (year not reported)	100	23	51	Incarcerated male adolescents; mean age 17.5 years (sd = 1.5); 57% Caucasian, 28% African American, 12% Hispanic	Exposure to Community Violence Scale-Adapted Version (self report), PTSD Checklist (self report), Clinician-administered PTSD Scale for Children and Adolescents (CAPS-CA).	Battery of self report instruments and semi-structured interviews by trained researchers	Descriptive analysis
Ford et al. (2008)	Cross-sectional single-group design; all juveniles sampled admitted during a 24–72-hour period	Connecticut pre-trial juvenile detention centers (January–September, 2005)	61	5	264	Juvenile detainees 10–17 years old (192 males, 72 females); 27% Caucasian, 43% black, 30% Latino	Traumatic Experiences Screening Instrument (TESI) (self report), UCLA PTSD Reaction Index (PTSD-RI) (self report)	Self report screen at the time of intake (24–72 hours of admission)	Logistic regression, ANOVA

(continued)

Table 12.3 **Major Findings of Empirical Studies That Examined Trauma and PTSD Among Youth in the Juvenile Justice System (1994–2009) (Continued)**

Author/s (Year)*	Research Design	Study Setting	Trauma (%)	PTSD (%)	Sample Size	Sample Description	Measures	Data Collection	Data Analysis
Kerig et al. (2008)	Cross-sectional single-group design, non-probability sampling	Juvenile detention centers in Midwestern United States (January–2007)	24.1 (females) 21 (males)	45 (females) 26 (males)	289	Juvenile detainees (199 male and 90 female juveniles); aged 10–17; European American (69%), African American (22%), Latino (4%), and Other (6%)	The UCLA Posttraumatic Stress Disorder Index for DSM-IV Adolescent Version, Clinician Administered PTSD Scale for Children and Adolescents (CAPS-CA)	Interview conducted by trained clinician, self report measures that used cross-sectional data collection	T-tests, SEM
Ruchkin et al. (2002)	Cross-sectional single-group design, non-probability sampling	Juvenile detention center in northern Russia (spring and winter, 1999)	96	25	370	Russian male juvenile delinquents aged 14–19 ($M = 16.4$, sd = 0.9) (only subsample of 289 youthful offenders completed the self report portion of the study)	PTSD module of Semi-structured Clinical Interview for PTSD (K-SADS-PL); Child Post Traumatic Stress Reaction Index (CPTS-RI) (self report); Survey of Exposure to Community Violence (self report)	Semi-structured psychiatric interview (conducted by psychiatrists), translation of measures into Russian, self report measures (interviewers were blind to the results of the self report measures)	Chi-square, ANOVA

Study	Design	Setting				Sample	Measures	Data collection	Analysis
Steiner et al. (1997)	Cross-sectional comparison group design, partial probability sampling (25% randomly selected; 75% referred psychiatric evaluation); comparison group-convenience sample	O.H. Close School in Stockton, CA (year not reported); comparison group from a local high school district in CA suburban area	50	31.7	164	85 incarcerated adolescent males aged 13–20 ($M = 16.6$, sd $= 1.2$); 37.6% African American, 26.9% Hispanic, 30.1% Caucasian, 5.4% other; comparison group of 79 male high school students from a previous study (average age 16, sd $= 1.4$); 72% Caucasian	PTSD module of the Psychiatric Diagnostic Interview-Revised	Semi-structured clinical interviews, case record reviews (clinical and field case files)	Chi-square, correlation, ANOVA; MANCOVA, Waller-Duncan K ratios
Thompson et al. (2007)	Cross-sectional comparison group design, non-probability sampling	Mid-sized urban detention centers and agencies in Western New York area (1999 to 2001)	Not reported	23 detention 31 shelter	277	$N = 121$ detention (M age $= 16$ years, sd $= 1.5$), 56.2% female; 40% Black; 37.2% White, 5% Latino, 17.2% other; comparison group–$n = 156$ emergency youth shelter (age $M = 16$, sd $= 2.4$); 55.8% female; 48.7% Black; 39.7% White, 9% Latino, 2.5% other	Trauma Symptom Checklist for Children (TSCC); Posttraumatic Stress Symptoms (PTS).	Self report questionnaires	T-tests, correlation, regression analysis

Table 12.4   Major Findings of Empirical Studies That Examined Trauma and PTSD Among Youth in the Juvenile Justice System (1994–2009)

Author(s) (Year)*	Major Findings
Abram et al. (2004)	The majority of juvenile detainees (92.5%) reported experiencing one or more traumas. About half of juvenile detainees with PTSD reported witnessing violence as the precipitating trauma. Significantly, more males (93.2%) than females (84.0%) reported at least one traumatic experience. Older youth (14 or older) compared to younger youth (aged 10–13 years) were significantly more likely to report traumatic experiences. There were no significant differences in overall prevalence among different racial ethnic group of juvenile detainees.
Ariga et al. (2008)	One-third (33%) of Japanese female juvenile detainees were diagnosed with PTSD and the majority (77%) had been exposed to trauma. The juveniles with PTSD showed a significantly high psychiatric comorbidity. PTSD symptoms were also significantly associated with depression, adverse parenting, and abnormal eating.
Brosky and Lally (2004)	The most common traumatic events among the sample of court referred adolescents were sexual and physical abuse. Female adolescents (75%) compared to male adolescents (51.3%) had significantly higher rates of trauma. Females also were more likely to be victims of physical abuse (38.2%) and sexual abuse (27.6%) compared to male adolescents (15.8%, 1.3%).
Burton et al. (1994)	One quarter (25%) of a sample of serious juvenile offenders met *DSM III-R* criteria for PTSD diagnosis. PTSD symptoms also were found to significantly correlate with exposure to violence and family dysfunction.
Cauffman et al. (1998)	Female compared to male juveniles had a higher rate of PTSD. A higher level of distress and lower level of self-restraint were found in female juveniles who were diagnosed with PTSD compared to male juveniles.
Dixon et al. (2004)	Rates of PTSD were higher for female juvenile offenders compared to female juvenile nonoffenders.
Erwin et al (2000)	All of the incarcerated adolescent males witnessed violence. The majority (92%) also reported exposure to unsafe situations and feeling unsafe in all environments. Self report measures compared to clinician administered interviews yielded higher PTSD rates.
Ford et al. (2008)	One in five (19%) juvenile offenders in pretrial detention had a complete or partial PTSD diagnosis. Approximately 61% reported psychological trauma. Types of trauma such as physical abuse, domestic violence, and neglect were significantly correlated with risk of suicide and drug and alcohol use. The risk of PTSD was not associated with gender, age, and ethnicity.
Kerig et al. (2008)	Females compared to male juvenile detainees reported higher scores on interpersonal trauma exposure and symptoms of simple and complex PTSD. PTSD mediated the relationship between trauma and mental health problems among the youth, especially among females.
Ruchkin et al. (2002)	Of the sample of Russian juvenile detainees, approximately 42% met partial criteria and 25% met full *DSM-IV* criteria for PTSD. The most common type of trauma reported was exposure to violence (being a victim or witness). Higher rates of PTSD were associated with higher rates of psychiatric comorbidity among juvenile detainees.
Steiner et al. (1997)	Incarcerated male offenders had higher PTSD rates than other adolescent community samples and county probation camps. PTSD showed elevated levels of distress and other psychiatric symptoms.
Thompson et al. (2007)	Youth in emergency shelters and in juvenile detention centers had high levels of trauma-related symptoms. Higher levels of PTSD symptoms among incarcerated youth included worries about family, greater number of runaway episodes, and living with a father who abused alcohol/drugs. In comparison, higher levels of PTSD symptoms among youth in emergency shelters were predicted by having worries about the family relationships.

Table 12.5   Themes of Major Findings Across Studies: Trauma and PTSD Correlates

Trauma and Stress			Well-Being	Other Individual Level and Social Environmental Characteristics
Trauma	Life events stressors	PTSD	Psychological and behavioral well-being	Youth characteristics
Location Family violence Community violence *Direct or indirect* Victim Witness	*Family factors* Adverse parenting Worries about family Parental substance abuse Family dysfunction	*Diagnosis* PTSD symptoms PTSD diagnosis	*Psychological well-being* Psychological distress Perceptions of safety Mental health problems Comorbidity w/ PTSD Conduct disorder Suicide risk	*Individual level factors* Gender Age *Social or environmental factors* Juvenile justice placement
Major subtypes Psychological trauma Physical abuse Sexual abuse Neglect Physical Assault			*Behavioral well-being* Abnormal eating Runaway episodes Self-restraint Delinquency Drug and alcohol use	

OTHER TYPES OF REPORTS

Social workers are also commonly required to write other types of reports in which there is some crossover with empirical research reports. These reports include evaluation reports, action research reports, and proposals, including grant proposals (Weinbach, 2005; York, 2009).

Evaluation Reports

Evaluation reports are generally prepared for agency or program evaluation projects after the project is completed. Sections may include "(a) summary, (b) purpose of the evaluation, (c) program background information, (d) description of the evaluation study and design, (e) results, (f) discussion of the program and its results, and (f) conclusions and recommendations" (Bouletmis & Dutwin, 2000, p. 143).

Despite many similarities, there are evaluation report characteristics that often distinguish evaluation reports from empirical research reports. For example, the evaluation report details the history of the agency and targets a specific audience, whether it is the agency personnel or funder. The conclusions and recommendations generally pertain to the specific agency as opposed to a broader application. The finding also may be part of a public presentation of results to the agency and interested stakeholders (Westerfelt & Dietz, 2010).

Action Research Report

Similar to an evaluation report, an action research report focuses on a specific group of people, an agency, or a setting. The common sections of an action report include (a) focusing and framing, (b) preliminary literature review, (c) methodology, (d) outcomes or findings, and (e) conclusion (Stringer, 2007).

What perhaps most distinguishes this report is the role of the participant throughout the report, particularly in the focusing and framing, outcomes or findings, and conclusion sections. The focusing and framing section describes how participants identified their problem for investigation. The outcomes or findings section describes how participants experienced and interpreted the problem investigated. This section also describes the steps participants took to resolve the problem studied and the outcomes of events and activities. The conclusion section compares and contrasts the participants' perspectives with those conclusions drawn from the existing research literature. Similar to the research report, it presents a broader perspective of the implications for the study of policies, professional practice, and future research (Stringer, 2007).

Proposals

Social workers often use their skills for proposal and grant writing (Gitlin & Lyons, 2008), often to obtain approval to start or fund a program and/or research or evaluation project. What distinguishes a proposal from a research report is a plan to conduct a study and future-tense language (Coley & Scheinberg, 2008). In contrast, a research report documents a research study that has been completed and is written in past tense (APA, 2009). Research proposals may be written for the purposes of dissertations or nonfunded or funded research projects (i.e., grants) (Locke, Spirduso, & Silverman, 2007).

Proposal Sections

The common sections of a proposal are (a) introduction, (b) background, (c) specific aims or hypotheses, (d) research design and methods, (e) preliminary data, (f) references, (g) budget, and (h) appendices (Coley & Scheinberg, 2008; Yuen & Terao, 2003).

Similar to the research report, the introduction provides an overview of the problem and rationale and significance of the study. The background provides a succinct review of the relevant literature. The specific aims and hypotheses, research design, and methods are similar to the research report but are written in the future tense. The specific aims or hypotheses state exactly what the study will do, what the research team will do, and what they expect to find out. The methods section details the proposed steps to conduct the study (Gitlin & Lyons, 2008; Marshall & Rossman, 2010; Yuen & Terao, 2003).

The proposal also generally highlights the research team's preliminary findings that provide a rationale for the current study and demonstrates the research team's expertise to carry out the project. The budget section documents the proposed expenses, including staff and supplies and a justification for these costs. The appendix or appendices generally include related documents, such as proposed timelines, sample measures, and informed consent forms. The length of a grant proposal may range from 15 to 30 double-spaced pages (Gitlin & Lyons, 2008). Dissertation proposals are generally much more comprehensive (Locke et al., 2007).

Funding Pointers

Social workers seeking grant funding should convey to funders how their research is important and how the proposed project will get done. Therefore, a proposal should convey a compelling argument for the study, a feasible plan to conduct the study, and clear indication the researcher and/or research team can carry out the project as proposed (Gitlin & Lyons, 2008; Marshall & Rossman, 2010).

There are common pitfalls that can be avoided. Many grant proposals are not funded because they do not follow the specific directions as to what is required (Gitlin & Lyons, 2008). Social workers can avoid this pitfall by becoming familiar with the federal and/or state funding, and private foundations proposal guidelines. Funding sources include the National Institutes of

Health, the National Institute of Mental Health, the Center for Disease Control and Prevention, and the National Institute of Justice. Private foundations that provide funding for research projects and programs include the William E. Casey Foundation and the John D. and Catherine T. MacArthur Foundation. It is helpful to become familiar with funding sources' lists of priorities. Additionally, social workers should carefully read the program announcement and consult with grant program officers about their projects.

Other important points relate to overall discipline. Social workers should strictly adhere to page limits and submission deadlines, and include all sections requested. The final submission should be flawless. A good strategy is to ask colleagues to review the proposal and recommend revisions (Gitlin & Lyons, 2008).

Presentations

Social workers often present their research or evaluation findings at research or professional conferences. The formats vary from oral presentations, poster presentations, or workshops. Oral presentations are generally an overview of a study's findings. In essence, an oral presentation is a succinct 20-minute presentation of the contents of the research report. This generally includes an overview of the problem, background of the literature, research questions or hypotheses, methods used, major findings, and implications. In some instances similar research studies in a topic area (about 3–5 research studies) are presented together as part of a symposium.

Poster presentations often combine a large group of research presentations using a large poster format. Posters are commonly 4 feet by 6 feet wide. An example of a poster presentation template can be found in Figure 12.5. Additionally,

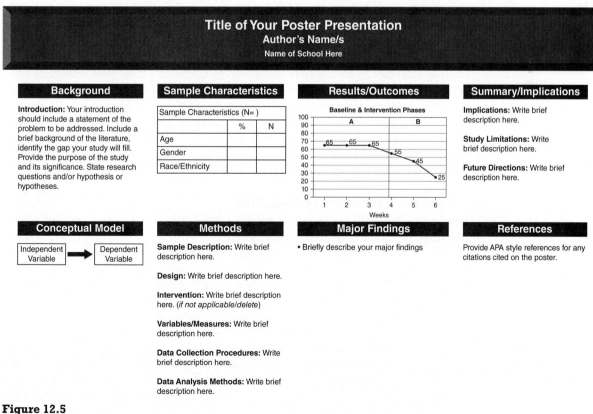

Figure 12.5
Poster Presentation Template

social workers often conduct workshops to share their research and practice evaluation knowledge. These workshops generally are 60 minutes long and provide lecture content and experiential learning exercises. For example, some research conferences may provide a workshop on learning qualitative data analysis software. Some professional conferences provide workshops on using specific evidence-based practices with a particular client population.

Research-Based Practice

Critical Thinking Question: What are your goals toward using research to inform practice and practice to inform research to advance human rights and social justice?

ADVOCACY AND RESEARCH FOR CHANGE

Another important avenue for the dissemination of research is for the purposes of advocacy efforts or policy debates (Centre for Civil Society, 2003). Mickelson (1995) defined advocacy as "the act of directly representing, defending, intervening, supporting, or recommending a course of action on behalf of one or more individuals, groups, or communities with the goal of securing or retaining social justice" (p. 95). Table 12.6 provides examples of different ways of disseminating research findings that involve advocacy.

The Relationship of Advocacy and Research

Social workers should be aware of two major types of advocacy: class advocacy and case level advocacy. *Case advocacy* refers to social workers who work directly with clients and advocate on their behalf in the agency or immediate community environment. In contrast, *class advocacy* refers to intervention to change the environment through social policy (Gibelman, 1995; Mickelson, 1995).

Before taking action, social workers must understand the situation, policies, public perception, client–environment intervention, and issues related to the problem. They must assess individuals and the community (Mayer, 2009). These different positions may necessitate different advocacy responses (Kuji-Shikatani, 2004). Case-level advocacy efforts may resemble case management, such as advocating for needed resources. In contrast, class-level advocacy may be as a political advocate. However, critical communication can also occur between case-level advocates who are privy to information from the field about a client population. This information can be shared with class advocates, who, in turn, can share this information with policy makers. The class advocate in return can provide the case advocate with critical information on laws, policies, and potential service loopholes to best help his or her clients (Mickelson, 1995).

Person-in-Environment Perspective

Use of the person-in-environment perspective allows the use of case advocacy because it connects individuals to their environment. The use of empowerment is to help increase individuals' ability to improve social justice outcomes. The use of this perspective also may assist agency administrators, public officials, and policy makers in learning how policies and laws can impact the individual (Mondros, 2009; Reisch, 2009).

Using the person-in-environment perspective, there are common steps in determining whether an advocacy approach or social action is needed. First, the social worker must determine whether there is a condition in the environment or social injustice that is an obstacle to the self-determination of an individual or a group. Second, he or she must determine whether the individual(s) or group(s) or community affected can be empowered to address the social condition. Third, they must determine whether advancement has

Table 12.6	**Possible Strategies and Venues to Present Research and Evaluation Project and Results**	
Actions	Potential Venues	Potential Activities
Share research and/or practice knowledge		
Write	Publications	Publish peer-reviewed research or practice journals
		Publish in e-journals
		Publish books or book chapters in area of expertise
Present	Professional research conferences–international, national, regional	Oral presentation
		Roundtable discussion
		Poster presentation
		Workshop
Broadcast	Internet	Your own or organization's website
	E-mail	E-mail newsletters
	Television or radio (local, national, or international)	Press release, documentary, news item, interview
	Magazines, newspapers (local, national, or international)	Editorial, press release
Events	Professional practice conferences–local, national, or international	Do a workshop or presentation
Advocate	Political events	Use research to advocate
	Charity events	
Network	Community stakeholders	Build coalitions

been made or could be made. If the individual or group cannot make or sustain the effort, the social worker or organization should advocate on their behalf. The social worker's knowledge of the existing empirical literature, the demographic statistics for the local population, and the common issues impacting this group help legitimize advocacy efforts (Humphries, 2008; Mickelson, 1995; Mondros, 2009).

Using Evidence to Facilitate Change

Research and evaluation can be a powerful advocacy tool, because it gives agency administrators and public policy makers evidence on which to base their decisions (Reisch, 2009). The use of research for advocacy purposes must move beyond the mere generation of findings to its application in community and policy practice arenas. This shift from conducting research to advocacy often lies with the social worker's ability to effectively communicate (oral or written) this information to key stakeholders (Chataway, Joffe, & Mordaunt, 2009).

Lightbulb effect   Research may serve as the lightbulb that brings a social issue out of the dark. For example, child maltreatment is not always considered a social problem. However, research can be a very effective tool for change as a simple lack of data and knowledge about an issue may be the cause of government inaction. When presented with research, the federal government may no longer be able to ignore an issue (Mayer, 2009).

For example, the "discovery" of child maltreatment in 1962 was the result of the "x-ray vision" of a team of radiologists and doctors who identified and documented visual signs of physical abuse, such as broken bones and fractures in infants and children. Dr. Kempe's naming of "battered child syndrome" put a face to the once hidden social problem of child abuse (Kempe, Silverman, Steele, Droegemueller, & Silver, 1962). The research that followed and the work of child advocates eventually made child maltreatment an illegal act with the passage of the 1974 federal Child Abuse Prevention Act (Finkelhor, Cross, & Cantor, 2005).

Empowerment tool   Research can be used as an empowerment tool that bolsters a cause with administrators and policy makers. In fact, many policy makers are open to consulting with experts, including staff from a community organization that is familiar with the population and the problem. Therefore, organizational staff is best prepared to advocate for their population's causes when they know the empirical literature as well as the local population profile (Chataway et al., 2009; Mayer, 2009). Social workers can use sound evidence to influence politicians' political positions.

Mobilization tool   Research also can be used to mobilize community members or groups (Humphries, 2008; McIntyre, 2008). For example, Alice McIntyre (2000) and a group of inner-city youth used participatory action research to determine a problem of community violence in the form of trash in their neighborhood. This information helped the youth mobilize for change.

Action Steps

Thinking Beyond Results

Policy advocates generally discuss strategies for using research for policy purposes. Chataway, Joffe, and Mordaunt (2009) recommended thinking beyond results in policy research and engaging stakeholders in all phases of the process. They recommended meeting with participants, funders, and other stakeholders to clarify issues, try out ideas, and determine what matters most to stakeholders. The research process is an iterative process and can deepen understanding and knowledge. Policy initiatives often may change, which may influence a research project. Therefore, if a reflexive dialogue occurs early in the process, it can help to refine the course of research to make it most relevant to all stakeholders involved (Mayer, 2009).

Communicating Results

Results should be communicated strategically. Some options include formal or informal presentations to stakeholders; breakfast, lunch, or dinner talks; and newspaper and popular journal articles. Public workshops with selected invitees from the policy world, experts, academics, and participants in the research also can be used (Chataway et al., 2009; Reisch, 2009).

The social worker should carefully consider the meeting format and how results will be communicated before committing to venues. The scope of the project effects, the environmental context, and level of stakeholders involved will influence the choice. The social worker also should be clear about the purpose of the meeting, the type of feedback desired, and the date and time of the meeting. Culture and context also can influence the communication of results (Chataway et al., 2009). For example, the language (e.g., formal versus informal) used for certain audiences, especially because research is often of a technical nature, should be carefully considered. Table 12.6 provides possible strategies and venues for presenting research and evaluation projects and results.

Global Evidence-Based Policymaking

Evidence-based policy is of growing interest among policy makers, including at an international level (Thomas & Mohan, 2007). Similar to evidence-based practice, evidence-based policy making draws on the best available evidence and knowledge to develop policies that help to improve health and well-being among individuals and communities and service provision (Mayer, 2009). However, Mayer (2009) noted some areas of concern. First, evidence is not always available to make policy decisions. Second, there are serious issues of legitimacy and power relations on an international level if the Western ways of knowing that revere logic and rationality and status of experts are the central frameworks used. Therefore, alternative ways of knowing relevant to underserved populations hold very little weight in policy debates.

Evidence-based policy making draws on the best available evidence and knowledge to develop policies that help to improve health and well-being among individuals and communities and service provision.

In reality, evidence-based policy making is complex when implemented in the field (Mayer, 2009). Mayer (2009) recommended strategies for improving the quality of research and its effectiveness in changing public policy and public action. Think critically about problems in advance and propose methods before acting. Social workers should carefully reflect to conceptualize the central issues and assess the feasibility of the research and data sources that will be needed to provide evidence. As described earlier, strategies include involving stakeholders throughout the process.

There also are sober realities to consider when using evidence to take action or to make changes in public policy. Perhaps most important, using empirical evidence will not always result in a shift in other people's views. An important strategy is to talk about evidence realistically. That is, avoid talking about results as if they prove something. This assertion makes it easy for others to attack, because all research results are to some degree inconclusive (Mayer, 2009).

Increasing Awareness

In addition to field-based knowledge and skills in evaluation, scholars and practitioners often speak to the critical importance of self-awareness and evaluation (Singer, 2006). Reeser (2009) offered some strategies that will help foster the activist and advocate within.

- ▶ *Awareness of the political nature of practice:* Social workers should be aware that there is a political nature of social work practice, including research and evaluation. Garnering a vision of a just society will help promote social justice, human rights, and well-being among all individuals, both locally and globally.

- ▶ *Awareness of the personal is political connection:* Social workers should be aware of the *personal is political* connection. This helps to remind social workers of the connection between the individual and the larger sociopolitical context.
- ▶ *Awareness of top-down strategies:* Social workers should be aware of top-down strategies, that is, strategies used by the status quo (e.g., those who hold power) to maintain power and control, and strategies that advance equity and fairness.
- ▶ *Awareness of bottom-up change power:* Social workers also should be aware of how power can be changed from the bottom up. That is, the rank and file has the power to change unjust structures. Social workers should be committed to helping empower people to recognize and use their resources. Frontline social workers also can realize the impact of building data from the ground up, which can help move the profession forward.
- ▶ *Engagement in reflection and action:* Social workers should engage in thoughtful reflection and action. This involves engaging in critical self-reflection and reexamining one's position (e.g, race, class, sex, class) and how it is linked to the larger environmental context (Reeser, 2009).

Policy Practice

Critical Thinking Question: What are the challenges to infusing research in policy practice? What are some strategies to overcome the challenges?

Future Directions: Think and Act Global

The Spread of International Social Work

Over the past 100 years, social work has grown from the industrial countries of the United States and England and spread to villages and cities, large and small, in all corners of the globe (Sowers & Rowe, 2007). International social work is referred to as "international professional action" by social workers (Healey, 2001, p. 7). These activities include international practice, policy development, and research and evaluation (Sowers & Rowe, 2007; Tripodi & Pitocky-Tripodi, 2007).

Social workers who integrate evidence-based research and evaluation efforts can be part of a powerful and collective force in effectively preventing or alleviating adverse social conditions.

Social workers who integrate evidence-based research and evaluation efforts can be part of a powerful and collective force in effectively preventing or alleviating adverse social conditions. Poverty; child abuse; HIV/AIDS; substance abuse; crime; and the structural oppression of women, persons of color, and individuals with physical and mental health disabilities are just some of the areas to make a contribution (Sowers & Rowe, 2007). Similar to our forefathers and foremothers, social workers can take ownership of community-based research practices and use them at local or global fronts (Austin, 2003; Zimbalist, 1977). Social workers can apply social work research and evaluation with action to shed light on undetected social problems at the collective level and also evaluate the effectiveness of practices, programs, policies, and laws.

From Domestic to International Research

Social workers can be involved in domestic and international social work research efforts. Using a "single country perspective," domestic social work research examines the population of one country, such as the United States. Only the literature of one country is used to frame the social problem, conduct the study, and apply the findings (Tripodi & Pitocky-Tripodi, 2007). A large majority of American social work research is conducted in the United States for the United States.

However, social workers who want to become involved in international research and evaluation efforts have several options. Compared to domestic research, international social work research efforts extend beyond a country's borders, such as outside the United States, to investigate social problems and solutions (Tripodi & Pitocky-Tripodi, 2007).

Tripodi and Pitocky-Tripodi (2007) categorized international social work research as three different types: (a) supranational (beyond borders), (b) intranational (within borders), and (c) transnational (across borders).

Supranational research   *Supranational research* is most concerned with research and populations from one country. However, the research can be conducted in any country. In contrast to domestic research, supranational research and evaluation use the empirical literature from two or more countries to frame research problems. Implications also are drawn for two or more countries (Tripodi & Pitocky-Tripodi, 2007).

Intranational research   *Intranational research* is conducted within one country's borders with immigrant populations, for example, the study of Mexican migrants within the United States. Intranational social work research uses the literature from the country of origin and country of emigration to frame research problems. Implications also are drawn for both countries (Tripodi & Pitocky-Tripodi, 2007).

Transnational research   *Transnational research* is conducted across national borders. Transnational research is comparative research using similar populations in two or more countries. The literature across the different countries' populations is used to frame research problems. Implications also are drawn across each population (Tripodi & Pitocky-Tripodi, 2007).

Think and Act Local: Practice-Based Research

Other innovative social work research methods are continually being developed for both local and global uses. The results can have direct relevance for practice and program decision making. For example, practice-based research or clinical data mining, which is a method defined as "practitioners' use of available agency data for practice-based research purposes" (Epstein, 2009, p. 3), has received considerable attention. It is a user-friendly approach, with feasible research methods, and the results are directly applied to agencies to improve services (Epstein, 2009). Epstein (2009) defined clinical data mining as follows:

> Clinical data mining is a practice-based retrospective research strategy whereby practitioner-researchers, alone or with assistance of a research consultant, systematically retrieve, codify, analyze, and interpret available qualitative and/or quantitative data from their own and other agency records in order to reflect on the practice, program, and or policy implications of their findings. (p. 71)

Steps   The first step in conducting a practice-based research skill involves obtaining agency support. Once that is obtained, the social workers gather information that can be used to help formulate practice-based research questions. In meeting with one or more staff persons the following questions are asked:

- What is your service or treatment program trying to achieve? (i.e., program goals and objectives)
- How do you go about achieving this? (i.e., program theory)

> ♦ Who are you trying to serve? (i.e., target population)
> ♦ How well do you do this? (i.e., perceived effectiveness)
> ♦ How do you know when you have done a good job? (i.e., indicators or measures used)
> ♦ What things get in the way? (i.e., perceived obstacles) (Epstein, 2009, p. 71)

Types of methods　　The information gathered from this query is used to craft research questions using the available agency data. Social workers' research knowledge and skills can easily be transferred for use in practice-based research. There are three methods choices to conduct analysis of the existing agency data. The first method is using quantitative data from agency records to conduct a quantitative data analysis. This method is similar to conducting secondary data analysis of existing datasets. The second method is to use qualitative data from agency records and convert them to quantitative data for quantitative data analysis purposes. The third method involves using qualitative data for the purposes of qualitative data analysis (Epstein, 2009).

Decision-making options　　Practice-based research involves a similar research design and decision-making process, but using existing data. The existing data offer a longitudinal portrait of the population's services, the services provided, and service effectiveness. Therefore, a variety of research questions can be pursued. For example, part of the decision-making process will involve design choices, such as the time frame (e.g., cross-sectional, longitudinal), sample selection (e.g., full sample or subsamples), program participation (e.g., mental health program, domestic violence program), and outputs and outcome variables (e.g., program completion, medication compliance, independent living), which are part of the decision-making process (Cresswell, 2006; Epstein, 2009). What is most useful about this approach is that it allows social workers to make a direct contribution in local communities. The knowledge and skill set also can be easily transported for social workers to assist agencies to develop or improve services in other countries.

IMPLICATIONS FOR HUMAN RIGHTS AND SOCIAL JUSTICE

The purpose of this text was to assist contemporary social workers in understanding the history of social work's research and evaluation efforts using a human rights and social justice framework. As evidenced in its history, social workers have used research and evaluation strategies to increase awareness of social issues and problems that impeded all individuals from achieving well-being (Zimbalist, 2007). Consistent with human rights principles, social work reveres the dignity and worth of the person and engages in strategies to help individuals achieve self actualization (Wronka, 2008). A recurrent theme in the results of these efforts is individual and social transformation. However, despite some progress, social workers have more work to do.

Mahatma Gandhi (n.d.) said, "Be the change you want to see in the world." This suggests that the process of change begins with critical self-awareness followed by actions. Even Clifford Beers did it, when the odds were against him, in a society dominated by stigma and discrimination against individuals with mental illness. Integrating the somewhat contradictory parts of professional identity, such as the empathic counselor, rational researcher, and passionate advocate, ultimately is helpful toward reaching and evaluating that goal. The takeaway message for social workers is this: Take back the research process. Owning the researcher and evaluator as part of one's professional identify will help social workers make a difference and be more confident.

Mahatma Gandhi (n.d.) also said, "a small body of determined spirits fired by an unquenchable faith in their mission can alter the course of history." With these words in mind, imagine for a moment the individual efforts of social workers as part of the collective. Imagine for a moment that we all did nothing. What might result? Now imagine for a moment that we all did something. What might result? Think about it. This century is in the hands of a new generation of social workers. Individually and collectively, there is the knowledge, the skills, the power, and the reach to promote human rights, social justice, and individual and community well-being. At this point, the next steps should come easy. And yes, the process is set, then the goals, then the objectives, then the plan, and then do it! And last but not least–evaluate how well it was done!

Exercise

Social workers use research and evaluation strategies to foster universal human rights, such as social, economic, cultural, and collective rights as outlined in the Universal Declaration of Human Rights (UN, 1948). This section revisits the strategies recommended by the United Nations (1994), which has recommended intervention strategies to help advance human rights (see chapter 2). At this stage, students' knowledge and skills in how research and evaluation facilitate the change process more than likely have increased.

For this exercise, individually or in groups of 3–6, review these strategies again (see next) and answer the following questions: (a) Which of the strategies are feasible in your current practice situation? (b) What knowledge, values, and skills of research and evaluation can be used? (c) If there are several feasible strategies, determine which one will have the most effective short-term outcomes and long-term impacts and indicate why. These intervention strategies include (a) work with local, regional, and national organizations to promote, develop, and implement needed changes in policy, planning, and programming on human rights issues; (b) recognize and adapt existing services to maximize effectiveness; (c) develop and involve appropriate and qualified leaders from the community to identify, plan, and implement needed services and advocacy efforts; (d) develop self capacities of those disadvantaged in their human rights; (e) organize previously unorganized disadvantaged groups for self help; (f) form alliances with like-minded social and political movements; (g) develop mechanisms to enhance local and global awareness, including the use of mass media; (h) fundraise for the cause; (i) assess the impact of actions undertaken in collaboration with persons and groups affected and associated groups and organizations; (j) document and disseminate information on human rights abuses; and (k) promote legislation that benefits disadvantaged groups (UN, 1994).

SUMMARY

This chapter reviewed the final stage of the research process, which includes disseminating the findings. This stage includes writing, sharing the findings, and action. As reviewed, writing can be a powerful tool to advance the aims of social work. Research findings are generally shared in journal articles in the form of research reports. These reports serve to enlighten others, including practitioners and policy makers, to social problems and practical solutions. Other methods to disseminate research findings include making presentations at local, national, and international research and professional association conferences.

Research for advocacy is a method used for agency and policy reform in the form of case-level and class advocacy. Strategies for communicating and presenting findings include the use of careful reflection about the problem, studies and the methods used, and the involvement of stakeholders. Twenty-first century social work practice awards social workers many opportunities to integrate the practitioner, advocate, and researcher. Social work has spread from its initial industrial roots in America and England and has extended its mission to all four corners of the globe. Social workers can be involved in moving the profession and its mission at the international level in international social work research efforts.

Of equal importance is the work done in the places and neighborhoods close to home. This may be in the form of practice evaluation, agency-based research, or the new development of practice-based research or clinical data mining. In the tradition of our foremothers and forefathers, social workers can integrate the practitioners, advocates, and researchers individually and collectively to advance human rights.

The use of sound research strategies to increase awareness of social problems and evaluate interventions is consistent with the profession's humanitarian roots and human rights and social justice process and outcomes. During the new century, contemporary social workers can use a bottom-up approach and reclaim their research knowledge and skills. These skills have always has been a rightful part of every social worker's professional identity and the means by which to confirm that each of us and our collective has made a difference.

Directions for the Social Work Research Students' Literature Review Project
Article Extraction Form

Use the following categories and corresponding guidelines for your content analysis data extraction for journal articles.

Article Background Information

1. Id_Code: Provide a number id for each extraction form. (Example code: TM001, in which TM= the reviewer's initials, 001 = first article reviewed). *Note: Label the corresponding PDF file with the same code.*
2. Full Citation: Use APA style (be consistent for articles, books, book chapters, etc.).
3. Year Study was Published: List the year the study was published.
4. Source: Was it a journal article, books, book chapters, and so on?
5. Database Retrieval Information: How did you find this information? What database did you use? What were the key word search terms? What other important information would you need to know to find this information again?
6. Study Type: (i.e., theoretical, quantitative, qualitative, or mixed methods) Also, specify whether the study is a descriptive, exploratory, explanatory, or evaluative design).
7. Study Location: In what city, country, geographic region was this study conducted?
8. System(s) Addressed: (e.g., child welfare, social services, health, educational, mental health, special education programs, substance abuse, juvenile justice) (or *not applicable*)
9. Problem Area, Policy, and/or Program Under Study: (i.e., What is the problem or focus of the study?)
10. Study Purpose: List study purpose or goal identified by authors.
11. Research Questions and Hypotheses: List the research questions and/or hypotheses explicitly stated by the author(s).
12. Significance of the Study: How does the author(s) describe the significance of the study to practice, research, and policy in the introduction?

What Are the Details of the Methods Section of the Articles?

13. Research Design: Briefly describe the research design, including sampling techniques.
14. Study Setting: Which country? If the United States, which geographic region? Describe characteristics of the study setting.
15. Sample Size: What is the number of participants in the study? Include subsample information, if applicable.
16. Sample Description: Briefly describe the sample (age, gender, race or ethnicity, and other relevant information) and provide numbers and percentages when available.
17. Variables and Definitions: List all the variables (i.e., independent, dependent, others, with the definitions for each).
18. Measures or Instrument Used: List variables with measures along with reliability and validity information, if available. If reliability and validity information is not provided, write *no information provided.*
19. Data Collection Procedures: How did the researchers collect data for this study? What plan was implemented?
20. Ethical Issues Addressed in the Study: How did the researchers obtain informed consent? What ethical issues were addressed?
21. Data Analysis: Describe the statistical tests for each relationship tested (if theoretical article is used, write *not applicable*).

Exhibit 12.1
Article Extraction Form Directions

Results and Discussion

22. Major Findings: If theoretical article is used, discuss model proposed; if research study is used, provide overview of major findings.
23. Study Implications (1): What are the implications mentioned by the authors for social work practice, research, and/or policy?
24. Study Implications (2): What are the implications explicitly mentioned by the authors for human rights and/or social justice?
25. Limitations of Study (which are mentioned by author[s])
26. Other Study Limitations (noted by reviewer)
27. Future Directions (recommended by author[s])
28. Reviewer Comments: About the quality of study (other limitations noted or other general comments).
29. Reviewer Views: About the implications for practice, research, and/or policy, and human rights and social justice.
30. Any Other Important Notes: List any additional comments here.

Exhibit 12.1

Continued

Social Work Research Students' Literature Review Project
Article Extraction Form

Use the following categories and corresponding guidelines for the extraction of articles for the content analysis. See instructions for more detailed explanations of categories.

Date Extracted:

Extracted by:

Article Background Information
1. Idcode:
2. Full Citation (Use APA):
3. Year Study Published:
4. Source:
5. Database Retrieval Information:
6. Study Type:
7. Study Location:
8. System(s) Addressed:
9. Problem Area, Policy, and/or Program Under Study:
10. Study Purpose:
11. Research Questions and/or Hypotheses:
12. Significance of the Study:

What Are the Details of the Methods Used By This Study?
13. Research Design:
14. Study Setting:
15. Sample Size:
16. Sample Description:
17. Variables and Definitions:
18. Measures or Instruments Used:
19. Data Collection Procedures:
20. Ethical Issues Addressed in the Study:
21. Data Analysis:

Results and Discussion
22. Major Findings:
23. Study Implications (1) for Practice, Policy, or Research (Stated by Authors):
24. Study Implications (2) for Human Rights and Social Justice (Explicitly Stated by Authors):
25. Limitations of Study Mentioned by Author(s):
26. Other Study Limitations (Evaluated by Reviewer):
27. Future Directions Recommended By Authors:
28. Reviewer Comments:
29. Reviewer's Views on Implications for Social Work and/or Human Rights and Social Justice:
30. Any Other Important Notes:

Exhibit 12.2
Article Extraction Form Template

Succeed with **PEARSON** **mysocialworklab**

Log onto **www.mysocialworklab.com** and answer the following questions. (*If you did not receive an access code to* **MySocialWorkLab** *with this text and wish to purchase access online, please visit* www.mysocialworklab.com.)

1. **Read the case study "Community Practice: Organizing Social Work in the Republic of Armenia, Part II."**

After reading, evaluate the quality of the evaluation report.

2. **Watch the critical thinking video "Demonstrating Effective Oral and Written Communication."** After listening to the commentary, describe how social workers can apply the communication strategies to oral and written communication about research.

PRACTICE TEST

The following questions will test your knowledge of the content found within this chapter. For additional assessment, including licensing-exam type questions on applying chapter content to practice, visit **MySocialWorkLab**.

1. The NASW Code of Ethics stipulates all but the following:
   a. Contribute to the knowledge base
   b. Contribute time and professional expertise
   c. Substitute other professions' ethical codes as needed
   d. Engage in social and political action

2. Which of the following draws on the best available evidence and knowledge to develop policies?
   a. Therapeutic jurisprudence
   b. Evidence-based policy making
   c. Policy reformation
   d. Resource analysis

3. A written paper that includes an introduction, methods, findings, and discussion sections generally refers to:
   a. A literature review
   b. An executive summary
   c. A summary analysis
   d. An empirical research report

4. A social worker who uses research to act on behalf of others to facilitate change is engaging in:
   a. Extracurricular activities
   b. Advocacy
   c. Assessment
   d. Conceptualization

5. Describe at least one social work strategy that can provide evidence that you can use in your practice to promote human rights and social and economic justice.

ASSESS YOUR COMPETENCE

Use the scale below to rate your current level of achievement on the following concepts or skills associated with each competency presented in the chapter:

1	2	3
I can accurately describe the concept or skill	I can consistently identify the concept or skill when observing and analyzing practice activities	I can competently implement the concept or skill in my own practice

_____ can demonstrate professional responsibility of generating knowledge for practice.

_____ can use research findings to advocate on behalf of others.

_____ can demonstrate clear oral and written communication skills in research.

_____ can engage in policy practice that advances human rights and social justice.

Appendix

INSTRUCTIONS FOR ASSESSMENT OF ORGANIZATIONAL CULTURAL COMPETENCE

The following Assessment of Organizational Cultural Competence is the work of an ad hoc committee of the Association of University Centers on Disabilities' (AUCD) Multicultural Council. Members include the following individuals:

Chana Hiranaka, Ad Hoc Committee Chair, University of Southern California UCE at Children's Hospital Los Angeles

Carolyn Richardson, Ad Hoc Committee Co-Chair, University of New Mexico

Allison Ball, University of Oregon

Rita Hohlstein, University of Wisconsin–Madison

Roberta Lopez, University of New Mexico LEND Fellow

F. John Meaney, University of Arizona, Tucson

Roz Parrish, University of Cincinnati

Linda Wilson, University of Oklahoma

In the current environment, many contracts and grants are requiring documentation of activities concerning cultural competence and/or sensitivity, including self-assessments and training. Therefore, the purpose of the instrument is to assist organizations to assess their progress toward cultural competence, both at the organizational and at the individual level.

In the development of the instrument, the term *culturally competent* means

Services, supports, or other assistance that is conducted or provided in a manner that is responsive to the beliefs, interpersonal styles, attitudes, language, and behaviors of individuals who are receiving services, supports, or other assistance, and in a manner that has the greatest likelihood of ensuring their maximum participation in the program involved. (Developmental Disabilities Assistance and Bill of Rights Act of 2000, Public Law 106-402).

The instrument consists of three sections: (1) Assessment of Organizational Cultural Competence, (2) Respondent Information, and (3) Assessment of Individual Cultural Competence. Section 1 is structured so that it can be individualized to the organization by inserting the appropriate information in the blanks provided; it also allows respondents to skip those functions that do not pertain to the organization.

It is imperative that all faculty, staff, consumers, and/or students know that their responses to sections 1 and 2 of the instrument are anonymous. Therefore, we suggest that you submit the two sections separately so that no respondent information can be used to identify responses on section 1 of the instrument. The respondent information should be used to determine if the respondents to section 1 reflect the individuals within your organization. Section 3 is solely for the respondents' use. We suggest that respondents be encouraged to keep a copy of this section so that they can refer to it and see their growth in this area.

Respondents should take no more than 10 minutes to complete sections 1 and 2, and an additional 5 minutes to complete section 3.

You can also access a database in ACCESS 2000 by contacting John Meaney at fmeaney@u.arizona.edu. This database will provide a means for entering and storing your data.

We hope that this instrument will assist your organization in identifying areas of strength and possible areas for improvement. The intent of the instrument is not to give an organization a "score," but to provide information as to where the organization may be on a continuum in moving toward cultural competence. The ad hoc committee is planning to develop a manual, which will provide activities to assist you with strengthening the cultural competency of your organization. The availability of the manual will be announced on its website.

If you have any comments or feedback regarding this instrument, we would very much like to hear from you. Contact either Chana Hiranaka at chanah@pacbell.net or Carolyn Richardson at crich@unm.edu.

Assessment of Organizational Cultural Competence

Our program is trying to identify our organization's strengths and our needs for further training and program development to become a more culturally competent organization. As a member of this program, your input into the assessment of our organization's cultural competence is important.

Your responses will be confidential and anonymous. The results of this survey will be utilized in aggregate and summary form only. If you have questions about the assessment of organizational cultural competence, contact _____. When you have completed the assessment, place it in (mailbox or location) _____. Thank you for your assistance in this most important effort toward becoming a culturally competent program.

Check below which of the following *best* describes your *major* function in the organization. *Check _only one_.*

☐ Administration   ☐ Clinical services   ☐ Research

☐ Support services   ☐ Education/training   ☐ Student/trainee

☐ Advisory board   ☐ Technical assistance/consultant

☐ Community/continuing education

Others specify: _____

Indicate your length of involvement with this organization:

☐ Less than 1 year   ☐ 1 to 5 years   ☐ More than 5 years

Please Check the *One* Answer That *Best Describes* Your Response to Each of the Statements

A.1 Organization	Yes	No	Do Not Know
Cultural competence is included in the mission statement, policies, and procedures.			
A committee/task force/program area addresses issues of cultural competence.			
Partnerships with representatives of ethnic communities actively incorporate their knowledge and experience in organizational planning.			
The organization supports involvement with and/or utilization of the resources of regional and/or national forums that promote cultural competence.			

Source: Association of University Centers on Disabilities. (2004). *Assessment of Organizational Cultural Competence.*

A.2 Administration	Almost Always	Often	Sometimes	Almost Never	Do Not Know
Personnel recruitment, hiring, and retention practices reflect the goal to achieve ethnic diversity and cultural competence.					
Resources are in place to support initial and ongoing training for personnel to develop cultural competence.					
Position descriptions and personnel performance measures include skills related to cultural competence.					
Participants for all advisory committees and councils are recruited and supported to ensure the diverse cultural representation of the organization's geographic area.					
Personnel are respected and supported for their desire to honor and participate in cultural celebrations.					
Fiscal resources are available to support translation and interpretation services.					

Source: Association of University Centers on Disabilities. (2004). Assessment of Organizational Cultural Competence.

A.3 Clinical services *Important:* If your organization does not provide these services, please check here and proceed to the next Section. _____	Almost Always	Often	Sometimes	Almost Never	Do Not Know
Clinical services are routinely and systematically reviewed for methods, strategies, and ways of serving consumers and their families in culturally competent ways.					
Cultural bias of assessment tools is considered when interpreting the results and making recommendations.					
Translation and interpretation assistance is available and utilized when needed.					
Forms of communication (reports, appointment notices, telephone message greetings, etc.) are culturally and linguistically appropriate for the populations served.					
Pictures, posters, printed materials, and toys reflect the culture and ethnic backgrounds of the consumers and families served.					
When food is discussed or used in assessment or treatment, the cultural and ethnic background of the consumer and family is considered.					

Source: Association of University Centers on Disabilities. (2004). *Assessment of Organizational Cultural Competence.*

A.4 Research and program evaluation *Important:* If your organization is not involved in these activities, please check here and proceed to the next Section. _____	Almost Always	Often	Sometimes	Almost Never	Do Not Know
Input on research priorities is sought from consumers and/or their families representing diverse cultures.					
Research projects include subjects of diverse cultures representative of the targeted research population.					
The researchers include members of the racial/ethnic groups to be studied and/or individuals who have acquired knowledge and skills to work with subjects from those specific groups.					
Consumers and families representing diverse cultures provide input regarding the design, methods, and outcome measures of research and program evaluation projects.					

Source: Association of University Centers on Disabilities. (2004). *Assessment of Organizational Cultural Competence.*

A.5 Technical assistance/consultation *Important:* If your organization is not involved in these activities, please check here and proceed to the next Section. _____	Almost Always	Often	Sometimes	Almost Never	Do Not Know
Technical assistance/consultation activities are routinely and systematically reviewed for methods, strategies, and ways of serving communities in culturally competent ways.					
When assessing the need for technical assistance/ consultation in communities, input from members reflecting the diverse cultural make-up of these communities is sought and utilized.					
Efforts are made to involve consultants who have knowledge of and experience with the cultural group requesting the technical assistance/consultation.					
Evaluation from the recipients of technical assistance/consultation activities includes components of cultural competence.					

Source: Association of University Centers on Disabilities. (2004). *Assessment of Organizational Cultural Competence.*

A.6 Education/training *Important*: If your organization is not involved in these activities, please check here and proceed to the next Section. _____	Almost Always	Often	Sometimes	Almost Never	Do not Know
Trainees/students are actively recruited from diverse cultures.					
Trainees/students from diverse cultures are mentored.					
Representatives of the diverse cultures are actively sought to participate in the planning and presentation of training activities.					
The training curriculum and activities incorporate content for the development of cultural competence.					
The training curriculum, materials and activities are systemically evaluated to determine if they achieve cultural competence.					

Source: Association of University Centers on Disabilities. (2004). *Assessment of Organizational Cultural Competence.*

A.7 Community/continuing education *Important:* If your organization is not involved in these activities, please check here _____.	Almost Always	Often	Sometimes	Almost Never	Do not Know
Participants are actively recruited from diverse cultures.					
Representatives of diverse cultures are actively sought to participate in the planning and presentation of these activities.					
The content and activities are culturally and linguistically appropriate.					
Participant evaluation of community/continuing education activities includes components of cultural competence.					

Source: Association of University Centers on Disabilities. (2004). *Assessment of Organizational Cultural Competence.*

Adapted in part from Promoting Cultural Diversity and Cultural Competency Self-Assessment Checklist for Personnel Providing Services and Support to Children With Special Health Needs and Their Families by Tawara D. Goode, Georgetown University Child Development Center, and Policy Brief 1: Rationale for Cultural Competence in Primary Health Care, developed by Elena Cohen, Consultant, and Tawara D. Goode, and Policy Brief 2: Linguistic Competence in Primary Health Care Delivery Systems: Implications for Policy Makers, developed by T. Goode, S. Sockalingum, M. Brown, and W. Jones, National Center for Cultural Competence, Georgetown University Child Development Center.

Respondent Information

Before completing this question, please review the statements on Assessment of Individual Cultural Competence. After reflecting upon the entire survey, please describe the subjects or topics in which you would like cultural competence training:

1. _____

2. _____

3. _____

The data on this sheet are collected to obtain information about the survey respondents. This information will allow us to determine if all groups have been represented.

Your information will not be shared with anyone in the organization. This information will not be linked to your responses on the other pages.

Please Provide the Following Information by Using a Checkmark.

Gender: ☐ Female   ☐ Male

Age: ☐ 18–35   ☐ 36–49   ☐ 50–65   ☐ 65+

Do you have a disability?   ☐ Yes   ☐ No

Are you a family member of a person with a disability?   ☐ Yes   ☐ No

Indicate your racial or ethnic identity using *one* of the following categories:

☐ African American/Black   ☐ American Indian/Native American (including Alaskan native)

☐ Asian   ☐ Hispanic

☐ Pacific Islander   ☐ White, European, non-Hispanic

Multiethnic or other specify: _____

Individual Assessment of Cultural Competence

As a member of the organization, the knowledge you have of yourself and others is important and reflected in the ways you communicate and interact. This individual assessment instrument was developed to assist you in reflecting upon and examining your journey toward cultural competence.

The following statements are about you and your cultural beliefs and values as they relate to the organization. Check the *one* answer that *best describes* your response to each of the statements.
Developed by the AUCD Multicultural Council.

A.8 Individual assessment	Almost Always	Often	Sometimes	Almost Never
I reflect on and examine my own cultural background, biases, and prejudices related to race, culture and sexual orientation that may influence my behaviors.				
I continue to learn about the cultures of the consumers and families served in the program, in particular attitudes toward disability; cultural beliefs and values; and health, spiritual, and religious practices.				
I recognize and accept that the consumer and family members make the ultimate decisions even though they may be different compared to my personal and professional values and beliefs.				
I intervene, in an appropriate manner, when I observe other staff engaging in behaviors that appear culturally insensitive or reflect prejudice.				
I attempt to learn and use key words and colloquialisms of the languages used by the consumers and families served.				
I utilize interpreters for the assessment of consumers and their families whose spoken language is one in which I am not fluent.				
I have developed skills to utilize an interpreter effectively.				
I utilize methods of communication, including written, verbal, pictures, and diagrams, which will be most helpful to the consumers, families, and other program participants.				
I write reports or any form of written communication, in a style and at a level which consumers, families, and other program participants will understand.				
I am flexible, adaptive, and will initiate changes, which will better serve consumers, families, and other program participants from diverse cultures.				
I am mindful of cultural factors that may be influencing the behaviors of consumers, families, and other program participants.				

Source: Association of University Centers on Disabilities. (2004). *Assessment of Organizational Cultural Competence.* Adapted in part from Promoting Cultural Diversity and Cultural Competency Self Assessment Checklist for Personnel Providing Services and Support to Children With Special Health Needs and Their Families by Tawara D. Goode, Georgetown University Child Development Center.

References

Abbott, E. (1942). *Social welfare and professional education.* Chicago, IL: University of Chicago Press.

Abram, K. M., Teplin, L. A., Charles, D. R., Longworth, S. L., McClelland, G. M., & Dulcan, M. K. (2004). Posttraumatic stress disorder and trauma in youth in juvenile detention. *Archives of General Psychiatry, 61,* 403–410.

Addams, J. (1910). *Twenty years at Hull house.* New York: The Macmillan Company.

Agnew, E. N. (2004). *From charity to social work: Mary E. Richmond and the creation of an American profession.* Chicago, IL: University of Illinois Press.

Alexander, J. F., & Sexton, T. L. (2002). Functional family therapy: A model for treating high-risk, acting-out youth. In F. W. Kaslow (Ed.), *Comprehensive handbook of psychotherapy: Integrative/eclectic* (Vol. 4, pp. 111–132). Hoboken, NJ: John Wiley & Sons, Inc.

American Counseling Association. (2005). *ACA code of ethics.* Retrieved from http://www.counseling.org/Resources/CodeOfEthics/TP/Home/CT2.aspx

American Medication Association. (2001). *AMA Code of ethics.* Retrieved from http://www.ama-assn.org/ama/pub/physician-resources/medical-ethics/code-medical-ethics.shtml

American Psychological Association. (2009). *Publication manual of the American Psychological Association* (6th ed.). Washington, DC: Author.

Angelou, M. (2007). *African American quotes: Maya Angelou.* Retrieved from http://africanamerican-quotes.org/maya-angelou.html

Ariga, M., Uehara, T., Takeuchi, K., Ishige, Y., Nakano, R., & Mikuni, M. (2008). Trauma exposure and post-traumatic stress disorder in delinquent female adolescents. *Journal of Child Psychology and Psychiatry, 49*(1), 79–87.

Aristotle. (2000). *The rhetoric and the poetics of Aristotle* (Rev. ed.). New York: MacMillan (Original work published 350 BC).

Armstrong, D. M. (1973). *Belief, truth and knowledge.* Cambridge, MA: Cambridge University Press.

Asmundson, G., Norton, G., & Stein, M. (2002). *Clinical research in mental health: A practical guide.* Thousand Oaks, CA: Sage Publications.

Association of University Centers on Disabilities (AUCD Multicultural Council). (2004). *Assessment of organizational cultural competence.* Retrieved from http://www.consumerstar.org/pubs/Assessment%20of%20Organizational%20Cultural%20Competence.pdf

Atkinson, R. (1998). *The life history interview.* Thousand Oaks, CA: Sage Publications.

Austin, D. (1983). The Flexner myth and the history of social work. *Social Service Review, 57*(3), 357–377.

Austin, D. (2003). The history of social work research. In R. L. Edwards (Ed.-in-Chief), *Encyclopedia of social work* (19th ed., Vol. 1, pp. 81–94). Washington, DC: NASW Press.

Bamberger, M., Rugh, J., & Mabry, L. (2006). *Real world evaluation.* Thousand Oaks, CA: Sage Publications.

Barker, R. L. (2003). *The social work dictionary* (5th ed.). Washington, DC: NASW Press.

Barnes, J. (Ed.). (1984). *Complete works of Aristotle: The revised Oxford translation.* Princeton, NJ: Princeton University Press.

Barnhardt, R., & Kawagley, A. O. (2005). Indigenous knowledge systems and Alaska native ways of knowing. *Anthropology and Education Quarterly, 36*(1), 8–23.

Bartlett, H. M. (1958). Working definition of social work practice. *Social Work, 3*(2), 5–8.

Bartlett, H. M. (1970). *The common base of social work practice.* Silver Spring, MD: NASW Press.

Beecher, H. K. (1966). Ethics and clinical research. *New England Journal of Medicine, 274*(24), 1354–1360.

Beers, C. (1908). *A mind that found itself: A memoir of madness and recovery.* West Valley City, UT: Waking Lion Press.

Belcher, W. L. (2009). *Writing your journal article in 12 weeks: A guide to academic publishing success.* Thousand Oaks, CA: Sage Publications.

Bem, D. J. (2000). Writing an empirical article. In R. J. Sternberg (Ed.), *Guide to publishing in psychology journals* (pp. 3–16). Cambridge, England: Cambridge University Press.

Berg, B. L. (2004). *Qualitative research methods for the social sciences* (5th ed.). Boston: Pearson Education.

Bernard, H. R., & Ryan, G. W. (2010). *Analyzing qualitative data: Systematic approaches.* Thousand Oaks, CA: Sage Publications.

Bisman, C. D., & Hardcastle, D. A. (1999). *Integrating research into practice: A model for effective social work.* Pacific Grove, CA: Brooks/Cole.

Blass, T. (Ed.). (2000). *Obedience to authority: Current perspectives on the Milgram paradigm.* Philadelphia, PA: The Psychology Press.

Bloom, M., Fischer, J., & Orme, J. G. (2009). *Evaluating practice: Guidelines for the accountable professional* (6th ed.). Boston: Pearson Publishing.

Bockting, W. O., Robinson, B. E., & Rosser, B. R. S. (1998). Transgender HIV prevention: A qualitative needs assessment. *AIDS Care, 10*(4), 505–525.

Bogo, M., Raphael, D., & Roberts, R. (1993). Interests, activities, and self identification among social work students: Toward a definition of social work identity. *Journal of Social Work Education, 29*(3), 279–292.

Boulmetis, J., & Dutwin, P. (2000). *The ABCs of evaluation: Timeless techniques for program and project managers.* San Francisco: Jossey-Bass.

Boynton, P., Wood, G., & Greenhalgh, T. (2004). Reaching beyond the White middle classs: Hands on guide to questionnaire design. *British Medical Journal, 328,* 1433–1436.

Breckinbridge, S. P., & Abbott, E. (1912). *The delinquent child and the home: A study of the delinquent wards of the juvenile court of Chicago.* New York: Russell Sage Foundation.

Briar, S., Weissman, H., & Rubin, A. (1981). *Research utilization in social work education.* New York: Council on Social Work Education.

Broadhurst, B. P. (1971). *Social thought, social practice, and social work education: Sanborn, Ely, Warner, and Richmond.* Unpublished doctoral dissertation, Columbia University, New York.

Bronfenbrenner, U. (1979). *The ecology of human development: Experiments by nature and design.* Cambridge, MA: Harvard University Press.

Brosky, B. A., & Lally, S. J. (2004). Prevalence of trauma, PTSD, and dissociation in court-referred adolescents. *Journal of Interpersonal Violence, 19,* 801–814.

Buchanan, I. (2010). *A dictionary of critical theory.* New York: Oxford University Press.

Burton, D., Foy, D., Bwanausi, C., Johnson, J., & Moore, L. (1994). The relationship between traumatic exposure, family dysfunction, and posttraumatic stress symptoms in male juvenile offenders. *Journal of Traumatic Stress, 7,* 83–93.

Butler, A. (1990). A reevaluation of social work students' career interests. *Journal of Social Work Education, 26*(1), 1–13.

Butler, A., Ford, D., & Tregaskis, C. (2007). Who do we think we are? Self and reflexivity in social work practice. *Qualitative Social Work, 6,* 281–299.

Calaprice, A. (2005). *The new quotable Einstein.* Princeton, NJ: Princeton University Press.

California Evidence-Based Clearinghouse for Child Welfare. (2010). *Information and resources for child welfare.* Retrieved from http://www .cebc4cw.org/

Campbell, D. T., & Stanley, J. C. (Eds.). (1963). *Experimental and quasi-experimental designs for research.* Chicago: Rand McNally & Company.

Cauffman, E., Feldman, S., Waterman, J., & Stiener, H. (1998). Posttraumatic stress disorder among female juvenile offenders. *Journal of the American Academy of Child and Adolescent Psychiatry, 37,* 1209–1216.

Cave, C. (2004). *Cultural competence, evidence-based practices and planning.* New York: New York State Office of Mental Health.

Centre for Civil Society. (2003). *An activist's guide to research and advocacy.* Retrieved from http:// www.csrsc.org.za/Documents%5Cactivism%20 and%20research%20manual.pdf

Chafetz, J. (1978). *A primer on the construction and testing of theories in sociology.* New York: F.E. Peacock Publishers.

Charmaz, K. (2006). *Constructing grounded theory: A practical guide through qualitative analysis.* Thousand Oaks, CA: Sage Publications.

Chataway, J., Joffe, A., & Mordaunt, J. (2009). Communicating results. In A. Thomas & G. Mohan (Eds.), *Research skills for policy and development: How to find out fast* (pp. 95–110). Thousand Oaks, CA: Sage Publications.

Chinman, M., Imm, P., & Wandersman, A. (2010). *Promoting accountability through methods and tools for planning, implementation, and evaluation.* Santa Monica, CA: Rand Corporation, TR-101-CDC. Retrieved from http://www.rand.org/pubs/ technical_reports/TR101/

Clinton, B. (1997, May 16). Remarks by the president in apology for study done in Tuskegee. *The White House, Office of the Press Secretary.* Retrieved from http:// clinton4.nara.gov/textonly/New/Remarks/Fri/ 19970516-898.html

Coady, N., & Lehman, P. (2008). *Theoretical perspectives for direct social work practice.* New York: Springer Publishing Company.

Coffey, A., & Atkinson, P. (1996). *Making sense of qualitative data.* Thousand Oaks, CA: Sage Publications.

Cohen, M., & Nagel, E. (1934). *An introduction to logic and scientific method.* New York: Harcourt.

Colcard, J. C., & Mann, R. Z. S. (Eds.). (1930). *The long view: Papers and addresses of Mary E. Richmond.* New York: Russell Sage Foundation.

Coley, S. M., & Scheinberg, C. A. (2008). *Proposal writing: Effective grantsmanship* (3rd ed.). Thousand Oaks, CA: Sage Publications.

Coller, B. S. (2006). The physician-scientist, the state, and the oath: Thoughts for our times. The *Journal of Clinical Investigation, 116*(10), 2567–2570.

Commission on Accreditation. (1988). Curriculum policy statement. In *Handbook of accreditation standards and procedures* (pp. 1–110). New York: Council on Social Work Education.

Compte, A. (2009). *A general view of positivism.* Cambridge, MA: Cambridge University Press.

Comstock, D., Hammer, T. R., Strentzsch, J., Cannon, K., Parson, J., & Salazar, G. (2008). Relational-cultural theory: A framework for bridging relational, multicultural, and social justice competencies. *Journal of Counseling and Development, 86*, 279–287.

Congress, E. P. (1999). *Social work values and ethics: Identifying and resolving professional dilemmas.* Belmont, CA: Wadsworth Group/Thomson Learning.

Congress, E. P. (2008). The culturagram. In A. Roberts & G. L. Greene (Eds.), *Social work desk reference* (2nd ed., pp. 969–973). New York: Oxford University Press.

Corey, G. (2008). *Theory and practice of counseling and psychotherapy.* Pacific Grove, CA: Brooks/Cole Publishers.

Corrigan, P. W. (2007). How clinical diagnosis might exacerbate the stigma of mental illness. Social Work, *52*(1), 31–39.

Council on Social Work Education. (1983). *Curriculum policy statement.* New York: The Lois and Samuel Silberman Fund.

Council on Social Work Education. (2002). *2001 Educational policy and accreditation standards.* Retrieved from http://www.cswe.org/File.aspx?id=14115

Council on Social Work Education. (2008). *2008 Educational policy and accreditation standards.* Retrieved from http://www.cswe.org/File.aspx?id=13780

Cournoyer, B. R., & Powers, G. T. (2002). Evidence-based social work: The quite revolution continues. In A. R. Roberts & G. J. Greene (Eds.), *Social workers' desk reference* (pp. 798–807). New York: Oxford University Press.

Creswell, J. W. (2006). *Qualitative inquiry and research design: Choosing among five traditions* (2nd ed.). Thousand Oaks, CA: Sage Publications.

Creswell, J. W. (2009). *Research design: Qualitative, quantitative, and mixed methods approaches.* Thousand Oaks, CA: Sage Publications.

Cross, T., Bazron, B., Dennis, K., & Isaacs, M. (1989). *Towards a culturally competent system of care: A monograph on effective services for minority children who are severely emotionally disturbed* (Vol. 1). Washington, DC: CASSP Technical Assistance Center, Center for Child Health and Mental Health Policy, Georgetown University Child Development Center.

D'Aprix, A. S., Dunlap, K. M., Able, E., & Edwards, R. (2004). Goodness of fit: Career goals of MSW students and the aims of the social work profession in the United States. *Journal of Social Work Education, 23*(3), 265–280.

Davidson, L. (2003). *Living outside mental illness.* New York: New York University Press.

Davies, M. (2000). *The Blackwell encyclopedia of social work.* Malden, MA: Blackwell Publishing.

Deal, K. H. (2007). Psychodynamic theory. *Advances in social work, 8*, 184–195.

Denzin, N. K., & Lincoln, Y. S. (2005). *The Sage handbook of qualitative research* (3rd ed.). Thousand Oaks, CA: Sage Publications.

Dewbry, S. (2004). The ethics of human subjects protection in research. *The Journal of Baccalaureate Social Work, 10*(1), 105–117.

Dix, D. L. (1975). *On behalf of the insane poor: Selected reports 1842–1862.* New York: Ayer Co. Publishers, Inc.

Dixon, A., Howie, P., & Starling, J. (2004). Psychopathology in female juvenile offenders. *Journal of Child Psychology and Psychiatry, 45*(6), 1150–1158.

Dobson, K. E., & Avery, J. (2010). *Ways of knowing: Selected readings.* Dubuque, Iowa: Kendall Hunt Publishing Company.

Drake, R. E., Goldman, H., Leff, H. S., Lehman, A. F., Dixon, L., & Mueser, K. T. (2001). Implementing evidence-based practices in routine mental health service settings. *Psychiatric Services, 52*(2), 179–182.

DuBois, B., & Miley, K. K. (2010). *Social work: An empowering profession* (7th ed.). Boston: Allyn & Bacon.

Dudley, J. (2008). *Social work evaluation: Enhancing what we do.* Chicago, IL: Lyceum Books.

Dudley, J. R. (2004). *Research methods for social work: Becoming consumers and producers of research* (5th ed.). Boston: Pearson Publishers.

Dybicz, P. (2004). An inquiry into practice wisdom. *Families in Society, 85*(2), 197–203.

Ehrenfreund, N. (2007). *The Nuremberg legacy.* New York: Palgrave MacMillan.

Ehrenreich, J. H. (1985). *The altruistic imagination: A history of social work and social policy in the United States.* Ithaca, NY: Cornell University Press.

Ellis, A. (1994). *Reason and emotion in psychotherapy.* Secaucus, NJ: Carol Publishing Group.

Ellis, A. (2003). Early theories and practices of rational emotive behavior theory and how they have been augmented and revised during the last three decades. *Journal of Rational-Emotive & Cognitive-Behavior Therapy, 21*, 219–243.

Elshtain, J. B. (2002). *The Jane Addams reader.* New York: Basic Books.

Ely, R. T. (1895). *Hull-House maps and papers. A presentation of nationalities and wages in a contested district of Chicago together with comments and essays growing out of the social conditions by residents of Hull-House.* New York: Thomas Y. Crowell & Company.

Emerson, R., Fretz, R., & Shaw, L. (1995). *Writing ethnographic field notes.* Chicago, IL: University of Chicago Press.

Emery, M., & Flora, C. (2006). Spiraling-up: Mapping community transformation with community capitals framework. *Journal of Community Development, 37*(1), 19–35.

Engel, R., & Schutt, R. K. (2010). *The fundamentals of social work research.* Thousand Oaks, CA: Sage Publications.

Engel, R. J., & Schutt, R. K. (2005). *The practice of research in social work.* Thousand Oaks: Sage Publications.

Epstein, E. (2009). *Clinical data mining.* New York: Oxford University Press.

Epstein, I. (1987). Pedagogy of the perturbed: Teaching research to the reluctant. *Journal of Teaching in Social Work, 1*(1), 71–89.

Erwin, B. A., Newman, E., McMackin, R. A., Morrissey, C., & Kaloupek, D. G. (2000). PTSD, malevolent environment, and criminality among criminally involved male adolescents. *Criminal Justice and Behavior, 27,* 196–215.

Evidenced-based practice in psychology: APA presidential task force on evidenced-based practice. (2006). *American Psychologist, 61,* 271–285.

Farnworth, M., Thornberry, T. P., Krohn, M. D., & Lizotte, A. J. (1994). Measurement in the study of class and delinquency: Integrating theory and research. *Journal of Research in Crime and Delinquency, 31,* 32–61.

Fetterman, D. M. (2010). *Ethnography: Step by step* (3rd ed.). Thousand Oaks, CA: Sage Publications.

Fetterman, D. M., & Wandserman, A. (2004). *Empowerment evaluation principles in practice.* New York: Guilford Press.

Finkelhor, D., Cross, T. P., & Cantor, E. (2005). *How the justice system responds to juvenile victims: A comprehensive model.* Washington, DC: Office of Juvenile Justice and Delinquency Prevention.

Fischer, J. (1973). Is casework effective? A review. *Social Work, 18*(1), 5–20.

Fischer, J. (1979). Isn't casework effective yet? *Social Work, 24*(3), 245–247.

Fischer, J. (2005). Reflections on destroying social work. *Reflections: Narratives of Professional Helping, 11*(1), 50–58.

Fisher, A., & Scriven, M. (1997). *Critical thinking: Its definition and assessment.* Edgepress, CA: Center for Research in Critical Thinking.

Flexner, A. (1915, May 12–19). *Is social work a profession.* In National Conference of Charities and Corrections, Proceedings of the National Conference and Corrections at the Forty-second annual session held in Baltimore, Maryland. Chicago, IL: Hildmann.

Fook, J. (2004). *What professionals need from research: Beyond evidenced-based practice.* London: Jessica Kingsley Publishers.

Foucalt, M. (1980). *Power knowledge: Selected interviews and other writings.* New York: Pantheon Books.

Foucalt, M. (1982). *The archeology of knowledge and discourse on language.* New York: Vintage/Anchor Books.

Fox, M., Martin, P., & Green, G. (2007) *Doing practitioner research.* Thousand Oaks, CA: Sage Publications.

Fraser, M., & Taylor, M. J. (1990). Social work and science: Many ways of knowing? *Social Work Research and Abstracts, 27*(4), 1–25.

Fraser, M. W., Jensen, J. M., & Lewis, R. E. (1993). Research training in social work: The continuum is not a continuum. *Journal of Social Work Education, 29*(1), 46–62.

Freud, S. (1996). *Three case studies.* New York: Touchstone Publishers.

Freud, S. (1997). *Dora: An analysis of a case of hysteria.* New York: Touchstone Publishers.

Friedman, B. D. (2008). *The research toolkit: Putting it all together.* Pacific Grove, CA: Brooks/Cole.

Furman, R. (2006). Autoethnographic poems and narrative reflections: A qualitative study on the death of a companion animal. *Journal of Family Social Work, 9*(4), 23–38.

Furman, R., & Bender, K. (2003). The social problem of depression: A multi-theoretical analysis. *Journal of Sociology and Social Welfare, 15*(3), 123–137.

Galtung, J. (1967). *Theory and methods of social work research.* New York: Columbia University Press.

Gambrill, E. (1999). Evidence-based practice: An alternative to authority-based practice. *Families in Society, 80,* 341–350.

Gambrill, E. (2005). *Critical thinking in clinical practice: Improving the quality of judgments and decisions.* Hoboken, NJ: Wiley & Sons.

Gettier, E. (1963). Is justified true belief knowledge? *Analysis, 23,* 121–123.

Gibbs, L. (2002). How social workers can do more good than harm: Critical thinking, evidence-based clinical reasoning, and avoiding fallacies. In A. R. Roberts & G. J. Greene (Eds.), *Social workers' desk reference* (pp. 752–757). New York: Oxford University Press.

Gibbs, L. (2003). *Evidence-based practice for the helping professions: A practical guide with integrated multimedia.* Pacific Grove, CA: Brooks/Cole.

Gibbs, L., & Gambrill, E. (1998). *Critical thinking for social workers: Exercises for helping professionals.* Thousand Oaks: Pine Forge Press.

Gibbs, L., & Gambrill, E. (2002). Evidenced-based practice: Counterarguments to objections. *Research on Social Work Practice, 12,* 452–476.

Gibelman, M. (1995). *What social workers do* (4th ed.). Washington, DC: NASW Press.

Gilbert, M. (2004). *The Second World War: A complete history.* New York: Holt Paperbacks.

Gilgun, J. (2005). The four cornerstones of evidenced-based practice in social work. *Research on Social Work Practice, 15,* 52–61.

Gitlin, L. N., & Lyons, K. J. (2008). *Successful grant writing: Strategies for health and human service professionals* (3rd ed.). New York: Springer Publishing Company.

Glaser, B. G., & Strauss, A. (1967). *Discovery of grounded theory: Strategies for qualitative research.* New York, NY: Aldine Publishing Company.

Glesne, C. (1999). *Becoming qualitative researchers: An introduction* (2nd ed.). New York: Longman Publishers.

Goldman, K. D., & Schmalz, K. J. (2005). Accentuate the positive: Using an asset-mapping tool as part of a community health needs assessment. *Health Promotion Practice, 6*(2), 125–128.

Goodman, A. (2007, July 24) Children's defense fund's Marian Wright Edelman calls on Congress & Bush Administration to help the country's nine million children without health insurance. *Democracy Now.* Retrieved from http://www.democracynow.org/2007/7/24/childrens_defense_funds_marian_wright_edelman

Gordon, D., Graves, K., & Arbuthnot, J. (1995). The effect of functional family therapy for delinquents on adult criminal behavior. *Criminal Justice and Behavior, 22*(1), 60–73.

Graham, J., Al-Krenawi, A., & Bradshaw, C. (2000). The Social Work Research Group/NASW Research Section/Council on Social Work Research, 1949–1965: An emerging research identity in the American profession. *Research on Social Work Practice, 10*(5), 622–643.

Grinnell, R. M. (1997). *Social work research and evaluation: Quantitative and qualitative approaches.* Itasca, IL: F. E. Peacock Publishers.

Grinnell, R. M., & Unrau, Y. (2005). *Social work research and evaluation: Qualitative and quantitative approaches.* Itasca, IL: F. E. Peacock Publishers.

Grobman, L. M. (2004). *Days in the lives of social workers: 54 professionals tell "real-life" stories from social work practice* (3rd ed.). Harrisburg, PA: White Hat Communications.

Grobman, L. M. (2005). *More days in the lives of social workers: 35 "real-life" stories of advocacy, outreach, and other intriguing roles in social work practice.* Harrisburg, PA: White Hat Communications.

Gruskin, S., & Ferguson, L. (2009). Using indicators to determine the contribution of human rights to public health efforts. *World Health Organization. Bulletin of the World Health Organization, 87*(9), 714–720.

Guba, E. G., & Lincoln, Y. S. (1994). Competing paradigms in qualitative research. In N. K. Denzin & Y. S. Lincoln (Eds.), *Handbook of qualitative research* (pp. 105–117). Thousand Oaks, CA: Sage Publications.

Guitierrez, L. (2003). Participatory and stakeholder research. In R. L. Edwards (Ed.-in-Chief), *Encyclopedia of social work* (19th ed., Vol. 1, pp. 115–123). Washington, DC: NASW Press.

Hall, F. (1937). *The social work year book.* New York: Russell Sage Foundation.

Hall, P., Backman, G., & Fitchett, J. (2010). Health and human rights education: Time to act. *The Lancet, 375*(9718), 894.

Hart, C. (1998). *Doing a literature review: Releasing the social science research imagination.* Thousand Oaks, CA: Sage Publications.

Haynes, R. B., Devereaux, P. J., & Guyatt, G. H. (2002). Editorial: Clinical expertise in the ear of evidence-based medicine and patient choice. *ACP Journal Club, 7*(March/April), 36–38.

Healey, L. (2001). *International social work: Professional action in an interdependent world.* New York: Oxford University Press.

Healey, L. (2001). Participatory action research and social work: A critical appraisal. *International Social Work, 44*(1), 93–105.

Healy, L. (2008). Exploring the history of social work as a human rights profession. *International Social Work, 51*(6), 735–748.

Held, D. (1980). *Introduction to critical theory: Horkheimer to Habermas.* Los Angeles, CA: University of California Press.

Hesse-Biber, S. N., & Leavy, P. (2011). *The practice of qualitative research* (2nd ed.). Thousand Oaks, CA: Sage Publications.

Hillier, A. (2007). Why social work needs mapping. *Journal of Social Work Education, 43*(2), 205–221.

Hollingshead, A. A. (1975). *Four-factor index of social status.* Unpublished manuscript, Yale University, New Haven, CT.

Holosko, M. J. (2005). *Primer for critiquing social research: A student guide.* Pacific Grove, CA: Thomson Brooks/Cole.

Hoopes, J. (1979). *Oral history: An introduction for students.* Chapel Hill: University of North Carolina Press.

Howard, M., Bricout, J., Edmond, T., Elze, D., & Jenson, J. (2003). Evidence-based practice guidelines. In R. L. Edwards (Ed.-in-Chief), *Encyclopedia of social work* (19th ed., Vol. 1, pp. 48–59). Washington, DC: NASW Press.

Huitt, W. (1998). Measurement, evaluation, and research: Ways of knowing. *Educational psychology interactive.* Valdosta, GA: Valdosta State University. Retrieved from http://www.edpsycinteractive.org/topics/intro/wayknow.html

Humphries, B. (2008). *Social work research for social justice.* New York: Palgrave MacMillan.

Ife, J. (2001a). *Human rights and social work: Towards rights-based practice.* New York: Cambridge University Press.

Ife, J. (2001b). Local and global practice: Relocating social work as a human rights profession in the new global order. *European Journal of Social Work, 4*(1), 5–15.

Institute of Medicine. (2001). *Crossing the quality chasm: A new health system for the 21st century.* Washington, DC: National Academies Press.

International Federation of Social Work. (1988). *International policy paper.* Retrieved from http://www.ifsw.org/en/p38000208.html

International Federation of Social Work. (2000). *Definition of social work.* Retrieved from http://www.ifsw.org/en/p38000208.html

International Federation of Social Work, and International Association of Schools of Social Work. (2004). *Ethics in social work, statement of principles.* Retrieved from http://www.ifsw.org/f38000032.html

International Federation of Social Workers. (1996). *International policy on human rights.* Retrieved from http://www.ifsw.org/en/p38000208.html

Jarvis, P. (1999). *The practitioner-researcher: Developing theory from practice.* San Francisco: CA: Jossey-Bass Publishers.

Jasek-Rysdahl, K. (2001). Applying Sen's capabilities framework to neighborhoods: Using local assets maps to deepen our understanding of well-being. *Review of Social Economy, 59*(3), 313–329.

Jayaratne, S., & Levy, R. L. (1979). *Empirical clinical practice.* New York: Columbia. University Press.

Jeter, H. R. (1937). Research in social work. In J. Hall (Ed.), *The social work year book,* (pp. 419–426). New York: Russell Sage Foundation.

Jiao, Q. G., & Onwuegbuzie, A. J. (1999, November). *I'll go to the library tomorrow: The role of procrastination in library anxiety.* Paper presented at the Annual Meeting of the Mid-South Education Research Association, Point Clear, AL.

Jones, J. H. (1993). *Bad blood: The Tuskegee experiment.* New York: The Free Press.

Jordan, C., & Franklin, C. (2003). *Clinical assessment for social workers: Quantitative and qualitative methods* (2nd ed.). Chicago, IL: Lyceum Books.

Jordan, J. V. (2010). *Relational-cultural therapy.* Washington, DC: American Psychological Association.

Kempe, C. H., Silverman, F. N., Steele, B. F., Droege-mueller, W., & Silver, H. K. (1962). The battered-child syndrome. *Journal of the American Medical Association, 181,* 17–24.

Kenagy, G. P. (2005). Transgender health: Findings from two needs assessment studies in Philadelphia. *Health & Social Work, 30*(1), 19–26.

Kerig, P., Ward, R. M., Vanderzee, K. L., & Moeddel, M. A. (2008). Posttraumatic stress as a mediator of the relationship between trauma and mental health problems among juvenile delinquents. *Journal of Youth and Adolescence, 38*(9), 1214–1225.

Killian, M. L., & Maschi, T. (2009). Defining collaborative forensic social work with diverse populations. In T. Maschi, C. Bradley, & K. Ward (Eds.), *Forensic social work: Psychosocial and legal issues across diverse practice settings* (pp. 3–11). New York: Springer Publishing Company.

Kirk, S. A., & Reid, W. J. (2002). *Science and social work: A critical appraisal.* New York: Columbia University Press.

Klemke, E. D., Hollinger, R., & Kline, A. D. (1988). *Introductory readings in the philosophy of science.* New York: Prometheus Books.

Kracker, J. (2002). Research anxiety and students' perceptions of research: An experiment. Part I. Effect of teaching Kuhlthau's ISP model. *Journal of*

the *American Society for Information Science and Technology, 53*(4), 282–294.

Kretzmann, J. P., & McKnight, J. L. (1993). *Building communities from the inside out: A path toward finding and mobilizing a community's assets.* Evanston, IL: Institute for Policy Research.

Krippendorff, K. (2004). *Content analysis: An introduction to its methodology* (2nd ed.). Thousand Oaks, CA: Sage.

Krueger, L. W., & Neuman, W. L. (2006). *Social work research methods: Qualitative and quantitative applications.* Boston: Pearson Education.

Krueger, R., & Casey, M. (2000). *Focus groups: A practical guide for applied research* (3rd ed.). Thousand Oaks, CA: Sage Publications.

Kuhlthau, C. C. (1983). *The research process: Case studies and interventions with exploring the thinking, feeling, and doing of research high school seniors in advanced placement English classes using Kelly's theory of constructs.* Unpublished doctoral dissertation, Rutgers University, New Brunswick, NJ.

Kuhlthau, C. C. (1988). Perceptions of the information search process in libraries: A study of changes from high school through college. *Information Processing & Management, 24*(4), 419–427.

Kuhlthau, C. C. (2005). *Seeking meaning: A process approach to library and information services* (3rd ed.). Norwood, NJ: Ablex.

Kuhlthau, C. C., & Tama, S. (2001). Information search process of lawyers: A call for "just for me" information services. *Journal of Documentation, 57,* 25–53.

Kuhlthau, C. C., Turock, B. J., George, M. W., & Belvin, R. J. (1990). Validating a model of the search process: A comparison of academic, public and school library users. *Library and Information Science Research, 12,* 5–31.

Kuhn, T. S. (1962). *The structure of scientific revolutions* (1st ed.). Chicago, IL: Chicago University Press.

Kuhn, T. S. (1970). *The structure of scientific revolutions* (2nd ed.). Chicago, IL: Chicago University Press.

Kuji-Shikatani, K. (2004). *Using research for advocacy.* Retrieved from http://ceris.metropolis.net/pac/pac11.pdf

Kvale, S., & Brinkman, S. (2008). *Interviews: Learning the craft of qualitative research interviewing* (2nd ed.). Thousand Oaks, CA: Sage Publications.

La Roche, M. J., & Christopher, M. S. (2009). Changing paradigms from empirically supported treatment to evidence-based practice: A cultural perspective. *Research and Practice, 40,* 396–402.

Lathrop, J. (1895). Middle class. In R. T. Ely (Ed.), *Hull-House maps and papers. A presentation of nationalities and wages in a contested district of Chicago together with comments and essays growing out of the social conditions by residents of Hull-House* (pp.140–155). New York: Thomas Y. Crowell & Company.

Leighninger, L. (2000). *Creating a new profession: The beginnings of social work education in the United States*. Alexandria, VA: Council on Social Work Education.

Levin, H. M. (2001). *Cost-effectiveness analysis* (2nd ed). Thousand Oaks, CA: Sage Publications.

Liebow, E. (1993). *Tell them who I am: The lives of homeless women*. New York: Penguin Books.

Lifton, R. (1986). *The Nazi doctors: Medical killing and the psychology of genocide*. New York: Basic Books.

Limb, G. E., & Organista, K. C. (2003). Comparisons between Caucasian students, students of color, and American Indian students on their view on social work's traditional mission, career motivations, and practice preferences. *Journal of Social Work Education, 39*(1), 91–109.

Lincoln, Y. S., & Guba, E. G. (1985). *Naturalistic Inquiry*. Newbury park, CA: Sage Publications.

Linn, J. W. (2000). *Jane Addams: A biography*. Urbana, IL: University of Illinois Press.

Littell, J. H., Corcoran, J., & Pillai, V. (2008). *Systematic reviews and meta-analysis*. New York: Oxford University Press.

Locke, L. F., Spirduso, W. W., & Silverman, S. J. (2007). *Proposals that work: A guide for planning dissertations and grant proposals* (5th ed.). Thousand Oaks, CA: Sage Publications.

Lofland, J. (1971). *Analyzing social settings: A guide to qualitative observation and analysis*. Belmont, CA: Wadsworth.

Lum, D. (1999). *Culturally competent practice: A framework for growth and action*. Pacific Grove, CA: Brooks/Cole.

MacKinnon, D. P. (2008). *Introduction to statistical mediation analysis*. New York: Erlbaum Publishers.

Madden, M. (2010). *Being ethnographic: A guide to theory and practice of ethnography*. Thousand Oaks, CA: Sage Publications.

Marlow, C. R. (2010). *Research methods for generalist practice* (5th ed.). Pacific Grove, CA: Brooks/Cole.

Marshall, C., & Rossman, G. B. (2010). *Designing qualitative research* (5th ed.). Thousand Oaks, CA: Sage Publications.

Martinez, P., & Richters, J. (1993). The NIMH community violence project: II. Children's distress symptoms associated with violence exposure. *Psychiatry: Interpersonal and Biological Processes, 56*(1), 22–35.

Maschi, T. (2010). *Research competence survey and graph*. New York: FUGSS Community Research Collaborative.

Maschi, T., Bradley, C., & Ward, K. (Eds.). (2009). *Forensic social work: Psychosocial and legal issues in diverse practice settings*. New York: Springer Publishing Company.

Maschi, T., Bradley, C., Youdin, R., Killian, M., Cleaveland, C., & Barbera, R. (2007). Social work students and the research process: The thinking, feeling, and doing of research. *Journal of Baccalaureate Social Work, 3*(1), 1–12.

Maschi, T., Jardim, A., & Georas, M. (2009). *Culturally competent oral history interview schedule for older adults with personal and/or family histories of immigration*. Retrieved from http://www.fordham.edu/belproject

Maschi, T., & MacMillan, T. (2009). *After school music program for youth satisfaction survey: Parent/caretaker version*. Unpublished instrument.

Maschi, T., Morgen, K., & MacMillan, T. (2010). *The inductive and deductive orientation survey* (IDOS). Unpublished instrument, New York: FUGSS Community Research Collaborative.

Maschi, T., Probst, B., & Bradley, C. (2009). Mapping social work students' perceptions of the research process: A qualitative exploration. *Journal of Baccalaureate Social Work, 14*(2), 63–78.

Maslow, A. H. (1943). A theory of human motivation. *Psychological Review, 50*(4), 370–396.

Maslow, A. H. (1954). *Motivation and personality*. New York: Harper Publishing.

Mayer, S. (2009). Using evidence in advocacy. In A. Thomas & G. Mohan (Eds.), *Research skills for policy and development: How to find out fast* (pp. 264–274). Thousand Oaks, CA: Sage Publications.

McIntyre, A. (2000). *Inner city kids: Adolescents confront life and violence in an urban community*. New York: New York University Press.

McIntyre, A. (2008). *Participatory action research*. Thousand Oaks, CA: Sage Publications.

McLeod, J., & Thomson, R. (2009). *Researching social change*. Thousand Oaks, CA: Sage Publications.

Medoff, P., & Sklar, H. (1994). *Streets of hope: The fall and rise of an urban neighborhood*. Boston, MA: South End Press.

Merighi, J. R., & Grimes, M. D. (2000). Coming out to families in a multicultural context. *Families in Society, 81*(1), 32–41.

Merinko, E., Novotney, L. C., Baker, T. K., & Lange, J. (2000). *Evaluating your program: A beginner's self evaluation workbook for mentoring programs*. Retrieved from http://www.austincc.edu/npo/library/documents/Evaluating%20Your%20Program.pdf

Merriam, S. B., & Associates. (2005). *Qualitative research in practice: Examples for discussion and analysis*. San Francisco, CA: Jossey-Bass.

Merriam-Webster. (2007). *Merriam Webster's collegiate dictionary* (11th ed.). Springfield, MA: Author.

Merton, R. K., Fiske, M., & Kendall, P. L. (1990). *The focused interview: A manual of problems and procedures* (2nd ed.). New York: Free Press.

Mickelson, J. (1995). Advocacy. In R. L. Edwards & J. G. Hopps (Eds.), *Encyclopedia of social work* (19th ed., pp. 95–99). Washington, DC: National Association of Social Workers.

Miles, M. B., & Huberman, A. M. (1994). *Qualitative data analysis.* Thousand Oaks, CA: Sage Publications.

Milgram, S. (2009). *Milgram experiment: An experimental view.* New York: Perennial Classics.

Minkler, M., Wallerstein, N., & Hall, B. (2010). *Community-based participatory research for health.* San Francisco, CA: Jossey-Bass.

Mirowsky, J., & Ross, C. (2005). Education, cumulative disadvantage, and health. *Ageing International, 30*(1), 27–62.

Mondros, J. B. (2009). Principles and practice guidelines for social action. In A. R. Roberts & G. L. Greene (Eds.), *Social workers desk reference* (2nd ed., pp. 534–544). New York: Oxford University Press.

Monette, D., Sullivan, T., & De Jong, C. (2008). *Applied social research: Tool for the human services* (7th ed.). Pacific Grove, CA: Brooks/Cole Publishers.

Morgan, D. (2001). *The best guide to eastern philosophy and religion.* New York: St. Martin's Griffin Press.

Morgan D. L. (1997). *Focus groups as qualitative research.* Thousand Oaks, CA: Sage Publications.

Mostes, P. S., & Hess, P. M. (Eds.). (2007). *Collaborating with community-based organizations through consultation and technical assistance.* New York: Columbia University Press.

Moustakas, C. (1990). *Heuristic research: Design, methodology, and applications.* Newbury, CA: Sage Publications.

Mullen, E. J., Dumpson, J. R., & Associates. (1972). *Evaluation of social intervention.* San Francisco, CA: Jossey-Bass.

Murphy, T. (2004). *Case Studies in biomedical research ethics.* New York: MIT Press.

Myerhoff, B. (1978). *Number our days.* New York: Simon & Schuster.

National Association of Social Workers. (1999). *Code of ethics of the National Association of Social Workers.* Washington, DC: NASW Press. Retrieved from http://www.naswdc.org/pubs/code/code.asp

National Associations of Social Workers. (2001). *NASW standards for cultural competence in social work practice.* Retrieved from http://www.socialworkers.org/practice/standards/NASWCulturalStandards.pdf

National Association of Social Workers. (2006). *Indicators for the achievement of the NASW standards for cultural competence in social work practice.* Washington, DC: NASW Press. Retrieved from http://www.naswdc.org/practice/standards/NASWCulturalStandardsIndicators2006.pdf

National Association of Social Workers. (2010). *What is social work research.* Washington, DC: NASW Press. Retrieved from http://www.socialworkers.org/research/researchMore.asp

Neuendorf, K. A. (2002). *The content analysis guidebook.* Thousand Oaks, CA: Sage Publications.

Neuman, K. (2002). From practice evaluation to agency evaluation: Demonstrating outcomes to the United Way. *Social Work in Mental Health, 1*(2), 1–14.

Norcross, J. C., Koocher, G. P., & Garofalo, A. (2006). Discredited psychological treatments and tests: A Delphi poll. *Professional Psychology: Research and Practice, 37,* 515–522.

Office of Human Subjects Research. (n.d.). *Nuremberg code* (Rev. ed.). Washington, DC: U.S. Government Printing Office, 1949. (Reprinted from *Trials of war criminals before the Nuremberg Military Tribunals under Control Council Law No. 10, 2,* pp. 181–182, 1949) Retrieved from http://ohsr.od.nih.gov/guidelines/nuremberg.html

Oleson, K. C., & Arkin, R. M. (1996). Reviewing and evaluating a research article. In F. T. Leong & J. T. Austin (Eds.), *The psychology research handbook* (pp. 44–55). Thousand Oaks, CA: Sage Publications.

Orcutt, B. A. (1990). *Science and inquiry in social work practice.* New York: Columbia University Press.

Osborne, R., & Van Loon B. (2003). *Introducing Eastern philosophy.* Minneapolis, MN: Totem Books.

Padgett, D. K. (2008). *Qualitative methods in social work research: Challenges and rewards* (2nd ed.). Thousand Oaks, CA: Sage Publications.

Pan, M. L. (2008). *Preparing literature reviews: Qualitative and quantitative approaches* (3rd ed.). Glendale, CA: Pyrczak Publishing.

Parents, Families, and Friends of Lesbians and Gays. (2009). Retrieved from http://community.pflag.org/Page.aspx?pid=194&srcid=-2

Patton, M. Q. (2002). *Qualitative research and evaluation methods* (3rd ed.). Thousand Oaks, CA: Sage Publications.

Patton, M. Q. (2008). *Utilization focused evaluation* (2nd ed.). Thousand Oaks, CA: Sage Publications.

Payne, M. (2000). In M. Davies (Ed.), *The Blackwell encyclopedia of social work* (pp. 521–522). Malden, MA: Blackwell Publishing.

Percy-Smith, J. (1996). *Needs assessment in public policy.* Philadelphia, PA: Open University Press.

Petrosino, A., Turpin-Petrosino, C., & Buehler, J. (2002). "Scared Straight" and other juvenile awareness programs for preventing juvenile delinquency. *Cochrane Database of Systematic Reviews, Issue 2.* doi:10.1002/14651858.CD002796

Pincus, A., & Minahan, A. (1973). *Social work practice: Model and method.* Itasca, IL: F. E. Peacock Publishers.

Platt, A. M. (1977). *The child savers: The invention of delinquency* (2nd ed.). Chicago, IL: University of Chicago Press.

Poll, C. (2002). Catching the richness of your heritage: The dos and don'ts of doing an oral history. In S. Seperson & C. Hegeman (Eds.), *Elder care and service learning: A handbook* (pp. 116–120). Westport, CT: Auburn House & Foundation for Long-Term Care.

Popkin, R. H. (1999). *The Columbia history of western philosophy.* New York: Columbia University Press.

Popper, K. R. (1959). *The logic of scientific discovery.* New York: Harper & Row.

Popple, P. R., & Leighninger, L. (2007). *Social work, social welfare, and American society* (9th ed.). Boston: Allyn & Bacon.

Potocky, M., & Farmer, A. (1998). *Social work research with minority and oppressed populations: Methodological issues and innovations.* New York: Haworth Press.

Powell, W. E. (2008). Sophia's window: Practice wisdom and selecting better paths. *Families in Society, Portularia, 7*(2), 91–102.

Primo, A. (executive producer). (1972). *Willowbrook: The last disgrace* [Motion Picture]. New York: WABC. Retrieved from http://www.mnddc.org/parallels/five/5f/5f_html/5f_1vid.html

Pyrczak, F., & Bruce, R. R. (2007). *Writing empirical research reports* (6th ed.). Glendale, CA: Pyrczak Publishing.

Reamer, F. G. (1995). *The philosophical foundations of social work.* New York: Columbia University Press.

Reeser, L. C. (2009). Educating for social change in the human service profession. In E. Aldarando (Ed.), *Advancing social justice through clinical practice* (pp. 459–476). Mahwah, NJ: Lawrence Erlbaum Associates.

Reichert, E. (2001). Move from social justice to human rights provides new perspective. *Professional Development, 4*(1), 5–13.

Reichert, E. (2003). *Social work and human rights: A foundation for policy and practice.* New York: Columbia University Press.

Reid, P., & Edwards, R. L. (2006). The purpose of a school of social work—An American perspective. *Social Work Education, 25*(5), 461–484.

Reid, P. N., & Gundlach, J. H. (1993). A scale for the measurement of consumer satisfaction with social services. *Journal of Social Service Research, 7*(1), 37–54.

Reid, W. (1995). Research and overview. In R. L. Edwards & J. G. Hopps (Eds.), *Encyclopedia of social work* (19th ed., pp. 2040–2054). Washington, DC: National Association of Social Workers.

Reisch, M. (2009). Legislative advocacy to empower oppressed and vulnerable groups. In A. R. Roberts & G. L. Greene (Eds.), *Social workers desk reference* (2nd ed., pp. 545–550). New York: Oxford University Press.

Reissman, C. K. (2008). *Narrative methods for the human sciences.* Thousand Oaks, CA: Sage Publications.

Richards, L. (2009). *Handling qualitative data: A practical guide* (2nd ed.). Thousand Oaks, CA: Sage Publications.

Richards, S., Taylor, R. L., Ramasamy, R., & Richards, R. Y. (1999). *Single subject research: Applications in educational and clinical settings.* Belmont, CA: Wadsworth Group/Thomson Learning.

Richmond, M. (1917). *Social diagnosis.* Philadelphia: Russell Sage Foundation.

Richters, J., & Martinez, P. (1993a). The NIMH community violence project: I. Children as victims of and witnesses to violence. *Psychiatry: Interpersonal and Biological Processes, 56*(1), 7–21.

Richters, J., & Martinez, P. (1993b). Violent communities, family choices, and children's chances: An algorithm for improving the odds. *Development and Psychopathology, 5*(4), 609–627.

Riis, J. (1890). *How the other half lives.* New York: Kessinger Publishing.

Ritchie, D. A. (1995). *Doing oral history.* New York: Twayne Publishers.

Roosevelt, E. (1958). *Eleanor Roosevelt.* Retrieved from http://www.udhr.org/history/Biographies/bioer.htm

Rose, G. (2010). *Visual methodologies: An introduction to the interpretation of visual materials* (2nd ed.). Thousand Oaks, CA: Sage Publications.

Rosenberg, M. (1989). *Society and the adolescent self-image* (Rev. ed.). Middletown, CT: Wesleyan University Press.

Ross, C., & Mirowsky, J. (2001). Neighborhood disadvantage, disorder, and health. *Journal of Health & Social Behavior, 42*(3), 258–276.

Rossi, P. H., Freeman, H. E., & Lipsey, M. (2004). *Evaluation: A systematic approach* (7th ed.). Thousand Oaks, CA: Sage Publications.

Rothman, J. C. (2008). *Cultural competence in process and practice: Building bridges.* Boston: Allyn & Bacon.

Royse, D., Thyer, B. A., Padgett, D., & Logan, T. K. (2006). *Program evaluation: An introduction* (4th ed.). Belmont, CA: Brooks/Cole.

Rubin, A. (2008). *Practitioner's guide to using research for evidence-based practice.* New York: Wiley Publishers.

Rubin, A., & Babbie, E. (2010). *Essential research methods for social work* (2nd ed.). Belmont, CA: Brooks/Cole.

Rubin, H., & Rubin, I. (2010). *Qualitative interviewing: The art of hearing data.* Thousand Oaks, CA: Sage Publications.

Ruchkin, V., Schwab-Stone, M., Koposov, R., Vermeiron, R., & Steiner, H. (2002). Violence exposure, Posttraumatic stress, and personality in juvenile delinquents.

Journal of the American Academy of Child and Adolescent Psychiatry, 41, 332–339.

Russell, B. (1940). *An inquiry into meaning and truth.* London: Allen & Unwin.

Ryan, M., & Sheehan, R. (2009). Research articles in Australian social work from 1998–2007: A content analysis. *Australian Social Work, 62*(4), 525–554.

Sackett, D., Rosenberg, W. M., Gray, J., Haynes, R., & Richardson, W. (1996). Evidence-based medicine: What it is and what it isn't. *British Medical Journal, 312,* 71–72.

Saleebey, D. (1996). The strengths perspective in social work practice: Extensions and cautions. *Social Work, 41,* 296–308.

Sales, B. D., & Folkman, S. (2002). *Ethics in research with human participants.* Washington, DC: American Psychological Association.

Sampson, R., & Laub, J. (1997). A life course theory of cumulative disadvantage. In T. Thornberry (Ed.), *Developmental theories of crime and delinquency* (pp. 133–161). New Brunswick, NJ: Transaction Publishers.

Satterfield, J. M., Spring, B., Brownson, R. C., Mullen, E. J., Newhouse, R. P., Walker, B. B., et al. (2009). Toward a transdisciplinary model of evidence-based practice. *Milbank Quarterly, 87*(2), 368–390.

Schram, B. (1997). *Creating small scale social program: Planning, implementation, and evaluation.* Thousand Oaks, CA: Sage Publications.

Secret, M., Jordan, A., & Ford, J. (1999). Empowerment evaluation as a social work strategy. *Health and Social Work, 24*(2), 120–128.

Seidman, I. (2006). *Interviewing as qualitative research: A guide for researchers in education and the social services.* New York, NY: Teachers College Press.

Shaw, I. (1999). *Qualitative evaluation.* Thousand Oaks, CA: Sage Publications.

Shaw, I., & Gould, N. (2001). *Qualitative research in social work.* Thousand Oaks, CA: Sage Publications.

Sieber, J. E. (1992). *Planning ethically responsible research: A guide for students and internal review boards.* Newbury Park, CA: Sage Publications.

Singer, J. (2006). *Stirring up justice: Writing and reading to change the world.* Portsmouth, NH: Heinenman Publishing.

Skinner, B. F. (1938). *The behavior of organisms.* New York: Appleton-Century-Crofts.

Smith, J., Flowers, P., & Larkin, M. (2009). *Interpretative phenomenological analysis: Theory, method, and research.* Thousand Oaks, CA: Sage Publications.

Smith, M. J. (2010). *Handbook of program evaluation for social work health professionals.* New York: Oxford University Press.

Soriani, F. I. (1995). *Conducting needs assessment: A multidisciplinary approach.* Thousand Oaks, CA: Sage Publications.

Sowers, K. M., & Rowe, W. S. (2007). *Social work practice and social justice: From local to global perspectives.* Pacific Grove, CA: Brooks/Cole.

Spitz, V. (2005). *Doctors from hell: The horrific account of Nazi experiments on humans.* Boulder, CO: Sentient Publications.

Stake, R. E. (1995). *The art of case study research.* Thousand Oaks: Sage Publications.

Stein, H. F. (2004). A window to the interior of experience. *Family Systems & Health, 22*(2), 178–179.

Steiner, H., Garcia, I., & Matthews, Z. (1997). Posttraumatic stress disorder in incarcerated juvenile delinquents. *Journal of the American Academy of Child and Adolescent Psychiatry, 36*(3), 357–365.

Stier, R. (2006). Anti-oppressive research in social work: A preliminary definition. *British Journal of Social Work, 1,* 1–15.

Strachan, H. (2003). *The First World War: Volume I: To arms.* New York: Oxford University Press.

Straus, S. E., Richardson, W. S., Glasziou, P., & Haynes, R. B. (2005). *Evidence-based medicine: How to practice and teach EBM* (3rd ed.). New York: Churchill Livingstone.

Strauss, A., & Corbin, J. (1998). *Basics of qualitative research: Techniques and procedures for developing grounded theory* (2nd ed.). Thousand Oaks, CA: Sage Publications.

Strauss, S. E., & McAlister, F. A. (2000). Evidence-based medicine: A commentary on common criticisms, *CMAJ, 163*(7), 837–841.

Stringer, E., & Dwyer, R. (2005). *Action research in human services.* Upper Saddle River, NJ: Pearson Publishers.

Stringer, E. T. (2007). *Action research* (3rd ed.). Thousand Oaks, CA: Sage Publications.

Suarez-Balcazar, Y., & Harper, G. W. (2003). *Empowerment and participatory evaluation of community interventions: Multiple benefits.* Binghamton, NY: The Haworth Press, Inc.

Substance Abuse and Mental Health Services Administration. (2006). *National Survey on Drug Use and Health.* Retrieved from https://nsduhweb.rti.org/

Szuchman, L. T., & Thomlinson, B. (2008). *Writing with style: APA style for social work* (3rd ed.). Belmont, CA: Brooks/Cole.

Tashakkori, A., & Teddlie, C. (1998). *Mixed methodology: Combining qualitative and quantitative approaches.* Thousand Oaks, CA: Sage Publications.

Taylor-Powell, E., & Henert, E. (2008). *Developing a logic model: Teaching and training guide.* University of Wisconsin-Extension, Cooperative Extension, Program Development and Evaluation. Madison, WI: the Board of Regents of the University of Wisconsin System. Retrieved from http://www.uwex.edu/ces/pdande/evaluation/pdf/lmguidecomplete.pdf

Thomas, A., & Mohan, G. (2007). *Research skills for policy and development: How to find out fast.* Thousand Oaks, CA: Sage Publications.

Thompson, S. J., Maccio, E. M., Desselle, S. K., & Zittel-Palamara, K. (2007). Predictors of posttraumatic stress symptoms among runaway youth utilizing two service sectors. *Journal of Traumatic Stress, 20*(4), 553–563.

Thyer, B. A., & Myers, L. L. (1999). On science, antiscience, and the client's rights to effective treatment. *Social Work, 44*(2), 21–32.

Tisa, A., & Tisa, J. (2010). *The Nuremberg trials.* New York: Skyhorse Publishing.

Tripodi, T., & Pitocky-Tripodi, M. (2007). *International social work research: Issues and prospects.* New York: Oxford University Press.

Turner, F. J. (Ed.). (1996). *Social work treatment: Interlocking theoretical approaches* (5th ed.). New York: The Free Press.

United Nations. (1948). *The universal declaration of human rights.* Retrieved from http://www.un.org/en/documents/udhr/

United Nations. (1994). *Human rights and social work: A manual for schools of social work and the social work profession.* Geneva: United Nations Centre for Human Rights.

United States Department of Health and Human Services. (2005a). *Overview of the uninsured in the United States: An analysis of the 2005 current population survey.* Retrieved from http://aspe.hhs.gov/health/reports/05/uninsured-cps/index.htm

United States Department of Health and Human Services. (2005b). *Regulations and ethical guidelines: Part 46: Protection of human subjects.* Retrieved from http://www.hhs.gov/ohrp/humansubjects/guidance/45cfr46.htm

United States Department of Health and Human Services. (2008). *Child maltreatment 2007.* Retrieved from http://www.acf.hhs.gov/programs/cb/pubs/cm07/

United States Department of Health and Human Services. (2009). *Making and screening reports of child abuse and neglect: Summary of state laws.* Retrieved from http://www.childwelfare.gov/systemwide/laws_policies/statutes/repprocall.pdf

Unrau, Y. A., Gabor, P. A., & Grinnell, R. M. (2006). *Evaluation in social work: The art and science of practice* (4th ed). New York: Oxford University Press.

Unrau, Y. A., & Grinnell, R. M. (2005). The impact of social work efficacy for social work students. *Social Work Education, 24*(6), 639–651.

Van Soest, D. (1994). Social work education for multicultural practice and social justice advocacy: A field study of how students experience the learning process. *Journal of Multicultural Social Work, 3*(1), 17–28.

Van Soest, D. (1995). Peace and social justice. In R. L. Edwards (Ed.-in-Chief), *Encyclopedia of social work* (19th ed., Vol. 1, pp. 95–100). Washington, DC: NASW Press.

Veysman, B. (2005). Physician, know thyself. *British Medical Journal, 331,* 1529–1530.

Videka-Sherman, L. (1995). Meta-analysis. In R. L. Edwards (Ed.-in-Chief), *Encyclopedia of social work* (19th ed., Vol. 2, pp. 1711–1720). Washington, DC: NASW Press.

Viney, W., & Zorich, S. (1982). Contributions to the history of psychology XXIX: Dorothea Dix. *Psychological Reports, 50,* 211–218.

W. K. Kellogg Foundation. (2004). *Logic model development guide.* Battle Creek, MI: Author. Retrieved from http://www.wkkf.org/knowledge-center/resources/2010/Logic-Model-Development-Guide.aspx

Waldron, H. B., & Turner, C. W. (2008). Evidence-based psychosocial treatments for adolescent abuser: A review and meta-analysis. *Journal of Clinical Child and Adolescent Psychology, 37,* 1–24.

Warner, A. G. (1894). *American charities. A study in philanthropy and economics.* New York: Thomas Y. Crowell & Company.

Weinbach, R. W. (2005). *Evaluating social work services and programs.* Boston, MA: Pearson Publishing.

Weiss, R. (1995). *Learning from strangers: The art and method of qualitative interview studies.* New York: Free Press.

Westerfelt, A., & Dietz, T. J. (2010). *Planning and conducting agency-based research* (4th ed.). Boston: Pearson.

Williams, T. T. (2004). Terry Tempest Williams. In D. Jensen (Ed.), *Listening to the land: Conversations about nature, culture, and eros* (pp. 321–322). White River Junction, VT: Chelsea Green.

Wisse, J. (1989). *Ethos and pathos: From Aristotle to Cicero.* Amsterdam: Adolf M. Hakkert.

Wood, A., & Wahl, O. (2006). Evaluating the effectiveness of a consumer-provided mental health recovery education presentation. *Psychiatric Rehabilitation Journal, 30*(1), 46–52.

Wooksoo, K. (2009). Drinking culture of elderly Korean immigrants in Canada: A focus group study. *Journal of Cross-Cultural Gerontology, 24*(4), 339–353.

Woolman, M. (2000). *Ways of knowing: An introduction to theory of knowledge (for use with international baccalaureate).* Victoria, Australia: IBID Press.

World Medical Association. (1964). *Declaration of Helsinki: Ethical principles for medical research involving human subjects.* Retrieved from http://ohsr.od.nih.gov/guidelines/helsinki.html

Wronka, J. (2008). *Human rights and social justice: Social action and service for the helping and health professions.* Thousand Oaks, CA: Sage Publications.

Wronka, J. (2008). Human rights. In T. Mizrahi & L. E. Davis (Eds.), *Encyclopedia of social work* (20th ed., pp. 425–429). Washington, DC: National Association of Social Workers.

Yin, R. (2008). *Case study research: Design and methods.* Thousand Oaks, CA: Sage Publications.

York, R. O. (2009). *Evaluating human services: A practical approach for the human service professional.* Boston, MA: Pearson Publishing.

Youdin, R. (2010). *Diagnosing older people: Mental health professionals' diagnostic accuracy.* Manuscript submitted for publication.

Yuen, F., & Terao, K. L. (2003). *Practical grant writing and program evaluation.* Pacific Grove, CA: Brooks/Cole.

Zeithami, V. A., Parasuraman, A., & Berry, L. L. (1990). *Delivering quality service. Balancing customer perceptions and expectation.* New York: The Free Press.

Zimbalist, S. E. (1977). *Historic themes and landmarks in social welfare research.* New York: Harper & Row Publishers.

Zlotnick, J. L., & Solt, B. E. (2006). The Institute for the advancement of social work research: Working to increase our practice and policy evidence base. *Research on Social Work Practice, 16*(5), 534–539.

Zlotnick, J. L., Biegel, D., & Solt, B. E. (2002). The Institute for the advancement of social work research: Strengthening social work research in practice and policy. *Research on Social Work Practice, 12*(2), 318–337. doi:10.1177/ 1087057106289725

Index